The Game of Science Education

Jeffrey Weld, **Editor**

University of Northern Iowa

PEARSON

Boston   New York   San Francisco
Mexico City   Montreal   Toronto   London   Madrid   Munich   Paris
Hong Kong   Singapore   Tokyo   Cape Town   Sydney

Editor: Traci Mueller
Editorial Assistant: Krista E. Price
Marketing Manager: Elizabeth Fogarty
Production Manager: Elaine M. Ober
Composition Buyer: Linda Cox
Manufacturing Buyer: Andrew Turso
Cover Administrator: Linda Knowles
Editorial-Production Service: Barbara Gracia
Interior Designer: Carol Somberg
Illustrator: Deborah Schneck
Copyeditor: Barbara Willette
Electronic Composition: Omegatype Typography, Inc.

Between the time Web site information is gathered and published, some sites may have closed. Also, the transcription of URLs can result in typographical errors. The publisher would appreciate notification where these occur so that they may be corrected in subsequent editions.

Library of Congress Cataloging-in-Publication Data

The game of science education/Jeffrey Weld, editor.
    p.   cm.
    Includes bibliographical references and index.
    ISBN 0-205-376304
    1. Science—Study and teaching (Elementary)—United States.   2. Science—Study and teaching (Secondary)—United States.   3. Science teachers—Training of—United States.   I. Weld, Jeffrey.

LB1585.3G.36 2004
507.1'2—dc21

                                                          2003046743

Printed in the United States of America

10   9   8   7   6   5   4   3   2   1   RRD–IN   07   06   05   04   03

Contents

PART I: THE COACHES   1

chapter 1

COACHING TO WIN   2

chapter 4

SINK OR SWIM: The Transformative Student Teaching Experience in Science 80

by Jill C. McNew

PART II: THE PLAYERS   103

chapter 5

LEARNERS IN SCIENCE: No Room on the Bench   104
by Karen Dawkins

chapter 6

FAIR PLAY IN SCIENCE EDUCATION: Moving beyond Science for All　136

by Rebecca Meyer Monhardt

chapter 7

ACCESSIBLE SCIENCE EDUCATION:
Every Student a Player   166
by John Stiles

PART III: THE EVOLVING GAME 197

chapter 8

THE NATURE OF SCIENCE: Understanding How the Game Is Played 198

by Michael P. Clough

chapter 9

THE WAVE: Community Evolution from Spectator to Supporter of Science Education 228

by Jeffrey Weld

chapter 10

TECHNOLOGY TRANSFORMS THE GAME OF SCIENCE TEACHING   254

by David R. Wetzel

chapter 11

TESTING AND ASSESSMENT IN SCIENCE EDUCATION: Setting Par for the Course   288

by Peter Veronesi

PART IV: REFLECTING ON THE GAME   317

chapter 12

REFLECTING ON THE GAME: Action Research in Science Education   318

by John W. Tillotson, Moses Ochanji, and Thomas J. Diana, Jr.

chapter 13

THE FUTURE OF THE GAME OF SCIENCE EDUCATION

346

by Robert E. Yager

appendix A

Building the Student-Centered Classroom   373

by Robin Lee Harris

appendix B

Teaching Standards of the National Science Education Standards   384

Preface

This book is dedicated to all students of science, that is to say, all citizens, who hold our collective future in their hands and minds. May science for all be a vital and welcoming enterprise, championed by professional science educators.

Inquisitive Young Scullions

"It isn't only art that's incompatible with happiness; it's also science. Science is dangerous; we need to keep it most carefully chained and muzzled," advised Mustapha Mond, World Controller on Earth 600 years hence, in Aldous Huxley's *Brave New World* (1932).

"But we're always saying that science is everything," said Bernard, his underling.

"Yes; but what sort of science?" asked Mustapha Mond sarcastically. "You've had no scientific training, so you can't judge. I was a pretty good physicist in my time. Too good—good enough to realize that all our science is just a cookery book, with an orthodox theory of cooking that nobody's allowed to question, and a list of recipes that mustn't be added to except by special permission from the head cook. But I was an inquisitive young scullion once. I started doing a bit of cooking on my own. Unorthodox cooking, illicit cooking. A bit of real science, in fact." He fell silent.

"What happened?" asked the dangerously free thinker, Watson.

The Controller sighed. "Very nearly what's going to happen to you young men. I was on the point of being sent to an island."

The islands to which Huxley's Mustapha eventually banished the inquisitive Watson and his ilk were intended for "all the people who aren't satisfied with the orthodoxy, who've got independent ideas of their own. Everyone, in a word, who's anyone."

I don't know about you, but I think I'd take my chances on the island, eschewing the stability of Huxley's caste system—reinforced with tranquilizers, prescribed sex, and sense-numbing entertainment—to mingle with the likes of Freud, Michelangelo, Frank Lloyd Wright, Buckminster Fuller, Marie Curie, Stephen Hawking, Maya Angelou, and all the other free thinkers. And who but the intellectually unconscious wouldn't? Yet ideas, with their potency manifested in science, were considered by Mustapha Mond to be "potentially subversive" of the status quo. They meant change. Thus, cookery book science that nobody's allowed to question was the only acceptable science. Good thing it's fiction.

Or is it? Huxley joins an elite science fiction fraternity that includes Isaac Asimov (proton-powered satellites), Gene Roddenberry (cell phone "communicators"), Mary Shelley (spliced body parts), and others who presciently described a modern reality. Science education in Huxley's 1932 *Brave New World* might sound eerily similar to the science classes many of us experienced at school in the 1970s, 1980s, or even now: cookery book laboratories and no opportunity to question, just to transcribe the collected "truths" as fast as our No. 2 pencils could scrawl. The sort of science education that prevails in too many schoolrooms across the United States continues to chain and muzzle science by rendering its students passive receptacles of its history rather than active apprentices of its methods.

Science is a game—an immensely exciting and competitive team sport—with special rules and a rich history that define the field. But science education has evolved to require Herculean stamina for absorbing nearly half a life's worth of indoctrination into those rules and history before finally getting a chance to play. It's a rare company—about 1 percent of the population—who actually suit up for science. The majority of Americans associate science with endless terminology and a parade of historic players of renown, mostly deceased Europeans. Of course, the size of textbooks, the length of lectures, and the duration of embryonic development needed to become a scientist have mushroomed to include the same knowledge that has irreversibly changed our ways of communication, leisure, transportation, health, and entertainment. The problem with this chaining and muzzling is that adult Americans end up distancing themselves from the science behind nearly every aspect of their lives at the very time when we all need to employ the logic and thought processes of the game of science in making decisions about an increasingly complex future. If only science were more accessible. Then everyone could get a taste, play a set or match of it, and engage in enough real science to know what it is like and to transfer some of that skill to other aspects of life.

This calls for new ways of looking at the way we teach science. Step back and consider what it is we need to know to teach most effectively:

- We need to know about our clients, our students—how they think, what they know, how they learn.
- We need to know the discipline we wish to teach—its foundational knowledge and its machinations.
- We need to know how best to represent our discipline to newcomers.

These overarching themes guided the development of this book. We, the contributing authors of *The Game of Science Education*, speak from a research perspective that informs practitioners of the latest thinking on science teaching and learning. And what a recent flurry of research there has been toward understanding science, learning, and teaching! Most notably perhaps, our understanding of learning itself has blossomed. Ninety-five percent of what we know about the capabilities of the human brain has been learned in the last twenty years (Gelb, 1998). This knowledge has spawned a revolution in the way we look at teaching while concomitantly we have examined science itself as a discipline: what it is and what of it ought to be taught to all citizens (National Research Council, 1996). With this backdrop, each of us has metaphorically represented science as a game in recognition of its active and exciting dimensions, facilitated by professionals who act more like coaches than pontificators. Included with each chapter is a Game in Action vignette in which we draw on the experiences of professionals in the field to represent theory in practice.

In Part I, four authors examine this game of science education from the perspective of the coach. So much of what we know about effective coaching in science today is the result of seminal work by John Penick. We know the most effective classroom climate, the techniques for establishing that climate, the teacher and student actions that characterize an effective learning atmosphere, and the ways for evaluating whether a science program is on target. In Chapter 1, "Coaching to Win," Penick deftly merges theory and practice to portray the winning science classroom.

In a practical sense, we all know expert science teaching when we see it. Getting an empirical basis for defining expertise has been a bit more slippery. Labeling teachers "expert" and clarifying the progression of practitioners along a continuum from novice to expert have only lately become the subject of fruitful research. In Chapter 2, "All-Star Performers: Science Teachers at the Top of Their Game," Gary Varrella exposes the intrinsic, social, and attitudinal dimensions that manifest themselves in science teacher expertise.

The science of science teacher preparation itself has rapidly evolved in concert with the changing needs of society, the dynamic nature of our student clientele, and our deeper understanding of the learning process. A shift toward a more reflective, encompassing science teacher education experience is the subject of Chapter 3, "New Science Coaches: Preparation in the New Rules of Science Education," by Pradeep Dass.

Calls for more practical experience in preparing science teachers are not only empirically derived and sound, but also steeped in anecdotal evidence. In Chapter 4, "Sink or Swim: The Transformative Student Teaching Experience in Science," Jill McNew shares her fresh perspective from the teacher preparation pipeline to blend research and reality.

In Part II, three authors examine this game of science education from the perspective of learners. Thanks to a quarter century's worth of science education research, we know that facts delivered to our students divorced from any meaningful context fail to make lasting impressions. Borrowing heavily from the work of Jean Piaget and other pioneers in learning theory, science education has been revolutionized. In Chapter 5, "Learners in Science: No Room on the Bench," Karen Dawkins frames this vision of science education as a constructivist pursuit.

Elegant research studies have substantiated persistent suspicions that the version of science many of us have in mind is not shared by all and that the game of science is not equally welcoming to all citizens. In Chapter 6, "Fair Play in Science Education: Moving Beyond Science for All," Rebecca Monhardt explores the critical intersection of science and culture where the prevailing paradigm must yield for science to be a "fair game."

Science has historically, notoriously, excluded diverse learners. A modern society can ill afford to miss opportunities for conveying the power—methods, knowledge, and skills—of science to all of its citizens. In Chapter 7, "Accessible Science Education: Every Student a Player," John Stiles calls on research aimed at effectively reaching students with disabilities, who stand to make great personal gain, as well as societal contribution, through a sound science education.

In Part III, four authors examine this game of science education as it reflects science itself. We know that the nature of the game of science, as it is played at the professional level in laboratories and universities, has been so poorly understood by observers (and often by participants themselves) that recreating it in school settings has been problematic. In Chapter 8, "The Nature of Science: Understanding How the Game Is Played," Michael Clough exposes those misunderstandings and distills the research on classroom remedies.

Science itself is a public enterprise; the sharing of research, findings, tools, protocols defines the culture of science. Its support—socially, politically, and financially— requires an engaged public, or fan base. In Chapter 9, "The Wave: Community Evolution from Spectator to Supporter of Science Education," Jeffrey Weld makes a research-based case for mirrored public engagement in the business of science education.

The very business of science has been advanced and transformed by technological innovation. Science education, then, has a dual responsibility to both reflect the inextricable technological links that underpin modern science and utilize advancing technologies in pedagogically sound ways. In Chapter 10, "Technology Transforms the Game of Science Teaching," David Wetzel explores the philosophical and practical dimensions of technology integration in science classrooms.

Our accumulated knowledge about how students learn has been brought to bear on how we measure what it is our students glean from the science education experience. Research on assessing learners' understanding of science concepts and processes has revolutionized the very notion of testing. In Chapter 11, "Testing and Assessment in Science Education: Setting Par for the Course," Peter Veronesi explores the resultant tension between informed practitioners and score-hungry laypeople.

Part IV represents an epilogue of sorts, in which reflections on this game of science education provide impetus for sustaining a revolution toward a type of science education labeled by Huxley as "unorthodox cooking."

Sustained revolution requires members who steel their commitment to change through continual reflection. And since science teachers, of all educators, base their practices on empirical notions of excellence, reflection and empiricism become the hallmarks of strong teachers. In Chapter 12, "Reflecting on the Game: Action Research in Science Education," John Tillotson, Moses Ochanji, and Thomas Diana, Jr., reflect on the increasingly prominent role of teachers' research into their own practices as a mechanism for professional growth.

Finally, science education's rich history informs us of the many triumphs and pitfalls in conveying the excitement and essence of science to our students. This history has undeniably shaped our present state, as it will our future. In Chapter 13, "The Future of the Game of Science Education," Robert Yager, whose influence on science education has been broad and profound, recounts the sometimes celebrated, sometimes scorned, and sometimes benign increments of change in science education and how history has shaped our horizon.

Two appendices round out this volume. Robin Harris eases the transition from theory to practice by interpreting research in "Building the Student-Centered Classroom," an exploration of the essential elements of a modern, inquiry science classroom (Appendix A). Also included are the Science Teaching Standards of the National Science Education Standards (Appendix B). Though the appropriate integration of Content Standards and the authentic measuring of student work according to the Assessment Standards are an omnipresent force in the development of this book, it is after all the practices outlined in the Teaching Standards that determine whether or not this game is celebrated by our learners.

This period in human history will surely be looked back on as pivotal in establishing sustainable, peaceful, responsible human habits of mind. Our adolescent grappling with issues at the interface of science, technology, and society will mature to management through an informed populace. The contributors to this book are optimistic that science, unchained and unmuzzled, can retain (or restore) the inquisitive young scullion in all of us. It all begins in the science class, where they're playing the game of science education.

On behalf of all the contributors I would like to acknowledge the valuable comments of the manuscript reviewers: Warren DiBiase, University of North Carolina at Charlotte; Do-Yong Park, Florida International University; Jon Pedersen, University of Oklahoma; Molly Weinburgh, Georgia State University; David Wetzel, Bloomsberg University; and David Winnett, Southern Illinois University.

References

Gelb, Michael J. (1998). *How to think like Leonardo da Vinci.* New York: Dell.

Huxley, Aldous. (1932). *Brave New World.* New York: Harper Perennial.

National Research Council. (1996). *National science education standards.* Washington, DC: National Academy Press.

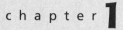

PART ONE

The Coaches

start

chapter 1

COACHING TO WIN

John E. Penick, Ph.D.
Head, Department of
Mathematics, Science, and
Technology Education, North
Carolina State University

ABOUT THE AUTHOR: Dr. John Penick, Professor and Head of the Department of Mathematics, Science and Technology Education at the North Carolina State University, started out as a biology and chemistry teacher in Miami, Florida. His leadership in science education has since included presidency of three professional organizations, including the Association for the Education of Teachers of Science, the National Association of Biology Teachers, and the National Science Teachers Association. Dr. Penick is an award-winning college teacher and researcher and the author of more than 275 articles, chapters, and books, including coauthorship of the innovative NSF-funded curriculum project *Biology: A Community Context* (2003).

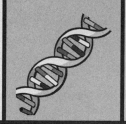

> ## Coaching is about change in light of goals.
>
> —Marv Levy
> *Coach of the Buffalo Bills*

CHAPTER WARM-UP

The goal of modern science education is to create scientifically literate citizens—lots of them. The objectives that support this goal require highly educated coaches of science who have a research-based rationale for the things they do on behalf of learners. Modern coaches of science find the National Science Education Standards essential for executing their rationale, especially in helping to shape the key components of an effective game plan. Those components are classroom climate, the role of the teacher, an appropriate curriculum, and valuable assessment.

INTRODUCTION: What's Winning?
(And What Does It Mean to Play?)

Just as Marv Levy sees coaching goals and processes changing, so too is teaching changing as we renew our focus on students and meaningful learning in a broad set of intellectual domains. Our new view of students includes how they learn and develop knowledge and ideas while at the same time we are setting our sights on expanded or additional goals for them. Our goals have moved from learning mere knowledge to developing conceptual understanding and applying knowledge to current problems and issues. Today, the most exemplary teachers count as theirs such goals as applications of knowledge, creativity, problem solving, and appreciation of knowledge as well as other, more traditional goals such as concept knowledge and skills.

When the singular goal was knowledge acquisition, teaching, especially in technical areas such as science, was considered by most to be synonymous with telling. The best teachers were usually those with the most skill in providing descriptions and analogies. In this model, the best students were those who could hear, read, remember, and repeat most accurately. As a result, the most verbal teachers were viewed as the best, and, of course, the best students were equally verbal, with excellent memories for their reading or what the teacher had said in class. Although an excellent teacher today should still strive to be knowledgeable and fluent in discussing the subject at hand, using analogies to help make a point, these skills are no longer sufficient. Now, with a renewed emphasis on a broader set of goals, teaching is changing such that all goals are important, and in our sights as we aim for educational excellence. As a result, exemplary teachers are those who have a powerful repertoire of ideas and techniques, including laboratory work, storytelling, discussion, debate, cooperative learning, applications of knowledge, and, yes, even telling. We must do more than ever if we wish excellence in today's education game. Has anyone ever viewed as excellent the coach who only taught players *about* the game but not *how* to do something with that knowledge: to execute the plays as a team in order to win at the game being played?

Some students succeed well in a fast-paced verbal environment; in this situation, those who are most like the teacher in learning style perform best, leaving behind those who differ or who are not yet fully capable of verbal learning. Until the mid to late 1960s, this situation was usually considered a normal (and even desirable) method for selecting out the academic students from the nonacademic ones. Then our goals for students began changing, reflecting simultaneously the changing demographics of our schools, our better understanding of learning and teaching, recognition that all citizens in all countries needed a basic understanding and appreciation of science and technology, and a trend toward more humanitarian ideals. By 1990, "Science for all; not just the elite" had become a common slogan around the world (Bowyer, 1990). And with science for all came a new vision of the successful and informed teacher.

This new teacher soon came to be seen as knowledgeable in his or her subject, open to personal learning, able to communicate in multiple ways, and having high standards and expectations for all students. Much as a coach must take all the players available and make the best team possible, the best teachers are now thought to be able to help all students learn as well as they can each year. Now teachers are thinking of the success of the class as a whole rather than just looking to a few select individuals as a winning measure. Just as the players together make a team, so a group of students with a successful teacher can make a class that functions better than single individuals. This perspective means changing from a typical competitive mode with a few winners and many losers (Yager, 1988) to a classroom in which all win, although not always at the same time and in the same way. Looking at a sports team, we don't expect all players to score goals. Instead, we set up plays in which some protect, some assist, and some make goals. Alone, none would win; together they can and will if each is performing at high levels as desired.

Bill Sanders (2002) notes that if each individual student learns and makes incremental progress each year, each will, across time, show notable progress, even though some will learn more than others. Although some will learn more and faster in this model, eventually all will succeed to a level that is deemed acceptable and useful to society. Just as a team that improves each game or season will win more in the future, so a classroom in which all students are learning consistently will in time be a winning class of winning individuals. A winning team or class will most likely have a winning coach or teacher who looks at each person as an individual, as a potential asset, and in light of what that person can do for the team or class.

Although many teachers view themselves as coaches of their students, as people who motivate, educate, and push their students, in science classes numerous studies have revealed that many teachers tend to coach only the elite—the natural-born winners (Goodlad, 1983; National Science Teachers Association, 1992; Project 2000+, 1992). Although allowing only the most talented to be on the team might ensure success for a few (and seeming success for the teacher), the majority of our students are left by the wayside, trying to play but with no help, no success, and no positive future. Rather than playing a losing hand over and over, they drop out, with no sense of commitment to the team, the game, or the institution that failed them. This is not the way to develop team spirit or even an appreciative audience for those who continue to play.

Rather, teaching to the elite leaves the rest of the class having generally to fend for themselves and possibly becoming labeled—by themselves and society—as losers in the game called school. In most games, there are equal numbers of winners and losers, letting players feel that they have excellent chances of winning. Unfortunately, in school, there have been far more losers than winners, a condition that leads many students to dislike school, schooling, and even teachers.

This dislike continues on into adulthood, with a large majority of our citizens reporting on several national assessments (Yager & Penick, 1986) that the science they learned in school was neither interesting nor useful. This is an intolerable situation and could be responsible for much of the antiscience sentiment and illiteracy that are present among today's students and citizens. Unfortunately, failing to be successful in school and finding science distasteful also limit career choices and aspirations in our increasingly technological and scientific work environment. What we need instead of winners and losers is for all students to learn science in ways that are useful and relevant. Or, as Bill Sanders points out, a person who improves academically each year wins each year and will eventually be quite capable and educated. Why must everyone learn and grow at the same pace and play exactly the same role on the team?

Considering our citizens' growing needs for science literacy, momentum has grown rapidly for teaching science to and for all students, not just the elite who are going on to study science professionally (Bowyer, 1990; Brandwein, 1981; Miller, Suchner, & Voelker, 1980; Mullis & Jenkins, 1988; National Science Teachers Association, 1990). Further, these critics say that we should focus our curriculum and instruction on understanding broad concepts rather than esoteric minutiae while emphasizing the processes and nature of science as well as the collaborative and social aspects of learning. Our winning science coach would recognize this new necessity of teaching all—of using all the players available and of wasting no minds, energy, or talents—and would develop strategies to see that all our students are in the winner's circle. Coaches recognize that if their players don't win, neither do they. Only when our students are all winners will we have maximal teaching and learning. Only then will we have a winning science teacher.

The Object of the Game

Our goals for students are the results we seek in teaching. Unless the coach and players all know the object of the game and how to score, they play randomly. No differently, students and teachers must know their purposes and goals in the classroom if they are to work together to achieve true academic success. Although there are an infinite number of goals for students that we might have, Penick and Bonnstetter (1993) identified a set of broad goals that hundreds of teachers and others reported as significant. They generalized these goals, saying that after an effective precollege science education, students should do the following:

- Have positive attitudes toward science
- Feel that their science knowledge is useful and applicable
- Use their knowledge in identifying and solving problems
- Be more creative
- Communicate science effectively
- Take action based on evidence and knowledge
- Appreciate and understand the nature of science
- Know how to learn science

If these are the goals—the criteria by which we determine how well the game was played—then both players and coach could well be expected to have their thoughts and focus on these goals continuously, especially as the action unfolds in the classroom. Every move made by the players and by the coach or teacher should somehow be related to that basic question one might (or, perhaps, should) be asking at any point: "How did (or will) that help win the game or achieve our goals?" The teacher who cannot answer readily is as suspect as the coach who has no particular rationale for a particular play, strategy, or substitution. Some have said that the norm in many classrooms around the world is to "teach, test, and hope for the best," but a competent coach or teacher has a strategic plan—a plan and strategy designed for and based on success, knowledge, research, and reflection. This plan for teaching has been referred to as a "research-based rationale for teaching" (Bonnstetter & Penick, 1990; Penick, 1999; Penick & Yager, 1988).

 ## A Rationale for Teaching

A research-based rationale for teaching includes a carefully stated set of goals for students, a thorough description of the roles of students and the teacher, and a plan for assessment and evaluation that corresponds, goal by goal, with the rationale. Unlike a mere "philosophy of education," the rationale is based on research, taking advantage of what we know from the research literature about learning, exemplary teaching, the nature of the subject we are teaching, and the role and impact of assessment. This plan is modified to take advantage of the strengths of players or students and the teacher (or coach), the present situation, and the playing field while never losing the focus on the original goals. Coaches understand the need for extensive strategy development as well as the logic of the game. Effective teachers must have a plan, a rationale, that is far more specific and far reaching than a lesson plan; and that rationale guides virtually every aspect of their teaching, the design of their classroom environment, and their assessment techniques and mechanisms.

Effective teachers not only have a rationale (Bonnstetter, Penick, & Yager, 1983; Krajcik & Penick, 1989; Penick & Yager, 1988), they have designed it even more carefully than they design their individual lessons. They begin by determining and justifying a set of goals for their students, goals that are desirable and attainable yet not so simplistic or specific that one could be said to have met them completely and perfectly at any point in time. For instance, if you look back at the list just mentioned, each of those goals can be achieved in some way, yet each can always be achieved at a still higher level. Then, not only do effective teachers have explicitly stated goals, they also use published research to justify them clearly and succinctly to others. These are not goals for the moment only; for the best teachers, these goals are a defining aspect of their teaching prowess and continuing success.

Once goals have been established, you next must investigate how best to achieve each and every one of them. For instance, if you wish your students to be creative, then go to the research literature. Find out the nature of creativity, what enhances and stimulates it, what inhibits creativity, what its benefits are, and what the roles of teachers and students are in settings in which creativity is being influenced positively. This is what will make your rationale research-based rather than just an editorial or opinion piece. Much has been written about each of the goals listed in the preceeding section, and papers relating to many other goals exist as well. Some teachers have gone so far as to publish their rationales for teaching science (Clough, 1992; Leonard & Penick, 1998), and many have described how a personal research-based rationale for teaching helped them explain to parents, administrators, and their students what they were doing and planning and why. A central part of any rationale is defining and creating an appropriate classroom climate in which we can reasonably expect success—in which the desired student goals can and will be met. A rationale is more than a game plan; a rationale explains and justifies the game in all its aspects. One aspect of a current rationale of teachers in the United States must be the recently developed U.S. National Science Education Standards (National Research Council, 1996).

The National Science Education Standards

With the development of the National Science Education Standards, the educational community developed new agreements about the science education game, including its goals, patterns, processes, and even how to measure success. The Standards provide us with three major focus areas to consider when planning or implementing lessons. These three areas are the content to be taught, how it should be taught, and assessment of learning. All aspects of the Standards consider research on teaching and learning, were widely validated, and have become the basis of the standards or frameworks of most states. In a sense, science education now has a complete and unified set of rules for play. While the Standards set the rules, individual teachers (just like all coaches) still develop their own rationales (playbooks, strategies, and curriculum). Yet, just as in sports, by necessity there is much overlap in these personal rationales. This overlap occurs because we are all playing much the same game in similar arenas, and some things make more sense than others do at a given moment. An overriding factor is that the research that applies to teaching and leaning is relatively specific in most instances. Because the Standards describe what students should be learning, how they should learn, and how we might best assess that learning, it is worth noting some of these specific aspects as they have been published.

The Nature of Science

While we (and the Standards) want students to learn facts, concepts, and skills related to science, we also want students to understand and appreciate the nature of science. Only a few of our students will continue in science or science-related fields of study and work. Even fewer will become scientists, engineers, or physicians. Every one of our students will be a citizen of an increasingly technological and scientific world, where they will be faced daily with numerous ideas and dilemmas with scientific bases. To function effectively in this world, they must understand how science is done, how scientific ideas and knowledge arise and are evaluated, and the roles of science and scientists in our society and future.

Rather than continuous inquiry, many citizens see science as static, believing that facts and explanations should never change and that scientists are supposed to be open minded and seekers of truth. Further, they see controversies in science as proof of the weakness and even falsity of the ideas and theories being discussed. Media stories regularly decry money and time wasted on seemingly trivial scientific pursuits such as the sex lives of African ground monkeys (*Good Morning America,* April 4–6, 2002) or the existence of almost unimaginably tiny subatomic particles. President Reagan was once quoted as saying, "We can no longer afford to support intellectual curiosity," implying that we can find value only in applied research that leads directly to new products or services.

The National Science Education Standards reflect science as philosophers and educators of science have emphasized for years. The Standards emphasize that science knowledge is tentative. By this, they mean that our understanding changes as data and evidence accumulate and change and as we develop more inclusive explanations. In science, we expect our explanations and ideas to change with time, experience, and investigation. We also expect controversy as different scientists offer different explanations for the same data set or phenomenon. This is not only normal and expected, it is the way science and scientists operate, with alternative ideas vying for acceptance. Eventually, evidence mounts, one idea prevails over the other, and new and equally controversial ideas come into being and focus.

Equally important to the nature of science is understanding that scientists do not discover knowledge. Rather, knowledge is invented to explain observations, facts, and phenomena. Just as knowledge is made up, it can (and probably will be) revised, discarded, and supplanted by new knowledge. This is not only acceptable, it is desired, because in this way ideas and what is considered knowledge are continuously being scrutinized, reviewed, examined, and investigated. This continual analysis of our understanding, paradoxically, helps to ensure the validity of our knowledge. At the same time, we know that our knowledge is not fixed or permanent but fluid and ever changing.

A classroom that reflects this understanding of the nature of science must be flexible and must stress how we know far more than what we know. The teacher in such a class is not all-knowing but is instead one who knows how to learn, how to investigate and analyze, and how to communicate understanding and explanation. Such a class is noticeably different from one in which students are expected to learn existing knowledge in rote and routine ways.

How Should Students Be Learning?

In any game, a knowledgeable and observant spectator can watch the players and, from their actions, eventually deduce the major objectives of the game and even many of the nuances of rules (except with cricket, for which few Americans can figure out the rules or the objectives!). In team sports, in which different players have specialized tasks, these, too, are evident. Equally visible are those players who are not playing the game as they should. In fact, even someone who knows little of the goals or rules of the game can spot slackers with little effort. So it is in the classroom. Each student has a role, and ideally, the roles fit with the individual student's abilities, personal goals, and aspirations and with the goals of the classroom and society. Yet unlike most games, in a classroom of students, we often do not have a singular goal for all to achieve simultaneously and by which success is determined. Rather, we have multiple goals, and winning in a well-run and well-taught classroom might be better described as occurring when all students achieve at a level that is commensurate with their individual abilities—when all are playing hard, producing well, contributing to the overall team effort, and developing personally.

Equally important, students must perceive that their efforts are more than mere practice. If they continually practice but never play the game, many will quit, seeking more meaningful activity (Yager, 1988, 1989). The teacher, then, must ensure that students have opportunities and encouragement to investigate real situations, to apply their knowledge to actual problems, and to communicate in ways that extend beyond school. In a series of studies, the National Science Teachers Association identified 165 school science programs that had impressive effectiveness in terms of student learning (Penick, Yager, & Bonnstetter, 1986). Without exception, the teachers in these programs found real science problems in their communities, made it possible for students to study these, and developed avenues for students to give their results to wider audiences. These teachers and classes modeled the standards that were being developed. In fact, many members of the search team and some of the teachers themselves served in formal roles with the National Research Council, the prime agent behind the National Standards; one, in fact, eventually became director of the national project.

The Standards state clearly that students should be learning science *through* inquiry, not merely learning *about* inquiry. The nature of inquiry and inquiry learning are both described fully in the literature. Thus, in the winning science classroom, we expect to see students engaged together in discussion, thought, and various types of action, such as experimentation, debate, and presentation. Students will be asking questions, often ones that they investigate directly. Although the teacher will be providing some explanations, we expect to hear even more explanations from students. If someone is talking, others will be listening and responding. And as befits such a class, the teacher continuously teaches the necessary skills, actions, and ideas that support thinking, inquiry, and science. Each of these collaborative behaviors is a part of the process and nature of science itself, and as a result, each should be reflected in the roles that are seen in the classroom.

Equally important if we are to reflect how science is done successfully by scientists, we should encourage and expect students to initiate ideas, actions, and conversation. As part of their roles, students should also be reflecting on and evaluating their own work—again, just as scientists themselves do. As science itself allows for numerous modes, directions, and procedures, so should our ideal science classroom reveal students engaged in numerous and different activities, beginning and ending at different points. Finally, because science is not really complete without communication of the results, the winning classroom provides systematic ways of fostering communication among all students—a sharing of ideas, results, evidence, and dreams. Of course, the teacher in this ideal and fully functioning classroom is not an idle bystander; he or she is planning, organizing, directing, revising, and considering continuously in the quest for student learning and winning at the game of science. And the learning is more than just concept knowledge and skills; the best teachers want their students to fully understand and appreciate science as an enterprise.

How Do We Assess Learning?

Even if all the other components are in place, the writers of the Standards recognized that a weak or faulty assessment system might well doom our other efforts. In the effective inquiry classroom, assessments must be fully compatible with all aspects of the educational game and the teacher's rationale for teaching. In addition, each of the goals must be included in the assessments. Goals that are not assessed receive less attention and class time than do those that are stressed. In traditional classrooms, the goal with primary assessment emphasis is content knowledge while goals relating to communication, creativity, and the nature of science are slighted at best. Looking at this from the sports analogy, in which assessment is defined in terms of scores, activities that do not provide scores are dropped in favor of those that put numbers on the board. Science classes are no different. Effective teachers teach for and overtly assess all of their desired goals for students; all goals count in the game of science education. If taught and assessed, these goals are far more likely to be accomplished than if they are only incidentally addressed. Thus, a significant portion of the Standards relates to the desired state of classroom assessment. Taken together, the elements of the Standards describe a total classroom climate that is poised for success.

Creating a Winning Classroom Learning Climate

Everyone who coaches team sports takes as a first task creating a team from the disparate group of individuals who present themselves. Although team building can take many forms, most authorities on the subject mention getting to know each other, communication, developing trust, and providing open avenues for structure, complaints, and concerns. And perhaps most important, the group must develop and believe in a common set of goals before success will occur. In many ways, each of these aspects of team building is the antithesis of what we find in the more traditional, teacher-centered classrooms. Although the teacher can and must still be the authority, to be successful, this authority must begin to focus on individuals, all the individuals, and their relationships to each other, the teacher, and the tasks and goals at hand.

If you ask most students (and even teachers!) about what they expect of the first day of a given class, they usually respond with descriptions of the teacher explaining the syllabus and grading, requirements, or getting textbooks. Rarely is much of academic substance mentioned or covered during the first class session. Even more rare is the first (or subsequent) class in which the students talk more than the teacher. Yet if building a team or getting to know each other is the goal, all must be involved, including talking—and why should this wait? In any adult social setting with strangers, our first inclination is to learn the names of new acquaintances, to talk to those we already know, and to meet newcomers. This is the beginning of team building, albeit undirected and somewhat random. The teacher who has a rationale for team building will begin directly and decisively.

Building a Team

The successful coach or teacher starts with exercises (often carefully structured) aimed at enabling students and teacher to get to know each other in a relaxed atmosphere. These exercises also reflect how the class will operate in the future, desired roles of teacher and students, and expectations. They usually have material to be learned as well. This is an opportunity for the teacher to learn more about the students as individuals: who is shy or aggressive, who speaks out, and who doesn't speak much at all. Often, students who would never raise a hand or speak out in class will talk animatedly in a more intimate, small group setting. While everyone is getting to know others in this setting, another positive aspect is taking place: This classroom is developing and being seen as different from the norm. In most classes, the teacher does most of the talking, but in this class, right from the beginning, the students are collectively talking more than the teacher. This is far more fun for the students (and usually the teacher as well). At the same time, students have opportunities for taking leadership responsibilities, and the teacher can learn from the students.

Now that the winning coach or teacher has established that this class (and this teacher!) is different, that the class can be fun, interesting, and relaxed; students are already feeling more at ease and wanting to remain and win. This is how a team forms. Contrast this with first-day classes in which students have their worst fears reinforced: This class will be hard, with lots of tests and term papers, good grades will be rare, it's boring already. Later classes do little to dispel these negative notions; most students say they are bored, they can't wait to get out, and find little of relevance. Meanwhile, most students attend class in fear, knowing that they are not the stars, not winners, that they are barely surviving.

Sure, with this team-building activity, we have spent an entire day doing nothing but getting to know each other. But if that day leads more students to be more willing to play the game and to play with confidence, we can all win and win consistently during the 179 days that follow. If most students don't want to play the game, the result is always going to be the same: losing. Winners get there by wanting to win, and the more students are fully in the game, the more winners we will have. Winning and team play are basic skills; we must devote time to the basic skills needed to win, and that is what effective teachers do, day after day, all year long.

Skill Building

Speaking of skills, if the goal of the initial class meeting is to communicate and build the team, why not structure it a bit and teach some specific communication skills at the same time? For instance, some of us like to have students interview each other and then introduce their partners to the entire class. In this way, each student gets to ask questions of her or his partner, take notes, and then paraphrase it all to the rest of the class. Each of these is a skill that we want to develop further during the year. This might also be a time to teach the basics of open-ended question-asking techniques.

Once students hear the difference in response from other students after asking "Do you like music?" versus "What kind of music do you like?," they will forever be hooked on asking questions that demand a full response rather than a simple "yes" or "no." And since the basis of inquiry in the science classroom is asking good questions, this is neither an idle activity nor one that is never to be repeated. A hallmark of the best teachers is purposefulness; even the smallest activities are looked at through the multiple lenses of the goals to be achieved. Exemplary teachers and coaches are always asking, "How will this move us toward our goals?"

The process of actively communicating and learning good communication skills is essential to another goal: developing trust. A teacher who trusts her or his own capability is more likely to be effective than is one with doubts. Students can feel comfortable if they trust the teacher. Students who know that their teacher trusts them are more likely to be reliable and cooperative. Such trust develops in an open environment where each person knows the other players and the rules, understands the goals, and feels empowered to structure to some extent how the events are played out. Trust reveals itself in the classroom as fewer aggressive complaints, more positive requests for change, and clear evidence of students taking initiative (Bandura, 1997). Trust opens direct and responsive avenues for the complaints and concerns that do arise. These avenues provide access to solutions as well, especially solutions that are negotiated and require involvement of both teacher and student. Trust means feeling comfortable, knowing that those around you are trying to create an environment where you belong and where you can succeed and win. Trust can be lost when you reasonably fear losing. The classroom should be a team, learning should be a team sport, and only a poor teacher (or coach) consistently leads an entire team to failure.

A Shared Vision

For success, however, the group must develop a common set of goals (the reason we are playing the game). Their playbooks (strategies and classroom procedures) must match, and they must all have a common vision of winning. This vision includes direction of play, scoring mechanisms, strategy, and even group reflection and criticism. But even members of a team don't all have the same personal goals. Football players on the same team all know how to score points and that points are what they want. But not all players expect to make points. Although a defensive tackle might dream of that fumble or interception, followed by a 99-yard run to the end zone, they do not measure their personal success in this fashion alone. Instead, each player knows personally what he or she can and must do to help the team, and each player determines personal success in terms of how much they helped the scoring effort. So, too, our students do not all have the same personal expectations (nor should they). Our students come with all varieties of background, accomplishments, and abilities. We should strive to get each to produce as best he or she can, to put forth maximal effort, each according to his or her own ability. In this way, we will encourage all to be productive, to learn, and to feel that school is a place where each can succeed, irrespective of how much others may accomplish.

The Role of the Winning Coach

Looking at the desired roles of students, the role of the teacher follows easily. Knowing what we want students to be doing when playing the game of science, we can identify aspects of the teacher's role that inhibit and those that encourage the desired performance (Penick & Bonnstetter, 1993). Although there is neither a single set of behaviors nor a single role that is optimal for all students at all times, we can identify teacher actions that are probably desirable and those that are never conducive to encouraging students to work together to achieve the goals we all have in mind. For instance, although there is no evidence that rejecting student ideas is motivating or even helpful to students, we know quite well that accepting ideas without evaluation leads to enhanced creativity (Penick, 1982), a sense of self-respect and confidence (Treffinger, 1978), and motivation to continue (Anderson & Brewer, 1946).

An Active Endeavor

Just as in tennis, players do not learn to play without holding the racquet, hitting the ball, and playing the game, students in science do not learn how to do science unless they, not just the teacher, do the work. This means that students need to be identifying problems to be solved, determining how to solve them, and deciding when they have been solved. This is what the Standards call for, not classrooms where students passively watch the teacher identify, solve, and evaluate. Students who are playing the game of science are active and eager and wish to learn more (Yager, 1988), but few students find it exciting or motivating to watch teachers play but never play themselves.

If we teachers wish students to reflect and self-evaluate, then we must refrain from doing the work for the students. Winning coaches know two things well: The players have to do the work, and the only way they will fully understand what they are doing is to analyze it themselves. As a result, effective coaches spend much time with players, not just analyzing prior events, but also teaching players how to analyze for themselves, to self-evaluate. After all, when the player is running down the field with the ball, there is no opportunity to call the coach in for a consultation. Instead, coaches prepare players for eventualities or help them to reflect on past events. Coaches do not and cannot play the game for their team. Independence of thought and action is what the excellent player is trained for. So, too, should we prepare and treat our students in classrooms.

To Inquire Is the Thing

If the game is science, all agree that the strategy to employ is inquiry. Inquiry implies observing, investigating, thinking and reflecting, talking to colleagues, and taking appropriate action. Inquiry, by definition, is not the same as following directions; inquiry assumes independence of thought and action and personal consultation with resources, be they people or reference materials. Inquiry cannot be mandated; it must be encouraged and nurtured. This, again, is where the winning teacher makes a significant mark.

Teachers who encourage inquiry provide a rich, stimulating environment filled with intriguing objects and ideas (Penick et al., 1986). These teachers provide significant opportunities systematically for students to explore, question, and pursue ideas, alone or together. Rather than answering students' questions, these teachers expect students to do the answering, relying on the resources available. The teacher's job is to prepare students for the game; the students' jobs are to play the game as it is meant to be played.

Because the teacher is to prepare students, there is more to this ideal classroom than merely turning students loose with the materials. Just as we would have little regard for a coach whose primary technique is to toss out the ball and say, "Go practice, and come back in an hour" so, too, we want a teacher who teaches *how* to inquire, investigate, use resources, and discuss the outcomes—how to do and learn science. This is what teachers truly are for: to teach how to do something and then offer the students opportunities to use what they have learned in real situations, not contrived textbook problems. And this is what students want to do: play the game for real. As Robert Yager (1988, 1989) noted several years ago, few students would participate in varsity sports if they were always practicing but never playing the game.

Curriculum for Success

Teachers and students normally interact with a specified curriculum. The curriculum necessary to provide science for all in a productive and successful manner must be different from the traditional curriculum that is appropriate for only a portion of the class. The curriculum that is suitable for all must provide options and opportunities; it must be flexible to take advantage of current events, local places, and individual students at any given moment in time. This is a tall order to fill. But if the teacher is flexible, it can be done. Just as the winning coach prepares for all eventualities, so too the winning teacher prepares alternatives for lessons that might not always work as expected. The effective coach or teacher has many other plays and lessons to try, always with an eye on the present context, who is playing, their skills, and what is necessary to win the game. In exemplary and quite successful classrooms, teachers usually invent much of their own curriculum rather than directly following a purchased curriculum (Bonnstetter et al., 1983; Penick et al., 1986; Tobin & Fraser, 1987).

What would we think of the new coach we just hired if we learned that she was using the same playbook as most of the other coaches in the league? Don't we usually hire coaches because they are planning to do something different from the prior (usually losing) coach? Why should teachers be expected all to do exactly the same thing? What do we want them to do? Although there are commercial curriculum materials that do provide much of the variety we desire in the best and most effective classroom (e.g., *Biology: A Community Context,* by Leonard and Penick, 2003; *Active Physics,* by Eisenkraft, Hobbie, Koser, Goerke, and Lee, 1998), even these need adaptations to fit all. None of them provide all possible activities, nor can they anticipate local events and resources that, if taken advantage of, can lead to student motivation and learning. Therefore, teachers need to learn how to adapt and modify, to select and create a curriculum that is best for the current group of students. To be winning teachers, they must know what curriculum can do and how to modify and use it. The best teachers are producers as well as consumers of curriculum.

 ## Assessment and Evaluation in the Winning Classroom

Evaluation in any classroom is often the major point of friction, for both students and teachers. Evaluation probably finds itself in this position because of its role as a tool of the teacher and the teacher alone. Advocates of teaching for relevance suggest using evaluation as part of the instructional strategy, not just as a mechanism for assigning grades (Yager, 1993). When evaluation becomes part of the instructional process, students view evaluation differently and with less anxiety (Druckman & Swets, 1988); assessment and evaluation become formative, helping students to grow and learn and decide what to do next rather than penalizing them for what they do not know.

Some teachers find it useful to discriminate between *assessment* (a measure of something—e.g., the score is 67 to 50) and *evaluation* (a judgment of value—e.g., we won the game by 17 points). Both are useful and necessary, and all students should learn to do both. As adults, we are all expected to self-assess and evaluate our efforts as well as our products. Why not begin in school, where opportunities for self-reflection, assessment, and evaluation are abundant? Assessment and evaluation occur when we can see the details of a process or product; it is one aspect of what differentiates experts from novices. James Pellegrino (in Bransford, Brown, & Cocking, 2000) notes that experts see patterns that are organized to support knowledge. We should be teaching our students to see these patterns, to become experts in their own learning.

In the same way, athletes are expected to take an active part in assessing and evaluating the progress and outcomes of the game being played. Even a mediocre coach would be appalled if the players continually asked, "Are we winning yet?" Equally disconcerting would be a team that was busily playing away but with no interest in the score. To avoid this, we teach all players the goals of the game, how to assess the current situation, to evaluate personal and team performance, and to recognize the types of efforts and knowledge necessary for winning. If we were to do the same in science classes, each of our students would be taught personally how to assess performance and learning continually, both of themselves and of the team. Students who can do this show a reduced need for the teacher's feedback and more self-reliance (Druckman & Bjork, 1994). If each of our students could evaluate as well as players on most teams, teachers would use evaluation instruments differently, as useful information for learning and designing learning atmospheres, and as a means to an end and not as an end unto themselves.

CONCLUSION: Reflection and Evolution of Goals, Ideas, Strategies, and Mechanisms

Although winning might not be everything, it is, as various sports figures have said, "a far sight better than losing!" No teacher or coach purposefully sets out to lose. But not all teachers view winning as an attainable or even desirable goal for all of their students. If we view high scores on the SAT or admission to prestigious colleges as the only meaningful goal of schooling, then, by definition, most of our students must be viewed as losers (and what does that make their teachers?). But if we set our goals wider and higher, to encompass those described earlier, then most of our students can succeed at winning levels. Because winning tends to be much more reinforcing than losing, perhaps teaching students and teachers how to be part of a team, a winning team, will lead to long-term improvements in all measures of school success. Society would become the big winner, and since we are all part of society, there would be no losers.

The Game in Action

A Coach Bridges Imaginations

For more years than I have been teaching, the best teachers, those who are interested in students learning concepts and applications, have been asking their students to design and test materials, structures, and machines in their science courses. As part of these lessons, students typically are asked to imagine a design, such as a bridge to be made of straws and pins or toothpick sand glue, and then to build it. Finally, they test it to destruction, much to the amusement of some students and the horror of others. Although this is fun for most students and they surely learn something in the process, I had never seen this lesson taught in a manner that provided the science education we hope for. Then I visited a middle school teacher with a different plan.

At this small school in central Iowa, the teacher presented a far more desirable and effective plan, which integrated science, technology, and mathematics into one motivating and interesting lesson. In an average-sized room, decorated with dozens of pictures of bridges, the teacher began by showing several short video segments of various bridges, including the famous one of the Tacoma Narrows bridge collapse. With each video clip, she would stop and ask open-ended questions, such as "How was the bridge designed?" or "What was different about this bridge?" She always waited after her questions, and after students answered, she would wait some more. This never failed to elicit a number of student responses.

After viewing all the film.clips, the teacher led the entire class in brainstorming various aspects of bridges, such as how they function, where and when they fail, and how to build them, all the while remembering types and examples of bridges. By accepting all answers with no evaluation at all, she soon had a sizable list on the board. Then, placing them in small groups, she asked them to categorize the various types of bridges. There was much argument and debate about this, and it was evident to me that some were getting rather creative in their ideas. Eventually, the class decided on about eight types of bridges, and the class was broken down into five smaller groups to further refine their categories.

The next day, the whole class came together again in a large group to raise ideas and in smaller groups to discuss in detail. After less than a half-hour, the groups had agreed on some definite classifications. After this, the class, as small groups, spent several days comparing the bridge designs, researching them, and trying to determine what each type would be best for. The teacher spent her time helping them find resources, asking questions, and providing information when it seemed necessary or useful. Sometimes she spoke to a single small group; at other times, she would call the whole class together if she had some information she thought would benefit all. During this time, they developed a vocabulary for discussing bridges, learned some terms in physics and mechanics, and seemed to be coming to an understanding of how individual components could be assembled to make the strongest possible working structure.

Student pairs then each selected a type of bridge to design and build, using white glue and toothpicks. Their task was to design and make a bridge of their type that would support the most center-hung load across a span of 30 centimeters. At the same time, the cost of the bridge, measured in toothpick units, would be considered in looking at the overall winner. By the third day, students were quite excited about their projects and had already been talking about bridges for more than three hours. They knew a lot of names and terms and had plenty of ideas about how to succeed. But unlike a lot of classes, they were not just turned loose to build. First, they had to submit a plan.

Each group's first task was to draw a 1:1 scale side-view plan for their bridge and submit it to the teacher. The teacher then called each pair up to her desk, where they had to defend their design and explain how the various parts of their bridge were designed. The emphasis here is on the word "design." Rather than beginning by just sticking parts together or drawing random lines on the paper, the students knew that they had to be prepared to defend each and every proposed toothpick in their design. These students were being asked to think.

And think they did. As I watched them on day five, they were arguing with each other about "what ifs" associated with each aspect of their bridges. Some students were engaging in less than covert "industrial espionage," seeking some advantage in their own designs. Of educational importance here is the fact that students were not just assembling a bridge, they were really designing it, thinking about it, and considering many elements. They knew that only after they had passed the design stage could they build their dream bridge. Without this design aspect, students could merely glue toothpicks together, test the bridge, and move on without much investment. Through the simple expedient of a design and review activity, the students were hooked into thinking and investing mentally and physically in their bridges. It also seemed that the anticipation of building but having to wait created an eager tension in the classroom. It was obvious that this class was busy, involved, and learning.

Thinking, testing, and analysis are key aspects of science and design under constraint, and methodical testing and measuring are aspects of technology. Merely building something is neither science nor technology. These students were really doing what we wanted them to learn. By the time they got to building their bridges, they knew the purpose of each structural element, had made predictions about where failure might occur, were creating structural changes to prevent failure, and were considering constraints of materials and costs. Many students were also now considering how the test weight would be suspended, making design changes to accommodate the point forces that would be applied to the center span. These students were doing the science in the only place it can be done: in their heads, thinking, communicating, and revising. Then they transferred this science to their design. All of this thinking did not occur spontaneously; the teacher had purposefully created a classroom climate that was conducive to thinking, communicating, and doing science.

The results of their thinking soon became more concrete and even more exciting as students began using their drawings as actual templates for gluing up the toothpicks. First, they duplicated their paper design so that each member of the two-person team had an identical print of the side view of the bridge. Then they literally glued the toothpicks to the papers, each assembling one side! After this, all

they had to do was build the bottom and assemble the two sides. Soon they were ready for a real-world application: testing to destruction. As you can imagine, when the test day came, all the students were all eager. No one was bored as the weights were added to a five-gallon pickle bucket hung under the bridge being tested. I can still hear their speculations about where they would fail and the groans and applause as bridges buckled and finally fell. These students will not quickly forget the lessons they learned in this interesting and effective science and technology classroom.

Reflecting on the Game

1. How would you describe the differences between learning about inquiry and learning through inquiry?

2. What is the role of the teacher in an inquiry classroom?

3. How does classroom climate relate to the goals you have for your students?

References

Anderson, H. H., & Brewer, J. E. (1946). Studies of classroom personalities. II: Effects of teacher's dominative and integrative contacts on children's classroom behavior. *Applied Psychology Monographs,* No. 8.

Bandura, A. (1997). *Self-efficacy: The exercise of control.* New York: W. H. Freeman.

Bonnstetter, R. J., & Penick, J. E. (1990). Building and assessing a teaching rationale. *Science Education International, 1*(2), 16–17.

Bonnstetter, R. J., Penick, J. E., & Yager, R. E. (1983). *Teachers in exemplary programs: How do they compare?* Washington, DC: The National Science Teachers Association.

Bowyer, J. (1990). *Scientific and technological literacy: Education for change.* Paper presented at the World Conference on Education for All, U.N. Educational, Scientific and Cultural Organization, Thailand, March 5–9, 1990.

Brandwein, P. F. (1981). *Memorandum on renewing schooling and education.* New York: Harcourt Brace Jovanovitch.

Bransford, J. D., Brown, A. L., & Cocking, R. R. (Eds.). (2000). *How people learn: Brain, mind,* *experience, and school.* Washington, DC: National Research Council, National Academy Press.

Clough, M. P. (1992). Research is required reading: Keeping up with your profession. *The Science Teacher, 59*(7), 36–39.

Druckman, D., & Bjork, R. A. (Eds.). (1994). *Learning, remembering, believing: Enhancing human performance.* Washington, DC: National Academy Press.

Druckman, D., & Swets, J. A. (Eds.). (1988). *Enhancing human performance: Issues, theories, and techniques.* Washington, DC: National Academy Press.

Eisenkraft, A., Hobbie, R., Koser, J., Goerke, T., & Lee, E. (1998) *Active physics.* Armonk, NY: It's About Time Publishing.

Goodlad, J. (1983). A study of schooling: Some findings and hypotheses. *Phi Delta Kappan,* March, *64*(7), 465–470.

Krajcik, J. S., & Penick, J. E. (1989). Evaluation of a model science teacher education program. *Journal of Research in Science Teaching, 26*(9), 795–810.

Leonard, W. H., & Penick, J. E. (1998). *Teachers guide for Biology: A community context.* Columbus, OH: Glencoe/McGraw-Hill.

Leonard, W. H., & Penick, J. E. (2003). *Biology: A community context.* Columbus, OH: Glencoe/McGraw-Hill.

Miller, J. D., Suchner, R. W., & Voelker, A. (1980). *Citizenship in an age of science: Changing attitudes among young adults.* New York: Pergamon.

Mullis, I. V., & Jenkins, L. B. (Eds.) (1988). *The science report card: Elements of risk and recovery,* Princeton, NJ: Educational Testing Service.

National Research Council. (1996). *National science education standards.* Washington, DC: National Academy Press.

National Science Teachers Association. (1990). *Qualities of a Scientifically and Technologically Literate Person,* NSTA Position Paper. Washington, DC: Author.

National Science Teachers Association. (1992). *Scope, sequence and coordination of secondary school science: The content core.* Washington, DC: Author.

Penick, J. E. (1982). Developing creativity through science instruction. In R. E. Yager (Ed.), *What research says to the science teacher,* Vol. IV. Washington, DC: National Science Teachers Association.

Penick, J. E. (1999). The rationale paper: Structured reflection for teachers. In P. Rubba, J. Rye, & P. Keig (Eds.), *Proceedings of the 1999 Annual International Conference of the Association for the Education of Teachers in Science* (pp. 1158–1169). Greenville, NC: Association for the Education of Teachers in Science. (ERIC Document Reproduction Service No. ED431626). Reprinted in *Model Clinical Teaching Connections,* Spring 2001.

Penick, J. E., & Bonnstetter, R. J. (1993). Classroom climate and instruction: New goals demand new approaches. *Journal of Science Education and Technology, 2*(2), 389–395.

Penick, J. E., & Yager, R. E. (November–December, 1988). Science teacher education: A program with a theoretical and pragmatic rationale. *Journal of Teacher Education, 39*(6), 59–64.

Penick, J. E., Yager, R. E., & Bonnstetter, R. J. (1986). Teachers make exemplary programs. *Educational Leadership, 44*(2), 14–21.

Project 2000+ (1992). *Toward scientific and technological literacy for all: A world conference for 1993.* Paris, France: UNESCO.

Sanders, W. (2002). Statistician: Test data underused. Cited in the *Tennessean,* January 30, 2002. See also www.sasinschool.com/TVAAS/.

Tobin, K., & Fraser, B. J. (Eds.) (1987). *Exemplary practice in science and mathematics education.* Curtin, Australia: Science and Mathematics Education Centre.

Treffinger, D. (1978). Guidelines for encouraging independence and self-direction among gifted students. *Journal of Creative Behavior, 12,* 14–20.

Yager, R. E. (1988). Never playing the game. *The Science Teacher, 55*(6), 77.

Yager, R. E. (1989). To prepare for the game—but never play it. *Teachers Clearinghouse for Science and Society Education Newsletter, 8*(3), 9.

Yager, R. E. (1993). The constructivist learning model. *The Science Teacher, 60,* 27–31.

Yager, R. E., & Penick, J. E. (1986). Perceptions of four age groups toward science classes, teachers, and the value of science. *Science Education, 70*(4), 355–363.

Additional Resources

American Association for the Advancement of Science. (1993). *Benchmarks for science literacy.* New York: Oxford University Press.

Becker, J. M. *Peer coaching for improvement of teaching and learning.* http://www.teachnet.org/TNPI/research/growth/becker.htm

Clough, M. P. (1992). Research is required reading: Keeping up with your profession. *The Science Teacher, 59*(7), 36–39.

National Research Council. (1996). *National science education standards.* Washington, DC: National Academy Press.

Sambar, C. On teaching and coaching students. www.sambarpress.com/chuck/onteach.htm

Yager, R. E. (1993). The constructivist learning model. *The Science Teacher, 60,* 27–31.

start

chapter

2

ALL-STAR PERFORMERS:
Science Teachers At the Top of Their Game

Gary F. Varrella, Ph.D.
Assistant Professor of Science Education, Graduate School of Education, George Mason University

ABOUT THE AUTHOR: Gary Varrella is a faculty member in the Graduate school of Education at George Mason University, specializing in science education. A former high school teacher in California, Dr. Varrella managed an NSF-funded project, the Iowa Scope, Sequence, and Coordination Project while a graduate student at the University of Iowa. Dr. Varrella is internationally recognized for his work in science teacher expertise, complemented by numerous leadership positions in science teaching organizations including the National Association for Research in Science Teaching, the Association for the Education of Teachers of Science, and Presidency of the National Association for Science/Technology/Society.

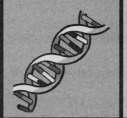

> ## The best and fastest way to learn a sport is to watch and imitate a champion.
>
> —Jean-Claude Killy
> *French Olympic gold medalist in Alpine skiing*

CHAPTER WARM-UP

Teachers' entry points, just like students', vary. Learning about teaching, like learning science, is a lifelong pursuit. The primary ingredient in becoming an expert science teacher is simply to believe in the goals and objectives set for students. Such beliefs are shaped by acquired pedagogical content knowledge, as well as motivation as a result of caring about students. The difference between expert and novice science teachers becomes a knowledge of when to act and why, what curricula to teach and how, and what effect these decisions might have on learners. Such knowledge is readily accessible by committed professionals.

INTRODUCTION: No End to the Season

I like to remind my students that a layup is a layup in basketball. There are striking similarities and differences between watching Kobe Bryant get some air and watching an eighth grader make the shot. The successful layup requires about the same number of steps, is completed on the same-sized court, and is worth two points on the scoreboard no matter who makes the shot. Beyond that, the differences between the novice's shot and the expert's are profound.

I find that when others watch an expert teacher "during game time," their responses and reactions vary widely. However, the majority of the comments and reactions are along a predictable continuum. At one end of the continuum is the individual who says, "I can't do that. I'm not that good. I'll *never* be that good." In the middle is the person who sees, understands, and either appreciates someone else performing on a level equal to their own or at least recognizes skillful execution and strives to learn from the example. On the other end of this continuum is the individual who does not see anything special or might even see something that is alarming or highly undesirable. On the "I can't" end of the continuum, we have an individual who needs serious conditioning in belief-in-self and more game time. The individual on the "so what" end of the continuum might need to enrich his or her understanding of teaching, readjust their binoculars for a clearer picture, or even reevaluate their understanding of the rules of the game. For some of these individuals, the root of the negative or passive reaction relates to the individual's beliefs about the "rules" of the game. For example, a Skinnerian behaviorist and a constructivist will never see the same event in the same way, since, although they are on the same court, they play by an entirely different set of rules.

This chapter explores the relationships of teachers' beliefs and their teaching practices. The constructivist paradigm (discussed thoroughly in Chapter 5 of this volume) provides an effective lens for viewing beliefs and practices. The deep roots of our rulebook for this chapter and this entire book come from the works of scholars such as Piaget, Vygotsky, Osborne and Wittrock, Kelly, Shulman, and von Glasersfeld. Teaching is about reaching the minds and life experiences of students, no matter their age. There are personal and social aspects, moments for direct instruction and moments for patience during the slow march to individual discovery. With time, practice, and reflection, we get better and better at this job that we love: teaching.

As professionals, the game is our occupation, just as is the case for the pro athlete. We hope that as you read this chapter, you imagine yourself on a continuum of growth and recognize that there is a beginning but, for the lifelong learner, there is no end to the season.

Shooting for the Top: A State of Mind, a State of Being

The professional athlete on the field of play, whether it is snow, ice, hardwood, or turf, operates on abilities that are guided by vision, attitude, and belief. Attitude and beliefs are not necessarily skills; however, for the all-star performer they are surely essential. Experts tend to have a rich belief structure that has grown from personal, social, and cultural influences (Bandura, 1977; Kelly, 1955; Pajares, 1992). The majority of the cultural influences and behaviors are expected, unspoken, and are taken for granted (Bandura, 1977; Hamilton, 1993; Kelly, 1955; Pajares, 1992). This collection of personal driving forces draws from the performer's declarative knowledge of the "content" of the game rules, social expectations, their personal playbook, and the procedural or "process" knowledge of the game witnessed through "skillful" play. When these are artfully melded, the player gets the win. In the mind and actions of the expert, these elements seamlessly blend and are applied harmoniously. No dichotomy exists for the expert between content and process (Rankin, 1999), whether one is swinging for the bleachers at Wrigley Field or engaging children in an inquiry-based science event on Thursday afternoon at Anytown Elementary.

The Teacher as Player-Coach

Every all-star teacher is a student of the game. They call themselves lifelong learners. These teachers believe in their ability to learn and carry that belief and commensurate attitude to their "coaching" assignment. They direct, moderate, facilitate, and are equally unafraid to *learn* right along with their students; hence think of the expert-like teacher as the consummate player-coach. This well of strength is deep and full of clear values and articulate beliefs. There is a solid body of literature supporting the premise that individual beliefs are strong indicators of the instructional choices and teaching patterns (Bandura, 1977; Beck & Lumpe, 1996; Prawat, 1992). For example, Pajares (1992) notes, "Individuals' beliefs strongly affect their behavior" (p. 326). Beliefs influence and inform personal values, which house evaluative and judgmental functions of beliefs, which further predispose individuals to specific actions (Pajares, 1992; Rokeach, 1970).

Pajares (1992) specifies that an individual's belief system be composed of three elements including beliefs, values, and attitudes. This very powerful personal triad guides the individual teacher's choices, producing markedly different performances by different individuals under the same circumstances (Bandura, 1977). This accounts, at least in part, for the broad array of successful teaching styles that one finds in a single school building and supports the premise that a rich and articulate belief structure is at the heart of a good teacher's effectiveness and is most certainly contextually situated.

A State of Mind: The Complex Construct of Beliefs

Star performers reflectively credit a state of mind, known as "the zone," for particularly stellar displays of performance. Clearly, there is a synergy of knowledge and belief, in some rare combination that only the well-prepared pro can tap, that accounts for the zone. The research on beliefs approaches the subject from many directions, using many different terms. Clandinin and Connelly (in Pajares, 1992) found a "bewildering array of terms . . . including teachers' teaching criteria, principles of practice, personal construct/theories/epistemologies, beliefs, perspectives, teachers' conceptions, personal knowledge, practical knowledge." Pajaras observes that in all cases, it was difficult to pinpoint where knowledge ends and belief begins. In contrast to this view, Kagan (1990) believes that terms such as "teacher cognition, self-reflection, knowledge, and belief" (p. 456) can each refer to different phenomena. She believes that the ambiguities rest with the epistemological traditions, the way theory is used, and the way the terms are defined. Kagan recommended that researchers define beliefs heuristically, that is, as self-educating mechanisms, according to which what we know is a function of how we personally come to know it (i.e., an epistemological tradition). The general definition of epistemology that is used here will be that of Fenstermacher (1988), who refers to epistemology as the "examination of knowledge, evidence, belief, and the credibility of our claims" (p. 40), that is, our personal philosophy about learning.

A State of Being: Teacher Beliefs Framed in Expertise

Others usually recognize expertise through skillful play. However, *being* an expert requires a personal link between beliefs and concrete actions. An effective method of exploring the link between teacher beliefs about constructivist teaching and expert-like teaching routines is to frame the characteristics of both elements and then consider relationships between those beliefs and commensurate practices. The literature on expertise is limited but robust and informative. The application of the novice-to-expert continuum provides a common referent and language for analysis of successful teaching in light of the teacher's beliefs and instructional strategies.

It is interesting to note that the development of much of the contemporary work on expertise occurred in the same time frame as the beginnings of contemporary thinking on teaching science, particularly the adoption of a science-technology-society (STS) thrust through a constructivist lens. STS was part of the response of science education to the inadequacies and struggles of Western education in the 1960s and 1970s (Berliner, 1986; Chi, Glaser, & Farr, 1988; Harms, 1981; Robinson, Enger, Varrella, & Yager, 1997; Yager & Roy, 1993).

In the Zone: Links to STS and Constructivism

Consider the melange of factors that come into play when the teacher takes the field: subject, context, materials, learners' preconceptions, and the interaction of curriculum, instruction, and understanding. A novice teacher can manage them. The proficient-to-expert teacher shapes them into something much greater than the sum of the elements. A quality of the expert teacher is that of holding a rich pedagogical content knowledge, or PCK (Gess-Newsome, 1999). This is a distinguishing characteristic of expert teachers and clearly separates them from content specialists (Clermont, Krajcik, & Borko, 1993). Pedagogical content knowledge represents a teacher's unique understanding of the subject in his or her personal playbook. This is in the context of instruction relating teaching of particular subject matter to specific metaphors, analogies, pedagogical strategies, examples, and contexts. The teacher draws on these elements to design and facilitate instruction to promote understanding among learners; in essence, the expertlike teacher creates the environment in which the subject or topic is learnable and teachable (Shulman, 1986, 1987; Wilson, Shulman, & Richert, 1987). Expert-like teachers draw on their PCK of a given subject matter area, considering the common student conceptions and preconceptions regarding the subject or topics, and then superimpose a repertoire of illustrations, contexts, explanations, and materials to promote further understanding of the subject or topic of study (Clermont et al., 1993) beyond those preliminary learner conceptions. The expert accounts for contexts that are specific to the learners and subject and to the school and prevailing local culture. This pattern parallels Berliner's (Berliner, 1987) conclusion that experts learn from reflection on experience, are more selective in their use of information, are more discriminating in their perceptions, and are more resourceful in their teaching activities than the average teacher is.

In this classroom milieu, constructivism symbolizes emancipation (Airasian & Walsh, 1997). Roychoudhury, Tippins, and Nichols (1995) assert that grounding instruction in a constructivist view of learning and teaching situates science learning in the lived experiences of students. This standpoint is synonymous with common STS strategies involving students in idea generation, consideration of multiple points of view, and collaborative inquiry and problem solving. A cooperative and supportive environment (i.e., a constructivist and STS-oriented environment) is an emancipatory one in which both male and female learners have the opportunity to make sense of their experiences in an interactive setting. In such an environment, individuals' learning needs can be expressed and addressed. These strategies are easily extended to circumstances in multicultural settings, with a notable record of success in that venue as well (Keating, 1997).

The Ever-Changing Scenery at the Front of the Pack

The label "expert" implies that an individual is at the forefront of his or her game. Working up to and maintaining a level of expert play demands discipline, investment of time, and a belief that each day can bring new rewards to the teachers and the students. Knowledge of content, context, and learners enables expert teaching but cannot ensure it. Motivation, born of caring enough to overcome institutional inertia, is the common denominator.

Prawat (1992) notes the centrality of the teacher in school improvement, which is normally designed to overcome institutional inertia, and points out a paradox. He notes that teachers are important agents of change in current reforms; paradoxically, teachers are often the major obstacles to change, owing to adherence to superficial and outmoded methods of instruction (i.e., individual inertia). Prawat argues that this paradox is evidenced by the still widely held beliefs in a transmissionist view of teaching and an absorptionist view of learning on the part of many teachers. This view and the corresponding teacher behavior underlie the continued maintenance of the status quo. This maintenance position is evidenced through "the ability to *manage* curriculum, to *run* activities, and to *organize* students" (Prawat, 1992). Eleven years earlier, in the landmark work of Project Synthesis, Harms (1981) arrived at a similar conclusion. One does not have to look far in the literature today to find that although there is clear evidence of progress, science is often still presented as "a rigid body of facts, theories, and rules to be memorized and practiced, rather than a way of know-ing" (van Driel, Beijaard, & Verloop, 2001, p. 138). Beliefs, values, and attitudes are tenacious and are apparently very slow to change. Overcoming institutional and per-sonal inertia is a hallmark of the expertlike teacher.

Prawat (1992) suggests that for teachers to rethink teaching and learning (i.e., to explore alternatives and accommodate a new set of beliefs about teaching and learn-ing), they must participate in learning communities that are similar to those we advo-cate for our students. This claim is supported elsewhere in the literature as well (Cohen, 2002; van Driel et al., 2001). This highlights the critical difference between the all-star players who will be discussed shortly and many of their colleagues. The all-stars have moved beyond these self-imposed constraints in beliefs and actions. The expert willingly participates in the learning communities, supporting, nurturing, and lead-ing as necessary. Hence, for the expert, who by virtue of beliefs and actions is at the front of the pack, the scenery is ever changing and therefore ever stimulating.

Expert teachers carry this philosophy of pursuit of that ever-changing scenery to their classrooms as well. STS is about science in the context of human experience. The expert teachers who are highlighted in a study discussed in the next section often used environmental issues as the subject of their STS, theme-driven and inquiry-based units of study (Varrella & Burry-Stock, 2001). This focus provided a frame of refer-ence for the learner that was as close as the recent newspaper's headlines. These expert teachers consistently tapped their students' existing conceptions and misconceptions, building a bridge of relevance between their general learning goals for their students and those students' interests. Science in the context of the learners' experience and the study of science through integrated, thematic, and concept-based instruction were the common tactics of these all-stars. Most used a direct or personally modified ver-sion of the learning cycle (see Chapter 6) as well.

Level and Art in Skillful Play

To explore expertise and the relationship of everyday teaching practices to teachers' beliefs, we must look at both tactical level and art in expertlike teaching. The lessons come from funded reform projects (Berliner, 1988; Burry-Stock, 1995a; Robinson et al., 1997) and from classroom research that examined the relationships between beliefs and practice (Varrella, 1997; Varrella & Burry-Stock, 1997; Varrella et al., 1999). These works stem from a variety of perspectives and locations, but all contribute evidence needed to understand all-star performers. One project in particular hinged on an STS-constructivist framework of thinking and pattern of teaching, which yielded insights into successful professional development activities and implications for preservice pro-grams (Robinson et al., 1997; Varrella & Burry-Stock, 2001; Varrella & Yager, 1998).

Novice to Expert: From the Farm to Fenway

Even the most gifted teacher works diligently at improvement. To help explore the roots of teachers' knowledge base for their practices, we must create a common con-ceptualization of that knowledge base. Shulman's (1987) work addressed this need in terms of pedagogical reason and action, building a series of implications for redirecting how teachers are prepared and how teaching should be understood. The questions of who can be called an expertlike teacher and how that person gets into the zone become one focal point. The spirit of these questions can be directed toward practices, beliefs, or the description of both and in relation to how the more *expert* among teachers go about their teaching duties. It gives a historical glimpse that can help to nurture future generations of experts as well.

Characterizing Expertise: Levels of Play

Much of our current thinking on expertise comes from the work of researchers in artificial intelligence (AI). This line of research grew along with the then infant computer science research agenda. The search for machines that could act as experts resulted in a collateral definition and systematization of previously nonformalized knowledge (Duda & Shortliffe, 1983). Duda and Shortliffe characterized the field as going from basic research to application as applied to systems of AI. However, the applications and thinking reached beyond that narrow technical perspective and back into the realm of human performance, without guidance by computer. The real richness of expert systems or expert thinking comes not just from the power of deductive or informational retrieval, but rather from those machines and people who have better ways to recognize and respond to specific patterns, using diverse and particular forms of knowledge and understanding for problem solving (Chi et al., 1988).

Two separate texts were published within one year of each other addressing expertise and artificial intelligence. One of these texts was *The Nature of Expertise* (Chi et al., 1988). The authors describe the organization of the knowledge base as a series of characteristics of experts:

1. Experts excel mainly in their own domain.
2. Experts perceive large meaningful patterns in their domain.
3. Experts are fast; they are faster than novices at performing the skills of their domain, and they quickly solve problems with little error.
4. Experts have superior short-term and long-term memory.
5. Experts see and represent a problem in their domain at a deeper (more principled) level than novices; novices tend to represent a problem at a superficial level.
6. Experts spend a great deal of time analyzing a problem qualitatively.
7. Experts have strong self-monitoring skills. (pp. xxvi–xviii)

This collection of characteristics represents a readily accessible, organized body of conceptual and procedural knowledge for the expert. This knowledge is used effectively by the expert through his or her "superior monitoring and self-regulation skills." (p. xxi)

The other text is *Mind over Machine* (Dreyfus & Dreyfus, 1986). Stuart Dreyfus, in researching AI, built an argument that human perception and understanding is not just "*knowing how*" (rather than *knowing that*) but is really the human capacity to pick up flexible styles of behavior. With his brother, Dreyfus began to consider and explore this thinking as it related to unsolved problems in artificial intelligence. They created an overall view of expertise described by a continuum. That continuum ranged from the simple analytical behavior of the detached observer, deconstructing events and the environment into recognized elements and following abstract rules, to involved and skilled behavior based on a holistic pairing of new situations with associated responses produced by previously successful experiences in similar situations. This represents an evolution from abstract toward concrete, which interestingly enough is the reverse of intellectual and developmental behaviors among young learners, certainly as described by Piaget. Eventually, Dreyfus and Dreyfus outlined a series of five steps from novice to expert: novice, advanced beginner, competent, proficient, and expert. David Berliner (1988) adapted and applied their framework to teaching referring to the novice-to-expert continuum as "stage theory" (p. 6).

Berliner began studying expert and novice teaching behaviors in the 1980s and, as was noted above, drew heavily on the work of Dreyfus and Dreyfus for a theoretical premise. Berliner studied teachers, scientists, and mathematicians with differing degrees of experience as classroom teachers (Andre, 1986; Berliner, 1988). A pivotal argument for expanded study of expertise in teaching related to the assumption that anyone who has subject matter knowledge can teach (Berliner, 1987). The study of routines, scripts, patterns, and the schema of experienced teachers provided valuable directions for new teachers as well as seasoned veterans. The continued study of experts also provided a model and frame of reference to assist the advanced beginner to become competent and to reach skillful levels of play more quickly. However, none of these supplants the "role of experience in acquisition of problem-solving skills" (Berliner, 1987, p. 78). Berliner used stage theory to study and develop a general model of expertise. Berliner (1988, pp. 2–6) described the distinguishing characteristics as follows:

Stage 1: Novice (basic fielding and batting): Here the common place must be discerned. The elements of the tasks to be performed need to be labeled and learned, and one learns a set of context-free rules to guide behavior. The behavior of the novice is rational, relatively inflexible, and tends to conform to whatever rules and procedures they were told to follow.

Stage 2: Advanced beginner (playing a few innings each game): Here experience can become melded with verbal knowledge, similarities across contexts are recognized, and episodic knowledge is built up. Strategic knowledge—when to ignore or break rules and when to follow them—is developed as context begins to guide behavior. The novice and advanced beginner, though intensely involved in the learning process, may also lack a certain responsibility for their actions. This occurs because they are labeling and describing events, following rules, but not actively determining through personal action what is happening.

Stage 3: Competent (playing in the AAA League): Competent performers of a skill have two distinguishing characteristics. First, they make conscious choices about what they are going to do. They set priorities and decide on plans. They have rational goals and choose sensible means for reaching them. In addition, while enacting their skill, they can determine what is and what is not important. From their experience, they know what to attend to and what to ignore . . . teachers at this stage feel more responsible for what happens [in their classroom]. . . . [However,] competent performers are not yet fast, fluid, or flexible in their behavior.

Stage 4:   Proficient (called up to the big leagues): This is the stage at which intuition or "know-how" becomes prominent. Nothing mysterious is meant in these terms. At some point in learning to ride a bike you no longer think about [it] . . . From the wealth of experience that the proficient individual has accumulated comes a holistic recognition of similarities which allows proficient individuals to predict events more precisely. The proficient performer, however, while intuitive in pattern recognition and in ways of knowing, is still analytic and deliberative in deciding what to do.

Stage 5:   Expert (star player): If novices, advanced beginners, and competent performers are rational, and proficient performers are intuitive, we might categorize experts as "a-rational." They have an intuitive grasp of situations and seem to sense in nonanalytic, nondeliberative ways the appropriate response to make. They show fluid performance, as we all do when we no longer have to choose our words when speaking or think about where to place our feet when walking. They are not consciously choosing what to attend to and what to do. They are acting effortlessly and fluidly; behaving in ways that are not easily described as deductive or analytic. The behavior of the expert is certainly not irrational. The writing of Schön (1983) about knowledge-in-action characterizes the behavior of the expert practitioner.

Berliner (1988) hypothesized that novices were generally student and first-year teachers, with individuals achieving abilities of an advanced beginner in the second or third year of teaching. He noted that with "talent and motivation," they might reach a level of competence by the third or fourth year. Proficiency might be achieved by the fifth year, and a subset of those proficient teachers will eventually reach the level of expert.

Acquiring Expertise in Teaching and Pedagogical Content Knowledge

A rich pedagogical content knowledge (PCK) is a trademark of the expertlike teacher. However, PCK does not just happen; the competent-to-expert teacher works at it every day. The body of accumulated pedagogical content knowledge embraces both subject matter knowledge and pedagogy. General pedagogical knowledge includes knowledge of theories and strategies of teaching and learning, sensitivity to the students and their learning habits, and skill and understanding in the principles of classroom management and student behavior. Subject matter knowledge includes concept, content and syntactic structures of the discipline (Wilson et al., 1987). PCK intertwines these elements for the purpose of effective teaching.

Much research on the topic of pedagogical content knowledge has been conducted with new teachers, specifically, how they convert their knowledge of subject matter into teachable classroom events and experiences (Shulman, 1986, 1987; Wilson et al., 1987). The studies indicate that growth is slow and is largely defined by the characteristics of the individual such as motivation, reflection, and creativity. Not surprisingly, these characteristics are common among teachers reaching stage 4 (proficient) and stage 5 (expert) levels of play.

Other studies of classroom teachers support these general premises. For example, Claremont, Borko, and Krajcik (1994) studied the demonstration skills of expert and novice chemistry teachers. They found that, as one might expect, expert chemical demonstrators possessed a greater repertoire of teaching concepts and adaptational habits when compared to novices. The experts also appeared more cognizant of the complexities that can interfere with learning and had rendered their demonstrations down to those factors that are essential for conceptual learning. An earlier and similar case study by Garnett and Tobin (1988) on two expert chemistry teachers arrived at similar conclusions. In this study, the two teachers focused on teaching for understanding by managing events and experiences and selecting strategies that facilitated student understanding. Context-based choices influenced these teachers' choices, and it can be inferred that these two experts' rich PCK guided their analytical choices and the natural or fluid adjustments that are common in the proficient-to-expert teachers' style.

Carter and her coauthors (Carter, Cushing, Sabers, Stein, & Berliner, 1988) examined information-processing differences between experts, novices, and postulants (those with no formal educational training but who expressed an interest in public school teaching) using slides of classroom situations and interviews. Their findings showed that experts made better decisions about the importance of one piece of visual information over another. They tended to form opinions quickly, easily connecting various bits of information, and generally had a richer personal framework for attaching meaning to the visual events that they were shown. As was the case with the other studies discussed above, these experts demonstrated traits common to both the theoretical and research-supported descriptions of proficient-to-expert teaching behaviors noted above.

The Study of Expertise in Constructivist Science Teaching

Each of the studies discussed above used a constructivist view of teaching and learning science (Clermont et al., 1993, 1994; Garnett & Tobin, 1988) for their analyses however, all of these studies used a qualitative approach to their research. A more recent study of expertise in science teaching used a mixed design, quantitative-dominant approach using a rubric referred to as the Expert Science Teaching Education Evaluation Model (ESTEEM) (Burry-Stock & Oxford, 1994). This model was founded on stage theory as described by Berliner (1988), using a behaviorally anchored continuum of novice to expert.

The ESTEEM instrument was developed by using both quantitative and qualitative analysis and involves more than just a classroom observation rubric. Also included was a self-assessment inventory of teaching practices using an expert-to-novice scale and complementary assessments of students' conceptual understanding.

Game Highlights Featuring Beliefs and Performance: Results of One Study

Let's talk about a few pros. Where did they come from? How do they play? What do they think? We will examine the pros in terms of the research that addressed these questions: What are the demographic characteristics of the proficient and expert teachers (i.e., the most expertlike science teachers) and the novice and competent teachers (i.e., the least expertlike teachers)? How can one evaluate the quality of their teaching and their thinking on the novice-to-expert continuum? Of course, because this section is based on a research study, confidence in measurement and instrumentation becomes pivotal as well. Focusing points include the following:

- The tools and strategies that are used to define and establish who might deserve the label of expertlike teacher
- A profile of the specific demographic characteristics of the subpopulation of teachers in the study, including comparisons of the most and least expertlike teachers
- A description of the teaching habits of the most expertlike teachers
- Considerations of key elements of the belief structures of the most expertlike teachers

The Tools of Analysis

Three instruments were used to define science teaching from different perspectives of expertise (Varrella & Burry-Stock, 2001). Two instruments were taken from the Expert Science Teaching Educational Evaluation Model (ESTEEM): the Teaching Practices Inventory (TPI) and the Science Classroom Observation Rubric (SCOR) (Burry-Stock, 1995b). These instruments describe ideal practices of expert science teaching from a constructivist perspective. The third instrument, the Beliefs About the Learning Environment (BALE), sought to describe and define expertlike beliefs (Varrella & Burry-Stock, 2001). All three incorporated Berliner's stage theory (Berliner, 1988) into their design, thus providing a consistent theoretical premise for analysis. The BALE also utilized Berliner's stage theory and was designed to evaluate teachers' responses to the open-ended "Teacher Beliefs Question" (Berliner, 1988; Burry-Stock, Yager, & Varrella, 1996; Robinson et al., 1997).

Where Do They Come From? What the Analysis Tells Us

The range of years of classroom teaching among the teachers in the study was from one to twenty-seven years. Twelve of the thirty-one teachers were teaching middle school at the time, and twelve of the thirty-one individuals had earned a master's degree. Earned credit hours past the baccalaureate among the group ranged from six to ninety hours. The range of years of participation in local and regional reform projects was from one to approximately twenty years. The gender was balanced, with fifteen women and sixteen men.

Statistically significant differences between the most expertlike and least expertlike teachers were found for five different demographic items. Differences were found in (1) years of participation in reform projects, (2) grade-level assignment (middle or high school), (3) master's degree designation, (yes or no), and (4) credit hours past the baccalaureate. Neither total years of teaching nor gender differences were statistically significant.

Did What They Think (Their Beliefs) Relate to How They Played (Taught)?

Each instrument helps us to understand the elements (the categories or scales) that were important and significant for the "major league" teacher. In addition to demographic characteristics that define major league teachers, the study sought relationships between beliefs and performance among the teacher sample. Multiple regression analyses were done to explore and describe these potential relationships between beliefs and practices (Peers, 1996). A regression helps to distill a large body of work down to those relationships that are most important. The bottom line is that teachers who are identified as expert by this study shared common beliefs about teaching and curriculum. What surfaced were four major findings:

1. Expert teachers value the learner as an individual.
2. Pedagogical approaches of experts are context-specific.
3. Experts are likely to go beyond the textbook to make instruction context-based.
4. Experts view learning and assessment as interwoven and interconnected.

Making Sense of the Results

The problem with expertise is how the concept is often misused or abused. If models of expertise are used to methodically cram teachers into the next newer and better mold, it becomes just another panacea, destined to fail and further widen the gap between the classroom teacher and reformers outside of the immediate school system. The advantage is to use expertise as a model and something that can be held up alongside the current beliefs, habits, and thoughts of practicing teachers. When expertise is put in the perspective of theory and practice and tied to longer-running enhancement efforts, teachers over time will take on more expertlike behaviors, each progressing farther than they might otherwise have imagined possible (Robinson et al., 1997). This transition coincides with changes in the individuals' articulated conceptions of teaching—beliefs and personal epistemologies, to be specific—and occurs over time through a personal conceptual change (Posner, Strike, Hewson, & Gertzog, 1982, Varrella, 1997).

Within this discussion, expertise is related to a series of common teacher characteristics. The influence of teachers' involvement with reform projects (that in this case emphasized STS and constructivism) was apparent among the proficient-to-expertlike teachers. Issue-based education was a priority and was described best by one of most expertlike teachers, "[learning events] are local, personal, and relevant." To use the phrase "local, personal, and relevant" without a context would usually be more indicative of a competent teacher than of a proficient-to-expert teacher, who is likely to include detail and description (Berliner, 1988). However, this teacher met this criterion in the statement preceding the one above, noting, "The student and teacher choose issues . . . [on the basis of] the needs of the student." All of the factors noted as outcomes of the regression support the premise that relating content to the student's experience (i.e., context) is critical, indeed expert.

Choices in The Classroom as an Indication of More Expertlike Beliefs

These most expertlike teachers established a tone and climate—that is, a culture—in the classroom. Their classrooms can be described as "working with" classrooms (Kohn, 1996), for example, "valuing the learner as an individual." Kohn considers everything from furniture to the teacher's voice and the climate around the school grounds, creating a list of "good signs" and "possible reasons for concern" (p. 55). In these most expertlike teachers' classrooms, an observer will see students addressing each other and asking questions of other students at least as often as they ask questions of the teacher. The atmosphere in these teachers' classrooms is more casual, and the students are active in experiential inquiries and problem-solving events. There is a deemphasis on facts and right answers, and the majority of exchanges include thinking, listening, problem solving, and a very obvious mutual respect between students and teacher bridging the learning and evaluative elements of the instructional program. Conversations are full of student queries and discussion rather than being dominated by teacher talk. Performance assessment is valued above traditional paper-and-pencil assessments. As one teacher among the most expertlike summarized, "by delegating some of the power, teachers can legitimately expect the students to see more value in what is going on. . . . It truly becomes their education."

Beliefs and Performance: The Instant Replay

Expert teachers from this study had common curricular tendencies that become a checklist for progression on the expertise scale. Common to experts is that they adapt content material, vary their instructional methods to emphasize conceptual understanding, are not overly dependent on the text as a source of their lessons, and codevelop content materials with their students (Varrella & Burry-Stock, 2001). These habits represent a conceptual change that occurred slowly over time. In addition to their curricular methods, experts display pedagogical habits that define expertise. Common to experts with regard to pedagogy is that they do the following:

- Not rely on the textbook
- Vary their teaching methods
- Maintain a high degree of student engagement in learning through application of exemplars, variation of teaching methods, and an emphasis on relevance
- Act as the facilitator, not the dictator
- Adapt to the needs of the moment on the basis of their studies conceptual and content understanding
- Emphasize understanding and the resolution of students' misconceptions

These teaching habits represent a state of mind—beliefs, values, attitudes—that guide teacher choices. The state of being—that of *being* in the classroom—represents the actualization of teaching on a daily basis. Hence, we have insight into the expertlike teachers in their zone.

Are Experts Born or Made?

Everyone searches for his or her fit in life. Once you find your career, what you make of it is in part based on talent, but an uncultured gift of talent will not get you past the minor leagues. We have considered key practices and complementary beliefs, but what of the journey? How do the most capable teachers become what they are? As our final elements, we should review the common demographic characteristics of the experts we have discussed and then consider, as our conclusion, a training routine.

Who Are These people?

A few common characteristics stood out among the most expertlike teachers in the study when compared to the least expertlike among them. A series of simple but important conclusions can be drawn from these data. The most expertlike teachers

- Have seniority in education (often ten years of experience)
- Are active in local, state and national school enhancement and reform efforts
- Represent an equal mix of men and women
- Are committed to lifelong learning, having earned additional degrees as well as continuing education credits (Compare to the least expertlike teachers, who tended not to have advanced degrees.)
- Show noteworthy consistency between what they do, defined by outside observers, and how they describe their philosophy and strategies for teaching
- Are often middle school teachers (No elementary teachers were involved in this study.)
- Are positively affected by their involvement in organized reform efforts as participants and particularly as teacher leaders
- In light of their relative level of expertise, provide further evidence that change, in this instance, in beliefs and pedagogical practices takes time (e.g., more than seven years of involvement in school reform and more than ten years of experience)

Change on the part of the study group, the system, and the individual is a time-hungry experience. Time has a multiple meanings here. Time also refers to the need for a radical change in the school day (Canady & Rettig, 1993). How can we extend our thinking and ideas in a sequence of unrelated, lockstep forty-three- to fifty-minute blocks of time separated by an obnoxious bell or buzzer? Finally, patience does not imply inactivity, just tolerance and support as participants in reform at the local level grow in their understanding and commitment to the larger agenda and further realize their individual potential to contribute to whole (Darling-Hammond, 1993).

Strength and Endurance Conditioning: A Framework for Thought and Action

The elements of conditioning that help the average teacher to become a good teacher or the good teacher to become a great teacher can be defined through a series of interlinked epistemological and pedagogical pivot points. The portrait of the expertlike teachers painted in this chapter hold a series of practical abilities and elements in their belief structures in common. Although these factors are apparent from the evidence and analyses presented above, it is only when the colors are mixed and applied to the canvas of the classroom that the true portrait of expertise can be appreciated. The resulting combination of these factors is more significant than the sum of either their teaching behaviors or beliefs. These expertlike teachers are all people who are proud to be teachers, remaining in their jobs by choice, not chance.

As was noted early in this chapter, great teachers are lifelong learners; for them, there is no end to the season. The evidence supports this premise that the conditioning routine is varied and of extended length. Expertlike teachers are committed to the expansion of their understanding of how people learn, how to teach effectively, and to expanding their understanding and mastery of the subjects that they teach. They are unafraid to take risks, working to make sense out of the natural and human-made world and always relating the new to familiar for themselves and for their students. Great teachers do not work in isolation. They seek out opportunities to collaborate, cooperate, and lead, as the situation requires. Moreover, they always work hard to model actions similar to those they expect of the students in their charge.

A framework for thinking and acting in and out of the classroom can be built around a series of six critical conditioning points (C^6):

The first point is that of *collaboration*. Seldom does someone reach expertise in teaching without having a collaborative nature, which always works best when in harmony with an open mind. However much one might learn by oneself, it is in collaboration with others that the power of the collective intellect eventually wins the day. Expertlike teachers are always interested in learning more about their subject areas, about effective teaching, and about what their students think and know. In particular, this latter element requires that the teacher be a good listener, which of course is the pivotal element of being a good collaborator.

Learning and teaching are oriented first toward *conceptual* understanding, which is the second C. All of the teachers in Varrella's (Varrella, 1997) original study followed a simple organizational scheme that emphasized a tenet of "phenomena before explanation." They tended to approach their instruction as suggested by the National Science Education Standards (National Research Council, 1996), which advocate "present[ing] broad unifying concepts and processes that complement the analytical, more discipline-based perspectives presented in the other [grade level content] standards" (p. 115). The expertlike teacher emphasizes the concept as a way to keep the big ideas ever linked to the details.

Content is our third C and embraces a wide variety of elements including facts, general knowledge, and skills. Content represents the critical details supporting the concept. As suggested in the National Science Education Standards, the unifying concepts and processes that govern the natural and human-influenced world are not the end, but rather the pivot for a deeper and broader understanding science. Required practice for and successful measurement of learning require that the students do something with what they have learned and can demonstrate an application other than on a paper-and-pencil test. That is, traditional and alternative practices must be included in the mix. The application might be in problem solving, simulation, or a performance-based situation. However, no matter the circumstance of the performance, a successful demonstration requires the inclusion of *details of content knowledge* at the appropriate development level.

Within the relationships among the domains of PCK, teacher understandings are those related to *context,* the fourth C. This includes the teacher's knowledge and understanding of community, of students and their ideas and existing conceptions, of the school's expectations, and of the world around us (Magnusson, Krajcik, & Borko, 1999). A commitment to context requires that the teacher connect with learners and help them to connect with their own existing understanding and experiences and with the larger world, whether it is just outside the door or a universe away. Attention to context is a high priority among those who are committed to STS-constructivist teaching; that is, the learning must be *relevant* to the student. This has developmental as well as practical implications when the teacher considers the students' ages, experiences, and abilities. The teacher can only tap the personal world of the child when the child is actively engaged in the learning experience. The idea of context has clear implications for curriculum planning that span the spectrum of curriculum design, scope, sequence, and appropriate methodologies.

Within the ideal learning event, which might be completed in forty-five minutes or forty-five days, depending on the topic and goals, the experience must link to the learners' frame of understanding. The learner's frame of understanding is constructed within and without the school. The expertlike teacher is cognizant of this generative, experientially based learning cycle (Osborne & Wittrock, 1985). These teachers strive to make sure that the learning events are relevant *both* to the learner and directly to the goals and target benchmarks of their unit, topic, or theme of study. Thus, we identify the fifth C, as *connectivity* or *connectedness,* a term that represents the complex interrelationship of the individual learner's experience, the curriculum, the leadership of the teacher. Many teachers wrongly assume that if all the lessons are on the same subject and perhaps are even theme-based, then the students will naturally make the connections across the series of individual lessons, all carefully constructed around a single topic, unit, or concept. The expertlike teacher understands the reality that this is not so! The expertlike teacher designs a curriculum and applies methodologies that include students' questions, interests, and existing adequate or inadequate conceptions. In essence, the expertlike teacher always begins and ends with what students *think that they know.* These curriculum frameworks incorporate inquiry and problem-solving techniques, pique and maintain interest and curiosity through novelty and context (relevance), and seldom if ever stray from the learning goals for the children. In essence, they build connectivity by encouraging collaboration among students, collaborating with their students, and continually emphasizing concept and content constructed around personally relevant big ideas, guiding questions, and problem-solving opportunities (Anderson et al., 1994; Brooks & Brooks, 1999; Driver, Asoko, Leach, Mortimer, & Scott, 1994; National Research Council, 1996; Osborne & Wittrock, 1983; Penick, Crow, & Bonnstetter, 1996; Varrella, 1996; Yager, 1991, 1995). As was noted earlier in the description of stage 5 of the novice-to-expert continuum, these teachers exercise their intuitive grasp of the situation to fluidly blend the components into a team effort that is akin to coaching their team to the pennant every season.

There is one last C, which some consider the most important of all: *caring*. Caring teachers not only care *about* subject and students, they also care *for* their students and strive to build connections in the learning environment between themselves and the content, between and among the students, between the teacher and the students, and, most important, at the intersection of the student, the content, and the teacher (Van Sickle & Spector, 1996). In this rich milieu of caring for and being cared for, the learners thrive (Noddings, 1984, 1992; Van Sickle & Spector, 1996). At this nexus of connectivity, the expertlike, caring teacher is in the zone, at the top of his or her game—hence the symbolic use of C^6, which much greater than the sum of $6 + 6 + 6 + 6 + 6 + 6$!

CONCLUSION: The All-Star Science Teacher

The most able teachers bring a vast body of practical and theoretical knowledge about teaching and about their subject(s) to bear for the benefit of their students every day. They care about the knowledge base and care for their students as they help them to grow intellectually and socially. These expertlike teachers emphasize and balance the key elements of partnerships between students and themselves, placing a large part of the ownership of the learning experience on the students through context, connectivity, and a focus on conceptual understanding and content knowledge. Thus do the expertlike teachers demonstrate their consistency in their practices and beliefs. These pivotal elements, including the rich and explicit belief system and commensurate practices, together represent within the very being of the expertlike teacher. In every instance, it is the result of years of work, constant reflection, and a burning desire to reach and stay at the top of their game.

These teachers see modeling an enthusiasm for learning as an endless and exciting journey, demonstrating how they care best for their students. One of the expertlike teachers in Varrella's (Varrella, 1997) study concluded an interview by saying, "We encourage students to be lifelong learners, shouldn't we as teachers model this as well? In the STS/constructivist classroom the teacher is a lifelong learner!"

The Game in Action

The All-Star and the Rookie

What follows are two true stories that frame the journey to the all-stars from two perspectives and in the teachers' own words. One perspective is that of the seasoned veteran, Bill, who has had an illustrious career teaching in Iowa. The other is that of Kim, who recently completed her internship and is now launching her quest toward all-star status in Virginia.

BILL'S STORY: Looking Back

My story begins in the fall of 1968 when, as a twenty-two-year-old rookie teacher, I was hired by an Iowa school district to teach science and social studies in a middle school. My first day at spring training, so to speak, I became aware that I was the junior staff person by nearly twenty-five years! The staff had an all-veteran line up—and me. To say that I might have been out of my league would be a gross understatement. These people had amassed years in the trenches, and I was aware very quickly of how inadequate my college preparation had been.

As the year began to unfold, I listened to and observed these people doing all sorts of wonderful things with students that I could only hope to do some day. They moved easily from subject area to subject area in what seemed to be a seamless flow from one day to the next. Their classes were somehow connected to each other, and it appeared that they always were aware of what each other was doing at any given time.

It soon became apparent that one of the critical pieces to their knowing and thus their artistry was the collaborative nature of the noon lunch hour. All morning happenings, both good and bad, were discussed, and any student who had wandered from the path was soon made aware that everyone knew of his or her transgressions. The lunch hour meetings were also a time to find out what was going on in each others classrooms, so there was never a time when opportunities to team across curricular lines was wasted.

While listening (I had nothing to share), I learned that most of these veterans had come up the hard way in one-room schools and teaching with Normal training until they could afford to finish their four-year degree. They had paid their dues and knew their craft. Most had learned early on that an integrated approach to teaching was the only way one could survive. In many one-room schools and multiple-grade classrooms, this meant that students were peer coaches teaching younger or slower students. The power of such cooperation was not left behind when these remarkable teachers moved from the country to the schools in town. Years of trial and error had honed their skills, and they operated in their classrooms as if they had written the text on all the modern-day education terms we use today.

It was in this environment that I spent the first ten years of my science-teaching career, being mentored by a senior faculty member, also named Bill, on what was really important for students to learn. Most of what Bill believed couldn't be found in hard copy or reproduced on worksheets. Most areas that we touched on just seemed to somehow get back to concerns about the planet and its resources. He was, as one soil conservationist said, almost a missionary when it came to the environment.

As inevitably happens, the day came for Bill to retire, and at age 32, I was left as the only science teacher in the school. Although Bill and I kept in close contact until his death two years ago, I soon began to revert to more traditional teaching practices. I found convenient excuses for retreating to text-driven, worksheet-bound methods, but in my heart, I knew that my students had to be as bored as I was. Student load, class size, and the emphasis on basic skills were all billboard-size excuses I readily hid behind because I lacked the self confidence to do the job.

Around 1984, a fellow science teacher and I heard of a professional development workshop at the nearby university on the topic of STS, and we applied for the one-week session. It was at this workshop that I again began to hear familiar ideas about teaching and learning that I had gradually put aside. My colleague Ron and I returned to our school thinking of ways to make the science classes we taught more student centered and less a dictatorship that they had become. A year later, I embarked on a master's degree program in science education and once again heard ideas about student-centered learning, learning theory, and a myriad of other theory-laden ideas that would soon change the way I delivered science instruction. Suddenly, I no longer looked for reasons not to try new ideas but fully embraced the challenge of implementing new practice in the classroom. In many cases, what my colleagues and I heard as possibility in Monday evening classes, we put into practice on Tuesday. For the first time in many years, we were responding to students' questions in meaningful ways, and the dynamics of our classrooms were changing rapidly. Students no longer could memorize for tests and pass courses. They were forced to think. New questioning techniques forced them to answer in depth, and we refused to let them be satisfied with superficial explanations from anyone.

Once these changes began, every other part of the curriculum had to be changed as well. Simple methods of assessing student progress no longer fit the way were operating in our classrooms. Multiple forms of assessment became the norm, and both teacher and student expectations of what was possible rose ever higher. We had moved in two short years from teacher-centered to student-centered classrooms in grades 7 to 12 in our science departments. From 1987 to 1989, most of our curriculum had changed to reflect local, relevant issue-based topics that both encompassed and were applied to traditional science. If we wanted to do titrations in chemistry, we used water from local streams, wells, and municipal sources and tested them for nitrates in parts per million. In retrospect, that strategy was no different from those I had eschewed only ten years earlier when I retreated to the seeming safety of the text! Students were a never-ending source of issues and questions that we were able to use to cover all the standard parts of our curriculum. When we needed things that related to force and motion, an Iowa highway patrolman or local sheriff was happy to come to class and explain how they used laws of physics to determine how fast a vehicle was traveling in an accident. The shift was subtle but profound. Students now owned the classroom while we covered science concepts in ways that were meaningful to all of us. All of us were now learners, and as a facilitator rather than a dictator, I found that my job was fun again.

Now I observe new teachers coming into our district who are not unlike myself thirty-four years ago. It strikes me that those who are really successful have a grasp of the needs of students and use that as a way of teaching their subject matter. As simple as it sounds, too often we only give lip service to what student needs really are and use all the trite excuses to explain why we deliver instruction that has little long-term value for our audience. If we are to teach, then we need not only to assess students, but, more important, also to assess our own teaching practices. Until that happens, little professional growth will occur, and teachers might well retire from the profession having taught the first year thirty-four times!

KIM'S STORY: Looking Ahead

Since I began my graduate courses in elementary education, I have moved from the novice T-ball player to the minors, and in a few short months, I will step to the plate as a major league player. The major league—it was my first dream as a child, it's what I've trained for, what I've sacrificed for, it's what I've dreamed of, it's the goal that helped me through tough times when I wondered, "Can I make it through this semester?" It's suddenly a realistic goal that somehow seemed far enough away that it was never quite understood as a reality. As I sit here now, with a full year of internship experience behind me, along with thirty-two graduate-level courses, I am aware for the first time the reality that I will be a teacher in the fall. I am nervous; there are no pinch hitters—or runners, for that matter—in this major league. There are fastballs and curve balls waiting for me that I haven't even imagined. There are bound to be some angry fans who won't like the way I play, and as Tom Hanks said, "There's no crying in baseball!" However, I am confident that my education thus far and my experiences in the classroom over the past year have prepared me to begin my rookie year.

My T-ball days were short and sweet. Oh, how naïve I was! I remember my first shock: "Kids don't sit in rows anymore?" Puzzled, I probed my professor to learn that teachers actually want students to talk to each other. "This is how we learn," she explained to me. I will never forget the drive home after that first night of classes. I was consumed in thought. We learn by talking to one another—could this be true? I started to think about all the lessons I have learned in life, both academic and general life lessons. The knowledge I have gained, that has remained with me, has come from both lessons that were modeled in some way and lessons in which I was encouraged to talk to others. I gained new insight, learned different perspectives, and deepened my understanding by simply talking to others. It was all coming together: Students don't sit in rows because we want them to talk to their peers and help each other learn. It wouldn't be until later, in my minor league days, that I would reflect on this epiphany and understand it as an example of connectivity. My professor was modeling a teaching philosophy; she was acting as a guide, a facilitator, guiding me to make connections and helping me to construct my own knowledge.

My minor league days have followed the pattern of enlightenment, reflection, enlightenment, reflection, with a few epiphanies here and there. I have had the amazing opportunity of observing and even collaborating with the veteran players who are so willing to coach, share their experiences, and offer support to the novice who is learning how to play. Textbooks, articles, and course assignments are all helpful and necessary, but I have learned how invaluable veteran teachers and actual experience are. I have learned more by talking to these veteran teachers about their experiences and ideas, even those that have different philosophies and styles than I do, than I have from any textbook. Because I am going through a program that teaches by modeling, I have learned how important it is not only for my own leaning but also for the students that I will one day teach. I have learned the importance of scaffolding, how if it is done properly, it will build confidence and prepare the student for independence. As I reflect on my teacher preparation courses thus far, I see how I was exposed to the constructivist theory, scaffolding, and connectivity in a way that has made all of these ideas relevant to my own life. Through connectivity, the program has set us up for success and guided us along the way to construct our own knowledge while making everything we have learned relevant and meaningful. This is what I hope to do for my students.

I have learned from professors who have acted as facilitators as they have guided me to make my own connections and construct my own knowledge. They have encouraged me to *do*, not simply memorize or think about what I have learned. Somehow I skipped the memorization step that I have become so accustomed to. In thinking about, talking about, and doing what I have learned, I have understood so much more than I would have by memorizing a theory or parts of a text. I have gained confidence in my knowledge and my ability because I have experience to support my learning as opposed to theory alone. This is why my students will do often. I want my students to learn through experiences and real-life examples that connect to what they know so that they will truly learn and understand the concepts of the curriculum. My title will be teacher, but my role will be facilitator. My goal is to make learning fun for my students. I want them to learn without initially realizing that they are learning. I realize that this is difficult and time consuming for the teacher, but teaching isn't about me. It's about the pride a child feels when she realizes that she read her first book or the growth of a child in knowledge and confidence in a year. It's about providing stability, support, and a routine for a child who has none of these things at home. It is about opening up the world to a child and giving him or her the skills to succeed in that world. It is about giving hope. Time is not a factor; heart, determination, and passion are required.

To be a good teacher, I need to continually grow. There are two ways I intend to do this. The first is to stay current with the latest research, reading all I can and talking to my colleagues about what is new, and not to be afraid to try new things. The second, which is extremely important, is to continually reflect. I will never grow and learn if I do not reflect on what I am doing well, what I need to improve, what went well in the classroom, what really stunk, where I have been, where I am now, and where I want to go and how to get there. I need to reflect

internally as well as share my reflections with others so that they can offer a different perspective and insight I might not be aware of. Luckily, I am a reflective person in general. However, I have perfected my technique throughout this past year. I reflect every day on the school day in general, lessons in particular, and my teaching. I have reflected on various lessons, then watched videotapes of these lessons (which I highly recommend!) and reflected on the video with a new perspective. I'm amazed at what I have learned about myself and my teaching along with my students by watching and reflecting on a taped lesson. If I reflect, I will grow.

I am excited and nervous as I approach my rookie year. I have had wonderful coaching and great models to emulate. I know that there will be days when I will strike out or hit a few foul balls, but I am confident that I will step to the plate armed with knowledge and passion and will one day hit a home run. Who knows, maybe one day I'll even make the Hall of Fame!

Reflecting on the Game

1. Every teacher has personal areas of expertise. Identify three of your greatest teaching strengths. What would a visitor see your students and you doing in your classroom that is a demonstration of this strength?

2. List your three key learning goals for your students in one of your classes. What would a visitor see your students and you doing in your classroom that indicates that you are attending to these goals?

3. How do people, regardless of age, learn? What do you do to help the students learn in terms of facilitating behaviors, that is, things that help the students meet the stated learning goals in your class? What blocking behaviors might get in the way of accomplishing these goals, and how can you modify those behaviors?

4. What evidence might be clearly seen by an outside observer related to your actions and those of your students that would support a claim that you are using the C^6 framework:?

References

Airasian, P. W., & Walsh, M. E. (1997). Constructivist cautions. *Phi Delta Kappan, 78,* 444–449.

Anderson, R. D., Anderson, B. L., Varanka-Martin, M. A., Romagnano, L., Bielenberg, J., Flory, M., Mieras, B., & Whitworth, J. (1994). *Issues of curriculum reform in science, mathematics and higher order thinking across the disciplines.* Washington, DC: U.S. Government Printing Office.

Andre, T. (1986). Problem solving and education. In G. D. P. T. Andre (Ed.), *Cognitive classroom learning: Understanding, thinking, and problem solving.* Orlando, FL: Academic Press.

Bandura, A. (1977). Self-efficacy: Toward a unifying theory of behavioral change. *Psychological Review, 84,* 191–215.

Beck, J. A., & Lumpe, A. T. (1996, January). *Teachers' beliefs and the implementation of personal relevance in the classroom.* Paper presented at the Annual Meeting of the Association for the Education of Teachers in Science, Seattle, WA.

Berliner, D. C. (1986). In pursuit of the expert pedagogue. *Educational Researcher, 15,* 5–13.

Berliner, D. C. (1987). Ways of thinking about students and classrooms by more and less experienced teachers. In J. Calderhead (Ed.), *Exploring teachers' thinking* (pp. 60–83). New York: Taylor and Francis.

Berliner, D. C. (1988, February). *The development of expertise in pedagogy.* Paper presented at the Charles W. Hunt Memorial Lecture presented at the Annual Meeting of the American Association of Colleges for Teacher Education, New Orleans, LA.

Brooks, J. G., & Brooks, M. G. (1999). *In search of understanding: The case for the constructivist classroom.* Alexandria, VA: Association for Curriculum Development.

Burry-Stock, J. A. (1995a). *Expert Science Teacher Evaluation Model (ESTEEM): Theory, Development, and Research.* Kalamazoo, MI: Center for Research on Educational Accountability and Teacher Evaluation.

Burry-Stock, J. A. (1995b). *Expert Science Teaching Evaluation Model (ESTEEM) instruments.* Kalamazoo, MI: Center for Research on Education Accountability and Teacher Evaluation.

Burry-Stock, J. A., & Oxford, R. L. (1994). Expert Science Teaching Education Evaluation Model (ESTEEM): Measuring excellence in science teaching for professional development. *Journal of Personnel Evaluation in Education, 8,* 267–297.

Burry-Stock, J. A., Yager, R. E., & Varrella, G. F. (1996, April). *An illustration of science education reform: The Iowa SS&C Project.* Paper presented at the National Association for Research in Science Teaching (NARST) Annual Meeting, St. Louis.

Canady, R. L., & Rettig, M. D. (1993). Unlocking the lockstep high school. *Phi Delta Kappan, 75,* 512–520.

Carter, K., Cushing, K., Sabers, D., Stein, P., & Berliner, D. (1988). Expert-novice differences in perceiving and processing visual classroom information. *Journal of Teacher Education, 39*(1), 25–31.

Chi, M. T. H., Glaser, R., & Farr, M. J. (Eds.). (1988). *The nature of expertise.* Hillsdale, NJ: Lawrence Erlbaum Associates.

Clermont, C. P., Borko, H., & Krajcik, J. S. (1994). Comparative study of the pedagogical content knowledge of experienced and novice chemical demonstrators. *Journal of Research in Science Teaching, 31,* 419–441.

Clermont, C. P., Krajcik, J. S., & Borko, H. (1993). The influence of an intensive in-service workshop on pedagogical content knowledge growth among novice chemical demonstrators. *Journal of Research in Science Teaching, 30,* 21–43.

Cohen, R. M. (2002). Schools our teachers deserve: A proposal for teacher-centered reform. *Phi Delta Kappan, 83*(7), 532–537.

Darling-Hammond, L. (1993). Reframing the school reform agenda: Developing capacity for school transformation. *Phi Delta Kappan, 74,* 752–761.

Dreyfus, H. L., & Dreyfus, S. E. (1986). *Mind over machine.* New York: The Free Press.

Driver, R., Asoko, H., Leach, J., Mortimer, E., & Scott, P. (1994). Constructing scientific knowledge in the classroom. *Educational Researcher, 23*(7), 5–12.

Duda, R. O., & Shortliffe, E. H. (1983). Expert Systems Research. *Science, 220,* 261–267.

Fenstermacher, G. D. (1988). The place of science and epistemology in Schön's conception of reflective practice. In P. P. Grimmett & G. L. Erickson (Eds.), *Reflection in Teacher Education* (pp. 39–46). New York: Teachers College Press.

Garnett, P. J., & Tobin, K. (1988). Teaching for understanding: Exemplary practice in high school chemistry. *Journal of Research in Science Teaching, 26*(1), 1–14.

Gess-Newsome, J. (1999). Secondary teachers knowledge and beliefs about subject matter and their impact on instruction. In J. G.-N. N. G.

Lederman (Ed.), *Examining pedagogical content knowledge* (pp. 51–94). Boston: Kluwer Academic Publishers.

Hamilton, M. L. (1993). Think you can: The influence of culture on beliefs. In C. Day & J. Calderhead & P. Denicolo (Eds.), *Research on teacher thinking: Understanding professional development.* Washington, DC: The Falmer Press.

Harms, N. C. (1981). Project Synthesis: Summary and implications for teachers. In N. C. Harms & R. E. Yager (Eds.), *What research says to the science teacher* (Vol. 3). Washington, DC: National Science Teachers Association.

Kagan, D. M. (1990). Ways of evaluating teacher cognition: Inferences concerning the Goldilocks Principle. *Review of Educational Research, 60,* 419–469.

Keating, J. F. (1997). Harvesting cultural knowledge. *The Science Teacher, 64*(2), 22–25.

Kelly, G. A. (1955). *The psychology of personal constructs.* New York: Norton.

Kohn, A. (1996). What to look for in a classroom. *Educational Leadership, 54*(1), 54–55.

Magnusson, S., Krajcik, J., & Borko, H. (1999). Nature, sources, and development of pedagogical content knowledge for science teaching. In J. Gess-Newsome & N. G. Lederman (Eds.), *Pedagogical content knowledge and science education* (pp. 95–132). Boston: Kluwer Academic Publishers.

National Research Council. (1996). *National science education standards.* Washington, DC: National Academy Press.

Noddings, N. (1984). *Caring, a feminine approach to ethics and moral education.* Berkeley, CA: University of California Press.

Noddings, N. (1992). *The challenge to care in schools.* New York: Teachers College Press.

Osborne, R. J., & Wittrock, M. C. (1983). Learning science: A generative process. *Science Education, 67,* 489–504.

Osborne, R., & Wittrock, M. (1985). The generative learning model and its implications for science education. *Studies in Science Education, 12,* 59–87.

Pajares, M. F. (1992). Teachers' beliefs and educational research: Cleaning up a messy construct. *Review of Educational Research, 62,* 307–332.

Peers, I. S. (1996). *Statistical analysis for education and psychology researchers.* Washington, DC: Falmer Press.

Penick, J. E., Crow, L. W., & Bonnstetter, R. J. (1996). Questions are the answer. *The Science Teacher, 63*(1), 26–29.

Posner, G. J., Strike, K. A., Hewson, P. W., & Gertzog, W. A. (1982). Accommodation of a scientific conception: Toward a theory of conceptual change. *Science Education, 66*(2), 211–227.

Prawat, R. S. (1992). Teachers' beliefs about teaching and learning: A constructivist perspective. *American Journal of Education, 100,* 354–395.

Rankin, L. (1999). Lessons learned: Addressing common misconceptions about inquiry. In National Science Foundation & Westat (Eds.), *Foundations: Inquiry—thoughts, views, and strategies for the K–5 classroom* (Vol. 2). Arlington, VA: National Science Foundation.

Robinson, J. B., Enger, S. K., Varrella, G. F., & Yager, R. E. (1997, October). *Iowa Scope, Sequence, and Coordination Project Final Report.* Iowa City, IA: University of Iowa Science Education Center.

Rokeach, M. (1970). *Beliefs, attitudes, and values.* San Francisco: Jossey-Bass.

Roychoudhury, A., Tippins, D. J., & Nichols, S. E. (1995). Gender inclusive science teaching: A feminist-constructivist approach. *Journal of Research in Science Teaching, 32,* 897–924.

Schön, D. A. (1983). *The reflective practitioner: How professionals think in action.* New York: Basic Books.

Shulman, L. S. (1986). Those who understand: Knowledge growth in teaching. *Educational Researcher, 15*(2), 4–14.

Shulman, L. S. (1987). Knowledge and teaching: Foundations of the new reform. *Harvard Educational Review, 57,* 1–22.

van Driel, J. H., Beijaard, D., & Verloop, N. (2001). Professional development and reform in science education: The role of teachers' practical knowledge. *Journal of Research in Science Teaching, 38*(2), 137–158.

Van Sickle, M., & Spector, B. (1996). Caring relationships in science classrooms: A symbolic interaction study. *Journal of Research in Science Teaching, 33*(4), 433–453.

Varrella, G. F. (1996). Using what has been learned: The application domain in an STS-constructivist setting. In R. Yager (Ed.), *Science/technology/society as reform in science education* (pp. 95–108). Albany, NY: State University of New York Press.

Varrella, G. F. (1997, March). *Voices of reform: The proficient/expert teacher.* Paper presented at the National Association for Research in Science Teaching Annual Meeting, Oakbrook, IL.

Varrella, G. F., & Burry-Stock, J. A. (1997, March). *Walking the walk and talking the talk: Teachers' beliefs and pedagogical practices.* Paper presented at the National Association for Research in Science Teaching Annual Meeting, Oakbrook, IL.

Varrella, G. F., & Burry-Stock, J. A. (2001, March). *Linking science teachers' beliefs and teaching practices.* Paper presented at the National Association for Research in Science Teaching, St. Louis, MO.

Varrella, G. F., Castle, T., Haas, B., Mays, D. W., Washburn Jr., D., & Toadvine, W. (1999). *Whatever it takes: The case study of Dawson-Bryant Elementary School.* Columbus, OH: Ohio Department of Education.

Varrella, G. F., & Yager, R. E. (1998, April). *Threads in the fabric of change: Characteristics of student-centered teachers.* Paper presented at the National Association for Research in Science Teaching, Annual Meeting, San Diego, CA.

Wilson, S. M., Shulman, L. S., & Richert, A. E. (1987). "150 different ways" of knowing: Representations of knowledge in teaching. In J. Calderhead (Ed.), *Exploring teachers' thinking.* (pp. 104–124). London: Cassell Educational Ltd.

Yager, R. E. (1991). The constructivist learning model: Towards real reform in science education. *The Science Teacher, 58*(6), 52–57.

Yager, R. E. (1995). Constructivism and the learning of science. In S. M. Glynn & R. Duit (Eds.), *Learning science in the schools: Research reforming practice* (pp. 44). Mahwah, NJ: Lawrence Erlbaum Associates.

Yager, R. E., & Roy, R. (1993). STS: Most pervasive and most radical reform approaches to "science" education. In R. E. Yager (Ed.), *What research says to the science teacher: The science, technology, society movement.* (Vol. 7, pp. 177). Washington, DC: National Science Teachers Association.

Additional Resources

Calderhead, J. (Ed.). (1987). *Exploring teachers' thinking.* London: Cassell Educational Limited.

Fullan, M. G. (1994). *Changing forces: Probing the depths of educational reform.* London: The Falmer Press.

Fullan, M. G., & Miles, M. B. (1992). Getting reform right: What works and what doesn't. *Phi Delta Kappan, 73,* 744–752.

Noddings, N. (1992). *The challenge to care in schools.* New York: Teachers College Press.

Osborne, J. F. (1996). Beyond constructivism. *Science Education, 80,* 53–82.

Schön, D. A. (1983). *The reflective practitioner: How professionals think in action.* New York: Basic Books.

Senge, P. M. (1990). *The fifth discipline.* New York: Doubleday.

Sergiovanni, T. J. (1994). *Building community in schools.* San Francisco: Jossey-Bass.

Van Sickle, M., & Spector, B. (1996). Caring relationships in science classrooms: A symbolic interaction study. *Journal of Research in Science Teaching, 33*(4), 433–453.

chapter 3

NEW SCIENCE COACHES:
Preparation in the New Rules of Science Education

Pradeep M. Dass, Ph.D.
Department of Biology and
Science Education, Assistant
Professor of Science Education
and Biology, Appalachian
State University

ABOUT THE AUTHOR: Dr. Pradeep Dass is an assistant professor of science education at Appalachian State University, teaching courses in science education and biology. He was a classroom teacher for fourteen years at Woodstock International School, Mussoorie, India, before pursuing his doctoral degree in science education. Dr. Dass is distinguished for his involvement in the preparation of preservice science teachers and professional development of in-service science teachers. His research and service expertise in science teacher preparation have been shared widely through professional science teacher organizations, including the Association for the Education of Teacher of Science and the National Association for Research in Science Teaching. He is currently active in professional development programs designed to promote the science-technology-society approach in school science instruction in several states within the United States.

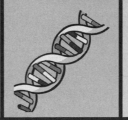

Success is where preparation and opportunity meet.

—Bobby Unser
Three-time Indianapolis 500 winner

CHAPTER WARM-UP

New rules for promoting scientific literacy are based on what we have come to know about the learning process itself. An exciting convergence has resulted in which modern science education mirrors the practice of science itself. Like science practitioners, learners of science develop knowledge and skills in several domains, including concepts, processes, applications, attitudes, creativity, and world view or nature of science. Teaching toward these domains requires rich experiences on the part of science teachers immersed in empirically derived practices and models.

INTRODUCTION: Changing Rules for the Game of Science in School Classrooms

The last two decades of the second millennium witnessed the emergence of new suggestions about how the game of science ought to be played in K–12 classrooms (Harms, 1981; Yager, 1987; Yager & McCormack, 1989). These suggestions stemmed from the recognition that the professional game of science itself has undergone drastic changes in the recent past (see Hurd, 1997, for examples of some of these changes). If the game has been changing at the professional level, its experience at the school level ought to mirror some of those changes so that the experience is somewhat authentic. Furthermore, greater understanding of how children learn has led to the recognition that the way we have played the game of science in school classrooms has been, for the most part, incongruent with the learning process. Thus, to be able to play the game so that it mirrors the professional game and is congruent with principles of effective learning, new rules must be employed. The Benchmarks for Science Literacy (American Association for the Advancement of Science, 1993) and National Science Education Standards (National Research Council, 1996) represent two commonly used sources of the new rules within the United States. Efforts to develop similar rules have been under way in other parts of the world too (e.g., Millar & Osborne, 1998). Collectively, these new rules promote teaching and learning of science that goes far beyond simple transmittal of the so-called scientific facts, figures, and processes learned in a rote manner for their own sake (which, unfortunately, happens to prevail even today in many school science classes). The key features of science instruction promoted by the new rules include enhancement of student understanding of the nature of science, student ability to critically analyze scientific information and apply it to real-life situations, and development of an attitude and desire for lifelong learning in science and matters related to science. Often these features are associated with being a scientifically literate person. Table 3.1 captures the spirit and goals of scientific literacy embodied in the new rules as found in three major U.S. documents.

As was mentioned earlier, one of the key principles that guided the development of the new rules is that "school science reflects the intellectual and cultural traditions that characterize the practice of contemporary science" (National Research Council, 1996, p. 19). This principle is evident in the areas of changing emphases presented in Table 3.2. These changing emphases can be regarded as changing rules.

The other factor that contributed to the development of new rules in the game of school science is significant improvement in our understanding of how children learn. On the basis of this improvement in understanding, Reinsmith (1993) proposed the following ten fundamental truths about learning:

1. Learning first takes place through osmosis.
2. Authentic learning comes through trial and error.
3. Students will learn only what they have some proclivity for or interest in.
4. No one will formally learn something unless the person believes that he or she can learn it.

Table 3.1 Goals of scientific literacy promoted by the new rules	
Document	**Scientific Literacy Goals**
Science for All Americans (American Association for the Advancement of Science, 1994, p. xvii)	[T]he science literate person is one who is aware that science, mathematics, and technology are interdependent human enterprises with strengths and limitations; understands key concepts and principles of science; is familiar with the natural world and recognizes both its diversity and unity; and uses scientific knowledge and scientific ways of thinking for individual and social purposes.
National Science Education Standards (National Research Council, 1996, p. 13)	The goals for school science that underlie the National Science Education Standards are to educate students who are able to • experience the richness and excitement of knowing about and understanding the natural world; • use appropriate scientific processes and principles in making personal decisions; • engage intelligently in public discourse and debate about matters of scientific and technological concern; and • increase their economic productivity through the use of the knowledge, understanding, and skills of the scientifically literate person in their careers. These goals define a scientifically literate society.
National Science Teachers Association Handbook (National Science Teachers Association, 1992 93, pp. 168–169)	Among other things, a scientifically and technologically literate person • uses concepts of science and of technology as well as informed reflection of ethical values in solving everyday problems and making responsible decisions in everyday life, including work and leisure; • engages in responsible personal and civic actions after weighing the possible consequences of alternative options; • defends decisions and actions using rational arguments based on evidence; and • considers the political, economic, moral, and ethical aspects of science and technology as they relate to personal and global issues.

5. Learning cannot take place outside an appropriate context.
6. Real learning connotes use.
7. No one knows how a learner moves from imitation to intrinsic ownership, from external modeling to internalization and competence.
8. The more learning is like play, the more absorbing it will be.
9. For authentic learning to happen, time should occasionally be wasted, tangents should be pursued, and side-shoots should be followed up.
10. Tests are a very poor indicator of whether an individual has really learned something.

Table 3.2 Changing emphases promoted by the National Science Education Standards

Less Emphasis on	More Emphasis on
Knowing scientific facts and information	Understanding scientific concepts and developing abilities of inquiry
Studying subject matter disciplines (physical, life, earth sciences) for their own sake	Learning subject matter disciplines in the context of inquiry, technology, science in personal and social perspectives, and history and nature of science
Separating science knowledge and science process	Integrating all aspects of science content
Covering many science topics	Studying a few fundamental science concepts
Implementing inquiry as a set of processes	Implementing inquiry as instructional strategies, abilities, and ideas to be learned
Activities that demonstrate and verify science content	Activities that investigate and analyze science questions
Investigations confined to one class period	Investigations over extended periods of time
Process skills out of context	Process skills in context
Individual process skills such as observation or inference	Using multiple process skills: manipulation, cognitive, procedural
Getting an answer	Using evidence and strategies for developing or revising an explanation
Science as exploration and experiment	Science as argument and explanation
Providing answers to questions about science content	Communicating science explanations
Individuals and groups of students analyzing and synthesizing data without defending a conclusion	Groups of students often analyzing and synthesizing data after defending conclusions
Doing few investigations in order to leave time to cover large amounts of content	Doing more investigations in order to develop understanding, ability, values of inquiry and knowledge of science content
Concluding inquiries with the result of the experiment	Applying the results of experiments to scientific arguments and explanations
Management of materials and equipment	Management of ideas and information
Private communication of student ideas and conclusions to teacher	Public communication of student ideas and work to classmates

Source: National Research Council, 1996, p. 113.

If the list on pages 50 and 51 represents fundamental truths about learning, then certain actions, approaches, and strategies ought to be used to engage students in the learning process so that real learning would take place. Perrone (1994) identified eight instructional elements that were found to be effective in engaging students in the learning process:

- Students helped to define the content.
- Students had time to wonder and to find a particular direction that interested them.
- Topics had a "strange" quality—something common seen in a new way, evoking a "lingering question."
- Teachers permitted, even encouraged, different forms of expression and respected students' views.
- Teachers were passionate about their work. The richest activities were those invented by the teachers.
- Students created original and public products, gaining some form of expertness.
- Students *did* something—participated in a political action, wrote a letter to the editor, worked with the homeless.
- Students sensed that the results of their work were not predetermined or fully predictable.

It is interesting to note that most of the elements listed above can also be found in the professional game of science. For instance, professional (science) players define the content of their inquiry; they wonder and pursue the direction that interests them; a lingering question often leads them to particular inquiry; they often invent experiments, activities, and procedures to conduct their inquiry; they create original and public products (models, theories, etc.); and they realize that the results of their work are not fully predictable or predetermined. Thus, it can be argued that mirroring the professional game of science in school science instruction actually has double advantage: It gives students a better sense of what science is all about, and, in congruence with the principles of effective learning, it leads to real learning.

When we understand the learning process better, recognize the changes in the professional game of science, and notice the commonalities between the two, we cannot continue to play the game of science in the school classrooms as before. We need to pay attention to the new rules (such as those promoted by the National Science Education Standards), learn them, and employ them on the playing field of our school science classes. Only then will school science experiences contribute to the development of scientifically literate people. Let us therefore turn our attention to some critical aspects of these new rules and then consider ways to prepare coaches (science teachers) who are well versed in these rules and are capable of getting their teams (science classes) to play by these rules.

Capturing the Essence of the New Rules:
Multiple Domains of Science

The changing emphases in the National Science Education Standards (see Table 3.2) clearly convey a view of science that is significantly richer and broader than that typically portrayed in most school science classes. The way science has typically been taught in K–12 classes gives the impression that science is nothing more than discrete facts, pieces of information, and specific processes. However, the Standards recognize and promote the view that information and processes are only a small part of the rich complexity of what we call the game of science. This rich complexity involves creative inquiry, feelings and values, increasing applications to issues of everyday life, and development of a scientific world view. Of course, the information (accepted body of scientific knowledge) and specific processes used in conducting scientific inquiry are an integral part of the game, but by themselves, they do not represent the entire game. A taxonomy of the domains of science initially proposed by Yager and McCormack (1989) and later revised by Enger and Yager (2001) identifies the following six domains of science: concepts, processes, applications, attitudes, creativity, and nature of science (scientific world view). A careful analysis of the Science Content Standards in the National Science Education Standards reveals at least two important messages:

1. The National Science Content Standards endorse the idea that school science instruction must address these multiple domains of science.
2. The National Science Content Standards indicate (as evident in Table 3.2) that science instruction that addresses these domains effectively will look radically different from the kind typically observed in most science classrooms.

Thus, addressing multiple domains of science in school science instruction can be regarded as the essence of the new rules. A look at the characteristics, significance, and shifting emphases of each of these domains therefore is in order at this point.

The Concept Domain

The concept domain is perhaps the most obvious and easy-to-teach domain of science. It includes facts, laws, principles, theories, and other accepted scientific constructs of specific disciplines of science as well as those related to all of the sciences. The concept domain is central to science and science instruction. It is central to science because it represents the fruit of scientific labor. It represents the knowledge base that developed in science during specific periods of time. This knowledge base guides future scientific activity. Thus, in the professional game of science, the concept domain is crucial for continuing to improve our understanding of the natural world. It is central to the game of school science instruction precisely because of its centrality in the professional game of science. Student understanding of science concepts is crucial to make sense of the world around them. Without proper understanding of science concepts, students would find it almost impossible to follow much of the public discussion of scientific results or to understand public policy issues pertaining to science and technology (Millar, 1989).

The concept domain has been thoroughly addressed in school science instruction. However, in most cases, students typically encounter science concepts in isolation as discrete pieces of information. They learn the concepts mostly through rote learning methods and usually have no reason for learning them other than the fact that the concepts exist and will be tested on various exams. For the most part, this rote learning of scientific concepts makes up a major portion of their science learning experience. Rarely do students learn scientific concepts within a context that establishes their importance beyond the class tests or exams; nor do they develop meaningful connections between the concepts themselves. As a result, students are usually not able to develop a fundamental, comprehensive understanding of basic scientific concepts. This problem is vividly demonstrated in *A Private Universe* (Harvard-Smithsonian Center for Astrophysics, 1987) and *Minds of Our Own* (Harvard-Smithsonian Center for Astrophysics, 1997), video documentaries in which Harvard and MIT graduates reveal their lack of a basic understanding of some of the most fundamental concepts in science (such as the cause of seasons, electric circuits, and photosynthesis). These documentaries also reveal that these Ivy League graduates' understanding of basic science concepts posed to them is hardly any better or more sophisticated than that of elementary grade students. That paints a rather tragic picture of the effectiveness of years of science education. Recognizing this problem, the National Science Education Standards provide us with specific directions for improving instruction in the concept domain. These directions, presented in Table 3.3, represent the new rules for concept domain.

The Process Domain

The process domain is closely tied to the concept domain. The accepted body of scientific knowledge, which makes up the concept domain, is a result of the use of a variety of processes by scientists as they go about playing their professional game. In this sense, the process domain is crucial to both science and science instruction. Just as there are processes in the game of basketball, such as dribbling, passing, and shooting that, when used carefully, can result in scoring points, there are processes in the

Table 3.3 Changing emphases related to the concept domain in the National Science Education Standards Content Standards

Less Emphasis on	More Emphasis on
Knowing scientific facts and information	Understanding scientific concepts and developing abilities of inquiry
Studying subject matter disciplines (physical, life, earth sciences) for their own sake	Learning subject matter disciplines in the context of inquiry, technology, science in personal and social perspectives, and history and nature of science
Separating science knowledge and science processes	Integrating all aspects of science content
Covering many science topics	Studying a few fundamental science concepts

Source: National Research Council, 1996, p. 113.

game of science that lead to specific knowledge. Different sports use different sorts of processes (often referred to as "skills") that are specific to each game. For instance, the processes that are used in basketball are different from those used in baseball. Yet there are also certain processes that are common to different sports. For instance, most sports require individual players to be able to run. Similarly, in science, there are actually several different games that are identified as specialty disciplines of science. Each specialty discipline employs specific types of processes unique to that discipline. At the same time, as in sports, there are some processes or skills that are common to most specialty disciplines of science. In *Science: A Process Approach,* the American Association for the Advancement of Science (1968) identified thirteen processes (see Table 3.4) that are common to most specialty disciplines of science.

It is important to recognize that although a listing of distinct and separate processes, such as the one presented in Table 3.4, is useful for identifying these processes, it does not imply that these processes occur separately, distinctly, and in a specific order during the game of science. Just like the processes in a game of basketball, the processes in the game of science are usually employed in a rich and complex combination in which the boundaries between individual processes might be so blurred that they are essentially nonidentifiable. Often, several processes are used in combination by scientists and employed in ways that a spectator might not have expected or predicted. This brings us to the issue of how the process domain is addressed in the game of school science instruction. To be sure, the process domain is addressed distinctly in most school science classes. Typically, however, science process skills are addressed in one of the early chapters, entitled "The Scientific Method," in most science textbooks. Teachers teach the specific process skills by engaging students in specific tasks, such as observing, hypothesizing, and inferring. For the most part, these tasks are done in an isolated manner. For instance, a teacher might start by saying, "In this activity, you are going to learn to observe." The processes are also presented, both in the textbook and by the teacher, in a specific order—observing, hypothesizing, data collecting, inferring, and so on—giving the impression that the

---

Table 3.4 Process skills common to most specialty disciplines of science

Observing	Using space and time relationships
Classifying, grouping, and organizing	Using numbers and quantifying
Measuring	Communicating
Inferring	Predicting
Identifying and controlling variables	Interpreting data
Formulating hypotheses	Defining operationally
Experimenting	

Source: American Association for the Advancement of Science, 1968.

game of professional science is always played using these processes in this specific order. This approach to addressing the process domain prevents students from developing an understanding of and an appreciation for the complex interplay of these processes in the professional game of science.

Recognizing the complex interplay of processes in the game of science and the need to portray that interplay in school science instruction, the National Science Education Standards provide some new rules to address the process domain in school science instruction. These rules appear as Science as Inquiry Standards within the Science Content Standards in the National Science Education Standards. According to these standards,

> inquiry is a step beyond "science as a process" in which students learn skills, such as observation, inference, and experimentation. The new vision includes the "processes of science" and requires that students combine processes and scientific knowledge as they use scientific reasoning and critical thinking to develop their understanding of science. (National Research Council, 1996, p. 105)

The Standards promote the use of scientific inquiries in which processes are employed much the same interactive way as they are in the professional game of science. They discourage teaching process skills discretely and encourage student involvement in scientific inquiries that integrate the use of process skills. Refer to Table 3.2 on page 52 for the changing emphases in the NSES with regard to the process domain.

The Application Domain

The application domain involves the use of previously learned material in novel situations. In the professional game of science, players (scientists) continually draw on previous knowledge and experiences to pursue new directions of inquiry and to solve new problems. Professional science is a game in which one builds on what the team (community of scientists) has previously accomplished. Of course, sometimes this building process requires abandoning what was built previously (as in the case of a paradigm shift resulting from what Kuhn [1962] called revolutionary science). In any case, application is a continual practice in the game of science. With regard to the learning process, Reinsmith (1993) proposed, "real learning connotes use." If that is true, it brings us immediately in the arena of the application domain. Application of knowledge in novel situations, to solve new problems, to pursue new directions of inquiry, to ask new questions, to design new experiments, and so on, is not only an obvious feature of the game of science, but also the best evidence that learning has taken place. It therefore follows that the application domain must be emphasized in school science instruction.

Enger and Yager (2001, p. 6) contend that for school students, there are two arenas in which application domain comes into play. The first is school studies, in which "application often involves problem solving or learning new material by using knowledge and skills acquired in previous studies." The second is daily life, in which "the crucial factor appears to be the ability to choose the concepts and skills pertinent and relevant for dealing with novel situations." They identify the following nine dimensions of the application domain that ought to be addressed in school science instruction:

1. Use of critical thinking
2. Use of open-ended questions
3. Use of scientific processes in solving problems that occur in daily life
4. Abilities to make intradisciplinary connections—integration of the sciences
5. Abilities to make interdisciplinary connections—integration of science with other subjects
6. Decision making related to personal health, nutrition, and lifestyle based on knowledge of scientific concepts rather than on hearsay or emotions
7. Understanding and evaluation of mass media reports on scientific developments
8. Application of science concepts and skills to technological problems
9. Understanding of scientific and technological principles involved in common technological devices

Of the four goals for school science that underlie the National Science Education Standards, three are directly related to the application domain: (1) Use appropriate scientific processes and principles in making personal decisions; (2) engage intelligently in public discourse and debate about matters of scientific and technological concern; and (3) increase their economic productivity through the use of the knowledge, understanding, and skills of the scientifically literate person in their careers (National Research Council, 1996, p. 13). Unfortunately, in most school science instruction, the application domain either is entirely absent or is a minor add-on at the end of a chapter or unit. This is primarily because of the isolated and fragmented way in which the concept and process domains are addressed in school science. As a response to this problem and to emphasize the importance of the application domain, the National Science Education Standards included two sets of standards that directly relate to the application domain. These are the Science and Technology Standards and Science in Personal and Social Perspectives Standards. The importance of these standards, and therefore the importance of the application domain, is further emphasized by the fact that these two sets of standards are part of the Science Content Standards. This implies that the application domain is as much a part of the content of science as the concept and process domains. Hence, according to the new rules, the application domain becomes a central component in the game of school science.

The Attitude Domain

In some ways, the attitude domain is the most nebulous of the six domains described here. If is often difficult to identify and certainly very difficult to measure. It is also a commonly neglected domain in school science. The way in which science is typically presented by authors in textbooks and teachers in classrooms gives the impression that science is primarily a body of knowledge that students ought to master. It gives the impression that scientists who have developed this knowledge are cold, emotionless people and that their work is not influenced by feelings, values, or morality.

Thus, students might come away with the idea that scientists are weird people who are detached from society and confined to their labs, where they work like machines. This picture is far from the truth, yet it is the picture that keeps many students from developing a keen interest in science and pursuing it as a desirable area of academic concentration and future career choice.

A careful survey of the professional game of science would reveal that the players in this game are passionate about what they do; they are committed to their work and have certain attitudes with which they approach their game. These attitudes can be considered under three categories: personal attitudes, team attitudes, and professional attitudes.

Personal Attitudes. For players in sports, a positive attitude is a critical factor for success. A determined personal resolve that "I can do it" is as important as the disciplined training and practice schedule. In the game of science, the same resolve has led to many important successes, discoveries and inventions. For example, Thomas Edison failed ninety-nine times before he was able to light up the first electric bulb. It was on the hundredth try that he met with success. Had he not had such resolve, he might have given up after several trials and would not have received the honor of being the inventor of the light bulb. A positive personal attitude sustains scientists through hours of grueling mental and physical activity that ultimately brings the joy of discovery, invention, and accomplishment.

Team Attitudes. When playing in a team sport, such as basketball, the players need to go beyond their personal resolve to a team resolve if they are to win. There are several things they ought to do as a team to win the ballgame. For instance, a team attitude of cooperation and coordination (sometimes known as teamwork) is very important. Without teamwork, it is extremely difficult for a team to win a game. Much of the professional game of contemporary science is a team sport. Hurd (1997, pp. 38–39) provides evidence for the fact that much of contemporary scientific research is conducted by teams composed of a variety of players. The ability and willingness to cooperate, coordinate, and collaborate as a team are essential for playing the game of science in its modern form.

Professional Attitudes. Science as a profession is marked by certain attitudes whose presence contributes significantly to its success. These include, but are not limited to, curiosity, questioning, testing of ideas, open-mindedness, healthy skepticism, honesty, open communication, and criticism. Collectively, the presence and practice of these attitudes within the profession ensure ethical behavior on the part of the professionals and prevent dogma from setting in. It is these professional attitudes that make science a self-correcting and progressive enterprise and distinguish it from other forms of knowledge generation.

Given the significance of the three categories of attitudes described above in the professional game of science, it is imperative that the attitude domain be an important component of the game of school science instruction. In *Science for All Americans,* the American Association for the Advancement of Science (1994, p. 203) recommends, "Science teaching should reflect scientific values." Clearly, this statement places the attitude domain in a prominent position within school science instruction. If science is taught in ways that help students see the presence and importance of these attitudes in science and get them to practice the same in their school science activities, then their own attitude toward science and scientists is bound to change. According to Enger and Yager (2001, p. 7), the attitude domain calls for learning experiences in school science that support the following developments in students:

- Exploration of human emotions (in science)
- Expression of personal feelings in constructive ways
- Decision making about personal values
- Decision making about social and environmental issues
- Development of more positive attitudes toward science in general
- Development of positive attitudes toward oneself (an "I can do it" attitude)
- Development of sensitivity to and respect for the feelings of other people

The Creativity Domain

Science is a creative endeavor in the sense that scientific knowledge, as well as all the processes, instruments, and apparatus that are used in the creation of scientific knowledge, are created by the community of scientists. Perhaps the best description of creativity as it relates to science was provided by Torrance (1969). His description characterizes creativity as the process of becoming sensitive to problems, deficiencies, gaps in knowledge, missing elements, and disharmonies. Identification of difficulties, search for solutions, making guesses, and formulating hypotheses about the deficiencies are also important components of creativity in Torrance's description. All of these components are regular features of scientific activity. Scientists regularly raise new questions, formulate hypotheses (that are put to repeated testing), devise tests to check the validity of their hypotheses, modify the hypotheses and tests in the light of new information or evidence, and finally communicate their results to others in the community of science. These activities, which are at the heart of the game of science, represent a profoundly creative process. According to Knorr-Cetina (1981), there are three aspects of scientific activity (particularly with regard to experimental work) that make the need for creative abilities paramount in science:

1. Scientists do not work with the natural world only *as it is*; rather, they manipulate the objects of study to make them more accessible for investigation.
2. Scientists do not always work with the natural world only *where it is*; rather, they bring the natural objects into an artificial setting (such as the laboratory).
3. Scientists do not wait to study an event only *when it happens*; rather, they can cause certain events to occur unnaturally when the situation demands it.

To succeed in accomplishing these three aspects of scientific activity, one must have an imaginative and inventive mind. In other words, a scientist must be a creative person. Without a creative mind, it would be difficult to figure out how to make natural objects accessible for investigation, how to go about investigating them in the artificial setting of the laboratory (designing experiments), and how to make certain events happen artificially. It follows then that creativity is essentially a prerequisite for scientific activity and must therefore be central to school science instruction.

Again, much like the application and attitude domains described above, very little attention has been paid to creativity in the science classroom. When it is present, it is usually not in the form that mirrors creativity in professional science. For instance, creativity in science classrooms often focuses on such things as the aesthetic qualities of student reports and projects, the decorative appeal of bulletin boards, and the media appeal of electronic presentations. Rarely are students challenged to raise new questions on their own, formulate their own hypotheses, and design their own experiments to test their hypotheses in science classes. Science labs and experiments are too often presented to students in a cookbook fashion. Students are expected to follow the directions (the recipe) and arrive at predetermined results and conclusions. Concepts, principles, and facts are presented in their final form in a manner that often ignores the creative process by which they were generated. As a result, the very prerequisite for science remains a foreign notion to many science students. The changing emphases in the National Science Education Standards to promote scientific inquiry in school science (see Table 3.5) clearly bring prominence to creativity in school science learning that mirrors creativity in professional science. The American Association for the Advancement of Science (1994, p. 204) calls for science teachers to promote and reward scientific creativity in their classrooms. So again, the new rules are bringing to the forefront a typically ignored domain of science. Enger and Yager (2001, p. 9) suggest the following instructional strategies that can promote the creativity domain in science classrooms:

- Visualization—production of mental images
- Divergent thinking
- Open-ended questioning
- Consideration of alternative viewpoints
- Generation of unusual ideas
- Generation of metaphors
- Novelty—combining objects and ideas in new ways
- Solving problems and puzzles
- Designing devices and machines
- Multiple modes of communicating results

The World View (Nature of Science) Domain

A world view about critical features of the game of science (often referred to as the scientific world view) has an effect on the way a person reacts to and deals with matters related to science. In sports, if you don't understand the rules and intricacies of a particular game, you will not be able to make sense of what goes on during the game, why players do what they do, and what contributes to the success of a team, except at a very superficial level. Similarly, understanding the critical features of the game of science is important for a person to be able to appreciate scientific activity, make sense of its results, and deal sensibly and effectively with the implications of those results. Several of the critical features of science, often collectively referred to as the nature of science (NOS), distinguish the game of science from other games of knowledge generation. A careful survey of the research literature addressing NOS reveals the following seven critical features of the game of science:

1. Science is a creative human endeavor pursued by the community of scientists (a team sport). Thus, it is an activity of a social nature.
2. Science is influenced by the social, cultural, political, religious, and geographical milieu within which it is practiced.
3. Science is not authoritarian.
4. Scientific activity blends logic, imagination, and creative thought in the generation of ideas, as well as the design of tests to check the validity of those ideas.
5. Scientists try to identify and avoid bias and try to reach consensus based on evidence.
6. Scientific knowledge is tentative yet durable, while not presuming to be the ultimate truth.
7. Accepted scientific theories are powerful instruments for explaining past and present phenomena and predicting future phenomena. Their acceptability is a function of the type and extent of evidence that supports the claims of the theory.

A proper understanding of these features, and hence of the nature of science, is as critical to scientific literacy as is mastery of the concept domain. In fact, much of what was discussed in the attitude, application, and creativity domains relates directly to the nature of science domain. Given the strong influence of science on contemporary society and the resulting choices and decisions people face at both personal and societal levels, it is imperative that our students gain a proper understanding of the nature of science to be able to function effectively as individuals and citizens. Too often, school science experiences have provided too few opportunities for students to explore and develop a proper understanding of the nature of science. Many school science experiences leave faulty impressions on students regarding the nature of science (for instance, that science provides objective, immutable truth or that theories are mere guesses, which, after accumulation of enough evidence or proof, get elevated to the status of facts). By identifying the Nature of Science Standards and placing them within the Science Content Standards, the National Science Education Standards convey the message that NOS is as much a part of the so-called content of science as is the collection of concepts, facts, and principles in any discipline of science. Further, by making NOS a part of the content of science, they clearly endorse the type of science instruction that fosters a proper understanding of the NOS. In other words, the new rules bring NOS to prominence within school science instruction. Enger and Yager (2001, p. 11) argue that the nature of science domain calls for school science experiences that address the following:

- The framing of questions for scientific research
- The methodologies used in scientific research
- The ways in which teams cooperate in scientific research

- The competitive side of scientific research
- The interactions among science, technology, economy, politics, history, sociology, and philosophy
- The history of scientific ideas

Coaching by the New Rules: Instruction in Multiple Domains of Science

If the rules are changing, as evident from Table 3.2, then the coaches (science teachers) ought to be trained in the new rules so that they can help their students play the game right and play it well. As established in the foregoing discussion of the six domains of science, the essence of the new rules regarding the changing game of science lies in proper recognition and clear understanding of all of these domains on the part of science teachers, followed by purposeful instruction that fosters the same recognition and understanding in their students. For the most part, science instruction has focused on the transmission of currently accepted scientific information from teachers to students and training in discrete scientific processes and skills such as observing, measuring, and using specific scientific instruments. This kind of science instruction usually addresses only two domains of science—*concept* and *process*—and presents a severely restricted view of science. Why do we have this situation? Most of the discipline-specific college science courses focus primarily on concept and process domains. As a result, potential coaches (science teachers) develop a limited perspective of the game of science that features only these two domains. Their perception of the game is influenced by what they experienced in their own science education. Hence, their coaching (science instruction) turns out to be rather limited in scope, out of sync with the new rules, and deficient in promoting the goals of scientific literacy presented in Table 3.1. A solution to this problem lies in getting science teachers to experience the multiple domains of science and develop an ability to affect student learning in these domains. Both pre-service and in-service science teachers should get the opportunity to participate in programs and activities that enhance their understanding of multiple domains and equip them with instructional approaches that will effectively engage their students in experiencing these domains within school science education.

Why is learning in multiple domains of science so important? If science involves more than just information and processes, then students must experience the other domains to develop a holistic understanding of science, an appreciation for what science is all about, and an ability to do science themselves. Instruction in multiple domains of science is not only important for students to become better scientists but also to understand and deal with the impact of science on their everyday lives. In other words, education in multiple domains of science is not only desirable but indeed essential to accomplish the goals of scientific literacy presented in Table 3.1. A variety of teacher education and professional development standards developed during the last decade also promote preparation of science teachers who can facilitate instruction that involves multiple domains of science (Danielson, 1996; National Council for the Accreditation of Teacher Education, 1999; National Research Council, 1996).

Therefore, preservice science teacher preparation programs and in-service professional development programs must strive to prepare teachers for affecting student learning in multiple domains of science.

How can teachers be prepared to affect student learning in multiple domains of science? Any program that aims to respond to this question will have to address the following three issues:

1. Teachers must become cognizant of the multiple domains of science.
2. Teachers must see the need for addressing these domains in school science instruction.
3. Teachers must be able to assess student learning in multiple domains of science.

At this point, it would perhaps be more useful to consider strategies for preservice and in-service programs separately.

Preservice Science Teacher Preparation

One of the best ways to change the limited perspective of preservice teachers is to get them involved in science activities in which they are required to ask new questions, explore resources to find answers, generate and test hypotheses, and share and discuss their findings in terms of both their experience with the activity and how they could apply this process in school science classrooms. In other words, the activities ought to engage teachers in multiple domains of science. In case of preservice teachers, the most likely place to begin experiencing such activities is the Science Teaching Methods course.

Short activities such as designing clay boats that would hold increasingly more weight than their own without sinking, candle suffocation experiments, and activities with batteries, bulbs, and wires and relatively longer investigations such as studying the behavior of mealworms or exploring a local environmental problem are just a few examples of the myriad activities that are routinely used in science teaching methods courses. However, their tremendous potential for introducing preservice teachers to the multiple domains of science is often not fully realized. Such activities and investigations, when designed purposefully to bring out the multiple domains of science, would help preservice teachers see that science involves more than just memorizing facts or developing specific skills (such as the use of a microscope). They would demonstrate the creative aspect of science and the importance of applying to new situations what one already knows and would help teachers to develop a better understanding of the nature of science as they take each activity to a higher level of sophistication or use them to answer new questions related to the concepts they are designed to explore. Of course, having only one or two experiences with such activities will not suffice. Methods courses must be infused with multiple opportunities for engaging in such activities, with explicit attention to the multiple domains that can be addressed through them.

Multiple opportunities to engage in such activities is a step in the right direction, but if the objective is merely to get the "right answer" and then move on to the next thing, this is not sufficient. Discussions following each activity are extremely important for bringing explicit attention to multiple domains. One cannot simply hope that doing these activities will suddenly enlighten the participants regarding these domains of science. They need to be engaged in discussions that require them to reflect on experiences with these activities and how they relate to the world of professional science. These discussions should focus on the identification of various domains of science through questions (raised both by the instructor and by participants themselves) that will serve to analyze the activities in terms of the domains. As much as possible, participants should be asked to relate their experiences with these activities to professional scientific research in order to identify the domains in professional science. Discussions need to also focus on strategies regarding the use of these activities (and others like them, which teachers could design themselves or locate from available resources) in ways that would help their students understand the multiple domains of science. Multiple assignments aimed at sharpening teachers' understanding of the six domains and their ability to employ particular instructional strategies that address these domains in school science would go a long way in preparing teachers who would be able to coach their science classes by the new rules.

Apart from understanding the multiple domains of science and their importance in the game of school science, teachers must also be prepared to assess student learning in multiple domains. This can be accomplished by having them develop rubrics for assessing growth in each domain within the context of the activities in which they participate. Whenever teachers engage in an activity that is meant to broaden their understanding of multiple domains of science, they should be asked to design rubrics for assessing growth in specific domains through that particular activity. This would help them practice how to assess student growth in multiple domains of science. Then, during student teaching and other practicum, clinical, or internship experiences, they could be required to design assessment items or activities that address various domains within every unit of instruction they design and undertake. Required assessment in multiple domains will ensure that teachers get into the habit of providing science experiences to their students that enhance learning in multiple domains of science and the assessment of this learning.

In-Service Professional Development of Science Teachers

Learning to coach by the new rules (of multiple domains) requires that in-service science teachers be provided with professional development opportunities that are substantially different from those typically offered in the name of in-service. Here again, the National Science Education Standards provide direction regarding what needs to be done. The Standards for Professional Development for Teachers of Science within the National Science Education Standards "provide criteria for making judgments about the quality of the professional development opportunities that teachers of science will need to implement the National Science Education Standards" (National Research Council, 1996, p. 55). In other words, coaches in action need to have specific types of opportunities that help them learn the new rules and learn how to implement them in their coaching. Of the four professional development standards in the National Science Education Standards, the first two, which are presented in Figures 3.1 and 3.2, focus on learning the new rules.

Professional development for teachers of science requires learning essential science content through the perspectives and methods of inquiry. Science learning experiences for teachers must:

■ Involve teachers in actively investigating phenomena that can be studied scientifically, interpreting results, and making sense of findings consistent with currently accepted scientific understanding

■ Address issues, events, problems, or topics that are significant in science and of interest to participants

■ Introduce teachers to scientific literature, media, and technological resources that expand their science knowledge and their ability to access further knowledge

■ Build on the teacher's current science understanding, ability, and attitudes

■ Incorporate ongoing reflection on the process and outcomes of understanding science through inquiry

■ Encourage and support teachers in efforts to collaborate

Figure 3.1 Professional Development Standard A
Source: National Research Council, 1996, p. 59.

A careful analysis of these two standards reveals that professional development opportunities based on these standards are most likely to bring to light multiple domains of science and ways of incorporating them in school science instruction.

An Overall Coaching Strategy: The Science-Technology-Society (STS) Approach

In coaching a particular sport, coaches engage their players in a variety of individual activities, drills, and techniques that are specific to that sport. However, if several coaches in the same sport are compared, it will soon become evident that each coach has a particular overall coaching strategy that makes him or her different from the others, even though they all prepare their teams according to the same rules to accomplish the same goal: victory. It will also not be a stretch to argue that although many factors determine the outcome of a particular game, specific coaching strategies have

Professional development for teachers of science requires integrating knowledge of science, learning, pedagogy, and students. It also requires applying that knowledge to science teaching. Learning experiences for teachers of science must:

- Connect and integrate all pertinent aspects of science and science education

- Occur in a variety of places where effective science teaching can be illustrated and modeled, permitting teachers to struggle with real situations and expand their knowledge and skills in appropriate contexts

- Address teachers' needs as learners and build on their current knowledge of science content, teaching, and learning

- Use inquiry, reflection, interpretation of research, modeling, and guided practice to build understanding and skill in science teaching

Figure 3.2 Professional Development Standard B
Source: National Research Council, 1996, p. 62.

a significant bearing on a team's victory. For instance, there must be something about Phil Jackson's coaching strategy that perennially brings his NBA team to playoffs.

The individual drills and activities of a sport can be compared to the individual science activities described in the section entitled "Preservice Science Teacher Preparation." However, just as an overall coaching strategy seems to be significant in accomplishing the goal of victory in sports, an overall instructional strategy is important in accomplishing the goals of scientific literacy in the game of school science education. So it is time now to turn our attention to an instructional strategy that has proved to be effective in enhancing student achievement in the six domains of science and hence effective in contributing to the goals of scientific literacy in school science education. This strategy is known as the science-technology-society (STS) approach. (For a complete treatment of the STS approach, see Yager, 1996.)

Identifying it as "the teaching and learning of science in the context of human experience," the *NSTA Handbook* (National Science Teachers Association, 1992–93, pp. 168–169) describes the STS approach thus:

> The bottom line in STS is the involvement of learners in experiences and issues which are directly related to their lives. STS empowers students with skills which allow them to become active, responsible citizens by responding to issues which impact their lives. The

experience of science education through STS strategies will create a scientifically literate citizenry for the 21st century.

So what are the STS strategies? How does the STS approach differ from traditional approaches to science instruction (i.e., lectures based on textbook chapters, followed by verification-type labs, and culminating in an end-of-chapter or end-of-unit test, which is most often of the multiple-choice variety)? The *NSTA Handbook* statement mentions that the emphasis in STS is on responsible decision making in the real world of the student, where science and technology are components (National Science Teachers Association, 1992–93). Yager (1998, p. 319) provides a list of circumstances that characterize an STS approach to the teaching and learning of science, which include the following:

- Students often identify the issue or question that forms the instructional module.
- Students see the issue as relevant.
- Students ask as many questions as the teacher does.
- Students are responsible for finding human and written resources for needed information.
- Students are involved in locating and engaging local human resources for the study.
- Students plan investigations and other activities.
- Teachers and students use varied evaluation techniques.
- Students are skilled and anxious to evaluate their own learning.
- Concepts and skills emerge as useful tools within the context of the original issue or question.
- Concepts and skills that are learned can be readily applied to new situations.
- Students do something with what they have learned, outside their own classroom, laboratory, or school.
- Students become experts in the eyes of other students and adults.
- Science learning affects the whole school and the community beyond the school.

Table 3.5 further helps characterize the STS approach by contrasting it with the standard (or traditional) science teaching approaches (Yager & Roy, 1993, p. 9).

However, one might still wonder how STS instruction is organized. What instructional components are involved in the STS approach? Answers to these and similar questions about STS may be found by examining the following key phases of STS instructional strategies: invitation, exploration, proposing explanations and solutions, and taking action. A brief description of each of these phases follows.

Invitation

The invitation phase focuses on students' questions, concerns, and curiosities. Students are invited to ask questions, brainstorm ideas, bring up unexpected phenomena, identify situations in which they might have varying perceptions, and observe their surroundings for points of curiosity. Alternatively, the teacher can present to the class some recent event, which might involve questions of science and technology and might have raised local, national, or global concerns. The teacher might invite students to express their views about the event and generate questions they would like

Table 3.5 A comparison of major characteristics of Standard and STS science classes	
Standard	**STS**
Surveys major concepts found in standard textbooks	Identifies problems with local interest or impact
Uses labs and activities suggested in textbook and accompanying lab manual	Uses local resources, both human and material, to resolve problems
Students passively assimilate information provided by teacher and textbook	Students actively seek information to use
Focuses on information proclaimed important for students to master	Focuses on personal impact, making use of students' own natural curiosity and concerns
Views science as the information in textbooks and teacher lectures	Views science content not as something that merely exists for student mastery because it is recorded in print
Students practice basic process skills but do not apply them for evaluation purposes	Deemphasizes process skills, which can be seen as the glamorized tools of practicing scientists
Pays little attention to career awareness, other than an occasional reference to a scientist (most of whom are dead) and his or her discoveries	Focuses on career awareness, emphasizing careers in science and technology that students might pursue, especially in areas other than scientific research, medicine, and engineering
Students concentrate on problems provided by teachers and textbooks	Students become aware of their responsibilities as citizens as they attempt to resolve issues they have identified
Science occurs only in the science classroom as a part of the school's science curriculum	Students learn what roles science can play in a given institution and in a specific community
Science is a body of information that students are expected to acquire	Science is an experience students are encouraged to enjoy
Science class focuses on what is previously known	Science class focuses on what the future might be like

Source: Yager & Roy, 1993, p. 9.

to pursue to better understand aspects of science and technology involved in the presented event. In either case, the questions and foci of investigations have been generated by students, and students are vested in pursuing answers to their questions.

Exploration

The exploration phase involves students working both in cooperative groups and individually in a variety of activities, mostly designed by the students themselves with guidance from the teacher as necessary, to seek answers to their questions or solutions to the problems that are identified in the invitation phase. The explorations include, but are not limited to, designing and conducting experiments, collecting and analyzing data, consulting live experts, locating and selecting appropriate resources, designing models, engaging in group discussions and debates, and evaluating results of various investigations.

Proposing Explanations and Solutions

This phase can occur simultaneously with the exploration phase and continue beyond the exploration phase. As students are engaged in various activities, they are encouraged to integrate their findings into explanations of the phenomena under investigation. These explanations are used in designing solutions to the problems that were identified during the invitation phase. This phase also involves assembling multiple answers or solutions, using peer evaluation to assess the validity of these answers or, solutions, and constructing appropriate explanations and solutions.

Taking Action

During this phase, students are encouraged to take action at personal or societal levels. It involves applying knowledge and skills that were gained to make specific decisions. Students are engaged in sharing information and ideas with peers, school and local communities, and experts for feedback and influencing decisions. Students develop products, promote ideas, raise new questions, and use the ideas and questions to generate discussion of issues and problems at various levels. They participate in the application of scientific knowledge outside the confines of their classrooms.

The STS instructional strategy represented in the four phases above engages students in science learning experiences that involve all six domains of science. Thus, as an overall coaching strategy, the STS approach is effective in implementing the new rules in a manner that leads to victory.

CONCLUSION: Science Literacy Through Informed Professionals

When rules of a game or sport are revised, it becomes the responsibility of coaches to ensure that they are current in their knowledge of the new rules and understand them thoroughly. A coach who is well versed in the current rules and employs them in effective coaching strategies is more likely to lead his or her team to victory. Similarly, science teachers who understand the changing rules in the game of science education and implement them in their classes using effective approaches such as STS will lead their students to *victory* in science. This victory involves developing the attributes of scientific literacy identified in Table 3.1. If we want our students to accomplish the victory of scientific literacy, our preservice science teacher preparation programs and in-service professional development programs must ensure that participating teachers are well versed in, and capable of effectively coaching their science teams by, these new rules.

The Game in Action

A Secondary Preservice Science Teaching Methods Course Organized by the STS Approach

Secondary preservice science teachers (PSTs) were given a semester-long science teaching methods course that was organized around the STS approach. The objective was to make them cognizant of the multiple domains of science and to enable them to use the STS instructional approach for learning in these domains. PSTs in this course were engaged in scientific explorations involving issues, questions, or problems drawn from real-life situations, identified and selected by the PSTs themselves. The intent was to have PSTs experience science learning in much the same way that their high school students ought to do for the goals of scientific literacy to be accomplished. Various aspects of science instruction, such as management and assessment, were dealt within the context of the scientific explorations, in which the PSTs were engaged. The entire semester-long methods course was organized around these STS investigations and PSTs gained hands-on experience in science instruction that embodies the spirit of the new rules in the game of school science education.

Science for Life: The Course Organizing STS Module

The Science for Life module was developed and used as an organizer for the secondary science teaching methods course so that the PSTs experienced the typical topics of a methods course (such as assessment and cooperative learning) within the context of this module throughout the semester. This module was developed with the recognition that the most desirable instructional strategies in the sciences during current times are those which relate science to the lives of students. Students should be able to see the relevance of science outside the classroom and apply scientific knowledge, principles, and processes to deal with real-life issues, problems, and concerns at both personal and societal levels. To this end, Science for Life engaged PSTs in exploring and experiencing science during the methods course in much the same way that they should use to engage their students in secondary science classes. Following the key elements of the STS instructional approach, PSTs were engaged in scientific explorations aimed at dealing with a real-life issue, concern, question, or problem selected by the PSTs themselves. Several major aspects of science instruction, such as assessment and classroom management, were addressed through discussions at appropriate times during the course within the context of the module. The module also involved extensive use of modern communication and information technology, thus providing PSTs with experience in integrating technology to enhance science instruction. By the end of the course, PSTs had developed an instructional module based on their own explorations, for use in secondary science classes so as to engage secondary students in science learning that has direct relevance to their lives. They were expected to use their instructional module during student teaching the following semester.

Goals of the Module

Drawing from NSTA's description of the STS approach, this module aimed to engage PSTs in experiencing science explorations based on real-life issues, concerns, questions, or problems. It was designed to accomplish the following goals with regard to preservice science teacher preparation, which in turn are expected to enable PSTs to further the goals of scientific literacy in secondary science classes:

- PSTs will learn to engage their students in scientific exploration and inquiry in the natural environment, stimulated by real-life situations, concerns, issues, and questions.
- PSTs will learn to relate science to the daily lives and interests of their students.
- PSTs will learn to create effective learning opportunities for students in a community of diverse learners, enabling them to construct meaning from specific science learning experiences.
- PSTs will develop an understanding of the national, state, and local science standards and will be able to organize science instruction that meets these standards.
- PSTs will learn to use a variety of authentic and equitable assessment strategies to ensure and evaluate student learning in multiple domains of science.

Resources for the Module

Several resources are important for this module. They can be divided into the following categories on the basis of the nature of resource.

Technology-Related Resources

The module requires the availability of computers with internet connection so that PSTs can (1) communicate electronically with the instructor, their peers, and resource people and organizations around the world and (2) access the World Wide Web for locating information and other resources. PSTs should have active e-mail accounts. They should also have access to word-processing, graphics, and presentation software.

Human Resources

The module involves communicating with scientists, experts, and organizations that are involved in work related to the specific problem, issue, or question selected by the PSTs. The purpose of this communication is to get firsthand expert information, learn about actions being taken, and get feedback from these experts on PSTs' proposed solutions and actions. PSTs are expected to locate appropriate human resources themselves.

Literature Resources

Research-based literature related to STS and specific questions being investigated in individual modules from various sources (journal articles, books, monographs, etc.) would be used. Some would be referred to or provided by the instructor, and some would be located by the PSTs.

Major Learning Activities

PSTs worked in self-selected groups of up to four individuals throughout this module. Because the module design is based on the STS approach, learning activities can be classified into the following phases.

Invitation

Two approaches were used in this phase. First, the PSTs were invited to brainstorm, search, and select one issue, question, or problem (henceforth referred to as TOPIC) based on real-life situations that would form the basis of their modules. The topic could be based on either a global or a local situation but should be something that would arouse the interest and curiosity of high school students. Several Internet sites were suggested to them as possible sources for ideas on current topics. PSTs were asked to develop a rationale for their topic selection and to identify critical questions that could possibly be addressed to explore the topic in a secondary science class within a semester.

Second, the PSTs were presented with a brief account of the manipulation of a specific gene by Harvard geneticists whereby a three-legged chicken had been produced. The PSTs were invited to generate a list of as many questions as came to their minds after reading the brief news report provided to them. Their questions were subsequently consolidated into a list of no more than three questions per group that could possibly be explored in a secondary science class within one semester.

Exploration

This phase focuses on activities aimed at gathering and analyzing scientific information and/or data needed to address the questions identified above. It involved the use of the Internet and the World Wide Web as well as traditional print resources to locate and collect relevant information. PSTs identified appropriate agencies, groups, or scientists who were studying issues and questions relevant to their topic and communicated with these sources electronically to gather latest information as well as to share their own findings, positions, and action proposals. PSTs also designed hands-on and minds-on investigations to conduct original research into questions that emerged. The exploration phase provided the basis for formulating hypothesis, designing explanations, and proposing solutions.

Proposing Explanations and Solutions

During this phase, PSTs synthesized the information that they had gathered during the exploration phase to formulate hypotheses, design explanations, and propose solutions to their specific questions. This phase involved communicating information and ideas to peers and to the external experts they communicated with during the exploration phase. Thus, PSTs made a formal presentation of all of their findings to their peers in the methods course. These presentations helped all PSTs in the course to benefit from each other's exploratory activities, their findings, and their unique ways of communicating those findings.

Taking Action

On the basis of synthesis described above, PSTs made informed decisions, took specific positions, and suggested appropriate actions. In essence, this is the application phase in which the knowledge gained is applied in terms of actions. Proposed actions could be at the local level, such as starting a new recycling program in the school, or at a more global level, such as communicating with policy makers to influence decisions about environmental issues. PSTs were required to develop action proposals that would be feasible in a secondary classroom context. They presented these action proposals to their peers in the methods class; however, in the secondary classroom setting, they would actually involve their students in carrying out these action proposals.

During each of the phases described above, issues such as assessment of student learning, managing cooperative learning groups, and effective use of modern technology were discussed and analyzed within the context of the module. They were discussed at appropriate time as the need to do so emerged during the progress of the module. The discussion sessions were facilitated rather than controlled by the methods instructor. During the course of the module, PSTs maintained journals to record the learning activities and to write reflective analyses of their own learning experiences. On the basis of their own explorations within this module, PSTs created an STS instructional module for a secondary science class, which they were expected to use during student teaching. In developing their STS instructional modules for secondary science classes, the PSTs were asked to consider the following ten questions:

1. How will the introduction of the unit help students in establishing the relevance of the topic?
2. How will the students be involved in the development of the unit?
3. Are the learning activities appropriate in terms of their relationship to the central module theme and developmental level of students?
4. Are a variety of resources, including print, on-line, and human, part of the plan?
5. What kinds of actions will students take (personal, political, community, etc.)?
6. What major science concepts will emerge as outcomes of the investigations in this module? Are these concepts appropriate in terms of standards and curricular frameworks for the particular grade level?
7. What will the assessment plans be?
8. Is the length of time spent on the module appropriate to the significance of the topic?
9. How will the module tie to other areas of the curriculum or to other departments in the school?
10. Could this module be expanded beyond the three-week plan?

Sample Instruction Modules

Following are brief descriptions of representative STS instructional modules developed by the PSTs.

Beetlemania

This module was an investigation of the Asian Longhorned Beetle crisis in Chicago, Illinois.

Our interest in pursuing the Asian Longhorned Beetle as an STS topic was sparked by several factors. At our homes, we received information regarding the beetle and its destructive feeding habits. We saw quarantine posters around the neighborhood. Numerous stories on the TV news and in the (news)papers were devoted to the crisis. Additionally, the beetles seemed to be the hot topic of discussion around the neighborhood. All of these factors combined to arouse an intense interest in the crisis. As teachers, we were interested in the crisis because it provided an excellent platform for the study of plant anatomy physiology, ecosystems, taxonomy, and entomology. Additionally, it provided a chance for the students to be part of real science in action.

Water Quality: Where Do We Get Our Water and Where Does It Go When We're Done with It?

This module was a study of the drinking water source and postuse treatment of water in Evanston, Illinois.

A water quality project can be created, adapted, and implemented in any classroom. Water, after all, connects everyone in a local community or a global one. We all need water to survive and we need to be aware of how we treat it. It would be reassuring to know that people that share the same water source treat it with the same concern. A water quality project begins with the water source itself. Where do we get our water? From that point, questions about raw water quality and water treatment can begin the questions of what factors are affecting our water and how that affects the people of the community. With that in mind, think of whose "used" water we are using. Where has it been? What has been in it? Is it healthy? If it isn't healthy, why isn't it? And what can be done to fix the problem? Other questions follow and are created by the specific situations that arise from the exploration. The connection question to other communities (locally, nationally, or internationally) is what happens to the water when we're done with it? In essence, what we do affects us as well as other people in our ecosystem.

What Is Death?

This module was an inquiry into the mortal weakness of human beings.

When students were first presented with the question "What is death?" some students looked at the microdeath as found in apoptosis and cellular death. Others were intrigued by macrodeath and searched for answers through the clinical route. How does one know that a person or an animal is dead? Is it by just looking at him or her? By searching the Internet, students were able to answer this and other questions. So far we know that if there is no pulse and no heartbeat, the person is dead. What if the person has a heartbeat and a pulse but no brain activity? This is known as being brain dead. Often times there is a debate on whether the person is clinically dead if he or she is brain dead. This is what we are going to investigate: "What defines clinical death?" For answers to this very difficult question, we researched the International Network for the Definition of Death. Here, issues about brain death, comas, and persistent vegetative state were the focus. Considering the state goals that are being covered in this module, students can demonstrate relationships between technology and medicine, show how beliefs

The final exam in the Secondary Science Teaching Methods course will be conducted in the form of a half-hour personal interview of students conducted individually by the instructor. In other words, this exam is an intense oral exam rather than a written exam. The following three questions will guide the interview conversation:

1. Describe some of the most important lessons you have learned this semester about the teaching and learning of science. Why do you consider them most important?

2. What are your most important goals for your students while you teach them science? Why do you consider these your most important goals?

3. In your opinion, what are some of the most critical elements in the teaching and learning of science? Why do you consider them most critical?

Figure 3.3 Final Exam Interview

and attitudes influence and have been influenced by new scientific and technological advances. In this section, students can make a difference by learning more about organ and tissue transplants because death can be the next step to life for someone else. Students may discuss with their family members the benefits of being an organ/tissue donor in case of the misfortune accompanied by death.

Tell Me What You Eat and I'll Tell You Who You Are: A Journey in Nutrition
This module was a study of human diet and nutrition to determine components of a healthy diet.

This lesson was designed to have students consider what they know about diet, nutrition, health, and how they are related. The quote "Tell me what you eat and I'll tell you who you are" was the starting point of a discussion about how food and a person could be interconnected. The discussion led to many questions, and from those questions several paths of inquiry were to be investigated. The class was divided into groups to work on different issues and culminate with a presentation. The students were allowed to form their own groups, but each student was responsible for an essay on any aspect of nutrition. Research would be conducted by using books, computers (Internet, spreadsheets, word processing), experimentation, and personal interactions with professionals. This scenario is how we see teaching a module. The teacher (ourselves) would have the position to guide the students with methods of inquiry, help students to focus their thoughts, and enable students to a better understanding of the subject. These objectives would be accomplished by having students research information, create and conduct experiments, and use their own real life situations as reasons to learn more. The study of nutrition can be used as a mechanism to introduce other topics such as human physiology and anatomy, microbiology (microorganisms found in food), organic chemistry (the breakdown of food), math and statistics, experimental design, politics (environmental versus agricultural methods), and culture (the diets of other nations and the statistics of the nation's health).

Results

For a methods course such as the one described above, the issue of effectiveness of the approach used is an important one. To elicit information about the impact of this STS approach on PSTs, three forms of qualitative data were accessed during the course: reflective journals during the semester as well as summary reflection at the end of the module, class presentation and discussion of STS instructional modules developed by PSTs, and in-depth interviews of all students individually at the end of the semester. Interviews served as the final exam for the course. Questions that guided the interview are provided in Figure 3.3.

It is important to mention that students' journals were not included in their course grade. Therefore, PSTs were able to share their thoughts and feelings rather freely without any fear that their writing would influence their course grades. The final exam interviews, which were included in course grades, were graded not on the basis of whether or not PSTs praised the STS approaches and experience, but on the basis of their ability to articulate specific viewpoints and defend their arguments in a reasonably convincing manner. Both the noninclusion of journals in course grades and the criteria for grading interviews were explained to PSTs in advance to minimize bias in these data sources, which could have resulted from concerns regarding course grades.

Reflecting on the Game

1. The "Beetlemania" module mentioned in this chapter was developed around the real problem of infestation of trees by the Asian Longhorned Beetle in Chicago during the semester of instruction. Identify a current local problem or issue faced by your community and develop an STS instructional module around it, using the guidelines provided in this chapter, for a grade level of your choice.

2. Identify ways in which your students will experience instruction in multiple domains of science as they work through this module in your class.

3. Identify which specific national and/or state science education standards will be addressed through your module and describe ways in which they will be met.

4. Develop succinct arguments to articulate a defense for addressing multiple domains of science through the use of STS approach in your class (for those skeptical or critical colleagues, administrators, and parents who might question what goes on in your class).

References

American Association for the Advancement of Science. (1968). *Science: A process approach*. Washington, DC: Author.

American Association for the Advancement of Science. (1993). *Benchmarks for science literacy*. New York: Oxford University Press.

American Association for the Advancement of Science. (1994). *Science for all Americans*. New York: Oxford University Press.

Danielson, C. (1996). *Enhancing professional practice: A framework for teaching*. Alexandria, VA: Association for Supervision and Curriculum Development.

Enger, S. K., & Yager, R. E. (2001). *Assessing student understanding in science: A standards-based K–12 handbook*. Thousand Oaks, CA: Corwin Press.

Harms, N. C. (1981). Project synthesis: Summary and implications for teachers. In N. C. Harms & R. E. Yager (Eds.), *What research says to the science teacher* (Vol. 3, pp. 113–127). Washington, DC: National Science Teachers Association.

Harvard-Smithsonian Center for Astrophysics (Producer). (1987). *A private universe* [Video Documentary]. (Available from Annenberg/CPB Video Cassette Sales and Customer Service, P.O. Box 2345, S. Burlington, VT 05407–2345 or www.learner.org)

Harvard-Smithsonian Center for Astrophysics (Producer). (1997). *Minds of our own* [Video Documentary]. (Available from Annenberg/CPB Video Cassette Sales and Customer Service, P.O. Box 2345, S. Burlington, VT 05407–2345 or www.learner.org)

Hurd, P. D. (1997). *Inventing science education for the new millennium*. New York: Teachers College Press.

Knorr-Cetina, K. D. (1981). *The manufacture of knowledge: An essay on the constructivist and contextual nature of science*. New York: Pergamon.

Kuhn, T. S. (1962). *The structure of scientific revolutions*. Chicago: University of Chicago Press.

Millar, R. (1989). Constructive criticisms. *International Journal of Science Education, 1*, 587–596.

Millar, R., & Osborne, J. (Eds.) (1998). *Beyond 2000: Science education for the future*. London: King's College School of Education.

National Council for the Accreditation of Teacher Education. (1999). *NCATE-NSTA standards*. Available: www.ncate.org.

National Research Council. (1996). *National science education standards*. Washington, DC: National Academy Press.

National Science Teachers Association. (1992–93). *National science teachers association handbook*. Washington, DC: Author.

Perrone, V. (1994). How to engage students in learning. *Educational Leadership, 51*(5), 11–13.

Reinsmith, W. A. (1993). Ten fundamental truths about learning. *The National Teaching & Learning Forum, 2*(4), 7–8.

Torrance, E. P. (1969). *Creativity*. Belmont, CA: Dimensions.

Yager, R. E. (1987). Assess all five domains of science. *The Science Teacher, 54*(7): 33–37.

Yager, R. E. (Ed.). (1996). *Science/technology/society as reform in science education*. Albany, NY: State University of New York Press.

Yager, R. E. (1998). STS challenges for accomplishing educational reform: The need for solving learning problems. *Bulletin of Science, Technology & Society, 18*(5), 315–320.

Yager, R. E., & McCormack, A. J. (1989). Assessing teaching/learning successes in multiple domains of science and science education. *Science Education, 73*(1), 45–58.

Yager, R. E., & Roy, R. (1993). STS: Most pervasive and most radical of reform approaches to "science" education. In R. E. Yager (Ed.), *What research says to the science teacher, Vol. 7: The science, technology, society movement* (pp. 7–13). Washington, DC: National Science Teachers Association.

Additional Resources

Enger, S. K., & Yager, R. E. (2001). *Assessing student understanding in science: A standards-based K–12 handbook*. Thousand Oaks, CA: Corwin Press.

Leonard, W. H., & Penick, J. E. (1998). *Biology: A community context*. Cincinnati, OH: South-Western Educational Publishing.

Yager, R. E. (Ed.) (1993). *What research says to the science teacher: Vol. 7. The science, technology, society movement*. Washington, DC: National Science Teachers Association.

Yager, R. E. (Ed.) (1996). *Science/technology/ society as reform in science education*. Albany, NY: State University of New York Press.

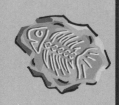

start

c h a p t e r

4

SINK OR SWIM:

The Transformative Student Teaching Experience in Science

Jill C. McNew
Street School, Tulsa, Oklahoma

ABOUT THE AUTHOR: Jill McNew received her B.S. in Biochemistry from John Brown University in 1998. After working in the pharmaceutical industry, she returned to graduate school at Oklahoma State University, completing teaching certification and a master's degree in curriculum and instruction in 2000. Jill now teaches science and math at Street School, an alternative high school in Tulsa.

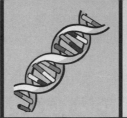

> **Your talent and reputation got you here. Your work ethic and personal conduct will determine how long you stay.**
>
> —Mike Shanahan
> *Denver Broncos coach, speaking to rookies*

CHAPTER WARM-UP

No preparatory experiences rival student teaching in educational value. The quality of the experience shapes or steels ideology, merges theory with practice, and establishes relational foundations for a successful career. Critical to a bright future in science teaching is the effective management and discernment of the duties of many role players: university supervisor, cooperating teacher, school and university administrator, and, of course, students. Knowing their roles and recognizing their contributions to the experience can help the rookie science teacher to make a smooth transition into the profession.

INTRODUCTION: Perspectives on Student Teaching

Some people compare student teaching to throwing a child into deep water to see whether she or he can swim. Student teaching can be exciting, informative, frustrating, exhausting, and any number of other kinds of experience. However the student might find his or her own experience, professional educators endorse the student teaching component as the most vital and promising in preservice teacher preparation. "Of all of the areas of the professional education curriculum, this area [student teaching] has received the highest endorsement as the foundation of a strong teacher education program" (Anderson & Mitchener, 1994, p. 18).

I recently completed my own field experience in a large urban high school in Tulsa, Oklahoma. My cooperating teacher and I could not have had more opposite approaches to teaching, but we were able to navigate our differences and develop a working relationship that allowed each of us to learn from the other's strengths. The experience was valuable and encouraging in that I was able to achieve some level of comfort in the classroom, gain confidence in my ability to navigate that environment successfully, and even implement investigative activities. I was also exposed to a style of teaching that was different from my own, which, rather than converting me, as researchers seem to fear (Croker and Wilder, 1999), served to further solidify my commitment to research-based, inquiry science teaching.

Student teaching has become increasingly important to teacher preparation since universities began considering specialized preparation necessary in the process of becoming a teacher. "Until the 1920's, student teaching remained a vocational, practically oriented course required for prospective elementary teachers. Secondary teachers were, however, graduated from liberal arts colleges with no professional teacher preparation" (Guyton & McIntyre, 1996, p. 515). Student teaching has evolved within the growing field of teacher education, becoming the unifying experience of teacher preparation. "Now most teachers learn about educational foundations and methods of teaching in the university classroom and are asked to apply what they have learned in school-based field experiences that typically fall in the range of 6–15 weeks" (Roth & Tobin, 2001, p. 741). Through their field experiences, preservice teachers become increasingly competent, and it is hoped that when they complete their assignment, they are prepared to continue their professional growth as first-year teachers. "Students begin with observation and eventually take over most, if not all, of the cooperating teacher's classroom responsibilities" (Anderson & Mitchener, 1994, p. 19). The transition from "being a student to being a professional" (Feiman-Nemser & Buchmann, 1987, p. 273) and the factors that facilitate it have been the subject of much speculation, but substantive research in this area is lacking:

> Considering its long history, there is a comparatively small amount of research on preservice science teacher education. In addition it is rather limited in scope and usefulness. . . . Research has produced little knowledge about how people actually become teachers, in spite of the fact that the problems of science teacher education have been explored in various ways. (Anderson & Mitchener, 1994, p. 28)

The existing literature does offer some insight and implications for maximizing the impact and effectiveness of the most common and current student teaching structures as well as improving the construction of field experiences to better prepare teacher candidates. Much of this research emphasizes the promise that the field experience holds for improving the proficiency of preprofessional educators:

> Student teaching holds promise for helping beginners learn because it is experiential; that is, it offers a chance to teach under guidance, to watch an experienced teacher close up and to find out how he or she thinks about teaching, to get to know children and how they think, to discover what it 'feels like' to be in charge of a class. (Feiman-Nemser & Buchmann, 1987, p. 256)

The importance that teachers and teacher educators place on the student teaching experience can make it seem threatening to prospective teachers. When learning to swim, you can see it done a thousand times, know a great deal about how it works theoretically, and still retain a deathly fear of the water. In an emergency, however, most people can at least tread water a little, and most novice teachers will experience marginal success in communicating a little science knowledge to a room full of students. This level of teaching, like treading water, takes a great deal of energy and is a slow, laborious process. With practice and the insight of more experienced teachers, the novice quickly gains proficiency and becomes increasingly more skilled as she or he picks up a few tricks and techniques and gets comfortable in the lab.

The Goals of Student Teaching

As the most experiential portion of teacher preparation, student teaching is prized by teacher educators, who have very high goals and expectations of students who are undergoing this phase of their training. Researchers have defined success in field experience in a variety of ways; for example, Barnes and Edwards (1984) described an effective student teaching experience as one "in which the acquisition of technical skills of teaching was accompanied by the development of a concomitant ability to make appropriate judgments with regard to the application of those skills" (p. 2). Feiman-Nemser & Buchmann (1987) offered a more detailed explanation of the characteristics of a successful field experience:

> Student teaching is teacher education when intending teachers are moved toward a practical understanding of the central tasks of teaching; when their dispositions and skills to extend and probe student learning are strengthened; when they learn to question what they see, believe and do; when they see the limits of justifying their decisions and actions in terms of "neat ideas" or classroom control; and when they see experience as a beginning rather than a culminating point in their learning. (p. 272)

Generally, researchers seem to consider student teaching successful when it includes four primary aspects. First and most basic, the field experience must give the student familiarity with the most basic aspects of schools and classrooms through a variety of experiences at many levels of teaching and school participation. Second, the experience should encourage the student's progression from the perspectives and modes of operation of a college student to those of a professional educator in a school or classroom setting. Third, the field experience should provide an experiential grounding for the current educative theory and best practice ideology being promoted in university classrooms. Finally, the preservice teacher must learn to navigate the various and complicated interpersonal relationships between different entities in the school setting.

The Experiential Dimension

Most preservice teachers enter student teaching having received their classroom experience exclusively through the eyes of a student. All of the prospective teachers' history as students comes into play in defining their perspective on education and teaching. Making the transition from the role of student to the role of educator requires a great deal of experience. As student teachers experience the classroom in their new-found role as educators, they must confront their own educative pasts from a completely new perspective:

> Preservice teachers begin to construct a reality about teaching in the student teaching experience. They learn to access their personal beliefs through the important questions and answers needed for assimilating their role as teacher and the characteristics contributing to the effectiveness of a teacher. (Collier, 1999, p. 173)

Researchers have described much of what experienced teachers do as "practical knowledge." Practical knowledge contains experiential knowledge that is mostly undocumented but of immediate importance for teachers' teaching practice (Zanting, Verloop, & Vermunt, 2001, p. 726). Researchers consider this important aspect of teacher behavior to be the experientially acquired reactions and behaviors from which an experienced teacher draws to deal quickly and appropriately with situations that arise in the classroom.

Competent teachers in their familiar classrooms almost always seem to do the right thing at the right time. They have a capacity to anticipate problematic situations. This capacity to anticipate, to make salient in the present certain aspects of the future, is acquired in praxis and in a familiarization with the field (Roth & Tobin, 2001, p. 750).

Because it is so experiential, this sort of knowledge is primarily obtained first-hand through teaching and coping with events in the classroom. It can also be acquired to some extent through classroom events shared in stories by other teachers. I found that stories about classroom experiences were readily available in the high school, and by sharing in experiences that they had not actually lived, novices learned some practices that they could apply in their own classrooms.

The Ideological Dimension

As prospective teachers gain classroom experience from which to draw in a variety of situations, they also must make a significant ideological shift. The ideology with which a teacher approaches a classroom must emerge from the student's history:

> At this level of professional development, student teachers are struggling to make the psychological switch from viewing themselves as college students to seeing their new daily role as a teacher, a learner-in-charge so to speak. Often they are so distracted by the process of teaching that they do not concede to the process of learning. (Collier, 1999, p. 179)

This transition comes through experience but also through a shift in focus: from considering learning activities for their own value, as distinct experiences, to seeing them as building to overall student learning. "Looking at teaching from the perspective of a pupil is not the same as viewing it from a pedagogical perspective, that is, the perspective of the teacher" (Feiman-Nemser & Buchmann, 1987, p. 257). As student teachers reflect on their observations and activities in the classroom, it is hoped that they will begin this progression to best promote student learning.

For many student teachers, this transition is made more difficult simply because they often look more like students than teachers to the rest of the students and staff. I cannot count the number of times a school official demanded my pass or a student aide walked into my room, looked directly at me, and asked, "Where's the teacher?" Such events emphasize the importance of adult presentation to students. Student teachers' dual roles as both learner and teacher contribute to identification difficulty, as does the inclination to identify with students who are often very close in age to student teachers and with whose role we are much more familiar. In my case, practice and direction from my cooperating teacher and university supervisor enabled me to gradually develop a management style that maintained accessibility to students while managing the classroom. By constructing a role for myself in teaching that reflected my own personality, I was able to develop my identity as an educator.

The Theoretical Dimension

Although most of the theoretical knowledge that is acquired in teacher education is attained primarily in university coursework, it is hoped that this knowledge will be reinforced and solidified through the experience of student teaching. This connection is vital to the university's aspiration to prepare transformative educators who will integrate the strategies and practices of inquiry science education into their classrooms and careers, because the new teachers' ability to connect theory to practice will determine their ability to apply that theory. "Key to the success of university-based teacher education is the linking of a theoretical foundation, provided through coursework, to the practical benefits of guided clinical experiences" (Turley & Nakai, 2000, p. 123).

One way in which students transition to applying the theories that they have learned at the university is through the formation of a language and form by which they evaluate teaching. Teachers are able to use such language to compare their own teaching to that of their peers and to incorporate the ideas and practices of other teachers into their own style. This language should include theories, observations, and comparisons between an image of ideal teaching and the real-world examples to which they are exposed:

> preservice teachers create a base of information from which they can examine their own and others' practices in light of readings from coursework, their initial beliefs about teaching,

and the effects of specific practices on students' school experiences. (Fairbanks & Meritt, 1998, pp. 47–48)

Like most new science teachers, I was a product of a great deal of traditional science education. I believed in the possibilities of inquiry science teaching before I could grasp a method for how it might actually work in the classroom. Fortunate student teachers work in tandem with experienced educators who strive to implement inquiry teaching in their classrooms. In such a setting, we witness experts at work and develop an image of the theoretical manifested in the practical.

The Relational Dimension

One of the most dreaded features of the student teaching requirement is how the preservice teacher will relate to the other participants in the school setting. A primary concern for both prospective teachers and their university supervisors, this is often a source of anxiety because it is so pivotal to the student teaching experience and because it depends equally on the teachers, administrators, and students in the school:

> Multiple layers of social activity underlie apprenticeships in teacher education: entering a social system as novice; negotiating with other, more experienced colleagues; juggling the various roles of teaching. Not only must preservice teachers contend with the dynamics of students, classrooms, and instruction, they must also find ways to work cooperatively and collaboratively with those whose classrooms they share. As a result, the role of the cooperative teacher in establishing the contexts of legitimate peripheral participation emerged as a critical element of the activity setting. (Fairbanks & Meritt, 1998, p. 66)

The student teacher must navigate several different sorts of relationships with people in a variety of roles: students, parents, school administrators, teachers, and other school personnel. Arguably the two most significant relationships during the field experience are with the cooperating or mentor teacher and with the university supervisor. The interactions with these entities are sometimes described as a triad relationship, as the two experienced educators work closely with the student teacher and one another to support, encourage, challenge, evaluate and provide an optimal learning experience:

> A typical student teaching experience brings together three people who are expected to work together for common purposes: a student teacher, a cooperating teacher, and a college supervisor. The working relationship is a well established and accepted one, and the work context and conditions are similar for the thousands of triads in existence at any given time. (Guyton & McIntyre, 1996, p. 522)

Throughout my field experience, maintaining constructive relationships with all of the parties involved at my site was one of the greatest challenges I experienced. The multiplicity of perspectives involved in student teaching promotes complicated interactions. The student teacher is not yet a professional but no longer a student. With much care, respect, and humility, the preservice teacher can navigate these relationships and promote his or her own interests, gaining an optimal experience.

The University Supervisor

The university representative plays a vital, though usually relatively removed role in the student teaching experience. This person is responsible for representing the pedagogy and ideals of the university, supporting the student teacher and giving feedback and advice regarding strategy and management, and ensuring that the student teacher fulfills all university requirements. My own university supervisor (who also happens to be the editor of this book) visited my site five or six times throughout the semester. He came and observed for an hour or two every other Thursday and generally brought an activity or evaluation. After he observed my progress, we shared a debriefing discussion, in which we discussed my performance, ways in which I could improve, and some things I might consider rethinking in my approach. We also discussed the site and my experiences. I had the opportunity ask for advice on management, meeting the requirements of my university and those of my cooperating teacher, and optimizing my field experience.

University supervisors participate in the field classroom in a variety of ways. Many drop in occasionally to observe the student teacher in action, then follow up their observation with an evaluative discussion that is intended to challenge the current practice of the teacher intern and to push her or him toward further growth. Others actually contribute to the teaching of the lesson that they attend, offering insight and ideas to enhance the lesson and broaden the experience of the student teacher. Researchers who promote this structure as a component of coteaching, argue:

> By working with another person, particularly with an experienced other, new teachers come to enact appropriate teaching as a way of being in the world. Working with others also brings out differences in perceiving and understanding. These differences, when brought out during the conversations about praxis, become the driving force for changes in praxis. (Roth & Tobin, 2001, p. 758)

In this model, university supervisors participate in lessons, either planned by the cooperating teacher or the student teacher or that they bring themselves. The three or more teachers share in the administration of the lesson, one taking a leadership role and the others supporting and contributing ideas, experience, and insight.

Aside from the primary role of facilitating and supporting the experiences of the student teacher, the university supervisor also holds the primary responsibility for evaluating the student teacher's experience and performance. "Feedback and evaluation are also a mechanism for helping the student teacher identify strengths and weaknesses in order to improve teaching" (Guyton & McIntyre, 1996, p. 525). This is a vital role, to determine both the student's preparedness as a professional educator and the university program's strengths and weaknesses in promoting the growth of the prospective teacher.

Evaluation of student teachers serves several purposes:

> Gatekeeping, or control of entry to the profession, is one of the major functions. . . . Assessing student teachers in terms of the goals of the teacher education program is another purpose that serves as a validating device for the program, as well as a source of feedback for program modifications. (Guyton & McIntyre, 1996, p. 525)

For me, the evaluation requirement for this portion of my teacher preparation was extremely frightening. Unlike most classwork, it is impossible to control all of the variables in the classroom when teaching. Because of this unpredictable aspect, the thought of being evaluated petrified me. Luckily, teacher educators recognize the growth process that is involved in learning to teach, and they look for progress, not perfection. My much-dreaded evaluations were encouraging and gave me valuable insight into myself and highlighted some areas in which I might improve. Ultimately, university supervisors provide important direction, support, and feedback to the student teacher, whose new role often feels cumbersome and confusing.

The Cooperating or Mentor Teacher

The role of the cooperating teacher is as complex as any role in education. Along with being ultimately responsible for providing a successful learning environment for all classroom students and for all of the other activities that fill the daily life of a classroom teacher, this person is now under pressure to provide guidance and support for a novice teacher. Although cooperating teachers seem to take this in stride, the duality of their role adds complexity to their already challenging job. The important role that cooperating teachers perform in teacher preparation is undeniable:

> The classrooms in which student teachers work affect the boundaries and directions of what can be learned through their characteristic interactions and curricula. Cooperating teachers set the affective and intellectual tone and also they conceive and carry out their role as teacher educators. (Feiman-Nemser & Buchmann, 1987, p. 256)

The practical, experiential and contextual knowledge that cooperating teachers offer serves a vital function in the process of becoming a teacher:

> It is clear that they [experienced teachers] have a body of practical knowledge which is not readily available to the university lecturer. Their knowledge of curriculum, for example, is detailed and situated in current practice in a way which could not be achieved by the academic study and analysis of curriculum documents, nor could it be convincingly maintained in the absence of practice. (Cope & Stephen, 2000, p. 921)

Although their role is universally recognized as invaluable, cooperating teachers' positive contributions are not necessarily automatic. Certain behaviors and practices of cooperating teachers are thought to be most effective in contributing to the growth of new teachers. Mentoring is a primary way in which cooperating teachers can promote development in student teachers: "mentoring consists of complex social interactions that mentor teachers and student teachers construct and negotiate for a variety of professional purposes and in response to the contextual factors they encounter" (Fairbanks, Freeman & Kahn, 2000, p. 103).

Mentoring involves intentional and purposeful action on the part of both the student and the mentor teacher, emphasizing growth and development of skills and ideology on the part of the student teacher. This is most often a give-and-take relationship in which both parties are engaged in considering, evaluating, and enumerating their own teaching practice and that of their partner. Mentoring, which is considered the most effective student–cooperating teacher relationship, maximizes the shared knowledge and professional growth of both parties. Fairbanks, Freeman and Kahn (2000) asked participants in a study of mentor-student interactions to define the most salient roles of mentor teachers. They found their participants' priorities to be "helping student teachers survive their beginning teaching experiences and define their relationships based upon dialogue and reflection; and building professional partnerships" (p. 104). In my student teaching, I benefited from this sort of reflection from a variety of teachers. In particular, a history teacher who was completing her doctoral dissertation challenged me to reflect on my teaching methods and ideology through challenging discussions and helpful advice. This type of mentor friendship is an optimal student–cooperating teacher relationship, but other site teachers can also serve in this capacity.

 ## The Student Teacher

The student teacher's role varies from assignment to assignment, and the cooperating teacher usually has the lead in determining the extent and level to which the student teacher is involved in the classroom. Most often, the role of the student teacher evolves from observer to helper to actually being in charge of teaching in a supervised role.

Preservice teachers are guided in their acquisition of teaching practices by more experienced mentors; they have opportunities to participate actively in classrooms, gradually taking on greater responsibility for teaching under the supervision of a mentor teacher and university faculty member, and they learn their practice through interactions with their peers and mentor teachers, in university settings, and through the teaching activities they undertake in classrooms (Fairbanks & Meritt, 1998, p. 49).

My own cooperating teacher offered me the opportunity to assume full responsibility for teaching from the first day of school. On the advice of my university representative, I declined this offer, gradually took over responsibilities for three physical science classes, and eventually accepted responsibility for the three biology courses as well. As they gradually assume more classroom responsibility, student teachers are allowed to view the hows and whys of the classroom with increasing depth: "[A]s mentor teachers reveal aspects of their teaching self to the student teachers, student teachers begin to recognize and to understand the tangle of practical and pedagogical issues that they may encounter as teachers" (Fairbanks et al., 2000, p. 107).

As preservice teachers become ready to tackle more of these responsibilities, they frequently encounter some conflict between their ideal of teaching and the practices of the cooperating teacher. This conflict is expected and can be positive, contributing to the prospective teacher's developing his or her own identity as an educator. Preservice teachers assemble their assessment and consider their adoption of teaching behaviors from mentor teachers in both positive and negative directions. They identify behaviors and models that they both would and would not themselves adopt in their teaching career: "Both negative and positive models served this function [helping to form student teacher identity], becoming an important aspect of the preservice teachers' socialization into the teaching community" (Fairbanks & Meritt, 1998, p. 62). This process is enhanced by the mentor teacher's willingness to share his or her underlying thoughts and reasons for an approach to the classroom. In my own experience, I was required to teach the traditional curriculum based on the district's recommended text, but I was able to integrate inquiry activities to ground areas of this curriculum. I was able to experience teaching in very different ways on a limited basis, and by combining this experience with discussions with teachers at my site and with my university supervisor, I was able to determine which was more palatable and effective for students and myself. "Sharing craft knowledge introduced the student teachers to the practices of experienced professionals, and they seemed to see these practices as sources of principled professional knowledge that ought to be emulated but not slavishly imitated" (Fairbanks et al., 2000, p. 107).

This form of reflective discussion is vital to the student teacher's growth, as it provides the reasons that underlie the actions of the experienced teacher: "If only observing them, student teachers do not find out about the mentors' knowledge, beliefs and reasons that may clarify their actions and decisions (Zanting et al., 2001, p. 726). As mentor and student teachers discuss their teaching philosophies, the student has opportunities to adopt the perspective and reasoning of the mentor or to disagree and apply this divergent experiential knowledge to his or her own teaching philosophy.

Many cooperating teachers recognize the value of the fresh perspective that student teachers bring to their classroom: "most teacher fellows made reference to the potential that students offered, both to schools and to the teacher fellows themselves, in terms of new ideas and a renewal of energy and enthusiasm" (Cope & Stephen, 2000, p. 921). In addition to renewed energy, student teachers can help to update the cooperating teacher's knowledge and experience with the most current theories and research in education. They also provide opportunities for the cooperating teacher to experience and try strategies and teaching theories that are different from their own. Although student teachers must always keep in mind their role as learner or intern in the classroom, they should not discount their potential to contribute to a richer, more lively classroom environment.

Often, as preservice teachers take on increasingly greater responsibility, they find the job of teaching overwhelming. This feeling is often what is remembered about the student teaching experience, contributing to its reputation as an extremely challenging and difficult portion of teacher education: "new teachers often struggle with the complexity and variety of their responsibilities" (Fairbanks et al., 2000, p. 105). For new teachers, one of the most overwhelming aspects of teaching is the constantly changing structural and curriculum demands made on professional teachers. This aspect is also a concern for their mentor teachers, who conclude that students should be exposed to all of the challenges of teaching: "In fact, although workload issues and the pace of change in the curriculum have been issues of some sensitivity with teachers . . . there was a clear sense that beginning teachers should be aware that change was a constant feature of teaching in the nineties" (Cope & Stephen, 2000, p. 918).

Another concern related to time restraints in student teaching is that the student and the mentor might find it difficult to prioritize time for reflection on practice among all of the other demands made on their time: "the 'busyness' of a teacher's life was such that they had little time for reflection" (Cope & Stephen, 2000, p. 917). This factor of student teaching came as a shock to me and to every student teacher with whom I have come into contact. Teachers handle a large number of tasks efficiently and as a matter of course; learning to fill all of these roles, however, can be a daunting task.

 ## Becoming a Teacher

In general, the student teaching experience can elicit a variety of emotional reactions in participants, as was mentioned in the introduction to this chapter. In the end, the conclusion must be drawn that learning to teach is a complex and multifaceted process that is difficult to define effectively. However this process occurs, it takes place through classroom experience alongside more experienced educators and negotiating a complex tangle of relationships and responsibilities:

> In methods courses at the university, student teachers crave concrete activities and specific directions. Yet, mentors and student teachers discover and rediscover that learning to teach, like teaching itself, is neither simple nor explicit. Instead, participants are involved in a complex negotiation, figuring out who they are as mentors, teachers, and student teachers. (Fairbanks et al., 2000, p. 111)

As was mentioned earlier, effective mentoring is particularly beneficial in learning to teach. Researchers also promote other practices to improve the experience and professional growth of student teachers. They encourage student teachers to reflect on how the classroom is experienced through the perspective of their students: "If novice teachers can be guided to understand their personal experiences through the mind of a learner first, they may be more likely to assimilate their understanding into the process of teaching" (Collier, 1999, p. 179). This practice encourages intern teachers to help their students to draw connections between lessons and activities and between the curriculum and student experience. It also encourages them to plan their curriculum around the interests and needs of students.

Another student teaching enhancement that researchers promote is coteaching, or teaching "at the elbows" of more experienced teachers. In this model, the student teacher participates at his or her assigned site as a member of a team of student teachers, mentor teachers, and university supervisors. Researchers argue that by teaching together with mentors and supervisors, students get to experience the decisions and reactions of the more experienced teachers, and they also see firsthand the results of these experiences. "Coteaching, that is, teaching at the elbows of peer(s), is a viable context for teacher education that better addresses the gap between explaining (theorizing) and understanding (living) teaching" (Roth & Tobin, 2001, p. 742). By participating in the classroom in this way, it is argued, the student is better able to evaluate and assimilate the practices of the experienced teachers, and the cooperating teacher and university supervisor are better able to understand and evaluate the actions of the student teacher because they are sharing in the lived experience of the teaching moment rather than observing at a distance. "We are convinced that in order to assess the knowledge enacted in teaching it has to be observed by experiencing it from a point of view of someone teaching rather than from the sidelines" (Roth & Tobin, 2001, p. 745).

During my university experience, I participated in a lecture section of an introductory biology course in a role similar to the one described in this research. Although the professor in this class definitely had the lead role, I was able to facilitate classroom activities with small groups as they attempted to unravel biological issues and situations that she gave them. I found this structure very helpful in initiating me to teaching and exposing me to the practical knowledge and problem-solving skills held by a far more experienced educator.

University Concerns

As the educational reforms proposed by the National Science Education Standards become increasingly prevalent, teacher educators seek to prepare new teachers with the skills and knowledge they need to enact these reforms in schools from the inside out. Thus, universities afford prospective teachers many theories and behaviors that researchers have identified as best teaching technique. Most schools, however, tend to be less advanced in their practices than universities would prefer. This creates a tension between the theoretical emphasis of the university setting and the practical, traditional setting of the school.

Although student teaching is the most widely accepted component of teacher preparation, it is criticized for lacking a theoretical and conceptual framework, for lacking commonly espoused goals, and for not fulfilling its potential (Guyton & McIntyre, 1996, p. 515). The danger in the student teaching experience is that in the hands-on world of teaching in a traditional classroom, prospective teachers will forget all of the transformative methods and ideals that they learned in their university coursework and continue in conventional teaching practices, as these will seem more practical and connected with the actual experience of the classroom:

> The notion of counteracting deficits by addressing them during the training of novices is a popular assumption. But it neglects the powerful socializing forces which operate on student teachers and contains at its heart a contradiction which assumes that students can learn selectively from experienced teachers. (Cope & Stephen, 2000, p. 923)

Therefore, the university must work to identify cooperating teachers who can model the teaching practices that the program emphasizes.

> The dilemma science teacher educators face is whether or not the experiences in the field have the focus they desire. Is it a setting in which prospective teachers can practice the new approaches they are learning in their teacher education program, or is it a setting in which they become socialized to entrenched and ineffective practices? (Anderson & Mitchener, 1994, p. 18)

Researchers have debated the actual influence of the skills and practices of the cooperating teacher. Some argue fervently that the strength or compatibility of the cooperating teacher affects the overall value of the student teaching experience: "For some STs [student teachers], being assigned a weak cooperating teacher, one whose teaching style was incompatible with the student teacher's, or one who had competing responsibilities was clearly a disadvantage" (Turley & Nakai, 2000, p. 128). Others contend that students learn as much from a difficult student teaching experience as they do from a generally positive one:

> Most of my colleagues insist that the best placement for a new teacher is with an exemplary cooperating teacher. This has not been my experience. In the long-term new teachers who learn most are those who have to contend with eventful classrooms. Teaching with an exemplary cooperating teacher might limit the diversity of the events that arise. . . . On the other hand, teaching with someone who has much to learn about teaching can provide experience with an event-rich environment that is conducive to the development of a robust teaching habits. (Roth & Tobin, 2001, p. 748)

My student teaching experience reflected the analysis of this researcher. As I was exposed to teaching through the more traditional method, my belief that learning science through inquiry is the most appropriate and promising method solidified. I also discovered that this strategy better fit my own personality and management style, although it is far more difficult to maintain at first than traditional teaching. My field experience convinced me that the results of inquiry were more than worth the extra work.

Some educational theorists argue that however prospective teachers find their field experience, all of the components of teacher education work together to contribute to the professional identity of the emerging teacher:

> [P]reservice teachers were influenced by the models they learned on campus and in school, the people and events they encountered during their teacher preparation, and their personal responses to these influences. Constructing a professional identity entailed the give-and-take of shaping and being shaped by the circumstances of their teacher preparation, by the interplay of all of these forces. (Fairbanks & Meritt, 1998, p. 67)

Part of the tension between the university setting and the school site involves a fundamental difference in focus. Whereas the university is focused on reform and theoretical foundations, the school is concerned with the various tasks of teaching in their most immediate priority.

Universities require explicit and analytical approaches to practice, and discourse that displays these features will be rewarded by high grades. The same type of activity is less likely to be valued by schools, which are more concerned with practical and immediate effectiveness in the classroom (Cope & Stephen, 2000, p. 914).

There is a concern that as university personnel promote transformative ideology, they will seem to students to be overly critical of teachers in the field, the cooperating teacher in particular: "One outcome of such programmes is that there is a very real danger that university courses end up criticizing the practices of the teachers with whom they have placed their students" (Cope & Stephen, 2000, p. 914). This would be an unfortunate result, considering the important role that experienced teachers play in the development of new teachers.

Optimizing the Student Teaching Experience

As student teachers are transformed from college students into professional educators, many struggle with adjusting to all that is expected of them to fill the shoes of a teacher. Researchers have identified several factors that affect the growth and adjustment of the prospective teacher, and I have included some aspects of my own preparation that I believe enhanced my experience.

Beginning Field Experience on Campus

As I approached student teaching, I found my early experiences of inquiry science teaching invaluable. As the study of science is transformed throughout primary, secondary, and university education, teachers who have been taught science through inquiry will be far better equipped to transmit this style of learning than will those of us who learned in a far more traditional style. Students of teaching can also be exposed to inquiry science teaching through opportunities to participate by helping to teach such courses on campus. At Oklahoma State University, for example, students in methods courses spend time helping out in inquiry-based introductory biology labs. Upper-level students can also earn advanced credits by assisting as facilitators in lecture sections of the same course. These students offer themselves as sources of good teaching theory and provide helpful assistance in the administration of these courses as they learn, teach, and observe a range of educators applying the inquiry approach.

Having Clear and Realistic Goals

One factor that affects the feelings that student teachers have about their student teaching experience is the expectations that they hold on entering the field. The prospective teacher who expects to be challenged, to gain experiential knowledge of teaching and learning and practical skills for running a classroom, and to begin a career-long process of teaching and professional growth often finds himself or herself successful in the student teaching experience. If the prospective teacher expects, on the other hand, for the student teaching experience to be an opportunity to practice and apply all of the knowledge that he or she has accumulated at the university, the experience will often be disappointing and frustrating:

> Student teachers have particular understandings and dispositions that influence their approaches to the experience and their capacities to learn from it. Social and intellectual skills, as well as expectations about themselves, influence their work. (Feiman-Nemser & Buchmann, 1987, p. 256)

Questioning and Conversation

One factor that seems to help to solidify the student teacher's classroom experiences is consistent and critical interaction regarding pedagogy and teaching strategy. Through conversations with other preprofessionals as well as with professional and university educators, prospective teachers consider and evaluate the foundation behind their own teaching and that of their peers and mentors:

> Although it is accepted that there are multiple ways of participating appropriately with the goal of learning to teach it also is a truism that there are multiple ways of participating that will not be productive. Accordingly it is desirable that discussions among participants with/in a community focus on the rationale for the most salient roles and associated modes of coparticipation. (Roth & Tobin, 2001, p. 757)

Doing Action Research and Philosophy of Education

In my own preservice teaching experience, I was required to complete two assignments that I believe encouraged me to further consider my own teaching strategies and behaviors relative to the theories I had absorbed in my university coursework. First and most formidable, before I entered the classroom, I was required to write and revise a detailed explication of my own personal teaching philosophy and goals, tying these to teaching behaviors that would promote the sort of learning to which I aspired for my students. This paper, called a rationale framework, forced me to judiciously consider what I desired for my students and how I expected to achieve my priorities. It also forced me to acknowledge how little I truly knew and understood about the actual process of teaching because I found it so very difficult to verbalize my plans and ideals on the topic. Incidentally, this paper also was an important contribution to my eventually landing a teaching job at an innovative alternative school.

Second, I was required to complete an action research project, to embark on an investigation on some question of my own formation within the context of my field experience. This activity forced me to make critical analysis of my classroom a priority and to concentrate on improving an area of my teaching that was lacking.

Seeking a Variety of Advice

As I came to the completion of my student teaching experience, I initiated my own opportunity, with the blessing of my university supervisor, to observe and converse with several highly admired teachers at my site. I observed their classrooms and interactions with students and took time to question them about the structures present in their classrooms and their own teaching theories and practices. Most were thrilled to share their knowledge and experience with me. I learned a great deal from these interactions and became the beneficiary of some excellent advice. Some of my favorite examples follow:

- "Your classroom should be an extension of yourself, don't let anybody make you someone you aren't."
- "Don't forget that it's as important to shape them [students] as people, not just fill their heads with language."
- "One thing they never tell you: Your classroom should be self-contained. You undermine your authority by constantly contracting out your discipline problems. Make a plan to take care of your problems yourself and stick with it. You'll gain the respect of both your students and the administration."

This advice proved quite valuable to me as I began my first year of teaching. Conversations with practicing teachers about teaching practice and the application of theory helped me to reflect on all that I had learned and how it could be applied in the classroom:

> Becoming critically reflective about personal reactions to teaching situations . . . may be the springboard to making connections among public theories and personal images of teaching. The result may be critical awareness of knowledge needs, with students posing their own questions and being motivated to seek knowledge that will help them be the teachers they want to be. (Black & Halliwell, 2000, p. 114)

Controlling the Context

Research has established the magnitude of the contribution that the classroom context contributes to a successful student teaching experience. It is also necessary to consider how the university can contribute to creating the most positive situation for prospective teachers.

Whatever the outcome, teacher educators must examine the impact of the context in which student teaching occurs and develop a strategy for gaining more control of the curriculum within that context. The framework, articulation, and integration of the curriculum of student teaching and school experiences are vital to the success of this component (Guyton & McIntyre, 1996, p. 520). One way in which most universities attempt to control the context is through screening the teachers who share their classrooms and practices with prospective teachers. Another method that some programs are attempting is to provide cooperating teachers with information and resources with which to better equip mentors to provide the best possible experiences for student teachers: "Some evidence exists that the preparation of cooperating teachers for their roles is effective in developing a more positive context" (Guyton & McIntyre, 1996, p. 520). Another method, which guarantees that the prospective teacher will benefit from a variety of perspectives and teaching styles, is that of placing groups of student teachers into a community of cooperating teachers who have continual assistance and support of the university in their mentoring endeavors.

One suggestion for improving the effectiveness and inclusion of pedagogic ideals in the student teacher experience is to organize student teachers in cohorts or community groups, in which students in a subject area are assigned as a group to an individual or department in a cooperating school.

> In either case, the objectives of the cohort arrangement include: creating a more coherent program and a stronger link between theory and practice; achieving a closer relationship between faculty and student teachers; establishing conditions conducive to mutual support among student teachers; and modeling a communal, collaborative approach to teaching and learning that student teachers can apply in their practicum settings and in their school and classroom after graduation. (Cope & Stephen, 2000, p. 914)

Maximizing Involvement

Throughout my student teaching commitment, I became involved in the high school in every way that I could. I took a position as the assistant coach of the swim team,

I volunteered to work with a youth organization, and I attended all of the sporting and recreational events that I could. All of this activity added significantly to the already demanding time commitment required by my internship, but I found that the opportunity to interact with students outside the classroom benefited me in two ways. First, the opportunity for students to see me in different environments allowed them to view me more as a holistic person. Second, I was able to experience the school community in a different way from the customary isolation of the classroom. By understanding the community of the school and having observed students in more social situations, I was better able to motivate students in learning science, and because students began to relate to me as a multifaceted person, rather than just their intern teacher, they began to offer me assistance in reaching my classroom goals rather than taking an oppositional, resistant stance.

CONCLUSION: Time to Dive In

Individual experiences of student teaching are as different as the individuals involved. Although the university and the field site can do a great deal to provide the best possible learning opportunities for their student teachers, it is up to the prospective teacher himself or herself to make the most of whatever opportunities are offered:

> Case studies of participants' experiences during their final year of teacher preparation revealed that learning to teach is a complex process determined by the interaction of personal factors such as the prospective teachers' knowledge and beliefs about teaching, learning, and subject matter; and situational factors such as expectations, demands, and feedback from key actors in the university and public school settings. (Borko & Mayfield, 1995, p. 501)

Bringing all of their educative histories to bear on the field experience, student teachers must form a new identity as a teacher: "Student teachers have particular understandings and dispositions that influence their approaches to the experience and their capacities to learn from it (Feiman-Nemser & Buchmann, 1987, p. 256). Student teachers should be vocal about their own ways of learning and ways in which their cooperating teachers and university supervisors can help them to maximize their field experience. In the end, the responsibility of maximizing whatever opportunities are afforded them in the field lies with the student teacher: "This interpretation may be informative insofar as it reminds us that, to some degree, becoming a teacher depends upon personal resources and dispositions" (McNamara, 1995, p. 59).

This chapter began with a comparison between learning to teach and learning to swim, and I alluded to the sink-or-swim method of learning to swim that is most commonly used as an analogy to student teaching. Every swimming coach knows that this is not an acceptable method for teaching small children to swim. Though unlikely to sink, most new swimmers would flail and sputter about in a terrifying introduction to the water. For the rare child who actually returned to swimming lessons after such a harrowing experience, the teacher would then have to overcome a great number of barriers in regaining that child's trust and getting him or her back in the water.

Swimming lessons are actually approached in a much gentler fashion, and I would suggest that this method presents a superior model for preservice teachers as well. New swimmers are allowed to enter the water at their own pace and then are supported by an instructor until they develop a level of comfort in the pool. The first task that is required of them is nothing more than to get their faces wet, maybe a few times if they want; then they are returned to the side of the pool, having succeeded in a small way in the direction of learning to swim. The next day, they might be ready to kick their feet with their faces in the water. Soon a child can kick a distance on his or her own without the physical support of the instructor, although the instructor is always within reaching distance, ready to offer help and support when necessary. Eventually, the process changes, and the instructor removes himself or herself from such close proximity and begins to collaborate with the student, showing the student how to move his or her arms in a crawl stroke and allowing the student time to practice and investigate how the water provides leverage and support. Student teaching that is analogous to this careful and gentle way of teaching swimming promotes the same self-sufficiency and confidence that can sustain new science teachers in those critical early years.

Researchers have provided educators and cooperating teachers with tools that they can use to improve the experiences of student teachers as they transform themselves into professional educators. Although this field has been fruitful, more research is needed to provide a complete model of an optimal student teaching experience. "Educational research and theorizing may not have spent time enough to make thematic that which makes teaching in praxis so different from teaching in theory" (Roth & Tobin, 2001, p. 745).

For all its imperfections and unpredictable dynamics, the student teaching experience in science can be the most powerful and gratifying part of professional preparation. With good lifeguards, the new teacher can be confident enough to dive right in.

The Game in Action

No Life Jacket Necessary!

Meet Emily, our superhuman student teacher. Emily, currently six weeks into her internship at Ultimate High School, is showing extraordinary aptitude for teaching science and much promise for becoming an exemplary high school teacher. Before we look any further into Emily's current status, let's look back at the teacher preparation that led up to this moment in her field experience. Having decided some time in middle school that she was destined to be a science teacher, Emily worked hard in school and graduated at the top of her high school class. She entered the State College science teacher preparation program, where she was assigned to a cohort, a small group of eight other perfect prospective teachers. On campus, these excellent preservice teachers completed all of the activities mentioned in this chapter in preparation for their internships. On completion of their university coursework, Emily and the rest of her cohort were split into two groups of four and assigned to two local high schools. These schools were perfectly appointed to accept the prospective science teachers, having entire departments of learner-centered teachers who were specially prepared to mentor new teachers and eager to assist in their progression to professionalism.

Emily was assigned to an energetic teacher with ten years of experience successfully teaching science as inquiry. Emily's cooperating teacher, Carol, had hosted three previous student teachers and was highly respected for her active and innovative classroom style, as well as her strong support of interns. She instructed Emily to take initiative in her own internship. Carol did not push Emily beyond her comfort and ability but encouraged her to take risks and try to incorporate as many different experiences into her internship as possible. Emily also interacted regularly with the other members of her cohort at her site, with the entire science department, and with her administrators at the high school, all of whom had taken a supportive stance in the teacher preparation program. In addition, a team of three university supervisors took turns spending one day a week at Emily's field site. The university supervisors, site teachers, and administrators had worked as a team for five years, providing excellent student teaching experiences to twenty-three students.

Initially, Emily participated in the classroom in a limited way. She passed out papers, answered questions, gave assistance to individual students, and led small groups of students in discussions and activities. In this way, Emily was participating in team teaching, but the responsibility for planning and administration of the lesson generally fell to Carol. Several times a week, one of the university supervisors participated in the lessons with Emily and Carol. Sometimes Carol planned and led activities with Emily and the university supervisor at her side; at other times, the university supervisor provided and led the lesson while Emily and Carol assisted. Emily found that one of the most important methods that the three teachers used to lead the class to deeper thought was to ask open and engaging questions, leading the class in an interesting and provoking dialogue or investigation. As Emily became increasingly comfortable with students and the classroom, she assumed more responsibility for the management of the classroom and lessons.

Finally, Emily is ready to teach her first lesson to Carol's two biology classes. She has planned and prepared and feels confident that her lesson will go over well, although she does not expect to be able to run it perfectly on her own. She is grateful for the presence of Carol and a university supervisor, who will participate actively in the lesson that they have reviewed together. The students respond well to Emily because they are already comfortable with her teaching and managing the classroom and assisting the other educators, so her landmark slips by them almost unnoticed. Emily's lesson goes generally as planned, but she sees that the students are confused by the complex topic about halfway through the activity. She pauses to regroup, and Carol takes advantage of the pause to ask a leading question that allows the students to tie the idea to a common, familiar experience, grounding the lesson in their lives. Emily is grateful for the added reinforcement, and the teachers help students to finish their activity and document their findings—a successful first lesson.

Emily plans to teach two lessons to the biology students next week, then three, then four, until she is responsible for all of the planning for biology. She will also periodically lead a few lessons in Carol's chemistry classes, but Carol has encouraged Emily to concentrate on building some excellent units in biology and not to spread herself too thin with full responsibility for multiple preparations. Emily feels comfortable that her internship will be a success. In many discussions with Carol, as well as with her cohort members, university supervisors, and other site personnel, she has been able to scrutinize her practices and strategies, and she has seen her style grow and improve significantly. Emily also recognizes that she has much room for teaching growth and plans to continue to seek discussions, environments, and literature that will challenge her and help her to persist in her professional development throughout her career.

Emily's experience appears to be an excellent one. The structure and support modeled here would allow her to grow and improve greatly, and I would expect that she would eventually parlay her experience into an exciting and transforming teaching career. I see one significant flaw, however: Education is never this perfect. As a human endeavor, involving a large number of people, and a great deal of politics, teaching is often the complicated navigation of a large number of variables with imperfect humans and illogical systems. The problem with Emily's experience is that she has not learned how to defend her ideas and practices, and she has not overcome obstacles. In the absence of challenges, she might be less able to implement her excellent ideas and practices; she needs to develop the security necessary to stand up to tradition and provide her own students with educationally transformative experiences. True, the structures described as Emily's case would contribute to excellent preparation for preservice teachers. But the nature of field experience is that the student teacher will confront many of the challenges that are present in the practice of teaching, and the most optimal situation that can be provided by a university will still contain these challenges. Student teachers who are equipped to implement learner-centered teaching strategies and have a vision and drive for this

methodology will have to defend their innovative approach to other participants at their site. The experience of defending their ideals, perhaps more than any other, will help to shape them into transformative educators.

Reflecting on the Game

1. What sorts of teachers might emerge from more and less optimal student teaching experiences? What unique strengths might be developed in a teacher who has a less optimal internship? What strengths might be developed in a more optimal partnership?

2. What do you think are the most important characteristics that a teacher might develop during her or his internship?

3. What do you think are the responsibilities of the student teacher in maintaining the theory and strategies promoted by her or his university department?

4. What do you think are the responsibilities of the mentor teacher and university supervisor in supporting and directing the student teacher?

5. In what ways might your current and past experiences as a learner inform your future identity as a teacher?

References

Anderson, R. D., & Mitchener, C. P. (1994). Research on science teacher education. In D. L. Gabel (Ed.), *Handbook of research on teaching and learning* (pp. 3–44). New York: Macmillan and National Science Teachers Association.

Barnes, S., & Edwards, S. (1984). *Effective student teaching experience: A qualitative-quantitative study* (Report No. 9060). Austin, TX: University of Texas at Austin, Research and Development Center for Teacher Education.

Black, A. L., & Halliwell, G. (2000). Accessing practical knowledge: How? why? *Teaching and Teacher Education, 16,* 103–115.

Borko, H., & Mayfield, V. (1995). The roles of the cooperating teacher and university supervisor in learning to teach. *Teaching & Teacher Education, 11*(5), 501–518.

Collier, S. T. (1999). Characteristics of reflective thought during the student teaching experience. *Journal of Teacher Education, 50*(3), 173–181.

Cope, P., & Stephen, C. (2000). A role for practicing teachers in initial teacher education. *Teaching and Teacher Education, 17*(2001), 913–924.

Croker, D. L., & Wilder, A. (1999). How can we better train our student teachers? *English Journal, 88*(3), 17–21.

Fairbanks, C. M., Freedman, D., & Kahn, C. (2000). The role of effective mentors in learning to teach. *Journal of Teacher Education, 51*(2), 102–112.

Fairbanks, C. M., & Meritt, J. (1998). Preservice teachers reflections and the role of context in learning to teach. *Teacher Education Quarterly, 1998*(3), 47–68.

Feiman-Nemser, S., & Buchmann, M. (1987). When is student teaching teacher education? *Teaching & Teacher Education, 3*(4), 255–273.

Guyton, E., & McIntyre, D. J. (1996). Science education. In John P. Sikula, Thomas J. Buttery, and Edity Guyton (Eds.), *Handbook of research on teacher education* (2nd ed., pp. 514–534). New York: Macmillan, 1996.

McNamara, D. (1995). The influence of student teachers' tutors and mentors upon their classroom practice: An exploratory study. *Teaching & Teacher Education, 11*(1), 51–61.

Roth, W.-M., & Tobin, K. (2001) Learning to teach science as practice. *Teaching and Teacher Education, 17*(2001), 741–762.

Turley, S., & Nakai, K. (2000). Two routes to certification: What do student teachers think? *Journal of Teacher Education, 51*(2), 122–134.

Zanting, A., Verloop, N., & Vermunt, J. D. (2001). Student teachers eliciting mentors' practical knowledge and comparing it to their own beliefs. *Teaching and Teacher Education, 17*(2001), 725–740.

Additional Resources

American Association for the Advancement of Science. (1990). *Science for all Americans: Project 2061.* New York: Oxford University Press.

Cummings, C. (2000). *Winning strategies for classroom management.* Alexandria, VA: Association for Supervision and Curriculum Development.

Haines, S. (2002). Preparing preservice teachers. *The Science Teacher, 69*(6), 46–49.

National Health Museum's website for health and bioscience teachers and learners: www.accessexcellence.com

Pacific Bell's e-learning toolbox for information and education: www.bluewebn.com

Trumbull, D. J. (1999). *The new science teacher.* New York: Teachers College Press.

PART TWO

The Players

chapter 5

Learners in Science: No Room on the Bench

Karen Dawkins, Ed.D.

The game of science education has changed dramatically since gaining the pioneering insights of learning theory. Coaches know that lasting impressions and the actions that spring from them require more than facts delivered to our students, divorced from meaningful experience. On an inquiry field of play, constructivism governs content, context, and pedagogy.

chapter 6

Fair Play in Science Education: Moving Beyond Science for All

Rebecca Meyer Monhardt, Ph.D.

Plenty of evidence has accumulated to indicate that science has not been a welcoming game for all of our students. Everyone deserves a fair shot at playing the game of science, and coaches bear great responsibility for creating an equitable playing field. Value for the diversity of learners results in a valuing of science by citizens.

chapter 7

Accessible Science Education: Every Student a Player

John Stiles, Ph.D.

Students with disabilities stand to make great personal gain, as well as societal contribution, through a sound science education. The inquiry skills of problem solving, critical thinking, and reasoning, coupled with deep conceptual understanding of science, represent a foundation for lifelong learning that all of our students deserve.

c h a p t e r

5

LEARNERS IN SCIENCE:

No Room on the Bench

Karen Dawkins, Ed.D.
Director of the Center For Science,
Mathematics, and Technology
Education, East Carolina University

ABOUT THE AUTHOR: Dr. Karen Dawkins taught high school science for more than twenty years in Kentucky, Mississippi, and North Carolina before moving to a position with the North Carolina Mathematics and Science Education Network. As director of the Center for Science, Mathematics, and Technology Education at East Carolina University, she now designs and implements professional development programs for K–12 science and math teachers. She recently led a team of high school teachers, high school students, and university faculty in a field research program on North Carolina's Outer Banks, gathering data and interviewing experts and residents as the basis for a curriculum product soon to be available in print, CD-ROM, and web-based versions.

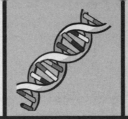

> # The country is full of good coaches. What it takes to win is a bunch of interested players.
>
> —Don Coryell
> *Ex-San Diego Chargers Coach*

CHAPTER WARM-UP

At the heart of modern science education lies constructivist learning theory: the belief that students construct their own understandings and that the new understandings that students construct rest on the foundations of knowledge and understandings that already exist. An appreciation for this learning theory shapes how teachers are prepared, how teachers view science, and how teachers approach the task of sharing science with learners. Constructivism provides a context for the everyday practices of science teachers: imparting knowledge, crafting investigations, assessing learning—indeed, facilitating science literacy as it emerges throughout this book.

INTRODUCTION: Bridging Research and Practice

All humans learn; we just do not fully understand how that happens. In the last thirty years or so, however, research has changed the way we think about learning, and that, in turn, has changed the way we think about teaching. Although practice always lags a bit behind theory, the influence of the National Science Education Standards (National Research Council, 1996) and associated reform documents has focused attention on learning and the implications of learning theory for our classroom practice. A major focus of the reform has been to bridge the gap between research and practice, an element that was long neglected in the world of education. In fact, researchers in the area of cognitive science are now quite likely to spend time with teachers, testing and refining their theories and the applications of those theories (Bransford, Brown, & Cocking, 1999).

Just as scientific theories serve to explain certain phenomena that we might observe in the natural world, learning theories seek to explain the learning process. The constructivist learning theory has evolved as a powerful idea that connects many current areas of research. Although constructivism is a complex concept, it offers many practical implications for science educators and science learners. Many of those implications can be understood in terms of team sports or games. Because the idea of constructivism is so big, however, a single metaphor will not suffice to explain it; therefore, this chapter will use a number of game references to illustrate different aspects of constructivism.

What Is Constructivism? Understanding the Game

The term "constructivism" is used a great deal in the education community. Although it is identified as a theory of learning, it is also used widely in relationship to teaching practice. You might hear educators talking about constructivist classrooms or constructivist teaching strategies. There is a fine line of distinction, but if you understand constructivism as a theory, you can build an understanding of what that means for classrooms and teaching. That is the primary purpose of this chapter: to connect the theory of learning (constructivism) to classroom practice.

Theories of Learning

The word "theory" is used in many contexts. For example, in everyday language, we might hear a person say, "If they would upgrade their weight training program, those offensive linemen wouldn't be allowing so many sacks—but that's just my theory." In this context, the speaker acknowledges that his theory is an opinion, probably based on limited information. He weakens his proposition by tacking on the phrase "that's just my theory." In science, theories are not weak statements; expressed as explanations based on evidence, they are at the heart of scientific knowledge. The strength of the theory rests on the depth and reliability of the supporting evidence as judged by the scientific community. To say, then, that a scientific explanation is "just a theory" is to misunderstand how theories are used in science to explain natural phenomena.

Constructivism as a Theory

To identify constructivism as a learning theory is to recognize two things: (1) It is an attempt to explain learning, and (2) it is based on evidence. Researchers acknowledge that coming to understand how people learn is an extremely complex undertaking. Despite recent findings in the area of brain research, we are in the infant stages of representing the complicated reality that we call learning. We do have a body of evidence, however, that provides a foundation we can use in improving the practice of teaching. As with any theory, different people interpret the evidence in different ways. This chapter will identify various perspectives on constructivism and the commonalities that allow us to make practical applications as we engage in the game of science education.

Constructivism Versus Behaviorism

Although some might argue that theories are recorded in books that are read only by academicians, widely accepted theories have profound influences on the way we live and work. In education, for example, the behaviorist theory of learning was a dominant factor for decades in determining pedagogy in the United States. Teachers who began their careers as late as the 1980s probably dealt with student behavioral objectives in their curriculum guides and teacher behavioral objectives in the tools used to evaluate teacher effectiveness. Teachers who continue to use this approach provide certain stimuli to students along with reinforcements over time to get students to respond appropriately. Yager (1991) says that this method works quite well if the goal of the experience is to prepare students to replicate a behavior that the teacher has identified. If the goal is to enable students to develop deep understandings of concepts, to connect related concepts, and to apply their knowledge to new situations, however, then the behaviorist model is ineffective. Although there are probably remnants of curriculum materials and other documents in use that reflect a behaviorist approach to learning, it is safe to say that constructivism is a much more influential force today. Fensham (1992) asserts that "the most conspicuous psychological influence on curriculum thinking in science since 1980 has been the constructivist view of learning" (p. 801).

Points of Agreement

Although a search through the literature on constructivism would probably unearth more than a dozen brands, each of which emphasizes a different aspect of learning, there are two principles that would likely be found in every one (Geelan, 1997a):

1. Students construct their own understandings.
2. The new understandings that students construct rest on the foundations of knowledge and understandings that already exist.

Without knowing any other aspects of constructivist learning theory, practitioners have in these two principles a basis for thinking about teaching strategies. A constructivist view of learning rejects previous ideas that pictured learners as vessels into which teachers could pour new ideas and information—straight from the teacher's brain to the student's brain, completely intact. Instead, it views learners as having complex networks of understandings that they have developed from their experiences. As they encounter new experiences through their senses, they attempt to fit these into their existing networks. Nobody can do this for another person; however, good teachers can provide environments that support learners in the process of establishing these connections and making sense of what they experience.

As an analogy, think about a child who played T-ball as a preschooler. She learned how to bat the ball, run the bases, and handle the ball in the field. When she got older and joined the softball team, she had to incorporate new elements into her game. The reflexive movements, hand-eye coordination, and running skills she had developed in T-ball all fit into the new scheme, but she had to learn new skills, apply the old skills differently, and fit them into the game of softball. She did not learn to play softball by reading the rulebook or watching the other girls play, although those sources of information were certainly helpful. Ultimately, she learned how to play by experiencing the game. After a more detailed look at constructivism, I will present additional connections to practice.

The Nature of Science and Science Education

There are certain philosophical issues that assert themselves when we consider constructivism as a theory of learning intimately tied to the development of knowledge. Interestingly enough, these issues are also elements that arise in discussions about the nature of science itself and what we can know about the universe.

The Nature of Reality: What Is Truth?

Much of science education involves learning about the world in which we live, and it might be productive to mention that scientists differ in their views on the nature of that reality and what we can come to know about it. For those of us who are not philosophers of science, it might seem a bit frivolous to waste our time debating such an esoteric matter. If we are serious about understanding the nature of science itself, though, it is worthy of consideration.

Some people, including many scientists, hold to the idea that there is an objective world independent of humans and that they can use objective critical methods to test hypotheses in regard to these realities. These realists maintain that there are objects, events, and processes that would exist even if there were no humans around to perceive them (Nola, 1997). At one end of the continuum, these scientists maintain that there are certain "truths" about the universe and we can learn what they are. At the far end of the spectrum are those who are skeptical that there are objective "truths" out there, or, more moderately, if there are, all that we can know of them is what we experience—and that experience necessarily involves subjectivity.

Connections with Science Education

Although some writers assume that what you think about the nature of science profoundly influences how you teach science, Nola (1997) rejects that claim. For example, if there is a direct connection, one would assume that if you subscribe to the notion of an objective reality and objective methods to learn about that reality, then you will probably teach in a very direct way. Gandy (1997) describes this approach as the "modified Dragnet theory of teaching" (p. 45)—nothing but the facts, ma'am (as well as definitions and theories). On the other hand, if you view reality from a more subjective perspective, then you are more likely to use a constructivist approach; that is, you emphasize using evidence to make explanations, without so much emphasis on "truth." In other words, if you think that scientists discover objects and relationships that exist in the universe, then you teach by telling. If you think that scientists invent concepts to explain what they observe and experience, then you teach in a constructivist mode. Matthews (1997) contrasts the two perspectives by using the phrases "finding out" for discovery and "making sense" for invention. The point is this: There is conflicting evidence for a direct connection between teachers' views of scientific reality and their ideas about good science teaching, but it is certainly a rich area for researchers and teachers to examine.

In regard to the ideas of being and knowing, Staver (1998) rejects the contention that a consideration of constructivism should address the nature of reality (being) at all. He focuses on "observations, objects, events, data, laws, and theory" (p. 503) as entities that exist as expressions of us, the observers. Constructivists do not deny or support the contention that there is an independent reality beyond us; according to Staver, they remain silent on this issue and instead emphasize a view that explains, interprets, and uses science as a way of knowing. Whatever the nature of the universe, how we come to know about it is within the bounds of constructivism. It is important for science teachers to confront various philosophies of science, including those that address the nature of reality; but even if they choose to ignore that aspect of their discipline, they can still embrace the practical implications of constructivism to facilitate the development of useful concepts by their students.

The Varieties of Constructivism

It is very difficult to develop a comprehensive list of perspectives on constructivism because there are many, and there is much overlap among them. An interesting scheme for categorizing perspectives was developed by Geelan (1997b), who focuses on two dimensions: (1) personal versus social learning and (2) objectivist versus relativist views of the nature of science. Although Staver suggests that consideration of the second dimension is unnecessary for constructivists, it is often included in the conversation. Geelan's dimensions are expressed in the coordinates illustrated in Figure 5.1 (adapted from Geelan, 1997b, p. 20).

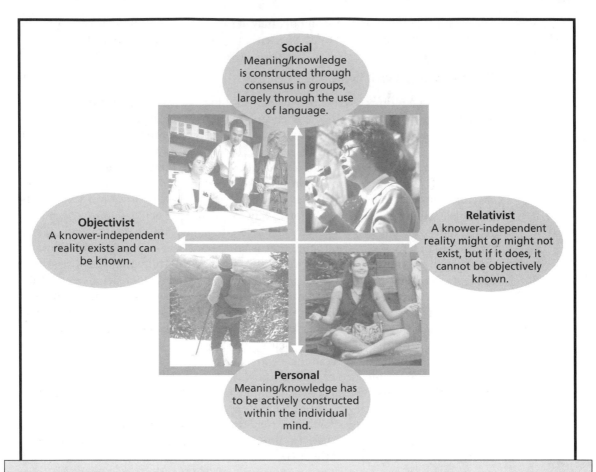

Figure 5.1 An adaptation of Geelan's organizational scheme for forms of constructivism

To explain more fully, the dimensions represented on the horizontal axis are those discussed previously in regard to the nature of science. One adheres to the idea of an objective external reality that can be perceived through scientific methods—or at least takes scientific knowledge as a given (objectivist); the other adheres to the idea of a reality that exists only through the experiences of the observers (relativist). The vertical axis emphasizes a contrast between individual learning and learning in a social context.

Geelan is careful to qualify his categories in three ways:

1. Writers may change their positions over time, and many have done so in respect to their views of both science and learning.
2. He indicates that in the historical development of constructivism, there has been a general movement from lower left to upper right, recognizing that the direction of movement could very well have been different if, for example, Vygotsky's

writings (emphasizing social and linguistic influences) had been available in the West before Piaget's work (emphasizing individual construction).

3. It is important to realize that the placement of any person's work on the scale simply shows a comparison relative to other positions. Notably, Geelan points out that no constructivist would be entirely objectivist; rather, some have less of a problem with the idea of scientific "truth." Those perspectives are therefore sited more toward the objectivist side of the scale. For the purposes of this paper, it is more important for us to deal with the vertical axis because those categories have important implications for science education.

Personal Construction of Knowledge. There are many brands of constructivism that might be considered in the broad category of personal constructivism. In general, they agree that individuals construct their own knowledge and that knowledge is not objective. Building on Piaget's ideas of accommodation and assimilation, von Glasersfeld (1993, 1995), who labels his views as radical constructivism, emphasizes that individuals do not passively receive knowledge; rather, they actively construct knowledge within their own minds. In addition, he recognizes that human minds do not have direct access to the external world. He does not deny the existence of an external world, but he argues that individuals construct knowledge for the purpose of making meaning out of experiences, not for the purpose of having certain knowledge about the world. Staver (1998) speaks of experience as our only interface with a world that is external to us. By "experience," he means all that we can perceive through our senses as well as the process of construction of knowledge from those perceptions, not the knowledge itself. Personal (or radical) constructivism has implications for conceptual change teaching, a topic to be explored later in this chapter.

Social Construction of Knowledge. One representative of social constructivism is Gergen (1985, 1995). Along with others, such as Driver, Leach, Milar, and Scott (1996) and Shotter (1995), Gergen emphasizes the central role of social interdependence and language in the development of knowledge. In fact, he represents the use of language in a society as a game with rules that are established locally by the participants. For social constructivists, making meaning of experiences (learning) occurs in the context of social interactions, primarily through the use of language. Through those interactions, the community negotiates meaning about knowledge as it is shared through language.

Personal and Social Constructivism: Room for Both. Because theories provide frameworks for thinking about concepts, multiple perspectives on a complex topic such as learning are not necessarily mutually exclusive. In fact, they may illuminate different aspects of a concept that is too complicated to be represented by only one view. Consider the origin of the wave-particle theory of light in physics; neither theory alone could account for the observed properties of light, but together they offered a more comprehensive explanation for a complex physical entity. Constructivism is a complex idea, not easily explained by a narrowly focused perspective. In reality, the personal and social constructivist positions often complement each other by emphasizing different aspects of learning. According to Hardy and Taylor (1997), a practical position for teachers is to consider that radical constructivism and social constructivism are complementary to each other.

Staver (1998) indicates that personal (radical) constructivism and social constructivism choose different problem to address, but they have much in common. He identifies four areas of shared belief (pp. 504–505):

1. Members of a community and the community itself construct knowledge from within; agreement between an individual's knowledge and the community's knowledge depends on the correspondence between the individual's knowledge and what the community agrees on as knowledge.
2. Social interactions (through language) in a variety of settings are essential to the construction of knowledge by both individuals and the community or society in which the individuals interact.
3. Cognition (learning) and the language used to express that learning serve a purpose; they are focused on what works (just as biological adaptations are based on what works for organisms in a particular environment).
4. The purpose of learning and language is to bring coherency to the experiences of the individual and to the knowledge base of the community of learners.

In summary, according to Staver (1998), "in radical constructivism, the focus is cognition and the individual; in social constructivism, the focus is language and the group" (p. 505).

More About the Role of Language

Because science education is usually conducted in a classroom setting, the role of language in learning is of particular importance. Even von Glasersfeld, noted for his radical constructivism, acknowledges a critical role for language in the development of complex concepts. In fact, there might be multiple roles of language, depending on the focus of science learning in the classroom. For example, school science often includes these two dimensions (among others perhaps): (1) involvement of students working in the role of scientists to learn about certain phenomena through their own investigations and (2) enculturation of students into the world of knowledge that professional scientists have developed. In the first case, emphasis is on making meaning out of data that students collect. The process is probably more important than the product, as students engage in arguments about the meaning of their experience. In this way, they are developing the skills to work scientifically—that is, to use evidence to support their thinking and to challenge each other in the process of generating new ideas. In the second case, the focus is on understanding the world as scientists have come to understand it—that is, to incorporate ideas about the world that are accepted by a majority of the scientific community (and that may be in conflict with students' everyday practical understandings). In this area of learning and teaching, it is impossible for students to reconstruct the complex processes by which scientists developed commonly accepted explanations about the natural world. They cannot "discover" atomic theory. They can, however, through the intervention of a knowledgeable person (the teacher or others), begin to fit these scientific ideas into their own frameworks of understanding. The effective use of language in this process is essential. This line of thinking will be continued in the context of teaching practice later in this chapter.

Constructivism as a Referent for Thinking About Teaching and Learning

After all is said and done, it is important to keep in mind that constructivism is no more a certainty than is any scientific theory. It is one way to look at learning, and its ultimate value is its usefulness in supporting meaningful learning. Some adherents of constructivism might seem to lift their model above all others, and particularly to tout its superiority to the outmoded and insufficient "transmission" model, by which teachers impart knowledge directly to students, primarily through talking and telling. In reality, constructivism is just one way in which we might look at learning. It is not the ultimate "truth," and it is useful only in specific contexts. Bauersfeld (1988) communicates a perspective that will resonate with wise teachers everywhere: "In the end, it is the life in . . . classrooms which processes and provides the evaluation of theories in . . . education" (p. 42). What constructivism does for practitioners is to provide a basis for reflection about student learning and practices that best support student learning. If it does nothing more than challenge the age-old practice of "teaching as we were taught," it will serve a noble purpose.

Summarizing the Nature of Constructivism

Table 5.1 presents summarizing statements made in the discussion of constructivism as a theory of learning.

Implications for Practice: What Does It All Mean?

Perhaps the reason constructivism has spilled over from the pages of research articles into publications that teachers actually read and find useful is that it does connect to sound teaching practices that have proved themselves effective with or without an explicit theoretical foundation. Academicians focus on theories; teachers focus on what works. Reflective teachers, however, are in the best place to test theoretical foundations for learning; their classrooms are the ultimate laboratories. In the case of constructivism, many aspects of the theory are supported by effective practices of resourceful and thoughtful teachers. This section focuses on the connections between the theory and the practices that logically follow.

Theory and Practice: Connecting for Success

At a university in the southeastern United States, a physicist and his research assistants use principles of mechanics to improve the efficiency of Olympic athletes. Using computer models, they simulate the forces and motion exerted by the human body in certain athletic endeavors, such as javelin throwing, shot put, or long jump. By altering certain aspects of the model, they increase the skill of the virtual athlete. When athletes come to their facility, they focus their training on one aspect of change that predicts improvement in their sport. It might be positioning of the elbow relative to

---

Table 5.1 Summarizing statements regarding constructivism

What Is Constructivism? Understanding the Game

Theories of Learning	The strength of the theory rests on the depth and reliability of the supporting evidence as judged by the scientific community.
Constructivism as a theory	To identify constructivism as a learning theory is to recognize two things: (1) It is an attempt to explain learning, and (2) it is based on evidence.
	If you understand constructivism as a theory, you can build an understanding of what that means for classrooms and teaching.
Constructivism versus behaviorism	Behaviorism works quite well if the goal of the experience is to prepare students to replicate a behavior identified by the teacher. If the goal, however, is to enable students to develop deep understandings of concepts, to connect related concepts, and to apply their knowledge to new situations, then the behaviorist model is ineffective.
	Although there are probably remnants of curriculum materials and other documents in use that reflect a behaviorist approach to learning, it is safe to say that constructivism is a much more influential force today.
Points of agreement	Although there are more than a dozen different brands of constructivism, there are two principles likely found in every one: Students construct their own understandings, and the new understandings that students construct rest on the foundations of knowledge and understandings that already exist.

Nature of Science and Science Education

The nature of reality: What is truth?	At one end of the continuum, scientists maintain that there are certain "truths" about the universe and that we can learn what they are. At the far end of the spectrum are those who are skeptical that there are objective "truths" out there, or, more moderately, if there are, all that we can know of them is what we experience—and that experience necessarily involves subjectivity. Some reject the notion that this should be a consideration at all in describing learning theory.

---

the shoulder in the javelin throw or angle of the head relative to the backbone in the shot put. Whatever the case, the human athlete is the ultimate test for the theoretical model. In many cases, the slight alterations result in increments of change in speed, distance, or force. In some cases, the theoretical model does not translate to improvement in the human athlete, but videotapes of the human athletes at work provide foundations for further thinking about the theoretical models. The point is this: Theoretical models about learning (such as constructivism) provide educators with a basis for examining their practice; in turn, the success of practitioners enables theorists to refine their models. If theory is separated from practice, there is no test bed in which its validity can be determined.

Table 5.1 Continued	

Nature of Science and Science Education (continued)

Connections with science education	There is conflicting evidence for a direct connection between teachers' views of scientific reality and their ideas about good science teaching.
The varieties of constructivism	Although there are dozens of brands of constructivism, two important categories are personal and social constructivism.
Personal construction of knowledge	Building on Piaget's ideas of accommodation and assimilation, von Glasersfeld, who labels his views as radical constructivism, emphasizes that individuals do not passively receive knowledge; rather, they actively construct knowledge within their own minds.
Social construction of knowledge	For social constructivists, making meaning of experiences (learning) occurs in the context of social interactions, primarily through the use of language. Through those interactions, the community negotiates meaning about knowledge.
Personal and social: room for both	Personal and social constructivist positions often complement each other by emphasizing different aspects of learning.
More about the role of language	Students can, through the intervention of a knowledgeable person (the teacher or others), begin to fit scientific ideas into their own frameworks of understanding. The effective use of language in this process is essential.
Constructivism as a referent for thinking about teaching	It is important to keep in mind that constructivism is no more a certainty than any scientific theory. It is one way to look at learning and its ultimate value is its usefulness in supporting meaningful learning.

Implications of Science Education Philosophy

From a philosophical perspective, there is a struggle in science education based on one's view of the extent to which students can construct their own scientific knowledge. According to Cobb (1994), "pedagogies derived from constructivist theory frequently involve a collection of questionable claims that sanctify the student at the expense of mathematical and scientific ways of knowing" (p. 4). When that view is taken to the extreme, the teacher's role is primarily as facilitator of student investigations, not necessarily including a responsibility to proactively support students' development of scientific ideas (ideas that are consistent with the views of the scientific community). Discovery learning is an example of such a pedagogy. Students in a pure *discovery learning* environment have primary responsibility for determining the focus of their learning, with only minimal guidance by the teacher. In such an atmosphere, there is no right or wrong; the science content is whatever students discover, regardless of how it relates to accepted scientific findings. Most science educators today agree that science makes legitimate claims about knowledge, although it certainly maintains a perspective that all knowledge generated by scientists is tentative, always subject to modification with new evidence. Moderate voices concede that there are important ideas about objects and events in the universe, accepted by the scientific community, that constitute appropriate content for science instruction. Unfortunately, teachers might feel guilty if they go beyond facilitating student problem solving and reflection. Although there is a place for open-ended investigations by students, teachers should not feel that they are politically incorrect if they build learning experiences for students that ultimately lead to conceptual understandings about accepted scientific knowledge. Most would see that a part of their job is the enculturation of science students into the community of science, not only in the processes of scientific inquiry, but also in the body of knowledge that has been generated by science. They recognize that students often come to them with conceptions of science that differ from those of professional scientists. Those alternative conceptions present difficult challenges for science teachers.

Alternative Conceptions in Science

If we agree that school science must include attention to scientists' ideas about natural objects and events, then teachers must address the conflicts that often exist between ideas that students have constructed through their experiences and ideas that scientists have constructed through disciplined study subject to the critical scrutiny of the scientific community. In regard to both personal and social construction of knowledge, the problem of alternative conceptions exists in every classroom situation. The problem of alternative conceptions has received a great deal of attention from the educational research community, resulting in a large body of research. Wandersee, Mintzes and Novak (1994) summarize much of that research into eight claims, each of which has implications for teaching:

1. Learners come to formal science instruction with a diverse set of alternative conceptions concerning natural objects and events.
2. The alternative conceptions that learners bring to formal science instruction cut across age, ability, gender, and cultural boundaries.
3. Alternative conceptions are tenacious and resistant to extinction by conventional teaching strategies.
4. Alternative conceptions often parallel explanations of natural phenomena offered by previous generations of scientists and philosophers.
5. Alternative conceptions have their origins in a diverse set of personal experiences, including direct observation and perception, peer culture, and language, as well as in teachers' explanations and instructional materials.
6. Teachers often subscribe to the same alternative conceptions as their students do.
7. Learners' prior knowledge interacts with knowledge presented in formal instruction, resulting in a diverse set of unintended learning outcomes.
8. Instructional approaches that facilitate conceptual change can be effective classroom tools. (pp. 181–191)

Learners' Alternative Conceptions. If we subscribe to the notion that our window to the world is our experiences, then the view of that world held by students is developed through the experiences they have had through the years. The kinds of experience students have are practical ones, not the controlled, carefully constructed experiences scientists use to learn about the world. For that reason, students come to logical conclusions about reality from observations that have not been subjected to scientific examination. Because they do not have all the data that scientists have, they come to conclusions that are based on insufficient information, and those conclusions often do not coincide with the conclusions reached by scientists.

Many researchers have focused on alternative conceptions in specific domains of scientific knowledge. As a result, teachers can access information about conceptions that students are likely to have in their particular science discipline. A majority of the alternative conceptions studied have fallen in the physical sciences. See Table 5.2 for representative areas.

Table 5.2 Representative areas of alternative conceptions in science

Physics

Forces and Motion
- If no force is being applied, either objects are at rest, or, if moving, they are slowing down.
- An object moves in the direction of the force applied to it.

Electricity
- Electricity leaves a battery and travels through one wire to a bulb, which is an electricity sink.
- Electricity leaves a battery from both ends and travels toward a bulb, where it is used up.

Heat and temperature
- Heat makes things rise.
- Heat and cold are materials substances that can be transferred from one thing to another.

Light/optics
- Light brightens objects so that they can be seen.
- Eyes play an active role in reaching out to intercept images.

Nature/states of matter
- Gas molecules are not in constant motion.
- Heating and cooling play no role in particle motion.

Earth/space science
- The orbit of the earth is highly elliptical (related to change of seasons).
- The earth is flat (second graders).

Biology

Life
- Living things show activity or usefulness.
- Living things show movement of any kind.

Animals and plants
- Animals are alive, have legs, move, have hair or fur, live outside or in the woods.
- Plants are not alive.
- Plants must eat (get food from the soil).

Human body
- The heart is shaped like a valentine.
- The heart cleans, filters, or makes blood.
- Tubes (other than blood vessels) carry air to the heart and other organs.

Continuity
- Some traits come from the mother and others from the father.
- Traits can change over time in response to the environment.

Chemistry
- Atoms vary in shape.
- Phosphorus atoms are yellow; water molecules are made of small drops (and other transferences of macroproperties to molecular level).

Source: Wandersee, Mintzes, and Novak, 1994.

If science educators have information about common alternative conceptions, they can plan instruction with that in mind. For example, a chemistry teacher who knows that students often have difficulty conceptualizing atomic structure and kinetic-molecular theory might decide to spend more time at the beginning of the course involving students in observing from a macroscopic perspective the behavior of different kinds of substances as they interact before consideration of microscopic (molecular level) interactions.

An interesting aspect of alternative conceptions is the idea that they are remarkably consistent across the boundaries of age, ability level, gender, and culture. A teacher might be surprised that a senior physics student in an honors class has views about certain phenomena that are as much at odds with accepted scientific thought as the views held by a younger student or a student operating at a lower level academically. The popular video *A Private Universe* (Harvard-Smithsonian Center for Astrophysics, 1997), surprised the science education world with the alternative conceptions of new Harvard graduates about causes of the seasons. The practical implication for teaching is this: Expect alternative conceptions, even among older students and academically gifted students. Identify what research says about specific alternative conceptions that are common in each scientific discipline, and plan teaching strategies that address those ideas proactively.

Despite intensive efforts by teachers to bring students' alternative conceptions into line with prevailing scientific thinking, many of those long-held conceptions are extremely resistant to change. The major difficulties seem to be in the physical sciences, especially in relation to counterintuitive phenomena. For example, students have a lifetime of experiences with forces and motion, but the kinds of experiences they commonly have lead them to notions that are not aligned with the notions of scientists who study forces and motion more systematically. It is important to note that some alternative conceptions are not so difficult to change. There is real practical value for teachers to distinguish between the two. For ideas that are relatively easy to alter, a less intensive approach might work quite well. For more resistant ideas, teachers might choose strategies specifically appropriate for promoting conceptual change. In the real world of classrooms, teachers recognize that time and energy are finite resources. For practical reasons, then, they are wise to budget more time and energy to address particularly stubborn alternative conceptions and to budget less time and energy to conceptions that can be changed by well-planned but less intensive strategies.

Another important consideration in dealing with alternative conceptions is the origin of the conceptions. It is impossible to know for certain where students' ideas originate, but researchers have proposed a few ideas. For example, students' observations from early childhood and their interactions with objects certainly influence their thinking. Those ideas serve them well in getting along in their world. They learn enough about gravity to know not to step off the top rung of a ladder, but they do not derive from those informal experiences the relationship of gravity to mass and distance.

Students also learn from their peer culture. The understandings that develop in their everyday interactions might share terminology with formal science, but they mean something else in their everyday world. The way they use the term "energy," for example, among their peers might include some elements that are consistent with a physicist's ideas about energy, but they might include other elements as well, and they certainly lack many of the scientific ideas about energy. The meaning that terms such as "energy" have for students in their everyday lives influences the meanings they construct in a formal science education setting and often obscure those formal meanings. Another example is one that was mentioned earlier in this chapter: People's ideas about the term "theory" in their daily lives (e.g., "just a theory") affect their ideas about scientific theories in such a way as to complicate the process of understanding the nature and role of theories in science.

Not only do students construct alternative conceptions under the influence of their informal experiences outside of school, they also construct them from the influences of their textbooks and their teachers. In regard to textbooks, a great deal of research has focused on textbook explanations that are at odds with the prevailing scientific views and on diagrams and pictures in textbooks that mislead students. Those misleading ideas occur in discipline-specific concepts and also in regard to the nature of science itself. For example, some biology textbooks have indicated that plants photosynthesize and animals respire (as though plants do not carry on respiration). Some textbooks have identified a scientific law as a theory that has been proved. Because textbooks often serve as the major authority on scientific knowledge for teachers and students, the detrimental effect on developing sound scientific ideas is enormous.

Teachers' Alternative Conceptions. Most teachers recognize that they themselves have developed many alternative conceptions during their informal and formal education; they have been subject to the same influences that affect their students' learning. Teachers often acknowledge that they leave their undergraduate programs with a relatively superficial understanding of science, especially in science disciplines that they might have encountered in only one or two courses. The reality is that their own science instructors were largely unaware of the enormously powerful influence of alternative conceptions and proceeded with traditional teaching strategies that addressed complex concepts with certain assumptions:

- Telling (or reading about it) suffices for teaching.
- If students listen, they will learn.
- If students do well on tests, then they must be proficient.

When they were students, most science teachers probably were conscientious about their work. More than likely, they read their textbooks, listened to their instructors, and did well on tests. Despite all of that, they might not have had sufficient opportunity to discuss in depth how their ideas are supported by evidence or how they compare to ideas held by scientists. It is quite unlikely that these teachers had a chance to confront their own alternative conceptions in the light of prevailing scientific thought in such a way as to rebuild their understandings. The implications for teacher education programs and for professional development of teachers are obvious.

A particularly troublesome outcome occurs when the alternative conceptions that students bring with them to their science classes interact with classroom instruction in such a way as to reinforce the students' preexisting ideas. Sometimes students' ideas are so entrenched that they use information presented by their teachers to support their alternative conceptions, even though the intent of the instruction is different. Just as scientists can use the same body of evidence to support differing conclusions, students can take a classroom experience and use it to support their unscientific concepts, and that process can go largely undetected unless the student has opportunities to engage in scientific discourse with peers and with the teacher. In fact, the student might perform very well on a traditional test while retaining concepts that are profoundly at odds with scientifically accepted views.

Conceptual Change Teaching

The problem of alternative conceptions has elicited a response in the form of what is often called conceptual change teaching. This approach is really an eclectic collection of strategies that recognize that "students come to new learning situations with a fund of prior knowledge and the teacher's primary role is that of meaning negotiator or change agent" (Wandersee et al., 1994, p. 191). Although there is a wide range of teaching strategies that addresses conceptual change, one approach is to provide students with experiences that provoke some degree of conflict in their thinking: that is, what they experience does not fit what they previously thought. In the context of the experience, students are then encouraged to develop new ideas that do fit the experience. In many cases, this process takes the form in classrooms of practical activities in which students engage, followed by group discussions about the experience.

Determining students' preexisting ideas is difficult work, and a number of strategies have been used, including interviews, concepts maps, open-ended and multiple-choice response items, classroom discussions, and journal writing (Wandersee et al., 1994). Considering that some ideas are more resistant to change than others, successful strategies for changing student conceptions involve careful planning, and the ultimate test is how well they work in classroom settings. Examples of conceptual change teaching often include a restructuring component in which students' ideas are carefully communicated and explicated, followed by confrontational strategies that attempt to replace a concept with another. For the process to work, it seems that the students must recognize that their prior conception poses problems for them in terms of effectively explaining what they observe. In addition, the concept proposed by the teacher must be understandable to the students and must be plausible to them.

In addition to confrontation strategies, another strategy that has met with some success is the use of analogies. Although analogies have been used by good teachers through the ages, connecting analogies explicitly to identified alternative conceptions has been documented only recently. As with other conceptual change teaching strategies, the use of analogies has met with only partial success. Some concepts are more susceptible to change through the use of analogies than other concepts are.

According to Wandersee, Mintzes, and Novak (1994), an area of research that holds promise for student learning is one that focuses on a generic strategy that enables students to examine their own learning (an exercise in metacognition) and exert some control in that endeavor. One example (Baird, 1986) makes use of student checklists, notebooks, and workbooks, all of which asked students to reflect on a variety of questions that focus on what students perceive they know about a topic, how they feel about the topic, what the most important facets of the topic are, what is required to understand fully, how the new knowledge compares with what they previously thought, how well they understand the topic, and how they will make use of the new knowledge.

Considering Personal and Social Perspectives

As was mentioned earlier in the discussion on the nature of constructivism, ideas about personal construction of knowledge and social construction of knowledge are not mutually exclusive. In fact, in the kind of conceptual change teaching described above, both elements are recognized. As expressed by Driver, Asoko, Leach, Mortimer, and Scott (1994), "classrooms are places where individuals are actively engaged with others in attempting to understand and interpret phenomena for themselves, and where social interaction in groups is seen to provide the stimulus of differing perspectives on which individuals can reflect" (p. 7). The role of the teacher in this kind of setting is to provide environments in which students have opportunities to engage in appropriate experiences, to reflect on their thinking, and to express their ideas. Teachers can stretch students' thinking by guiding the discussions. Duckworth (1987) shows how this can be accomplished:

> What do you mean? How did you do that? Why do you say that? How does that fit in with what she just said? Could you give me an example? How did you figure that? In every case these questions are primarily a way for the interlocutor to try to understand what the other is understanding. Yet in every case, also, they engage the other's thoughts and take them a step further (pp. 96–97).

In this kind of atmosphere, students argue their ideas, but how do they connect their ideas to those of the scientific community? How do they enter into a larger discourse about science than the one occurring in their classroom? How do they submit their views for confirmation or correction? Teachers can use students' discourse as a springboard to consider the body of knowledge generated by scientists. For example, at the end of the discussion described by Duckworth above, the teacher could very easily pose an additional question: "What do scientists say about this?" At this point, students consult the views of experts through readings, through conversations with a knowledgeable teacher, or through other avenues. They then compare their thinking with that of the experts. If their conclusions are consistent with those of the scientific community, that is a real achievement. If they are not, the students' task is to reconcile the inconsistencies.

An Example

For example, consider a class of fourth graders exploring the properties of light. They used flashlights and mirrors to investigate how light travels. Once they finished their activities and discussed their findings, they came to a shared conclusion that light can bend around corners. Their teacher then had them read a passage from their textbook that presented a different idea: Light can travel only in a straight line. The students reexamined their evidence and discussed new possibilities. They decided that they had based their conclusion primarily on the fact that there was light on the wall behind the mirror and they assumed that the light came from their flashlight, struck the mirror, bent around the edges, and struck the wall. They tried their experiment again, using different-sized mirrors, different sized-flashlight beams, and different distances between the flashlight and the mirror. After discussing their new findings, they concluded that the only time light appeared on the wall behind the mirror was when they used a flashlight with a relatively large beam and located it at a relatively large distance from the mirror. They drew pictures to show what might have happened in different versions of the experiment. At the end of the discussion, they were able to reconcile their ideas with the prevailing scientific view.

There are several important considerations here for the practice of science teaching:

- Students can, at some level, experience the kind of discourse that occurs in the scientific community, using evidence as a basis for arguing their positions; this is in itself a valuable aspect of science content.
- Although each student constructs certain personal ideas about the event, those ideas are powerfully influenced by the experience of manipulating materials and observing the results.
- Merely manipulating the materials (doing hands-on activities) does not necessarily lead a student to an understanding of a scientific concept; the student must make meaning from the experience through discussions with peers (facilitated by the teacher). Furthermore, the student must look at his or her ideas in comparison to accepted science and reconcile differences.
- In a classroom setting, personal learning cannot be separated from social processes if those classrooms are designed to be communities of learners.

Implicit in the elements described above is the role of language as the vehicle by which meaning is negotiated. Teachers who are skilled at facilitating this kind of discourse in their classrooms use language as a very powerful tool to accomplish important educational objectives. In the first place, the rich discussion between and among students and teachers provide a window into the complex frameworks of understandings that students bring with them to the science classroom. Although a pretest might provide some evidence of prior understandings, it necessarily must focus on a limited number of aspects of the concepts. Conversations, especially those facilitated by masterful teachers, reveal at a much deeper level what students understand and, perhaps more importantly, what they understand differently from conventional science. In addition to enabling the teacher to understand more fully students' alternative conceptions, classroom discourse uses language to develop both individual and community understandings of scientific concepts.

Playing the Game

Returning to our ongoing game metaphors, consider the difference between team sports and individual sports. The high school football coach devises plays that involve each position in a certain way. Each player has an assignment, but that assignment connects integrally with everybody else's assignment. Only when an individual's actions relate to the intent of group (the team) does the expected outcome occur. Each player must be constantly aware of the actions of every other player on his or her team, some of which can be anticipated. To complicate matters, the player must also read the actions of the opposing team and adjust his or her actions accordingly. Although language is essential in developing an understanding of the play in the locker room and on the practice field, communication on the field involves spoken language and also the body language that provides clues that affect decisions by individual players. We have all heard sports announcers comment on certain players' ability to read the defense or sense where the ball is. Although the type of communication on a ball field is different from that in a classroom, it is essential for individuals to coordinate their play for the good of the team. The point is that even in a team sport, each individual has responsibilities and makes contributions to the success of the team.

For individual sports, such as tennis, the player must develop skills through intensive practice. Although personal commitment, natural abilities, and individual effort contribute to the success of the player, it is doubtful that any tennis player would deny the importance of interactions with a coach and with other players in the development of her expertise. We often hear players talk about the role of opponents in elevating their level of play. We are also likely to recall players who have publicly expressed the importance of their coaches who diagnose problems and prescribe solutions in the process of building expertise.

Just as team sports require individual responsibility and individual sports require interactions with peers, the process of learning in a science classroom incorporates both elements. Personal and social learning are essential components.

Constructivism as an Implicit Element in Reform Documents

Recent publications by the American Association for the Advancement of Science (1993) and the National Research Council (1996) have been at the forefront of the reform movement in science education. By providing standards, benchmarks, and other recommendations for teaching practice, they influence science education at all levels. Although they do not necessarily use the term "constructivism," many of their recommendations for teaching and assessment are consistent with constructivist theory.

For example, the National Science Education Standards (National Research Council, 1996) summarizes many of its recommendations in sections at the end of each chapter that feature changing emphases. Table 5.3 lists selected phrases related to

---

Table 5.3 Changing emphases in the *National Science Education Standards*

Less Emphasis on	More Emphasis on
Focusing on student acquisition of information	Focusing on student understanding and use of scientific knowledge, ideas, and inquiry processes
Presenting scientific knowledge through lecture, text, and demonstration	Guiding students in active and extended scientific inquiry
Asking for recitation of acquired knowledge	Providing opportunities for scientific discussion and debate among students
Maintaining responsibility and authority	Sharing responsibility for learning with students

Source: National Research Council, 1996, adapted from pp. 52 and 100.

teaching and assessment that seem to be strongly connected to what has been described in this chapter on constructivism and its implications. In general, these emphases in teaching and assessment paint a picture of classrooms that are communities of learners with very active involvement of students in developing scientific understandings through engagement with materials and with each other.

Table 5.4 summarizes the major points made previously in regard to implications of constructivist theory for practice.

Table 5.4 Summarizing statements regarding implications for practice: What does it all mean?

Implications of science education philosophy	Although there is a place for open-ended investigations by students, teachers should not feel that they are politically incorrect if they build learning experiences for students that ultimately lead to conceptual understandings about accepted scientific knowledge.
Alternative conceptions in science	Learners come to formal science instruction with a diverse set of alternative conceptions concerning natural objects and events.
	The alternative conceptions that learners bring to formal science instruction cut across age, ability, gender, and cultural boundaries.
	Alternative conceptions are tenacious and resistant to extinction by conventional teaching strategies.
Learners' alternative conceptions	The practical implication for teaching is this: Expect alternative conceptions, even among older students and academically gifted students. Identify what research says about specific alternative conceptions that are common in each scientific discipline and plan teaching strategies that address those ideas proactively.
Teachers' alternative conceptions	Most teachers recognize that they themselves have developed many alternative conceptions during their informal and formal education; they have been subject to the same influences that affect their students' learning.
Conceptual change teaching	Conceptual change teaching is really an eclectic collection of strategies that recognize that students come to new learning situations with a fund of prior knowledge and the teacher's primary role is that of meaning negotiator or change agent.
Considering personal and social perspectives	Classrooms are places where individuals are actively engaged with others in attempting to understand and interpret phenomena for themselves, and where social interaction in groups is seen to provide the stimulus of differing perspectives on which individuals can reflect.
Constructivism as an implicit element in reform documents	Although reform documents do not necessarily use the term constructivism, many of their recommendations for teaching and assessment are consistent with constructivist theory.

CONCLUSION: The Best Fit

Perhaps the most important aspect of constructivism that is communicated in this chapter is that implied by the title "No Room on the Bench." Despite our continuing efforts to understand the complexities of learning and the implications for teaching, researchers and practitioners agree that meaningful learning occurs best when students are active participants, not passive recipients. Just as players learn the game through involvement of their minds and bodies on the field of play, so do students become enculturated into the world of science through investment in the process. Like athletes, they might suffer some aches and pains as they confront the standards of scientific knowledge with their own preconceptions, but the intensity of the struggle is matched by the value of new understandings. By playing the game, they understand their world better, and they develop skills that will serve them in all aspects of their lives.

The Game in Action

Team Players Construct Meaningful Learning

Carolyn, Fran, and Marge were three high school teachers who had the luxury of time to plan instruction for a new course in earth/ environmental science that had recently been inserted into the state requirements for high school graduation. Although they were from different school systems, they met at a university summer institute and had stayed in touch through the years, often attending the same professional development courses when possible. None of the three teachers had a strong content background in the earth sciences; their college preparation and teaching experience had been primarily in the life sciences. There were very few teachers in the state who were prepared in the earth sciences, and because Carolyn, Fran, and Marge had a strong background in science (although not earth science) and successful teaching experience, their principals reassigned them to teach the new course when it was instituted in their schools. When the opportunity to participate in a statewide project focusing on the new course became available, they decided to apply. All three were accepted into the program and participated fully in the summer courses and the school year follow-up meetings.

The project focused on three aspects of earth/environmental science: content, teaching, and leadership. Because of their expertise and interest, Carolyn, Fran, and Marge became leaders within the group, working with the university instructors in planning and execution of program activities. At the end of the second year of the three-year project, the focus of the professional development was on preparing teaching materials for use in classrooms. Although all forty-five teachers were involved in the process, Carolyn, Fran, and Marge worked with the university instructors to develop standards for the materials as well as lessons that would exemplify the standards.

Considerations for Curriculum

Unlike the circumstances in which most teachers find themselves, the project provided time for the development team to carefully consider issues of learning and teaching, to reflect on their implications, and to discuss them with each other before actually constructing lessons. The team consisted of Carolyn, Fran, Marge, and Kate (the university instructor). The materials they produced would be used by many other teachers, and for many, the quality of the lessons would have a great influence on the quality of teaching. Because the teachers were aware of not only the philosophical considerations, but also the practical matters that teachers face in real classroom with real children, they began the process with a list of guidelines to provide direction for their work. Table 5.5 below shows the list with which they started. Many other considerations entered into the mix once they began.

Where to Begin

After deciding on general guidelines, the team began to try to make sense out of the topics that were included in the state's mandated

Table 5.5 Guidelines for developing lessons

Think about Learning	Think about Implementation
Focus on important science concepts and identify the ideas students commonly have that are in opposition to conventional science.	Establish guidelines for group work, rules for orderly discussion, etc.
Provide ample opportunity for students to discuss and debate their ideas prior to instruction.	Plan student assignments that use easily accessible and cheap materials.
Provide a variety of learning experiences, including highly structured ones as well as more open-ended ones.	Plan a system for orderly distribution of materials.
Distinguish between activities designed to teach the methods of science and those designed to teach other science content.	Decide ahead of time what kinds of assessments will be done for the purpose of grading and what kinds will be used for determining students' understandings.
Sequence learning activities to maximize connections.	Devise suggestions for assessments that do not take unreasonable amounts of time (for teacher or students).
Identify connections among topics.	Incorporate strategies that give students more responsibility for their own learning.
Connect school science to students' everyday experiences.	Incorporate state-mandated curriculum objectives.
Provide common experiences as a basis for discussion.	Provide a list of sources for teachers that can give content background.

course of study. The content was organized in a linear fashion with no explicit connections between and among topics. The major competency goals were as follows:

- Build an understanding of lithospheric materials, processes, changes, and uses with concerns for good stewardship.
- Develop an understanding of tectonic processes and their human impacts.
- Build an understanding of the origin and evolution of the earth system.
- Build an understanding of the hydrosphere and its interactions and influences on the lithosphere, the atmosphere, and environmental quality.
- Build an understanding of the dynamics and composition of the atmosphere and its local and global processes influencing climate and air quality.
- Acquire an understanding of the earth in the solar system and its position in the universe.
- Build an understanding of alternative choices facing human societies in their stewardship of the earth.

In addition to the content identified in the competency goals, the team also had to consider incorporation of strands that were foundational to the entire K–12 curriculum: (1) the nature of

science, (2) science as inquiry, (3) science and technology, and (4) science in personal and social perspectives.

What an overwhelming job! Was one sequence better than another? Did it make a difference? A long discussion ensued.

Carolyn: Well, we have to start somewhere. Let's forget the strands for now and work them in later. Just looking at the major goals, is there a logical way to sequence them?

Marge: It's hard to look at these things as separate from each other. You can't teach about lithospheric materials without talking about tectonics, and you can't talk about the hydrosphere without bringing in weather and climate.

Kate: And you certainly can't just stick on the stewardship thing at the end. It has to be included along the way with every topic.

Fran: The way I look at it, I can see starting with the universe and working down to the earth. Since this is earth science with a major focus on environmental science, I think it would be a mistake to spend half the year on the universe and solar system—but we have to include it.

Marge: One way of looking at it is to consider the universe and the solar system just as a setting for the earth; just as a way of placing the earth in space relative to other bodies. We just can't get bogged down with a lot of details about the universe or we will never get back to the earth.

Kate: I like that idea. I think it will work. Start with the universe, then to the solar system within the universe, and then to the earth within the solar system.

Fran: I think that might be the easy part. I cannot imagine a best way to sequence the rest of the stuff. It is all too interdependent.

Carolyn: Maybe we can capitalize on the interdependence—show an organizational scheme that helps us see the connections. That will certainly help teachers see the links and they can use the plan to help students see the links. For once, maybe we can get away from teaching discrete lessons and units.

Fran: Let me take what we're saying and make a design on the computer [see Figure 5.2]. What do you think?

Designing Lessons That Conform to Guidelines

After agreeing on a plan for the big picture, the team set out to design specific lessons related to the curriculum goals. The conversation focused on priorities for learning.

Fran: We know that teachers will adapt these lessons to meet their needs, but if we build in components that we know to be supportive of meaningful learning, maybe the curriculum can actually be a source of professional development for the teachers.

Kate: You're right. I know that good curriculum materials helped me become a better teacher. The format we establish could really make a difference.

Marge: Even though we want a lot of variety, maybe it would be good to start with a general format that we

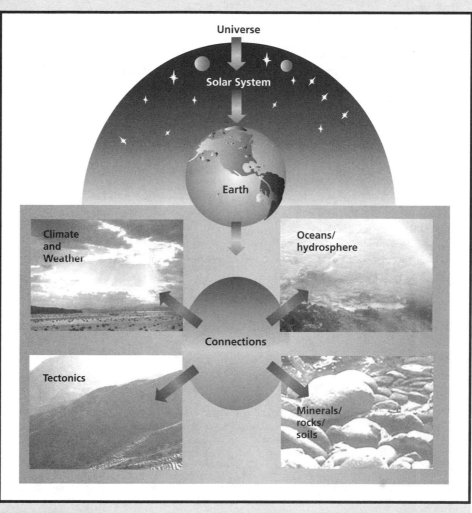

Figure 5.2 Possible perspective on organizing the entire year's course

can modify as needed—one that will support the ideas about learning that we know we want to emphasize.

After many attempts, the team decided on a general format that was, in essence, a type of learning cycle (see Figure 5.3). The three teachers had not had experience with learning cycle materials, but Kate pointed out that the model they developed had characteristics in common with learning cycle materials that had been used with success for many years.

The next step was to try out the format as a tool in developing specific lessons. The team decided to use hydrology as a starting point, since they had focused on ground water and rivers in their

UNIT TITLE

I. Teacher Background

Big ideas and connectiones among them (advance organizer)

Alternative conceptions commonly held by students regarding concepts in this unit

This is for teacher only—not for students at this point.

II. Student Inquiry Cycle (either in small groups or whole group)

   A. Question 1: (Pose question appropriate for the unit.)
      What do you know (prior knowledge)?
      What evidence do you have (for what you know)?
      If you don't know, what do you think?
      Where would you look or what would you do to find out?

   B. Guided Inquiry (May be lab, outdoor activity, library research, assigned reading, etc.)

   C. Making Sense (teacher helps students make sense of data they gathered—helps them develop scientific language to describe what they learned)
      * This is where the content is developed—**AFTER** students have already done initial exploration.

   D. Making Connections
      1. To previous concepts
      2. To next inquiry cycle

REPEAT

   A. Question 2

      What do you know (prior knowledge)?
      What evidence do you have (for what you know)?
      If you don't know, what do you think?
      Where would you look or what would you do to find out?

   B. Guided Inquiry

   C. Making Sense

   D. Making Connections

[Continue through all the major questions related to the topic.]

Figure 5.3 Lesson development format

previous summer's fieldwork. They spent a great deal of time discussing sequencing of ideas, how to make connections, common misconceptions students have, and learning experiences that a teacher could lead without expensive materials and equipment. They decided that they needed to talk with a scientist in the field before developing the content background, but they had enough expertise among them to flesh out the beginnings of a unit on hydrology (see Figure 5.4).

HYDROLOGY

Teacher Background

Big ideas and connections among them (advance organizer)

This is for teacher only—not for students at this point.

STUDENT INQUIRY CYCLE

Question 1: In what forms does water occur on earth?
What do you know (prior knowledge)?
What evidence do you have (for what you know)?
If you don't know, what do you think?
Where would you look or what would you do to find out?

Guided Inquiry (teacher demo)
Show three beakers:
No. 1 with ice
No. 2 with liquid water
No. 3 with liquid water set on hot plate (or over flame)

Discussion:
What differences do you observe in the three beakers?
What is happening?
Where in nature do we find water in these three states?

Making Sense (Teacher helps students make sense of data they gathered—helps them develop scientific language to describe what they learned.)
  * This is where the content is developed—**AFTER** students already have gathered data.

Making Connections
To previous concepts
To next segment of inquiry cycle

Question 2: Why does water occur in three states on earth but not on other planets?
What do you know (prior knowledge)?
What evidence do you have (for what you know)?
If you don't know, what do you think?
Where would you look or what would you do to find out?

Guided Inquiry (Student document research)
To students: From your notes, your textbook, library resources, or internet resources, find information needed to complete this sheet:

Names of Planets	Surface High Temperature	Surface Low Temperature	Atmospheric Composition

Making Sense
Concepts to develop:

Water is not found on all planets.
Some planets are too cold or hot for liquid to exist.
Earth is the only planet with three states of water (partly because of temperature range).
[Continue through learning cycles, using questions to focus study assignments.]

Figure 5.4 Beginning lessons on hydrology

Classroom Implementation

The team decided that they needed to try their lessons with their students before they proceeded too far with the development process. Marge was at a point in her instruction at which she could work in the hydrology unit before the next team meeting. She agreed to implement a series of lessons, set up video cameras to record the classroom, and bring the tapes back to the group for analysis.

Marge began her first class with a whole group discussion, using the questions in the lesson format. In response to the first question (forms of water on the earth), students agreed that water could be liquid, gas, or solid (ice). Their evidence consisted of their direct observations of the three forms and of the processes by which water changed forms. After having the students record their conclusions in their notebooks, Marge showed the class the three beakers: one with ice, one with liquid water, and one with liquid water on a hot plate. Here is an excerpt from the ensuing discussion:

> *Marge:* What do you think is happening in these beakers?
>
> *Melissa:* I can see that the ice is melting. There is some liquid water in the bottom of the beaker. The water on the hot plate is boiling.
>
> *Marge:* What do you predict would happen if we kept the boiling water on the hot plate for five more minutes?
>
> *Melissa:* It would begin to boil off.
>
> *Marge:* What do you mean by that?
>
> *Melissa:* The water would start to disappear.
>
> *Jeff:* It's not really disappearing. It's going up in the air.
>
> *Marge:* How do you know?
>
> *Jeff:* You can see the steam up over the beaker—just like you can see it when you're boiling water on the stove at home.
>
> *Heather:* I didn't think you could see steam. I thought it was a gas. I guess you can, though, because we know the water is turning into steam, and you can sure see the little cloud up there.
>
> *Marge:* Can anybody help Heather with her problem?
>
> (Long silence)

Heather's conflict provided Marge with a perfect opportunity to have students confront an idea that was obviously confusing. Although Heather voiced the issue, other students admitted their own conflict. With probing questions, Marge facilitated a discussion that resulted in these three conclusions that were agreed on by the class:

1. Steam is a gaseous form of water that occurs at high temperatures.
2. Not all gaseous water is steam; water vapor in the air may be cool, and it is not steam.
3. When you see "steam" above boiling water, it is really water droplets that have condensed back from the gaseous steam when the steam hits colder air. The cloud is made of liquid water, not gaseous water.

The lesson continued with a discussion of the occurrence of water in nature in its three states and the natural processes that determine those states. Marge segued to the next day's lesson with a question about the occurrence (or nonoccurrence) of water on other planets, connecting the lesson to a previous unit on the solar system. Students worked in small groups to investigate the question.

Evaluating the Results

When the team met again, Marge brought some of the videotaped lessons as well as student work products. Marge reported on her successes and failures, with suggestions for refinement:

- In general, using questions to focus the investigations was effective.
- Knowing ahead of time some of the alternative conceptions to anticipate was extremely helpful; for example, Marge found studies regarding students' ideas about groundwater that showed a variety of views inconsistent with scientific thinking.
- Students were hesitant to participate in discussions at first, but they became more comfortable after a few days.
- Students were uncomfortable with assessment formats that were unfamiliar to them, especially the high-achieving students, who were accustomed to memorizing information and successfully reporting it on tests.
- Finding appropriate sources of information outside the textbook was a problem. Marge anticipated that any lessons the team developed would need to include readings on topics that were not likely to be in a textbook. Schools with easy Internet access and well-stocked libraries would be at a real advantage.
- Students showed frustration when Marge refused to answer their questions and urged them to conduct their own research to find out.
- The lessons took more time than the team envisioned.

Despite the difficulties, the ultimate consideration was this: Did the students come to understand important science concepts and learn to work scientifically? The team agreed that they did. They established a plan for the next steps of the process: to make refinements to the lessons that had already developed and to expand the scope of their work. As their assignment proceeded through the next several months, the format underwent many refinements, but careful attention to learning ensured that these principles were always observed:

- The learning experiences challenged students to investigate important questions.
- Students were given opportunities to communicate their ideas before the instruction.
- Adequate time was provided each day to describe, explain, and present arguments in relation to investigations.
- Students were constantly challenged to provide evidence to support their ideas.
- Although students' ideas were always respected, in key content areas those ideas were scrutinized in relation to scientific views to reconcile inconsistencies.
- At every opportunity, connections were made to students' out-of-school experiences.

A Few Months Later

After a year, the development and implementation process continues. The team has learned that although their experiences had prepared them to use learning theory as a basis for developing curriculum, many teachers who attempted to use the lessons were very uncomfortable. Some gave up because they did not feel as though they had control of their classrooms. Others adapted the materials to fit their previous, more traditional mode of teaching, fearful that their students would not learn what they needed to know for the state tests if they wasted so much time on activities. A few took full advantage of the student investigations, but they did not see a need for the extended discussions following each inquiry activity.

Those teachers who are committed to the process, however, are beginning to produce students who think for themselves, who use evidence to support their ideas, who have confidence in their ability to learn science, and who will ultimately be "the proof of the pudding." Carolyn, Fran, and Marge have many colleagues who have now joined the team and who are transforming classrooms into dynamic learning communities.

Reflecting on the Game

1. Consider how your learning experiences reflect constructivist ideas. What kinds of experiences have you had that promoted meaningful learning?
2. In what ways does your teaching exhibit practices consistent with social constructivism? With personal constructivism?
3. How do you resolve the conflict between a pure "discovery learning" environment and one that promotes understanding of traditional science content (the knowledge base developed by scientists)?
4. In what practical ways can you use constructivist theory to address alternative conceptions held by students?

References

American Association for the Advancement of Science. (1993). *Benchmarks for science literacy.* New York: Oxford University Press.

Baird, J. (1986). Improving learning through enhanced metacognition: A classroom study. *European Journal of Science Education, 8,* 263–282.

Bauersfeld, H. (1988). Interaction, construction and knowledge: Alternative perspectives for mathematics education. In D. Grouws, T. Cooney, & D.

Jones (Eds.), *Perspectives on research on effective mathematics teaching.* Reston, VA: Lawrence Erlbaum and Associates.

Bransford, J. D., Brown, A. L., & Cocking, R. R. (Eds.). (1999). *How people learn.* Washington, DC: National Academy Press.

Cobb, P. (1994). Constructivism in mathematics and science education. *Educational Researcher 23,* 4.

Driver, R., Asoko, H., Leach, J., Mortimer, E., & Scott, P. (1994). Constructing scientific knowledge in the classroom. *Educational Researcher, 23*, 5–12.

Driver, R., Leach, J., Millar, R., & Scott, P. (1996). *Young people's images of science*. Buckingham: Open University Press.

Duckworth, E. (1987). *"The having of wonderful ideas" and other essays on teaching and learning.* New York: Teachers College Press.

Fensham, P. (1992). Science and technology. In P. Jackson (Ed.), *Handbook of research on curriculum* (pp. 798–829). New York: Macmillan.

Gandy, R. (1997). Constructivisms and objectivism: Disentangling metaphysics from pedagogy. *Science and Education, 6*, 43–53.

Geelan, D. (1997a). Prior knowledge, prior conceptions, prior constructs: What do constructivists really mean, and are they practicing what they preach? *Australian Science Teachers Journal, 43*, 26–29.

Geelan, D. (1997b). Epistemological anarchy and the many forms of constructivism. *Science & Education, 6*, 15–28.

Gergen, K. (1985). The social constructionist movement in modern psychology. *American Psychologist, 40*, 266–275.

Gergen, K. (1995). Social construction and the educational process. In L. Stefe & J. Gale (Eds.), *Constructivism in education* (pp. 17–39). Hillsdale, NJ: Erlbaum.

Hardy, M., & Taylor, P. (1997). Von Glasersfeld's radical constructivism: A critical review. *Science & Education, 6*, 135–150.

Harvard-Smithsonian Center for Astrophysics (Producer). (1997). *A private universe.* (Available from Annenberg/CPB Video Cassette Sales and Customer Service, P.O. Box 2345, S. Burlington, VT. 05407-2345 or www.learner.org.)

Matthews, M. (1997). Introductory comments on philosophy and constructivism in science education. *Science & Education, 6*, 5–14.

National Research Council. (1996). *National science education standards*. Washington, DC: National Academy Press.

Nola, R. (1997). Constructivism in science and science education: A philosophical critique. *Science & Education, 6*, 55–83.

Shotter, J. (1995). In dialogue: Social constructionism and radical constructivism. In L. Steffe & J. Gale (Eds.), *Constructivism in education* (pp. 41–56). Hillsdale, NJ: Erlbaum.

Staver, J. R. (1998). Constructivism: Sound theory for explicating the practice of science and science teaching. *Journal of Research in Science Teaching, 35*, 501–520.

von Glasersfeld, E. (1993). Questions and answers about radical constructivism. In K. Tobin (Ed.), *The practice of constructivism in science education* (pp. 23–28). Washington, DC: AAAS Press.

von Glasersfeld, E. (1995). *Radical constructivism: A way of knowing and learning*. Washington, DC: Falmer Press.

Wandersee, J. H., Mintzes, J. J., & Novak, J. D. (1994). Research on alternative conceptions in science. In D. Gabel (Ed.), *Handbook of research on science teaching and learning* (pp. 177–210). New York: Macmillan.

Yager, R. (1991). The constructivist learning model. *The Science Teacher, 67*, 44–45.

Additional Resources

Constructivism, Instructivism, and Related Sites: www.emtech.net/links/construc.htm

Constructing Knowledge in the Classroom: www.sedl.org/scimath/compass/v01n03/understand.html

Essays on Constructivism and Education: www.towson.edu/csme/mctp/Essays.html

Constructivism and the Five E's: www.miamisci.org/ph/lpintro5e.html

Constructivism Explained: http://carbon.cudenver.edu/~mryder/itc_data/constructivism.html

chapter

6

FAIR PLAY IN

SCIENCE EDUCATION:

Moving Beyond
Science for All

Rebecca Meyer Monhardt, Ph.D.
Department of Elementary
Education, Utah State University

ABOUT THE AUTHOR: Dr. Rebecca Monhardt is an associate professor in the Department of Elementary Education at Utah State University, teaching undergraduate and graduate classes in science education. Her research is related to diversity issues in science education, more specifically those related to Navajo students. Dr. Monhardt has worked with Navajo students, teachers and parents at Mexican Hat Elementary School since 1997, where over 250 of her undergraduates have enjoyed field experiences. She has also developed culturally responsive science materials as an extension of her work with diverse learners of science.

> No one gets an iron-clad guarantee of success. Certainly, factors like luck and timing are important. But the backbone of success is usually found in old-fashioned, basic concepts like a fair chance, hard work, determination, good planning and perseverance.

—Mia Hamm
U.S. Olympic Soccer team, 2000

CHAPTER WARM-UP

The rallying cry "science for all" rings hollow to many learners who possess a unique vantage or background for interpreting knowledge, a uniqueness born of culture and ethnicity not shared by the majority population. The goals of modern science education, including science literacy and science pursuit as a career, can be achieved only when the scientific enterprise is taught and learned as an inclusive and welcoming way of knowing about the natural world. The valued knowledge and skills that make up our discipline are only strengthened when diversity of views, definitions, and contributions gain presence in science class.

INTRODUCTION: An Inclusive Language

To play any game, it is necessary to understand the rules that govern the playing of that game. Without that understanding, it is virtually impossible for all players to have an equal shot at winning. Furthermore, most people will not even attempt to play a game if they do not understand the rules. Could this also be true for those wishing to play the science game—to participate in the field of science? Are the "rules" in science universally agreed on and understood by all those who wish to play? Are they fair for all who wish to play? Does everyone have an equal chance simply by being familiar with the rules? Research indicates that where science is concerned, the answer to these questions is no.

Despite the emphasis on "science for all students" in the National Science Education Standards (National Research Council, 1996), minority achievement and participation in science remain low. In this chapter, I look at equity and fairness of opportunity in science education and explain why even knowing the rules of the game is not always enough. As an illustration of the latter principle, I present here the outline of a game that is probably not a familiar one to most science educators: the Navajo Shoe Game.

Various explanations of the game exist. I have chosen the one described by Vernon Mayes and Barbara Lacy (1989):

> Two teams are chosen, one black, one gray. One person acts as an official. Pits are dug on the north and south sides of the hogan or playing field. Four [shoes] are placed in each pit. A disc (about the size of a quarter blackened on one side, made from the base of an ear of corn) is dropped from waist height by the official. The team of the person who blackens the disc is automatically the "blacks". The team that wins the disc drop is first to hide the turquoise. Holding a blanket in front of them, they hide the turquoise in the toe of one of the [shoes]. The other side must guess where the stone is. As the game is played, 102 songs associated with the game are sung. Score is kept with 102-yucca leaf counters (about 6 inches long). Points are awarded by the number of guesses it takes to find the turquoise: 10, 6, or 4 points are awarded accordingly. The game ends when all the counters are held by one side. But before the game starts, a turquoise offering is made to the yucca plant that furnished the counters. A final offering (usually a turquoise) is made with a prayer at the end of the game, and the counter and other game equipment are buried at that time.

As an Anglo woman, I was a bit confused when I first read about this game, and I reread the directions several times, trying to understand it. I had many questions about exactly how to play. Finally, I realized that the basic rules of the game are clearly described, but no matter how many times I read the directions, I still just didn't quite "get it." I knew where to find yucca leaves even though it would require some effort on my part to obtain them. The songs proved to be one of the biggest problems; I didn't know them, and I couldn't find anyone who was willing to teach me. These songs were not "my knowledge," and the consensus of "the knowers" was that I had no need to have this information. Probably even more significant for me was the fact that I really didn't get the point of the game; you hide rocks in shoes, you say the right words, and you try to guess where the rocks are. It seemed like an incredible amount of effort just to find some rocks. But, of course, my world view is not rooted in Navajo culture.

To a Navajo, on the other hand, this description of the game might be very understandable. It is easy to obtain the necessary yucca leaves almost anywhere in the territory of the Navajo Nation. If you are a Navajo, you know the 102 songs and the ending prayer, and if you don't, you know someone who can and will teach you. Most important, you also understand the point behind this game: It is a sacred game that stems from the Navajo creation stories of how day and night came to be. It has a point—a very important one.

The Navajo Shoe Game as perceived by me, an Anglo woman, provides an interesting metaphor for examining the way in which students from diverse racial, cultural, and social class groups might view the discipline of science. As in the case of the Shoe Game, participating and succeeding in science require certain knowledge and someone to help in the teaching and learning of this knowledge. Science also has to make sense for students. Just as the Shoe Game might seem foreign to non-Navajo players, so minority students might also perceive science as a strange game, one that does not seem to coincide with their personal view of the world. It is a game for those who understand how to play.

Cause for Concern: Minority Success and Participation in Science

Concern over the continued lack of success and participation by minority students in science has prompted a focus on equity in major recent science reform efforts such as those documented in *Benchmarks for Science Literacy* (American Association for the Advancement of Science, 1993), the *National Science Education Standards* (NRC, 1996), *Project 2061: Science For All Americans* (American Association for the Advancement of Science, 1989), and the materials that accompany the National Science Foundation's State Systemic Reform Initiative (Heck, 1998; Laguarda, Breckenridge & Hightower, 1994). That increased emphasis on providing a better science education for all students stems from data indicating that students from culturally and/or linguistically diverse backgrounds, with the exception of Asian Americans, perform at a level below that of Anglo students on standard measures of academic achievement (Barba, 1998; Clark, 1999; Rodriquez, 1998). In looking at the most recent science scores from the National Assessment of Educational Progress (NAEP) in the area of science, results indicate no significant changes in student scores for grades 4, 8, and 12 since the last time the NAEP was administered, in 1996. However, African American, Hispanic and Native American students continue to perform at lower levels than Anglo students in science.

Gatekeepers

School success functions as a gatekeeper in science. The lack of achievement in science classes by minority groups often results in their lack of participation in science careers. Although culturally diverse individuals and females have significantly improved participation rates in business and industry in recent years, this trend is not the case in fields of science and technology (Barba, 1998). The National Science Foundation (1994) reports that although African American, Hispanics and Native Americans make up 19 percent of the total labor force in our country, they make up only 8 percent of the science, math, engineering and technology work force. For women, the statistics are similar. Although the percentage of women in the workforce is estimated to be 46 percent, only 22 percent work in the fields of science, math, engineering and technology (Clark, 1999).

The seriousness of the current problem is compounded by the fact that minorities are the most rapidly growing segment of the population. Hodgkinson (1992) predicts that by the year 2050, minority subgroups will outnumber white subgroups at the elementary school level. There is cause for concern. Lack of participation of minority students in science and science-related fields could have far-reaching implications. According to George D. Nelson, director of Project 2061 for the American Association for the Advancement of Science, "If the United States is to continue to lead the world in scientific research and technology development, then future generations of scientists, engineers, and technicians must reflect our nation's diversity" (National Science Teachers Association, 2001/2002).

A Matter of Access

Why are minority students not entering science fields? Many of the barriers, both legal and social, that have historically prevented minority participation have been eliminated (Barba, 1998). Low performance of minority students on standard measures of achievement certainly appears to be a factor, but lack of success in school science is not the only reason that minority students are choosing not to pursue science careers. To some students who have the skills and abilities to play the science game well, the game itself just does not seem appealing. Lewis and Collins (2001) investigated the career decisions of three academically successful African American students and found that the two students who chose not to pursue science careers did so because they perceived a mismatch between a career in science and their life goals. Conversely, the student who had a clearer understanding not only of the nature of science but also of the actual work that scientist do chose to continue in a science career. Many minority students have no firsthand knowledge of what scientists or those working in science related fields actually do. They might have misperceptions about what it is like to work in the various fields of science, and these misperceptions could paint a not-so-appealing picture of science as a career. Minority students, through firsthand experience with those who working in science or science-related fields, can gain a clearer understanding that science is indeed a human endeavor and can be quite different from the school coursework that must be done in preparing for these careers. Findings from this study suggest that minority students need more information about various science careers entail and should have access to people who are actually working in fields of science.

Science Education: Who Are the Players?

Central to any game are its players. In team sports, the success of the team often depends on the different skills and talents each player brings to the field. Diversity is viewed as a positive aspect in developing a winning team. How successful would a baseball team be if all the players were great hitters but none of them could run or catch a ball? There are many in the field of science education who believe that the game of science could perhaps gain something from including players who bring a variety of knowledge, skills, and abilities to the field. Historically, science has not taken advantage of the diverse perspectives and the choice of potential players and has taken a more exclusive than inclusive stance. Since 1993, when Derek Hodson proposed a rationale for multicultural science education advocating an inclusive framework that had a place for all students, interest in this topic has continued to grow. As Project 2061 states, "Ultimately, reform is more about people than it is about politics, institutions, and processes" (American Association for the Advancement of Science, 1989, p. 211). The true success of reform must be measured in terms of its effect on those underserved students whose lack of success was a major catalyst for seeking reform in the first place. In other words, it's all about the players.

Unique Needs, Unique Solutions

In discussions of "science for all," there is a tendency to write about minority groups as if they were all the same. They are not. In seeking ways to meet the needs of minority groups, it is important to view the various groups as unique and distinct with concerns that might or might not be similar. The term "minority group" is a very broad one, including many separate and distinct groups of people. Latinos/Latinas, African American, American Indians, women, and people with disabilities all fall into this category. Furthermore, there are subgroups within these larger groups. For example, there are more than 550 federally recognized American Indian tribes within the United States alone, and although certain commonalties exist between these tribes, to assume that all are exactly the same is incorrect. The commonality that bonds all minority groups together is that they have been traditionally and are currently underserved and underrepresented in science. However, in seeking solutions to this concern, the specific and often different issues within unique minority groups must be addressed.

Enhancing Visibility

Rodriquez (1997) underscores this point with his view that even the National Science Education Standards (National Reseach Council, 1996) promotes a "discourse of invisibility" (p. 19) by not directly addressing the complex ethnic, socioeconomic, gender and theoretical issues that influence the teaching and learning of science in school. Central to his concern is the way in which the NSES chose to portray individuals from minority groups in both text and photographs. The specific names of minority groups were not given in the text, and although diversity is portrayed in the pictures, the terms

"Latina/Latino," "African-American," "Cambodian American," "Ute," and others are not used. To people from minority populations, this nonacknowledgement stands out like a flashing neon light and sends an important and unacceptable message. Listening to concerns from representatives from the diverse population of underrepresented players is essential in framing solutions to problems related to equity in science education. Multiple pairs of eyes will help all of us to improve our vision and see what we as individuals situated in one particular culture might be unable to see on our own.

As science educators, not only do we need to recognize distinct differences in minority groups, but we must also acknowledge what these unique players bring to the game. In addressing the needs of these students, we should not lose sight of the fact that students who have constructed knowledge of the world in a different cultural context from the mainstream also have much to offer (Barba, 1998).

Making Sense of the Game

Hodson (1993) suggested that science could be made more relevant for all students if real-life situations were addressed in science classes and instruction began with and built on what students already knew. The importance of helping students understand the relevance of science to their everyday lives has since become a major national science educational goal (Barton et al., 2001). Often, however, students see little personal relevance in the topics that are commonly addressed in science classes. Consider the following window into a science classroom:

> The teacher began the class by giving the sixth graders a worksheet entitled "The Cohesive Property of Molecules of Water." Next, he wrote the title of the investigation and the problem statement on the overhead, and the students copied it onto their worksheet. The problem stated, "What makes water molecules attract other water molecules?" The teacher told students to think about raindrops running down a window. He said that the drops didn't just flow down, they go other ways. The students stared blankly at the teacher. The example they were asked to imagine meant nothing to them. It was not raining that day, nor could these students, who lived on a reservation situated in the desert Southwest, readily recall what happens when raindrops run down a window. The silence and blank stares did not discourage the teacher from moving forward. He wrote the following statements on the overhead: (1) Different kinds of water attract each other. (2) Molecules attract each other to make bigger molecules. The students were allowed to select one of these as their hypothesis. A girl shyly asked, "What does molecule mean?" and the teacher responded with a definition taken right from the glossary of the science textbook. This was the only question that any student asked that day. Next, the teacher had students copy the procedure, word for word, from a previously prepared overhead onto their worksheets. The step-by-step procedure was a great deal for students to copy, and this activity took most of the class period. When students finally finished copying, they had about ten minutes left in the class period to actually carry out the procedure they had spent so much time copying. What students were to do was to make drops of water on a piece of waxed paper and poke the drops with a pencil to push them together. Students seemed to enjoy this activity, and one boy shouted excitedly for the teacher to see what his group had observed. Unfortunately, students had to stop after just a few minutes so that they would have time to finish copying the conclusion from the overhead onto their worksheet before the bell

rang. At the end of class, I asked one of the students what she was trying to find out in this investigation, and she began to read aloud the procedure she had copied word for word from the overhead onto her paper. As she stumbled over the words, I stopped her and asked her just to tell me in her own words what she had found out. After a moment of awkward silence, she told me to ask the teacher and that he could explain it to me.

What did students learn about science from this experience? They saw no connection to their lives, nor did the teacher seek any of their prior experiences as a starting point for this lesson. School science is often foreign to the lived experience of many students and is often disconnected from students' day-to-day life (Bouillion & Gomez, 2001). Even when students' natural curiosity provided a window of opportunity for the teacher, the regimented classroom procedure limited any opportunity for students to make their own sense of the phenomena. This classroom scenario would not be a positive learning situation for any group of students, but for minority students, it helps to reinforce the idea that science is someone else's knowledge, not a part of their lives. This lesson began with the teacher's frame of reference, not the students', and seemed to go from bad to worse.

The Power of Context

Roberta Barba (1998) emphasizes the power of providing students with culturally familiar examples in content acquisition. The particular students in the preceding classroom example, while not being able to relate to the example of water running down a window, had other experiences with water that they could have shared if they had been given the chance to do so. Students in the desert Southwest *do* have memorable experiences with infrequent yet dramatic instances of rainfall in the desert. One does not soon forget how tiny droplets of rain turn the desert into raging torrents of water, red with the particles of earth they have taken with them. This example would have provided a frame of reference for the students, and they could have used their personal experiences to make sense of the concept the teacher was trying to teach. Valuing the everyday experiences of diverse students and their families is a way of making science more inclusive (Atwater, 1996). For students in inner-city Chicago, a different example would have been warranted.

The instructional strategies that this teacher used, however, are universally inappropriate in any setting. The methods that this teacher employed removed all opportunities for students to have any ownership whatsoever of the information. Science was portrayed not as a process of making sense of the world but rather as a body of static knowledge to be transmitted from the teacher to the students. Was this classroom scenario a fictional account? Unfortunately, it was not. Even more unfortunately, it is an example that is replayed often in other settings with other groups of students.

Seeking a Culture Link

A large body of research suggests that students from underrepresented groups often struggle to find relevance and meaning in the way science is taught in school (Atwater, 1998; Barton, 1998; Hammond, 2001; Rosser, 1990). This is especially true of students from indigenous cultures. In the United States, Native Americans are the least likely to pursue scientific careers (Indian Nations at Risk Task Force, 1991), nor do many Native students successfully complete science and math courses that would prepare them for scientific and technical careers (Nelson-Barber & Estrin, 1995).

Few of the models used with these groups of students are culturally based, a factor that a growing number of researchers believe hinders their success (Allen & Crawley, 1998; Cahape & Howley, 1992; Indian Nations at Risk Task Force, 1991; Mercer, 1993; Nelson-Barber & Estrin, 1995; Posey, 1998; Schik, Arewa, Thomson, & White, 1995). Although many students from Native communities often have a wealth of knowledge rooted in firsthand experience with the natural world, this knowledge often goes unrecognized in school settings, and it remains untapped and ignored (Ascher, 1991; Nelson-Barber & Estrin, 1995). When the values and perspectives that students bring with them are not acknowledged, it is not surprising the Native students view the game of science as something that is simply "not for them." In a study of Navajo students in grades 4–6, Monhardt (in press) found that when asked to draw a scientist, students overwhelmingly portrayed scientists as Anglos. Of the ninety-six students who completed the drawing, only one drew a Native American scientist. When the same students were asked whether they could or would like to be scientists, the common response was an incredulous "No!"

How STS Bridges Science and Culture

A science-technology-society (STS) approach to science instruction shows great promise in working with all students and perhaps even more so with students from indigenous cultures. The use of this philosophy can help students to make sense of the science game. STS identifies problem of local interest and impact and incorporates local resources, both material and human, to resolve problems. Cultural connections with Native communities can become an important part of the process, and science is not sacrificed in the process. Students must seek out content knowledge from the viewpoint of Western science as well as taking into account the values of their own communities. Multiple perspectives have relevance to the problem that is being addressed because it is a local concern. All players must have input. Students engaging in such projects feel that science can help them to make a difference in their lives and the lives of those in their community. They also become aware of their responsibilities as citizens as they attempt to resolve the issues they have identified. Students feel that they are indeed real players of the game, not just outsiders who are being forced to participate in an artificial and irrelevant experience.

What might this approach to science education for Native students look like in practice? One example is the Indian Summer Program, now in its seventh year (Galindo & Rinehart, 2002). This project, which involves Shoshone-Bannock students, has several main goals:

- To build on local culture and values
- To collaborate with Shoshone-Bannock tribal members in the incorporation of tribal environmental knowledge with the methods of Western science

- To encourage lifelong learning by extending teaching and learning beyond the classroom
- To create a research-based education model that can be shared with others.

The project strives to integrate traditional knowledge with new knowledge as a way of helping students feel connected to who they are and to science as well.

An example of traditional knowledge for students is learning about the willow weir basket. The Shoshone-Bannock people view willow as a great gift that has helped them to survive for many generations. Willow has traditionally had many uses, such as a material for making the weir baskets that are used for catching salmon, as a tool for cooking meals, as a raw material used in the construction of cradleboards and as a traditional medicine. Tribal mentors help students make willow weir baskets as a way to gain appreciation for the gift of the willow plant. Although some might view this as not being connected to a "regular" science curriculum, this knowledge forms a strong cultural foundation for one of the many science experiences that the students have been engaged in as part of the Indian Summer program.

The students participate in a project called "Dances with Salmon" that addresses a real world local problem: the decline of salmon and steelhead. Beginning in 1995, students became involved in this fish recovery project in the Salmon River basin. Previous attempts by others to address this problem used single-species recovery efforts, but the Indian Summer program took a different approach. Building on traditional values of giving back to the earth rather than taking from it, young tribal members looked at the problem holistically and focused their efforts on preserving habitat as well. Not only is an ecosystem approach compatible with traditional values, it is also more cost effective than a single-species approach. With the help of the community members, students gathered basic physical and biological data as they examined the current fish population and the habitat conditions. From this information, they determined what factors could be affecting the fish population and chose a way to address these factors. To increase the number of salmon, students created streamside hatcheries for salmon, using a device called a Whitlock Vibert (WV) box developed in France in 1950 by Richard Vibert. Eggs are placed in the nursery portion of the box, where they are protected until they hatch. The fry remain in the nursery until the yolk sack is absorbed. The fry then escape through slots in the box and live in a streamside incubator until they are ready to enter the stream.

Students constructed their own streamside incubator boxes from old refrigerators that would otherwise have made their way into the local landfill. They modified the interior of the refrigerators to create a secure environment for the WV boxes and to provide a secure environment for the developing fish. Water from the stream entered the incubators though a one-inch pipe and exited through a two-inch outlet pipe that controlled the water level and provided a way for the fry to leave the incubator when they were ready. Traditional knowledge of salmon was considered in the construction of the boxes, and care was taken to provide an almost natural environment for the eggs to develop in. Students recreated the conditions that would be found in a small stream, including the addition of rocks on the bottom. Humans never touched the eggs after they were placed in the box.

Hatching Promise

What impact has this project had on the problem it was intended to address? Since its beginning, the streamside incubator project has expanded to incorporate fourteen different sites. In 2001, a total of 271,900 eggs were placed in the boxes, resulting in an amazing live hatch rate of 96 percent. Idaho has experienced salmon and steelhead runs for the first time in years. This year, students added Global Positioning Systems technology to collect data from their sites. The use of this technology greatly enhanced data collection, and students were able to monitor dissolved oxygen levels, water flow, and fish migration. The system makes it possible to monitor the streamside hatcheries during the winter months, when the harsh Idaho climate covers them with feet of snow.

Not only has this project positively affected the natural environment, it has had a positive effect on the Native students as well. And this is just one of several meaningful and successful projects that are a part of Indian Summer.

The project staff strives to ensure success for all students involved in various projects. They state, "As educators our task is to integrate science and technology with Native American culture so that our students may cope with modern living as consumers, producer and citizens. We understand traditional Native views and we strive to foster curiosity, problem solving skills, and recording techniques. All these are basic techniques of being a good scientist" (Galindo & Rinehart, 2002, p. 8).

Parents as Part of the Team

Parental involvement has been identified as an important element in children's success in school (Epstein, 1987; Funkhouser & Gonzales, 1997; Moles, 1993; Smith & Hausafus, 1998). However, some researchers believe that educational reform movements often place too much emphasis on the schools and too little emphasis on parents and the community. This would seem to be true for reform efforts in science education, as evidenced by the lack of published research on the area of parent involvement (Barton et al., 2001). As early as 1981, Tobias emphasized the need for parental encouragement as a key factor in involving students with science. It is believed that success in mathematics and science is founded on attitudes that are established early in life (Tressel, 1984), at a time when parents are their children's most influential teachers. Chapter 9 of this book addresses parental involvement in science education more deeply.

Hurdles to Parental Involvement

Involving minority parents in their children's schooling is a complicated process and involves changing the attitudes of parents as well as those of educators. This process requires that all parties rethink their individual roles as well as their understanding of where science learning takes place. The boundaries of where learning takes place must reach beyond the school to include the home and community context (Barton, 1998).

Unfortunately, many parents feel that they have inadequate science knowledge to do science at home with their children (Belfiore & Barton, 1999; Brickhouse, 1994;

Scribner-Maclean, 1996). Like their children, parents often perceive science to be simply school-related and see little authentic or real-world connection to science. They view science ideas as having been constructed by others and do not see themselves to be constructors of science knowledge in home settings. Yet parents of minority students often have a wide range of valuable everyday knowledge that they do not recognize as science. Lori Hammond (2001) describes a unique teacher education program at California State University–Sacramento which helped to establish a community of trust between the school and the surrounding community. Many of the parents in the school community are immigrants from Southeast Asia and have a wealth of knowledge about everyday skills such as obtaining and preserving food, construction skills, growing fibers to produce textiles, and metalworking. Within this program, these skills were recognized as important, and parents assumed the role of experts. Though not without problems resulting from exceptions and assumptions on both sides, the project was successful in validating knowledge that parents and community members had to offer.

Valued Partners

Williams-Norton, Reisdorf, and Spees (1990) found that families who do science together at home demystify the subject and identify the everyday nature of science and technology. When children do science activities that are related to topics of real-world relevance at home, they become more enthusiastic about science, and their parents become more confident as promoters of education (Monhardt et al., 2002; Smith & Hasafus, 1998).

The general premise supporting parental involvement is that when schools and families create productive partnerships, all stakeholders benefit. The families become empowered, the schools become more effective in achieving their educational goals, and all students experience success (de Carvalho, 2001).

Minority parents must have a real voice in their children's education and be empowered to participate in the actual decision-making process. Many schools involved in site-based management have included minority parents on decision-making committees, but their membership is often only a token effort. Research indicates that parents have little real voice in making decisions of consequence, especially curriculum—related decisions (Malen, Ogawa, & Krantz, 1990). A great deal of previous research touts the benefits of parental involvement; however, many of these studies have focused on predominantly white, middle-class families. When findings from these studies are generalized to disadvantaged or minority families, the recommendations are often unsuccessful. The research with marginalized groups has identified barriers that prevent this group of parents from becoming involved in their children's schooling, but few have looked at what strategies are successful within specific minority groups.

Strategies for parental involvement should be culture-specific if values of learning promoted at home are to be synchronized with those promoted at school. For instance, strategies for working with Native American parents must be tribe-specific as well as community-specific. In working with minority students and their families, understanding the differences and similarities between the education children receive at home (traditional education) and the education they receive at school (formal education) is essential information for educators who want to work effectively with children and their families (Sipes, 1993). School programs that want to include minority parents must be based on the needs and interests of these specific families. Current research supports the idea that educators who take the time to learn about the culture and values of minority families will not only help to maintain the integrity of the families but also succeed in involving parents in children's schooling.

Creating Equitable Contexts for Playing the Game

How should the needs of culturally diverse students be met in the science classroom? Traditionally, the cultural deficit model has informed instruction for culturally diverse students (Sleeter & Grant, 1987). This model is based on the idea that students' lack of success in school is due to their lack of preparation for learning, and the blame for this lack of preparation is placed on the families and the communities from which they come. Often, students are perceived as not caring or unmotivated to learn. Those who subscribe to the cultural-deficit model label culturally diverse students "at risk"—in need of fixing—and view it as the school's responsibility to fix them (Barba, 1998). Unfortunately, it is a common practice to group minority students together and label them as "low ability." Data from the National Science Foundation (1994) indicate that in grades 9 through 12, 29 percent of the classes with few minority students are labeled "low ability," whereas 42 percent of classes with at least 40 percent minority students are so labeled. These labels affect student achievement because teachers as well as students tend to see this as a self-fulfilling prophecy and have lower expectations.

Elrich (1994) describes his experiences as a teacher in a culturally diverse classroom where his students saw their diversity as an indicator of their impending and unavoidable failure. His African-American and Hispanic middle school students exhibited low self-esteem, had low expectations for themselves and saw no value in education. This scenario is a common one. Many minority students themselves buy into the cultural deficit model and believe that they are indeed "broken beyond repair."

A multicultural model is in direct contrast to the cultural deficit model (Sleeter & Grant, 1987). This model is guided by the idea that diversity is not a problem but is actually a strength. All students can benefit in a context in which different ways of knowing and different constructions of science are brought into the science classroom. Rather than viewing diverse student populations as the ones who need fixing, this model advocates that the school system itself needs to change to accommodate and celebrate what diverse students bring into the classroom.

Are the Rules the Same for All?

Rakow and Bermudez (1993) found that teachers of Hispanic American students indicated that they did not differentiate in the teaching strategies they used for Hispanic students and their Anglo counterparts. For these teachers, "equitable practice" was interpreted as treating all students the same. Helping practitioners, researchers, and policymakers to rethink this view of equity is important in making sure that all students receive the best science education possible.

A democratic society is founded on the principle of equality—equal opportunity for all. Equality implies "sameness" and is often interpreted to mean that what is good for one should be good for all. Shouldn't the rules of fair play be the same for everyone? Unfortunately, it is not that simple. In looking at how to create contexts in which all students can succeed and learn science or any subject, this idea of "sameness" is flawed. Equity, the elusive goal that we continue to strive for in educational practice, is a somewhat different idea, requiring different strategies on the part of the teacher. Banks (1994, p. 5) defined equity pedagogy as "modified teacher behaviors that facilitate the academic achievement of students from diverse racial, cultural and social class groups."

As many researchers have reported and many practitioners are currently experiencing, this is a very complex problem, one that does not have prescriptive solutions. Addressing the problem requires examining some of the fundamental assumptions about the discipline of science and how it is taught in our schools.

Equity Does Not Mean Sameness

Recent thinking from many within the science education community advocates that a "one size fits all" approach to curriculum, instruction, and/or assessment is ineffective in meeting the needs of culturally and linguistically diverse learners (Lee, 1999; Lynch et al., 1996; Rodriquez, 1997). "Equity" in science education does not mean treating all students the same. A look into any classroom in the country at any grade level will illustrate quite clearly why this approach has proven to be ineffective. Students are simply *not* the same.

The importance of meeting learners' individual needs is an idea that is stressed in colleges of education throughout our country. Addressing individual differences is certainly not a new idea in the field of education. When it comes to science education, however, accommodating differences in language and culture in science classrooms is somewhat of a novel idea. Individual differences exist in all classrooms, and effective teachers are the ones who can address these differences, whatever they might be. As any practicing teacher will tell you, meeting the individual needs of students is one of the most challenging tasks for teachers.

Who Is Teaching the Rules of the Game?

Teachers are entrusted with the daunting task of teaching the rules of the science game to their students. The degree to which teachers are able to accomplish this task is affected by many factors, including how well teachers are trained to teach their particular subject, the match between gender and ethnicity of teacher and student, and the training and experience teachers have in working with diverse populations.

It would make sense that students whose levels of achievement and participation in science are below what we would hope should have the very best teachers to help prepare them to be successful. However, minority students typically have less access to highly qualified teachers. Classes with high minority populations are less likely to have teachers who are subject area specialists than are classes with low proportions of minority students (National Science Foundation, 1994).

Rethinking Race, Culture, Ethnicity

Another factor in teacher success with minority populations involves how well the teacher's gender and ethnicity matches the population the teacher serves. Where gender is concerned, 49 percent of all high school science teachers are female. In looking at how these numbers are distributed, it is perhaps not surprising that the highest percentages of female science teachers are in the biological sciences (42 percent) and only 24 percent of physics teachers are female (Blank & Gruebel, 1995). These percentages seem similar to the numbers of females who later choose to enter these particular fields of science. The numbers are much worse when we look at teachers from minority cultures. Minority cultures are underrepresented in the teaching profession in general, representing only 14 percent of the total teacher workforce. Where science is concerned, the numbers dwindle even more. Only 28 percent of minority teachers teach biology, chemistry, or physics (Blank & Gruebel, 1995).

Another concern is how well science teachers are trained in teaching minority population. Teachers often receive little or no training in working with minority populations, yet teacher educators, principals, and practicing teachers identify this as an essential area in which more training is urgently needed (Moles, 1993). Although some programs for preservice teachers attempt to change the practices and beliefs of prospective teachers (Bullock, 1997; Ross & Smith, 1992; Smolkin, Surnia & Mecado, 1995), most devote little time to preparing teachers to work in diverse settings. Recommendations for change include the development of teacher preparations programs that move beyond the focus on curriculum and toward a framework in which prospective teachers are encouraged to challenge their existing beliefs about equity, diversity, teaching and learning (Luft, Bragg, & Peters, 1999). Preservice teachers are often ill equipped to meet the needs of students in our increasingly diverse society and could greatly benefit from actually spending time teaching science in diverse settings. It has been shown that preservice teachers' abilities to work in diverse settings are enhanced when they actually have this experience firsthand (Grant & Tate, 1995; Monhardt et al., 2002). Banks (2001, p. 12) states,

> [T]eacher education students must be helped to critically analyze and rethink their notions of race, culture, and ethnicity and to view themselves as cultural and racial beings. They also need to reconstruct race, culture, and ethnicity in ways that are inclusive and that reveal the ways in which these concepts are related to the social economic and political structures in U.S. society.

 ## Culturally Familiar Role Models

Within the field of science education, culturally diverse role models have seldom been included in discussion of the history of science. The "additive model" (Gilbert & Gay,

1985) is aimed at providing minority students role models in the field of science by adding the contributions of those who were somehow omitted from the history of science. Who "discovered" the smallpox vaccination? Was it Dr. Boylston, a European male who was acknowledged by the scientific community for this discovery? Or was Onesiumus, an African American slave who shared traditional tribal knowledge with his master about how transmitting a less virulent form of smallpox to children prevented them from contracting a deadly form of the disease? His master shared this information with Dr. Boylston, who used accepted scientific methods to validate this knowledge (Barba, 1998, p. 59). This is just one example of how diverse cultures have made contributions to the field of science that are rarely acknowledged. The inclusion of such examples could communicate to culturally diverse students that their heritage has also played an important role in the development of scientific knowledge.

The use of culturally familiar role models can significantly increase students' interest in pursuing science careers (Healy, 1990; Pitman, 1989). Role models have been shown to be important in encouraging all students in science, but this is perhaps especially true for minority students (Barba, 1998; Clark, 1999). Historical accounts are important, but to students who live in a world of "right now," it is also essential to provide role models that are currently contributing to the field of science. Exposing students to people from their own culture who are making contributions to the field of science can help students to identify with the discipline of science (Rakow, 1988). The vignette accompanying this chapter illustrates that the best role models are those with whom students can identify.

Does this mean that minority students can be taught only by those from their own culture? No, in reality, that is not always possible. But Anglo teachers must realize the importance of proving opportunities for minority student to interact with people in science with whom they can identify. Learning the rules from someone who interprets them though your eyes is much more effective than learning them from a person who does not travel in your reality. Teachers must seek out people who can have a profound ability to encourage students to see the possibilities that are available to them within science.

The Language of the Game

Students from ethnic minorities whose first language is not English face challenges in the science classroom related directly to the use of language. Not only do language minority student need to navigate the everyday school tasks of speaking, reading, and writing in an unfamiliar language, but they are also faced with what some have considered a foreign language of its own: the language of science. Almost every game has its own specialized language, and knowledge of this language is one of the first steps in learning to play the game with any success. Football has terms such as "blitz," "clipping," and "encroachment"; basketball uses phrases such as "full-court press," "man-to-man defense"; and in ice hockey, it is important to know what is meant by "clearing the zone," a "backhand shot," and "carom." Are these familiar terms? Simply knowing that the vocabulary will not automatically guarantee that you will be a successful player of the game. However, not knowing the language of the game will almost certainly guarantee failure. The game of science is quite similar: You have to understand the language before you can play.

Meanings Transfer Even If Language Does Not

Often, teachers incorrectly assume that linguistically diverse students have deficiencies not only in the language skills they need to make sense of science concepts, but in actual content knowledge as well (Duran et al., 1998). Rather than viewing the knowledge of science students have constructed in a language other than English as relevant, teachers often do not acknowledge it at all or view this knowledge as problematic. This belief can result in lower expectations for language minority students. In popular sports, we do not take this view. Football as played in the United States is quite a different game from the football that is played in other countries. Yet do we devalue the skills that European players possess in playing their game of football? Certainly not. We view these skills as not only valuable, but also transferable to our game of football. Perhaps we should view the knowledge that linguistically diverse students have constructed of science in the same manner.

The Basic Skills Trap

Students' success in school science is often related directly to their skills in reading and writing. Students who have difficulty with reading and writing also have difficulty in science, and this is especially true for students whose first language is not English. Scores on standard measures of achievement in science often reflect a student's reading ability rather than evidence of his or her understanding of science concepts. Teachers believe that for limited-English-speaking students to be successful in science, they must develop literacy skills. Certainly, it is important for students to become fully literate in English. This will help them to achieve success not only in school, but in other areas of life as well. Unfortunately, in science classrooms, this belief often results in a basic skills approach, in which emphasis is placed on teaching the basic skills of reading and writing rather than a focus on developing an understanding of science. A basic skills approach to the teaching of reading and writing often begins in elementary school and actually does more harm than good. Students do not learn science in this way, and they develop low-quality literacy skills as well (Duran et al., 1997; Duschl & Wright, 1989; Reyes & Molner, 1991).

An elementary science teacher allowed me to spend some time in her classroom. What I observed on this particular day, I found to be quite interesting:

> Mrs. McDermott (a pseudonym) began her fourth grade science class by lecturing about living things. Most of her students were poor readers and were unable to read their science textbook. The majority of these students had grown up hearing Navajo, yet most students were not fluent speakers of this language. In school, students struggled with reading and writing in English. Mrs. McDermott thought that the best way to get the necessary science information across to her students was simply to tell them what they needed to know. There was so much information to cover in the state curriculum, and she told

me that lecture provided the very best way to get through all the information the students would need for the end-of-year science test. She used the overhead to illustrate the information she was attempting to cover. The lecture was focused on the meaning of many science words that were unfamiliar to the students. They furiously scribbled notes into their science notebooks at Mrs. McDermott's prompting. "Copy this definition. You'll need to know this." Near the end of class, Mrs. McDermott was pronouncing some of the terms the students had copied from the overhead: Moneran, Protista, Fungi, and so on. A fourth grade girl sitting next to me leaned over and earnestly asked me, "Do you know that language?" By the look on her face and the tone of her voice, it was obvious that she did not. The child asking this question was the only Anglo child in this class. If science seemed like a foreign language to her, what must the Navajo children have been thinking?

Listening to teacher talk and memorizing vocabulary words become paramount in classrooms where the emphasis is on basic skills instruction. The important part of learning science is the meaning making function rather than the learning of vocabulary and repeating what the teacher has said (Duran et al., 1997). Unfortunately, language minority students often do not understand the sense-making function of science because of the teaching methods they experience. In working with linguistically diverse students, overemphasis on the use of precise terminology too early in the learning process can actually alienate students from learning science altogether (Hodson, 1993). Students become overly dependent on what teachers say and do not understand that science is about making their own sense in order to actually apply science learning to the real world (Duran et al., 1997).

Learning the Language of the Game

The ways in which people first use language are acquired within their home culture. Learning a language involves more than just speaking the words of that language. Language also transmits values, attitudes, and understandings that are a part of the culture (Garcia, 2001) Young children begin by mimicking language patterns of those around them until they are able to use language for their own purposes (Wertch, 1991). Students who have learned a language other than English in their home often have difficulty in adapting to different ways of language in school. In much the same way that students learned their first language at home, teachers can help students learn not only English but also the language of science. At first, students might simply mimic the language of science, just as they did when they were learning their first language. Eventually, their use of the language of science will move away from simple mimicry to using the language to express their own understanding. The language of science is much more than just repeating the words. Attached to the words must also be a mechanism for making meaning.

Talking, reading, writing, and listening play important roles in science understanding. In helping students to learn the language of science, teachers should focus on key concepts in science rather than isolated bits of information. Helping students to see how these big ideas fit together will help them begin to see science as more than just a collection of facts. In teaching students with limited English skills, supplementing teacher talk with visual presentation of content has been shown to be effective.

Students benefit from strategies that make thinking and learning visible, such as the use of real-world objects, icons, and pictures as well as diagrams and concept maps that show how concepts are connected (Duran et al., 1998).

Student talk is an essential way of making meaning in science classrooms (Lemke, 1990), and all students should be given the opportunity to do science and make meaning of what they are doing through the use of everyday language. Linguistically diverse students come into the science classroom with existing knowledge that they have constructed in their native language. New science knowledge can be learned when students have the opportunity to reconcile and often reconstruct their previous knowledge within new frameworks.

Roberta Barba (1998, pp. 198–202) describes a classroom model for culturally diverse learners that builds on the three-part learning cycle approach to science instruction (Karplus, 1974), as shown in Table 6.1. The SCALE (Science Content and Language Expansion) model incorporates language acquisition skills in helping

Table 6.1 Learning cycle and SCALE sequences toward science for all

Learning Cycle	SCALE
Exploration phase: Students explore science concepts through hands-on engagement with concrete, real-world experiences as they interact with materials and each other to explore events, materials. The teacher's role is an indirect one as he or she observes what students are doing and interacts with individuals or small groups.	*Activation stage:* Students recall what they already know as they explore events, materials, and science concepts with their peers. Social interaction is emphasized. As students explore the science concepts, they also develop their English language skills as they talk about what they are doing with their peers.
Concept invention phase: The teacher assists students in developing science concepts. Names are given to the concepts that students experienced in the previous phase. The teacher assumes a more direct teaching role as he or she helps students to develop the concepts they are learning through multiple modes of instruction.	*Actualization phase:* The teacher introduces the "language of science" as vocabulary is attached to the concepts that the students experienced in the previous stage. The teacher uses multiple strategies to help student develop understanding of the concept such as the use of textbooks, fotonovelas (picture books), and audiovisual materials. The teacher's explanations may be in the students' home language. Peer interaction is again encouraged.
Concept application phase: Students apply what they have learned to a new situation, generalizing their newly learned concepts to different situations.	*Application phase:* Students apply what they have learned to new situations and also connect what they have learned to examples in their own lives. Students are able to use new concepts to explain previous experiences.

students with limited English skills learn science. Students develop their English skills and their understanding of science in cooperative group settings, where they are tutored in their native language by their peers. Students are given the opportunity to bring the understandings they have constructed in their native language into the school setting.

The use of students' home language, peer tutoring, and working in cooperative groups have numerous benefits for students who are second language learners. Not only have these strategies been shown to increase students' self-esteem and improve attitudes toward school in general, they also are useful in helping students to acquire content knowledge (Barba, 1998).

Whose Game Is It?

Since discussions of establishing equitable learning contexts for all students in science first began, one of the greatest stumbling blocks relates to the question "What is science?" Arguments against a multicultural approach to science instruction center on conflicting claims of what actually "counts" as science and whether or not the knowledge of other cultural groups should be included in this definition. This definition is viewed as important because ultimately what is deemed "science" is what will be taught in school. Within the science education community, the majority view has historically focused on a universalist perspective or what is referred to as the "Standard Account" (Cobern & Loving, 2001). Often referred to as "Western modern science," this is the kind of science currently taught in most schools and has come to be regarded by many as the only true scientific enterprise (Good, 1995; Gross & Levitt, 1994; Matthews, 1994). Science achievement of non-Western cultures is often viewed outside the realm of "true" science. This philosophy not only excludes creationism but also excludes the knowledge of science constructed over generations by indigenous peoples (Snively & Corsiglia, 2001).

What Counts as Science?

From a pedagogical standpoint, what effect does acceptance of a Western modern science approach have on students who may not subscribe to this viewpoint? World view, as defined by Cobern (1996, p. 584) is a "nonrational foundation for thought, emotions and behavior, which provides a person with presuppositions about what the world is really like and what constitutes valid and important knowledge about the world." Studies by Jegede and Okebukola (1991) and Lawson and Worsnop (1992) indicate that when world views collide in the science classroom, learning is impeded. When new knowledge conflicts with existing cultural beliefs, the leaner is unable to accommodate the knowledge into his or her belief system. All students come into the school setting with intuitive understandings that are grounded in cultural experience, and these existing understandings are the framework for acquiring new knowledge (Brown, Collins & Duguid, 1989; Cole, 1985; Lave, 1988; Nelson-Barber & Estrin, 1995; Ovando, 1992).

Uncommon Frames of Reference

When the values and perspectives that students bring with them into the classroom are not appreciated, acknowledged, or accepted, they might feel in conflict with the institutional norms. Some students are able to negotiate between conflicting world views, but others have tremendous difficulty. These students might deny their previous cultural beliefs and become assimilated into the culture of the dominant group or hold onto these beliefs and experience exclusion (Aikenhead, 1996; Costa, 1995). The students who remain on the outside do not understand the science game. The rules are not "universal" for them. They do not play the game because they simply don't understand it. These marginalized students do not experience success in school science and ultimately do not become part of the science and technology workforce.

All cultures generate knowledge in order to make sense of the world (Selin, 1993), but is this knowledge science? There is growing concern that discussions about the relationship of science and culture tend to take on a decidedly antiscience tone (Norman, 1998). Good (1995), Cobern and Loving (2001), and many others argue that good science explanations will always be universal even if we do incorporate "indigenous knowledge" as scientific and broaden what is currently taught as science. In other words, when placed alongside the beliefs of other cultures, Western science will triumph because it offers the better explanation. Other ways of knowing are viewed outside the realm of science and are viewed as valid only to the degree to which they correspond to present beliefs of Western science (Deloria, 1992).

Valuing Knowledge

The idea of calling the knowledge of one cultural group "better" than another's causes uneasiness for many. For example, I asked a young Navajo college student whether he personally viewed traditional Navajo beliefs as better than the beliefs of the mainstream science community. The obvious annoyance in his tone of voice when he responded let me know quite clearly that he did not personally consider this a valid question to ask. Interestingly, he also equated religion (i.e., Christianity) with the majority viewpoint as he responded quite passionately:

> Here's the thing, see that's the thing about Christianity, it always has to put things in good or bad, good or evil and to us, you can't really put it [that way] because what my grandfather used to say is, "Look, you know, we gave you this belief, from us and our grandparents, and their grandparents, and it came from the Creator, that's how it came down." So that doesn't make us right or wrong. But for me, I think my tradition is a great influence. I think it builds values and it builds identities.

In looking even superficially at how indigenous cultures view the world, it is obvious that traditional beliefs differ greatly from those of Western modern science. The mainstream science community reacts with uneasiness to the idea of a belief system rooted in sacred objects and sacred places and transmitted through the use of stories. Beliefs of many indigenous groups fall into the realm of pseudoscience, myth, religion, or New Age beliefs when viewed though the lens of Western modern science. These beliefs might be considered religion by many and dismissed as being in a category different from science. However, important knowledge related to environmental concerns often exists at the core of spiritual explanations of indigenous people; this is relevant knowledge that is needed today (Johnson, 1992).

The scientific community does not accept reliance on the oral tradition as a valid method of transmitting information (Barba, 1998; Snively & Corsiglia, 2001). Knowledge that is transmitted through the use of stories handed down from generation to generation is often difficult to understand for outsiders to the culture, making it difficult for them to see past the story itself and into the specialized knowledge that is contained within it (Snively & Corsiglia, 2001). In the Navajo culture, for example, the older members of the community who have the most traditional knowledge about their culture use stories to explain certain points to a listener. Knowing the Navajo language is important for understanding the stories because there are many words in Navajo that have no English equivalent and vice versa. The stories are used as teaching tools and are subject to different levels of analysis based on the degree of analytical abstraction applied by the listener. Knowledge of Navajo culture is based on four main levels of knowledge that can be subdivided into three additional levels of abstraction (Schwarz, 1997). If stories are shared at all with people outside the culture, they are told in the way in which they would be shared with a young child. Future tellings of the same story add additional important points. The message that is conveyed by the story is not explicit, and the listener is left to think about the story and what it means. Questions can be asked that the storyteller might or might not answer. It is not up to the storyteller to explain the story; rather, it is the listener's responsibility to make his or her own sense of it.

It is not uncommon for a storyteller to express to the listeners that he or she does not possess total understanding of the story. While an elder was relating a story that had been told to him many times as a child, he stopped at a certain point and said in a puzzled way that he didn't know why something was as it was in the story because "they never told me why" (Monhardt, 1999). This is not unusual, considering the traditional Navajo belief that young, inexperienced people should not ask too many questions, especially of older people. It indicates disrespect to attempt to take a shortcut to obtain the knowledge that it took the elder person a lifetime to acquire. Rather, it is best for a young person to gain knowledge gradually through actual experiences. Accounts in the literature seem to repeat the idea that the exact meaning of stories is not always exactly or completely known (Benedek, 1995; Left Handed, 1938). Although to those from Western cultures this might seem an odd and unreliable way of transmitting information, the oral tradition is essential to the Navajo culture and to other indigenous groups.

Common Ground

The late Dean Jackson, former president of Navajo Community College (now Diné College), advocated "establishing relevancy and meaning" between the Western world and the Navajo world to capitalize on the best of both the Western ways of knowing and traditional Navajo beliefs. When the focus moves away from the specifics of indigenous belief systems to a more general approach, the possibility of common ground with Western science views begins to seem feasible. Themes such as interrelationships and interdependence, change, or equilibrium in natural systems are all possible organizers for science instruction that would serve the indigenous cultures as well as mainstream science. In learning from the oral tradition, students listen and then actively try to make sense of this information on their own. They don't simply ask questions and get answers. It is their responsibility to make their own meaning. Is this so different from inquiry-based science classrooms in which students investigate questions they have in order to develop their own understanding? As students learn more, their previous ideas might be challenged or changed, and additional meanings might be made, similar to the different levels of understanding within the oral tradition of indigenous people.

Over the past twenty-five years, scientists in many different fields have been carefully studying and documenting traditional knowledge of indigenous groups. Snively and Corsiglia (2001) give an in-depth account of this "new" field of study. TEK is defined as "traditional ecological knowledge which is both the science of long resident-oral peoples and a biological science label for the growing literature which records and explores that knowledge" (p. 8). This area of study offers promise in finding a way to incorporate other beliefs into the study of Western modern science.

The possibilities for incorporating knowledge from groups outside the realm of Western science are already becoming a reality at some institutions such as the predominately Navajo Diné College on the Navajo reservation. A bi-cultural group of scientists and educators believe that when Navajo science students draw on both Native and mainstream world views, they improve their ability to formulate hypotheses and think critically (Semken & Morgan, 1997). Wouldn't looking at science from multiple perspectives benefit non-Native students as well and, at the same time, satisfy the tenets of Western science?

Fractions Within Cultures

As Ortiz de Montelano (2001) states, when it comes to teaching multicultural science, "the devil is in the details" (p. 79). A holistic, general approach to the incorporation of indigenous knowledge into science classrooms seems much more desirable than focusing on specifics. Opposition to the incorporation of specific cultural belief comes not only from the mainstream science community; it comes from two opposing factions within indigenous community as well. In the Navajo community, some nontraditional Navajo parents do not wish the teaching of cultural beliefs to be a part of their children's school education. The goals some parents have for their children are related to learning the ways of the mainstream culture. They do not want their children to speak Navajo, nor do they want them to learn their traditional cultural background. At the other end of the spectrum, traditional Navajo parents are uneasy with the idea of their cultural beliefs being transmitted in a school setting. These traditional parents do not see this as a responsibility of the school but rather as a family responsibility. Their argument is a valid one. Within the Navajo culture, there are many things that are inappropriate to talk about openly, stories that should be told only at certain times of the year, and other specific but important cultural beliefs. Often, when well-intentioned non-Native teachers attempt to incorporate Native beliefs into science classrooms, these beliefs become trivialized and seem to be simply bits of nature lore or the "arts and crafts of science" rather than the sacred beliefs of a culture. The inclusion of specific knowledge from nonmainstream cultures in the science classroom must be approached with sensitivity. Parents and others with school community can provide guidance to teachers on what is and is not appropriate to include.

CONCLUSION: Education for All Becomes Education for Each

Wouldn't all students benefit from teaching strategies in which all points of view were accepted and acknowledged, not simply labeled as correct or incorrect? When science is taught as a body of accepted knowledge and presented in a way that allows for only one interpretation, those who do not share this view are alienated. When student knowledge that is grounded in cultural beliefs is acknowledged and perhaps even valued, a different sort of effect will occur. Rather than being on the outside of the game, students will become a part of it. To those who view science simplistically as the process by which we make sense of the world, the door is opened to many ways of knowing, not only the ways of Western modern science. Rather than one way to "do" science, there are many different ways and multiple legitimate sciences (Ogawa, 1995).

Other voices are beginning to be heard as this debate continues. Norman (1998) states that past shortcomings of science related to issues of race, class, and gender should be dealt with forthrightly, and Roth (1995) suggests that the history of Western science is not all a story of progress and consensus, as it is commonly portrayed. Rather, it includes issues of power, bias, and discrimination that are often conveniently overlooked.

The new voices that are speaking out for equity focus on making students, their lives, and their experiences central to science teaching. Rather than teaching students the rules of the game, this approach suggests that perhaps the game itself should be transformed to incorporate and value many different ways of knowing. Would this transformation irreparably damage science, as the keepers of the Standard Account fear? Or would changes in science both as a discipline and as a practice expand our way of looking at the world, making it a better game in which all can really participate? Achieving equity in science education does not involve a single correct prescriptive approach that will work for *all* students. As J. Francis Rummel said, "Now that we have achieved education for all, let us now seek education for each" (Gilliland, 1988, p. 8).

The Game in Action

Connecting Science and Culture

I was already an experienced teacher when I began teaching science at Meadows Middle School. For the previous eight years, I had taught in predominantly white, upper-middle-class schools where my students had experienced success and I had been recognized for my expertise in teaching science. Yet after just one day at my new school, I realized that I was in no way prepared to teach this group of students. Over 85 percent of the students in my science classes were of Mexican American ethnicity. For most of them, English was their second language. Academic success was equally foreign to these students, and they were the lowest-scoring students in the district on standardized tests. Virtually all of them came from low socioeconomic backgrounds, and many of their parents often worked at more than one job just to make ends meet. Low self-esteem was the norm, and many of the students had already given up on school, turning to gang membership as a way to belong. The school administrators saw fit to lump all of these student together into six classes taught by one team of teachers. The teachers, myself included, were specially selected not on the basis of our expertise in working with minority populations, but rather because we could "manage students behavior" and had the least number of office referrals.

Our team of marginalized students was even situated on the fringe of the school environment, housed in the most remote section of the building, as far away from the "others" as possible. Like the other subject area teachers on my team, I tried the best I could without any special training in how to meet the special and unique needs of these students. We struggled, and the best you could say about us as teachers was that we cared about our students. But it was painfully evident to all of us that caring was not enough.

As a science teacher, I tried to make science relevant and meaningful for students, bypassing the study of atoms and molecules in favor of more pressing concerns such as environmental hazards existing in the neighborhood, the dangers of tattoos, especially the do-it-yourself kind, and why it is not a good idea to use a pen as eyeliner. Was this the right approach? Was I doing students a disservice by not focusing on the standard knowledge of science that students with college in their future needed to have? I didn't know whether I was taking the right approach or not, but at least the students seemed somewhat interested.

As a team, teachers focused on building our students' self-esteem and constantly gave the message to students in subtle and not so subtle ways that they could succeed at whatever they wanted. Of course, they didn't really believe us, and I have to wonder whether we really believed it either. It was a source of great frustration for all of us to realize that what we were doing was simply not enough but not knowing what to do differently.

I was especially concerned about the young women in my classes. In some ways, they were typical adolescent females, interested in things other than school, but in their case, the problem was much more serious. Many of these young women were involved in risky behaviors outside of school, and some had already become part of the juvenile justice system.

One day, one of those rare, serendipitous events took place that teachers live for. It made a difference in the way students perceived themselves and their options for the future and in the way I viewed my role as a teacher. I had arranged for Wildlife on Wheels to come to my science class. The program was highly regarded, and wildlife biologists brought actual animals of all sorts into classrooms for students to experience firsthand. I must have subconsciously expected an Anglo male to do this presentation because I was as shocked as the students when a young Latina woman walked into my classroom with a fascinating array of live animals. Not only was this woman young and Latina, she was also what my students referred to as "Bad!," which of course translates into "really cool." She had the clothes, the fingernails, the jewelry, and absolutely everything that my students admired. I even heard one student whisper, "Is that Selena?!" It wasn't the famous Latina pop star, but it might as well have been. The students in my class, male and female alike, were spellbound. They could not take their eyes off this intelligent, articulate young woman, and they hung on her every word. She seemed to know everything there was to know about animals and answered each student's questions with care, consideration, and accuracy. Sometimes she spoke to them in Spanish. The female students in the class glanced at each other with amazed expressions. Science had suddenly become a wonderful thing for them, something that real people do. Forget the fact that boa constrictors were not found anywhere near our immediate environment. The relevance was not in the content but rather in the person who delivered it. This person looked like someone my students wanted to be like.

When the presentation was over, a group of five girls I worried about the most hung around in the classroom, talking quietly among themselves. Finally, one young woman, designated as the spokesman, quietly asked me, "Hey Miss, do you think we could do that?" The emotion I felt at that moment has not diminished to this day. I am still overcome when I remember the sincerity of her question and the timidity not often seen in this outwardly bold girl. The fact that she and the other girls saw a glimmer of possibility for themselves, options that they had not realized before, was amazing. After getting a hold of myself, I replied, "Of course you can. Why not?" It was the same message I had repeated time and time again. The difference was that this time, the students actually believed me.

Reflecting on the Game

1. What factors would you consider in creating an inclusive learning environment in a science classroom?
2. Why should the lack of minority participation in science be of concern to everyone?
3. Explain why a "one size fits all" approach to science education is ineffective.
4. What are the characteristics of effective role models for all students?
5. What can teachers do to encourage minority parental involvement?
6. What can teachers do to accommodate different world views in the science classroom?

References

Aikenhead, G. S. (1996). Science education: Border crossing into the subculture of science. *Studies in Science Education, 27,* 1–52.

Allen, N. J., & Crawley, F. E. (1998). Voices from the bridge: Worldview conflicts of Kickapoo students of science. *Journal of Research in Science Teaching, 35,* 111–132.

American Association for the Advancement of Science. (1989). *Science for all Americans.* Washington, DC: Author.

American Association for the Advancement of Science. (1993). *Benchmarks for science literacy: Project 2061.* New York: Oxford University Press.

Ascher, M. (1991). *Ethnomathematics: A multicultural view of mathematical ideas.* Pacific Grove, CA: Brooks/Cole.

Atwater, M. (1996). Social constructivism: Infusion into the multicultural science education research agenda. *Journal of Research in Science Teaching, 33,* 821–838.

Atwater, M. (1998). Science literacy through the lens of critical feminist interpretive frameworks. *Journal of Research in Science Teaching, 35*(4), 375–377.

Banks, J. A. (1994). *An Introduction to multicultural education.* Boston, MA: Allyn and Bacon.

Banks, J. A. (2001). *Cultural diversity and education,* 4th ed. Boston: Allyn and Bacon.

Barba, R. H. (1998). Science in the multicultural classroom. Needham Heights, MA: Allyn and Bacon.

Barton, A. C. (1998). *Feminist science education.* New York: Teachers College Press.

Barton, A. C., Hindin, T., Contento, I. R., Trudeau, M., Yang, K., Hagiwara, S., & Koch, P. D. (2001). Underprivileged urban mothers perspectives on science. *Journal of Research in Science Teaching, 38,* 688–711.

Belfiore, J., & Barton, A. C. (1999). *Report: Supporting parents through advocacy, reform and science knowledge* (Technical Report). New York: Wildlife Conservation Society.

Benedek, E. (1995). *Beyond the four corners of the world: A Navajo woman's journey.* Norman, OK: University of Oklahoma Press

Blank, R. K., & Gruebel, D. (1995). *State indicators of science and mathematics education 1995: State-by-state trends and new indicators from the 1993–94 school year.* Washington, DC: Council of Chief State School Officers.

Bouillion, L. M., & Gomez, L. M. (2001). Connecting school and community with science learning: Real world problems and school-community partnerships as contextual scaffolds. *Journal of Research in Science Teaching, 38,* 878–898.

Brickhouse, N. (1994). Bringing in the outsiders: Reshaping the sciences of the future. *Curriculum Studies, 26,* 401–416.

Brown, J. S., Collins, A., & Duguid, P. (1989). Situated cognition and the culture of learning. *Educational Researcher, 18*(1), 32–42.

Bullock, L. D. (1997). Efficacy of a gender and ethnic equity in science education curriculum for preservice teachers. *Journal of Research in Science Teaching, 34*(10), 1019–1038.

Cahape, P., & Howley, C. B. (Eds.). (1992). *Indian Nations at Risk: Listening to the People.* Washington, DC: U.S. Department of Education. (ERIC Document Reproduction Service ED 339 588)

Clark, J. V. (1999). Minorities in science and mathematics: A challenge for change. *ERIC Review K–8 Science and Mathematics Education.* 2(6), 40–42.

Cobern, W. W. (1996). Worldview theory and conceptual change in science education. *Science Education, 80*(5), 579–610.

Cobern, W. W., & Loving, C. C. (2001). Defining "science" in a multicultural world: Implications for science education. *Science Education, 85,* 50–67.

Cole, M. (1985). The zone of proximal development: Where culture and cognition meet. In J. V. Wertsch (Ed.), *Culture, communication and cognition: Vygotskian perspectives.* Cambridge, England: Cambridge University Press.

Costa, V. B. (1995). When science is "another world": Relationships between worlds of family, friends, school, and science. *Science Education, 79*(3), 331–333.

de Carvalho, M. E. P. (2001). *Rethinking family-school relations: A critique of parental involve-*

ment in schooling. Mahwah, NJ: Lawrence Erlbaum Associates.

Deloria, V. (1992). Ethnoscience and Indian realities. *Winds of Change, 7*(3), 12–18.

Duran, B. J., Dugan, T., & Weffer, R. (1997). Increasing teacher effectiveness with language minority students. *The High School Journal, 80,* 238–246.

Duran, B. J., Dugan, T., & Weffer, R. (1998). Language minority students in high school: The role of language in learning biology concepts. *Science Education, 82,* 311–341.

Duschl, R. A., & Wright, E. (1989). A case study of high school teachers' decision making models for planning and teaching science. *Journal of Research in Science Teaching, 26,* 467–501.

Elrich, M. (1994). The stereotype within. *Educational Leadership, 8*(51), 172–175.

Epstein, J. (1987). Parent involvement: What research says to administrators. *Education and Urban Society, 19,* 119–136.

Funkhouser, M., & Gonzales, J. (1997). *Family involvement in children's education.* Washington, DC: U.S. Department of Education.

Galindo, E., & Rinehart, B. (2002, Spring). *Indian Summer VII.* (Available from Native American Science Research and Education Program, Sho-Ban High School, P.O. Box 709, Fort Hall, ID 83203)

Garcia, R. L. (2001) Language, culture, and education. In J. A. Banks (Ed.), *Cultural diversity and education* (pp. 268–292). Boston: Allyn and Bacon.

Gilbert, S. E., & Gay, G. (1985). Improving the success in school of poor black children. *Phi Delta Kappan, 10,* 133–137.

Gilliland, H. (1988). *Teaching the Native American.* Dubuque, IA: Kendall-Hunt.

Good, R. (1995). Comments on multicultural science education. *Science Education, 3*(79), 335–336.

Grant, C. A., & Tate, W. F. (1995). Multicultural education through the lens of the multicultural research literature. In J. A. Banks & C. A. Banks (Eds.), *Handbook of research on multicultural education.* New York: Macmillan.

Gross, P., & Levitt, N. (1994). *Higher superstition: The academic left and its quarrels with science.* Baltimore, MD: Johns Hopkins University Press.

Hammond, L. (2001). Notes from California: An anthropological approach to urban science education for language minority students. *Journal of Research in Science Teaching, 38,* 983–999.

Healy, J. M. (1990). *Endangered minds: Children's learning in today's culture.* New York: Simon and Schuster.

Heck, D. J. (1998). Evaluating equity in statewide systemic initiatives: Asking the right questions. *Journal of Women and Minorities in Science and Engineering, 4*(2), 161–181.

Hillebrand, G. M (1996, March). *Writing in/forms science learning.* Paper presented at the annual meeting of the National Association for Research in Science Teaching, St. Louis.

Hodgkinson, H. L. (1992). *A demographic look at tomorrow.* Washington, DC: Institute for Educational Leadership, Center for Demographic Policy.

Hodson, D. (1993). In search of a rationale for multicultural science education. *Science Education, 77,* 685–711.

Indian Nations at Risk Task Force. (1991). *Indians nations at risk: An educational strategy for change.* Washington, DC: U.S. Department of Education.

Jegede, O. J., & Okebukola, P. A. (1991). The relationship between African traditional cosmology and students: Acquisition of a science process skill. *International Journal of Science Education, 13*(1), 37–47.

Johnson, M. (Ed.). (1992). *Lore: Capturing traditional environmental knowledge.* Ottawa, Ontario: Dene Cultural Institute, International Development Research Center.

Karplus, R. (1974). *Science curriculum improvement study: Teachers handbook.* Berkeley, CA: Lawrence Hall of Science.

Laguarda, K. G., Breckenridge, J. S., & Hightower, A. M. (1994). *Assessment programs in the statewide systemic initiative (SSI) states: Using student achievement data to evaluate the SSI.* Washington, DC: Policy Studies Associates.

Lave, J. (1988). *Cognition in practice.* Cambridge, England: Cambridge University Press.

Lawson, A. E., & Worsnop, W. A. (1992). Learning about evolution and rejecting a belief in special creation: Effects of reflective reasoning skill, prior knowledge, prior belief and religious commitment. *Journal of Research in Science Teaching, 29*(2), 143–166.

Lee, O. (1999). Equity implications based on the conceptions of science achievement in major reform documents. *Review of Education Research, 69*(1), 83–115.

Left Handed. (1938). *Left Handed, Son of Old Man Hat: A Navajo autobiography.* New York: Harcourt, Brace and Company.

Lemke, J. L. (1990). *Talking science: Language, learning, and values.* Norwood, NJ: Ablex.

Lewis, B. F., & Collins, A. (2001). Interpretive investigation of the science-related career decisions of three African-American college students. *Journal of Research in Science Teaching, 38*(5), 599–621.

Luft, J. A., Bragg, J., & Peters, C. (1999). Learning to teach in a diverse setting: A case study of a multicultural science education enthusiast. *Science Education, 83,* 537–543.

Lynch, S. Atwater, M., Crawley, J., Eccles, J., Lee, O., Marrett, C., Rojas-Medlin, O., Secada, W., Stefanich, G., Willeto, A. (1996). *An equity blueprint for Project 2061 science education reform: Second draft.* Washington, DC: American Association for the Advancement of Science, Project 2061.

Malen, B., Ogawa, R. T., & Krantz, J. (1990). Site based management: Unfulfilled promises. *The School Administrator, 8*(47), 30–32, 53–57.

Matthews, M. (1994). *Science teaching: The role of history and philosophy in science.* New York: Routlege.

Mayes, V. O., & Lacy, B. B. (1989). *Nanisé: A Navajo herbal.* Tsaile, AZ: Navajo Community College Press.

Mercer, N. (1993). Culture, context and the construction of knowledge in the classroom. In P. Light & G. Butterworth (Eds.), *Context and cognition: Ways of learning and knowing.* Mahwah, NJ: Lawrence Erlbaum Associates.

Moles, O. C. (1993). Collaboration between schools and disadvantaged parents: Obstacles and openings. In N. F. Chavkin (Ed.), *Families and schools in a pluralistic society* (pp. 21–49). Albany, NY: State University of New York Press.

Monhardt, R. (1999, January). *The compatibility of the Navajo worldview and the nature of science: Implications for science education.* Paper presented at the AETS Annual International Meeting, Austin, TX.

Monhardt, R. M. (in press). The image of the scientist through the eyes of Navajo children. *Journal of American Indian Education.*

Monhardt, R. M., Spotted-Elk, N., Bigman, D., Valentine, D., & Dee, H. (2002). It's about people: A successful school/university partnership. *Winds of Change, 17*(1), 14–17.

National Research Council. (1996). *National science education standards.* Washington, DC: National Academy Press.

National Science Teachers Association. (2001/2002). NAEP 2000 science scores show no significant change since 1996. *NSTA Reports, 13*(3), 1, 3.

National Science Foundation. (1994). *Women, minorities, and persons with disabilities in science and engineering.* Washington, DC: National Science Foundation.

Nelson-Barber, S., & Estrin, E. T. (1995). Bringing Native American perspectives to mathematics and science teaching. *Theory into Practice, 34*(3), 174–185.

Norman, O. (1998). Marginalized discourses and scientific literacy. *Journal of Research in Science Teaching, 35*(4), 365–374.

Ogawa, M. (1995). Science education in a multi-science perspective. *Science Education, 79*(5), 583–593.

Ortiz de Montellano, B. R. (2001). Multicultural science: Who benefits. *Science Education, 85,* 77–79.

Ovando, C. (1992). Science. In J. Reyhner (Ed.), *Teaching American Indian students* (pp. 223–240). Norman, OK: University of Oklahoma Press.

Pitman, M. A. (1989). *Culture acquisition: A holistic approach to human learning.* New York: Praeger.

Posey, J. D. (1998). Exploring indigenous pedagogies: Why is this knowledge important to today's educators? *The Researcher, 13*(1), 71–78.

Rakow, S. J. (1988). Famous minority scientists as role models for elementary science. *The Texas Science Teacher, 17,* 18–20.

Rakow, S. J., & Bermudez, A. B. (1993). Science is "ciencia": Meeting the needs of Hispanic American students. *Science Education, 77,* 669–683.

Reyes, M. L., & Molner, L. A. (1991). Instructional strategies for second language learners in the content areas. *Journal of Reading, 35,* 96–103.

Rodriquez, A. J. (1997). The dangerous discourse of invisibility: A critique of the National Research Council's National Science Education Standards. *Journal of Research in Science Teaching, 34*(1), 19–37.

Rodriquez, A. J. (1998). Busting open the meritocracy myth: Rethinking equity and student achievement in science education. *Journal of Women and Minorities in Science and Engineering, 4,* 195–216.

Ross, D., & Smith, W. (1992). Understanding preservice teachers' perspectives on diversity. *Journal of Teacher Education, 43,* 94–103.

Rosser, S. (1990). *Female friendly science.* New York: Teacher's College Press.

Roth, K. J. (1995, April). *Stories of alienation and connection: Examining the neighborhood of science from the margins.* Paper presented at the annual meeting of the American Educational Research Association, San Francisco. pp. 18–22.

Schik, J. M., Arewa, E. O., Thomson, B. S., & White, A. L. (1995). How do Native American children view science? *The National Center for Science Teaching and Learning Research Quarterly, 4*(3), 1–4.

Schwarz, M. T. (1997). *Molded in the image of Changing Woman.* Tucson, AZ: The University of Arizona Press.

Scribner-Maclean, M. (1996). Science at home. *Science and Children, 34,* 44–48.

Selin, H. (1993). Science across cultures. *The Science Teacher, 60*(3), 38–44.

Semken, S. C., & Morgan, F. (1997). Navajo pedagogy and earth systems. *Journal of Geoscience Education, 45,* 109–112.

Sipes, D. S. B. (1993). Cultural values and American-Indian families. In N. F. Chavkin (Ed.), *Families and schools in a pluralistic society* (pp. 157–173). Albany, NY: State University of New York Press.

Sleeter, C. E., & Grant, C. A. (1987). An analysis of multicultural education in the United States. *Harvard Educational Review, 57*(4), 421–444.

Smith, F. M., & Hausafus, C. C. (1998). Relationship of family support and ethnic minority students' achievement in science and mathematics. *Science Education, 82,* 111–125.

Smolkin, L., Surnia, J. H., & Mercado, M. (1995, April). *Preparing teachers for diversity: A cross-cultural rural/urban teacher preparation program.* Paper presented at the American Educational Research Association Meeting, San Francisco, CA. pp. 18–22.

Snively, G., & Corsiglia, J. (2001). Discovering indigenous science: Implications for science education. *Science Education, 85*(6), 6–34.

Tressel, G. W. (1984). A museum to touch. In *Encyclopedia Britannica, 1984 Yearbook of Science and the Future.* Chicago: Encyclopedia Britannica.

Wertsch, J. V. (1991). *Voices of the mind; A sociocultural approach to medicated action.* Cambridge, MA: Harvard University Press.

Williams-Norton, M. E., Reisdorf, M., & Spees, S. (1990). Home is where science is. *Science and Children, 27*(6), 12–15.

Additional Resources

Avery, S., & Skinner, L. (1992). *Extraordinary American Indians.* Chicago: Children's Press.

Cajete, G. (2000). *Native science.* Santa Fe, NM: Clear Light Publishers.

DeLoria, V. (1995). *Red earth, white lies: Native Americans and the myth of scientific fact.* New York: Scribners.

McPherson, R. S. (1992). *Sacred land sacred view.* Salt Lake City, UT: Signature Books.

Miller, D. S. (1997). *Stars of the first people.* Boulder, CO: Pruett Publishing Company.

Slapin, B., & Seale, D. (1998). *Through Indian eyes. The Native experience in books for children.* Los Angeles: American Indian Studies Center.

Weatherford, J. (1988). *Indian givers: How the Indians of the Americas transformed the world.* New York: Fawcett Columbine.

start

chapter

7

ACCESSIBLE

SCIENCE EDUCATION:

Every Student a Player

John Stiles, Ph.D.
President of Science Education
for Students with Disabilities and
Science Education Consultant,
Milbridge, Maine

ABOUT THE AUTHOR: Dr. John Stiles has been an educator for over thirty years in three states and four countries. Having taught from elementary to graduate levels, he is currently a high school principal in Thailand. He received a B.A. in biology and an M.S. and Ph.D. in science education. As an advocate for students with disabilities, Dr. Stiles has published widely on practical and theoretical dimensions of inclusive science education. He is the president of Science Education for Students with Disabilities.

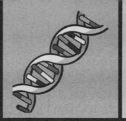

> **The mandate for equal opportunity doesn't dictate disregard for the differences in candidates' qualities and skills. There is no constitutional right to play ball. All there is is a right to compete for it on equal terms.**
>
> —Tim Ellis
> *U.S. District Judge, Virginia*

CHAPTER WARM-UP

Eleven percent of school-age children in the United States fall into the category of "disabled." This presents both a challenge and a pressing national priority to present science as an accessible and engaging enterprise for all our students who will become voters, consumers, parents, and professionals who rely on sound science education. The strategies for meeting the challenge include the same modern techniques that make science a successful pursuit for all learners: a relevant, active, stimulating curriculum in the hands of compassionate, creative practitioners.

INTRODUCTION: To Be Science-Minded

If science education were the Olympics, U.S. students—by international rules—would be far down the medal tally list. Our students tend to perform, well, average on international tests designed to measure achievement in math and science (National Science Teachers Association, 2001/2002). For decades, this has not sat well with some educators, many parents, and most politicians.

Science education, like sports, has its critics. These academic versions of "armchair quarterbacks" frequently second-guess coaches and players in the science education game. Yet these criticisms are most likely to be seen as misguided only by teachers themselves. For example, when the dismal results of U.S. students on international tests in math and science were reported a few years ago, National Public Radio solemnly announced the findings and included some of the questions that were often missed by students who took the test. Then NPR did a curious thing: It gave the answers on the air. The irony in this is that the very basis for school criticism—that kids don't have all the answers—turned out to be the case for NPR listeners as well. If the answers were obvious, why the need to air them?

Likewise, in the newsletter of the National Science Teachers Association, test results were reported, examples were noted, and *the answers were given!* The world's largest science teacher organization thought that it was necessary to give the answers to the teachers of the kids who took the test. Maybe science education reform advocates are right: Few of us have enjoyed a style of science education that makes science a permanent part of our understanding of how the world works.

But do our students' performances on international exams really merit the familiar rhetoric of school shortcoming? How can our mediocre students and their failing schools be leading the world in science, engineering, and technology advancement?

Perhaps science educators hinted at this dilemma some years ago. Long Beach State University science educator Alan Colburn (1990) warned that our children might well pay a heavy price for the rush to make our students "number one" in science. In an article in *Education Week,* Colburn cautioned that we should not compare U.S. students to students in countries where sorting by testing occurs at a very early age, often as young as fourth grade, such as Singapore, which usually scores ahead of the United States on international tests. Even if we did decide to pursue the necessary means to outperform such countries, Colburn argues, the damage done to our kids by "teaching to the test" would not be worth the effort.

It would appear to many that Colburn was right. Now that the United States has in place a system for national tests (No Child Left Behind Act, 2001), many concerned educators have predicted that curricula will be narrowed, standardized curricula will be adopted, and much time will be spent in preparing students for testing. This hits hard at the core of U.S. education, which was originally designed to decentralize control and add creativity and flexibility.

This trend is also worrying to those who advocate for students who have disabilities. The winnowing process in science still occurs in most countries and results in a separation of the haves and have-nots. Until recently, the U.S. education system has been able to resist that kind of thinking. But the political clamor for standardized education and testing portends a tough road ahead for students who have special needs. (The topic of testing in general is addressed more thoroughly in Chapter 11.)

This trend mirrors the process by which most sports teams are chosen. Everyone might be allowed to try out, but in the end, most end up on the sidelines cheering their superiorly talented fellows on to victory. Is that where U.S. education—and science education in particular—is headed? Should science education be more than a filtering and processing plant for future scientists?

Societies have tended to devalue people with disabilities and have had lowered expectations for them, resulting in low self-esteem of the disabled and diminished academic performance by students who have disabilities (Stefanich et al., 2001). With lowered expectations and lack of confidence, disabled people often end up pursuing careers below their abilities.

If our society is to reverse this attitude, science teachers can be leaders in the effort. Although science has historically been the last place in schools where students with disabilities find support and encouragement, it could easily be the first. Science is well suited to students who have disabilities, as long as teachers are aware of the modifications and adaptations that have to be made. Inquiry-based science is an effective vehicle by which all students can experience success. Add to that the lengthy list of outstanding scientists who have disabilities, and the picture looks bright for equal access in science. This chapter will help to explain how science teachers can and do make a difference.

Sports Games Versus Science Education

Allowing equal opportunity but keeping requirements the same as they were in the past does not guarantee equal treatment or outcomes. These people who prevail are the ones for whom the game or sport was initially created. Thus, the more physically abled remain as participants while others watch or have parallel games created that are specially designed for the less able. Even with equal opportunity for females, the games of sport are largely segregated, with a few notable exceptions such as mixed doubles in tennis.

Olympic events, for example, have top male and female participants in gender-segregated competitions, and disabled athletes hold their own "Paralympics" and "Special Olympics." Understandably, these sporting events would lose appeal if the most able did not compete in them.

A Different Kind of Game

The game of science, however, is a very different kind of game. The greatest difference between science and sports is that in a team sport, various degrees of high physical ability are usually involved, whereas in science, many different kinds of abilities are at play simultaneously. Kinesthetic manipulation and coordination, intellectual problem solving, creative thought, various types of communication (reading, speaking, signaling, writing), and use of process skills (observing, recording, measuring, analysis) are all important in science classrooms and laboratories. Although a few talented individuals might possess most or all of these diverse abilities, most scientific endeavors are done in teams in which individual strengths contribute to the success of the investigation or research.

This allows scientists to focus on what they can do rather than on what they cannot do. Such a model gives the term "equal access" a boost in implementation, particularly in schools. Indeed, the game of science boasts a long list of individuals whose talents far outweigh their perceived limitations.

Success Despite Barriers

In highlighting just a few modern-day scientists who often overcame tremendous barriers to become researchers, inventors, or teachers, it becomes an obvious error in judgment to assume that these scientists were ever incapable of scientific work. It also begs the question of how many would-be scientists were discouraged from contributing to the field by well-meaning but misguided advisors who assumed that science was not a proper career choice.

Opportunity Is the Key

Blinded at an early age, Geerat Vermeij, now professor of evolutionary biology and paleontology at University of California–Davis, followed his passion of investigating the natural world thanks to his parents and caring teachers, who encouraged him to take risks (Vermeij, 1997). Despite obvious barriers in science, which is often a visual endeavor, Vermeij proved that a blind biologist could succeed by interpreting nature through sensations other than sight. Indeed, his success is partly attributed to his sense of touch, which allowed him to discern minute differences in shell structure. "Seeing" from a different perspective and having a fierce passion for the study of nature vaulted Vermeij to the ranks of international renown in evolutionary marine biology.

"A conscious effort must be made," says Vermeij, "to acquaint a blind person with those aspects of the environment that cannot be heard, smelled, or easily grasped by hands and fingers" (Vermeij, 2002). Vermeij reminds teachers that even things that can be heard, for example, must be pointed out to blind students, drawing attention to what is "often just part of the background noise."

What does Vermeij say that a blind person needs to succeed in science? Like any other person, a blind student must have "opportunity, curiosity, intelligence, and a willingness to work hard." If teachers encourage these things, then blind students can—and do—succeed.

"We teach science," says Vermeij, "by putting the theory and methods of science into practice and by letting opportunity, observation, hypothesis, adaptation, and the power and beauty of scientific explanation do their work."

From Autism to Invention

Temple Grandin, assistant professor of animal science at Colorado State University, is an internationally known consultant, educator, and inventor of livestock-handling equipment. She has appeared on television shows such as *20/20, 48 Hours,* and *CNN Larry King Live* and has been featured in *People Magazine,* the *New York Times,* and *U.S. News & World Report.* She has also published over 300 articles in scientific journals and livestock periodicals (Grandin, 2002).

Diagnosed with autism at a very early age, Grandin was highly sensitive to stimulation, particularly sounds. Like many scientists, Grandin is a visual thinker; her entire thought process comes in the form of pictures (Grandin, 2000). She was fortunate to have caring teachers who recognized her needs and structured the classroom in such a way that she received consistent instruction by "teachers who know how to be firm and gentle" (Grandin, 2000).

The Silence of Physics

Harry Lang, now professor of physics at Rochester Institute of Technology, was stricken with meningitis at age fifteen, which left him profoundly deaf (National Science Foundation, 1998). Supported and encouraged by his family, Lang graduated from the Western Pennsylvania School for the Deaf in Pittsburgh, then went on to major in physics at Bethany College, where he succeeded despite a lack of support services (interpreting, note taking), which were not available in the late 1960s (Lang, 2002).

During the course of his studies and teaching at RIT, Lang noticed that there were no books about deaf people in science-related careers. Determined to do something about it, Lang read hundreds of resources, finding information about more than 800 deaf scientists. He has written four books on science and technology, the contributions of deaf men and women in the history of science, and implications of educational research for teaching. An author of more than fifty scholarly works, Lang is currently directing projects that connect interested students and parents to resources for deaf education, particularly in science (see "Additional Resources" at the end of the chapter).

Lang relies on his communication skills of lip reading, oral speech, sign language, and writing to relay and gain information. He is an enthusiastic supporter of the use of the Internet for communication, finding it a wonderful way to break down barriers. He looks forward to advances in speech recognition and speech-to-print technologies, which will further facilitate communication with others.

These few notable examples of current scientists and educators give reasons why the game of science must include all students from a very early age. It is not enough to stir them into the classroom pot. Teachers must give them complete access to the joys of learning and find ways to tap into their special gifts rather than basing assumptions on perceived limitations. This is particularly crucial in this age of standardization, in which students with disabilities can be pushed aside in the rush to raise test scores. Education must be more than that. As teachers, we need to renew the passion to find that spark in each student that will drive her or him forward to success.

One might well wonder how many other students, for one reason or another, were discouraged from enrolling in science courses or seeking science-related careers. Surely, the numbers must be significant. These scientists were educated in an age in which accessibility in science was not supported by legislation and was simply deemed impossible or frivolous by educators as well as by society as a whole.

Changing the Rules

For decades, students with disabilities were isolated from their peers while being educated in "special" schools or classrooms. Those were the lucky ones. For many, their disability was never recognized or diagnosed; and others were simply ignored for a number of bureaucratic reasons: The school had no money to give special services; teachers had no training in working with special needs students; social attitudes had not gotten to the point of advocacy or action; or their plight was simply not considered important enough to take away resources from "normal" students.

As students with disabilities gained more support from the changing social structure of the United States in the 1960s and 1970s, classrooms became more accessible. Special programs funneled money into education for disabled students, and the number of teachers who were trained in special education grew. Education of disabled students was still mainly done in isolation, however, though some students were partially or fully "mainstreamed" into the regular classroom.

More Players into the Game

In 1973, Congress passed the Individuals with Disabilities Education Act (Individuals with Disabilities Education Act, 1973); it was amended in 1990 (Americans with Disabilities Act, 1990) and in 1997. Congress realized the need for people with disabilities to have the same experiences, services, and opportunities that had always been accessible to the general public but often were denied to the disabled (previously referred to as "handicapped").

Although some educators complained that these amendments drained needed resources from the "regular" classroom or gave resources to special needs students at the "expense" of other students, those eventually became minority sentiments. However, it is not unusual to hear such comments today. For some, this game will never be the same, now that we have removed barriers to the "less able." According to those opponents, our teams will now suffer from the addition of those for whom the game was not originally designed. Greg Stefanich, a nationally recognized expert in science and disabilities, has responded to these criticisms. In a paper presented at the National Science Teachers Association's annual convention (2001a), Stefanich noted that disabled students "are not receiving something extra; they are gaining access to what the general population has taken for granted as being universally available."

In contrast to the basketball court or football field, the K–12 classroom is ideally suited for inclusive participation, including science. Multimodality instruction is exciting for children and can be achieved with great success in classrooms where teachers not only are well aware of the benefits, but also are experienced or trained in its implementation. As Stefanich notes, "Group synergism can become more powerful than the collective output of each person acting independently." This includes students who have one or more disability. Their passion is no less than that of any other student; often what they lack is support from caring teachers. If given this, they can become productive members of the classroom team.

What the New Rules Say

The IDEA legislation has changed the way in which the game of science (and general education) is played. These rules now involve modifications in the child's educational environment as well as the responsibilities of the science educator (Stefanich, 2001a).

Regular classroom teachers, including science teachers, are now part of a student's Individual Education Plan (IEP) team. The teacher must now be an active player in the review and development of educational plans that best suit the individual student.

Classroom teachers now collaborate with parents, special education teachers, administrators, and students to coordinate plans to implement interventions and adaptations recommended by the IEP team. This can be an exciting opportunity for science educators to include science in the IEP; in the past, unfortunately, science was ignored in the IEP in favor of language arts and math. However, science can be one of the best vehicles for disabled students to become engaged in meaningful and collaborative learning in the classroom. Science teachers can now take advantage of the legislation to push for inclusion and a recognition of science as a natural environment for students who have disabilities.

Access to—and placement in—the regular classroom is mandated by law at the federal, state, and local levels. This requires classroom teachers to modify classroom expectations to fully meet the needs and abilities of all students. Again, science is an excellent format for modification. With sometimes minor adjustments in strategies and materials, all students can enjoy science.

Despite the clear mandate for schools to include all students in the least restrictive environment, there is sometimes confusion about, or downright foot-dragging in, the process of abiding by the new game rules. This is seen in sports all the time; but with universal application, the rules eventually become incorporated into each venue, and the game goes on.

The Old Rules Often Still Prevail

Outside of the United States and in isolated pockets within this country, the new rules have had a difficult time taking hold. In the former, the laws simply do not apply, giving practitioners free rein to play by their own rules, while in the latter, it is often a case of a lack of oversight or support.

Making Their Own Rules

In the early 1990s, as a member of an international school faculty in a large Southeast Asian city, I took part in a comprehensive one-year plan to design a new state-of-the-art school that was to be built in a new location far from the polluted city center. Science teams met throughout the year to discuss and design our "dream" facility, as did educators in all other academic areas.

During one of the all-faculty meetings to discuss our progress, the conversation turned to accessibility for disabled students. After a very brief discussion, much to my surprise and dismay, the consensus was that because we were a private school and we could have a very selective admission policy, the new school should not admit special needs students. The reasoning was that we simply "did not have the services required" to admit students who were disabled. Although the initial discussion centered on wheelchair accessibility, there was no distinction between disabilities, and the policy eventually included physically as well as learning or intellectually disabled children.

Keep in mind that this discussion occurred in a country in which schools were not compelled to serve special needs students. Students in government schools were taught in separate facilities, and private schools were under no legal obligation to admit students who had disabilities. The thinking was that they could "go somewhere else."

At the next meeting, I pointed out that if our school were to adopt such a policy, we would, in effect, be barring a Stephen Hawking from attending. Hawking is the British physicist who is the leading thinker in finding a way to resolve the differences in relativity and quantum mechanics in the search for a unified theory. Hawking has amyotrophic lateral sclerosis, or Lou Gehrig's disease, which not only confines him to a wheelchair, but has rendered him practically speechless as well. I added that this would also preclude any future student who might have a paralyzing accident or parents and visitors who might need assistance in entering and moving throughout the school.

Eventually, the school was built with accessibility in mind and is truly a fine facility. I wonder whether the design might today be different had the subject not arisen. I also wonder how many simple design changes could have been made—but weren't, owing to lack of advocacy at the time. There are plenty of examples of inaccessibility around the world, despite our progress in access design.

Often, it is not malicious intent, but ignorance that affects decision making. As games evolve, so do the rules. In fact, it is rather like coevolution in nature: Sometimes it is difficult to determine which caused the other.

Games, like education, have rules that are set up according to the goals of the inventor, and many times these rules are laid out without thought about future modifications that might become necessary. Can you imagine basketball being played with a lane that is a mere six feet wide? Yet it was originally designed that way, and the tiny lane was used until Wilt Chamberlain came along, forcing changes in the rules. In science education, the "rules" excluded impaired students until a stream of talented students with disabilities proved that the rules needed to be changed despite the misgivings of purists, as always exist in any endeavor, including sports.

Ignorance of the Rules Is No Excuse

A small liberal arts college on the coast of New England prides itself on its pristine location and environment: Ocean waves gently massage the shoreline on which the college sits, offering unparalleled views of coastal serenity, and shaded footpaths wind through the campus landscape. The majestic administration building, a former mansion built in the 1800s, provides a strikingly beautiful center to the college. It is, one would think, the perfect place to study—perfect, that is, if you are not disabled.

The college's small faculty (approximately twenty-five) includes an influential core group of scientists who have great power over the college's curricula and philosophy. In the mid-1990s, the college admitted several students with disabilities, both learning disabled and physically challenged. These students found it increasingly frustrating to succeed owing to enormous barriers that existed. For example, although a wheelchair ramp allowed access into the administration building, the entrance hall was as far as any wheelchair could get. The administration offices on the second and third floors were accessible only by stairs, as were several of the faculty offices and one classroom. Unable to get to the offices, physically disabled students and visitors had to bear the humiliation of waiting for people to come downstairs to talk with them. The building could have accommodated motorized railing seats on a staircase as a solution to the problem.

Similarly, the gravel pathways and drives were impossible for wheelchairs to traverse, and winter ice made locomotion on crutches particularly hazardous. Faculty offices located in pastoral cottages scattered about the campus were also inaccessible to these visitors, either because the cottages did not have ramps or because they were situated on hillsides.

For learning-disabled students, the most difficult aspect of being at the college was the perceived lack of understanding or compassion by faculty, particularly those in the sciences. For most, it was a struggle, even with faculty advocates, to get basic accommodations such as extra time for tests. Science faculty members were reluctant to modify what had proudly become a rigorous academic experience. One faculty member, who based her entrance requirements on a timed essay, noted that although some students might find that difficult, "We all have some kind of disability."

During a visit by a well-known expert on science and disabilities, science faculty members continued to rationalize their de facto exclusionary practices, maintaining that they did not see why they had to change their curricula for one student. The visiting science educator took them to task by bluntly telling them that "unless your class cannot learn the material without venturing onto terrain inaccessible to a disabled student, then by doing so, you are breaking the law."

Often, the inertia of those who wield power inhibits progress until legal action is taken. The above scenario did take place—and likely is continuing at that school, as in many other places. The game has new rules, but they have yet to be fully embraced or even acknowledged in some cases.

 ## The Player as Coach

Not many years ago, I was supervising student teachers in middle and high school science classrooms. I particularly enjoyed visiting one high school biology class, as the student teacher was doing a fabulous job of implementing inquiry science into a traditionally lecture-format classroom.

One of the students in the class was blind. Accompanying her during every class was an aide, who assisted her with note taking and interpretation of visual teaching activities. The student teacher and I spent a good deal of time brainstorming ideas for instructional modification, and he was able to move toward a more student-centered approach, which offered hands-on learning.

Despite the successes, we were not satisfied with the limits his teaching had for the blind student. During a break, I sat with the student and chatted with her about her impressions of the class and the current lessons in genetics. What I learned from this brief encounter was monumental in its implications for perceiving the needs of the blind. The student had mentioned that although she was able to follow the text and lessons due to the Braille translations, nonetheless she was stumped by the concept of X and Y chromosomes. To her, they didn't make sense.

It suddenly occurred to me that the reason for this was that the chromosomes had gotten their names from their physical structure. That is, they looked like the letters X and Y to sighted people. To a blind person, who had never seen the chromosomes, or any representation of them, describing them as a series of what the student read as Braille dots was confusing! Sometimes the simplest assumptions are the greatest barriers. The student teacher made three-dimensional figures for the student, who immediately grasped the connection and gained a greater conceptual understanding of genetics.

I later learned from Geerat Vermeij (2002) that there are several low-tech methods for making visual material in science accessible to the blind. One way is to take a standard sheet of paper, place it on a soft, yielding surface such as a pile of newspapers, and then with a sharp pencil or pen trace an illustration by pressing firmly while drawing. "On the back side of the sheet, a mirror image of what you have drawn will emerge in a raised format"—simple, but effective. It is not so simple unless the method is taught, however.

From these lessons, two things become clear: Students with disabilities are quite capable of learning in an inclusive classroom setting, and the question of whether they can succeed or not often depends on the attitude and commitment of their teachers. As in sports, it is usually the most perceptive and caring coach who notices a buried potential in a player and brings it to fruition through perseverance and compassion.

 ## Learning to Play by the New Rules

Whenever new rules are proposed or implemented, whether in sports or education, old habits and attitudes often linger, slowing the transition to the new rule or paradigm. Let's look at what the three situations described previously offered in terms of learning, as outlined in Table 7.1.

A question arises from these lessons: Is it worth the time and energy to provide classroom modifications and accessibility for all students, or is it just a few talented individuals who do well and might succeed just as well without intervention anyway?

Table 7.1 Old rules versus new

Learning Example	Old Rule	New Rule
International school	Make plans for the desired environment.	Plan for contingencies.
New England college	Teachers plan the lessons. Try to fit in.	Students have right to the least restrictive environment.
High school biology	Teachers know best.	Ask the student.

What Research Says About Science and Disabilities

In any setting, classroom teachers have two choices when students have difficulty learning: Either they can do nothing and "let the chips fall where they may," or they can make modifications to make the learning experience successful for the disabled student. By doing the former, a teacher takes the historically prevalent road that prohibited special needs students from reaping the benefits of a quality education. By doing the latter, teachers become partners in success. Their students receive the benefits of reduced barriers to learning and are able to enjoy their school experience.

All science students, whether disabled or not, can become excited about learning and work successfully to their potential. First, the lessons must have meaning for the students and relate to their lives (Kyle, Bonstetter, McCloskey, & Fults, 1985; Lang, 1990; Pankiewicz, 1992). Second, students tend to learn more if the lessons are of interest to them personally (Torrance & Meyers, 1970). Third, students must be actively involved in and responsible for their own learning (Romance & Vitale, 1992; Shymansky, Kyle, & Alport, 1982). Fourth, students must be aware of standards that are attainable but that also guarantee high-quality work (Glasser, 1990; Paredes & Frazer, 1992). Fifth, a variety of instructional strategies and modalities must be used to ensure that students with disabilities reach desired instructional objectives (Scruggs & Mastropieri, 1994).

If a teacher or coach is to get the most out of a student player, the teacher must be able to engage the student in a way that brings meaning, interest, active involvement, and challenge to the experience from a variety of perspectives. For teachers of disabled students, this might mean modifying the learning environment to achieve maximum success. Although this might seem reasonable, students with disabilities are often denied the opportunity to use materials or have access to technology to help them express what they have learned. For example, at the basic level of assessment, the unit or course examination, most standardized tests do not allow the use of any assistive tools for students who may need them (Stefanich, 2001b).

Special needs students do as well or better academically and socially in regular classroom placement than in noninclusive settings and achieve more as adults in employment and education (Ferguson & Asch, 1989). Although the literature is well-stocked with supportive evidence for inclusion, many general educators continue to experience a level of apprehension regarding the practice of inclusive education (Owens, Welton, & Broadway, 2002).

Teaching and Instruction

By its very nature, U.S. education is inclusive, and virtually all mission statements in K–12 schools include quality and equity as foundations (Stefanich, 1995). By any standard of reason and compassion, students who have disabilities are entitled to the measures that will enhance their educational experience in such a way as to meet their needs for academic success.

According to the U.S. Department of Education (1990; see also Keller & Keller, 2001), approximately 11 percent of school-aged children in America fall into the category "disabled." Of these, nearly half are considered having specific learning disabilities, and almost a quarter have speech or language impairment. What this means is that in a typical classroom of twenty-five students, about three of them will have some type of disability. One or two will have learning disabilities. In a typical middle, junior high, or high school day, that could mean that a teacher will have up to eighteen disabled students in his or her classes. Because each student is unique, each of the eighteen will require different modifications, although many general strategies can be used for several students.

Although these students are generally identified and have teams that are involved in developing an IEP, there has been a lack of sufficient progress in science classroom adaptations for students with disabilities. Some science teachers have the perception that modifications for disabled students are the responsibility of the special education teacher, and special education teachers often look on their responsibility as helping the student with reading, writing, and test taking (Stefanich, 1995). Thus, modifications within the science classroom are often inadequate.

A lack of responsiveness in science class on behalf of disabled students can often result in learning-disabled students receiving science grades of D or F (Cawley, Kahn, & Tedesco, 1989). When students appear to be failing to work successfully, it might be due to an inability to understand concepts within the instructional context. For others, it might be due to confusion in attempting to sort out the various bits of information. In a recent one-on-one tutoring session, an eighth grade student with learning disabilities responded to a question by saying, "The periodic table is where you can find all the carbohydrates you smell in the air." On further questioning, it was found that the student had confused three different lessons: the periodic table, food groups, and the sense of smell. These units had been presented in sequence, and the student had simply lumped them all together. Had the tutor not happened to ask her to relate what she had been studying, the mix-up probably would have never come to light.

Another eighth grade student (with excellent math skills and high academic achievement in science) recently told me that she believed "the earth was soft, and if you touched it, your hand would go through the surface." Puzzled, I probed further and discovered that she saw the earth as an enclosed box, much like the maps in her textbooks, complete with a border (the "sides" of the box).

Any student might have such confusions and misconceptions, but they perhaps occur more frequently in those who have learning disabilities. Therefore, it is essential that teachers ask questions for understanding as often as possible and attempt to address any mix-ups immediately.

It might be a good idea to change strategies, such as using activities that directly relate to the students' world or using tactile models, such as Punnett squares (see Figure 7.1). If problems persist, refer the students for assessment. Successful coaches do this all the time. If an athlete is struggling in a skill area, a good coach can spot the problem and modify training for the individual. The coach does not automatically assume that the athlete is incapable of improvement or of reaching higher standards.

Science should be an exciting, active enterprise. If students are not engaged, it might not be their fault. Insightful science teachers can spot this and reach out to help. Knowing that learning disabilities are by far the most significant disability in

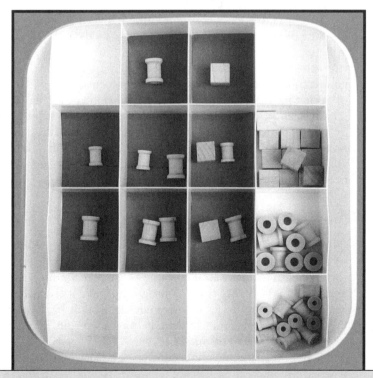

Figure 7.1 A manually adaptive Punnett square activity
Source: Joan Bradley, The Ohio State University.

terms of proportion of students can prompt a teacher to look at ways to act in response to students' struggles rather than to chalk the resulting grades up to "disinterest" or "laziness."

Recent research has been consistent in its understanding of how we learn science concepts—so much so that it is now generally accepted practice for effective teachers to provide a stimulating, active, and investigative framework by which students study science. Constructivist theory explains that we construct our own meaning of nature, the world, and our universe, and the best way to do this is by direct, sensory observation and manipulation. One of the best ways to reach learning-disabled (and all!) students in science is to provide a hands-on environment that actively engages the students in interesting activities. Once this is done, the hook is set, and students look forward to science learning with great anticipation. Sometimes the only modification in such cases is in the mind of the teacher. Teachers who make the switch from lecture-driven, book-centered science to exploratory science are frequently amazed at the difference in students' attitudes and performance.

For students with physical disabilities, teachers must be careful not to reduce their role to that of observers in science classes. Students with motor impairments and sensory loss can and do make significant contributions to their classroom activities if given the chance and responsibility.

In sports, there is a constant battle between proponents of competition and proponents of cooperation. For those whose goals is the production of an elite class of athletes, their sports teams will be small, turning away any but the physically superior athletes. But for coaches who value participation more, their squads will comprise a much greater number of happy athletes, who will always remember the thrill of taking part. Science in our modern world needs a big team of interested players.

In science, we do not have to choose between teaching only to the top academics or arranging for a wider array of playing fields. In teaching active, engaged, investigative science, teachers will find a great satisfaction in knowing that they have contributed not only to the well-being and growth of each individual, but also to the eventual improvement of science literacy in the general population.

Preservice and In-Service Instruction

Obviously, legislation is not enough, nor is awareness. In-service instruction and preservice education programs must focus on helping teachers become familiar and comfortable with inclusive strategies and assistive technology. If K–12 schools and college and university teacher training programs make a commitment to develop skills and knowledge in this area, inclusive education will become a dynamic and embraced method of teaching every student, helping each child reach her potential in an atmosphere of enjoyment and success.

School districts must make inclusive education teaching strategies a requirement if we are to succeed in helping all students achieve their potential. In doing so, it is essential that modifications and adaptive strategies in science classes be underscored. In the interactive, inquiry-based science classroom, modifications go beyond the adjustments needed for reading, listening, and test taking. Science has accessibility issues specific to the discipline, as well as the same general needs in other academic areas.

Teachers do not have to go far to find help with inclusion strategies. Seeking out colleagues, forming cross-disciplinary teams for informal and formal collaborations, and participating in national organizations are all ways in which science teachers can improve their instructional strategies for students with disabilities (Moeller & Wahl, 2002).

Preservice teacher education programs in colleges and universities can be proactive in teaching strategies to those who are preparing to be classroom science teachers. As part of science methods classes, instructors can model innovative techniques, create class simulations, put students in practica that involve working with students who have disabilities, have preservice teachers become familiar with legislation and research concerning students with disabilities in school settings, and have preservice teachers use adaptive technology and build or use modified equipment. Preservice science teachers and college faculty have reported positive results and desire to improve teaching strategies for students with disabilities when given opportunities to work with classroom teachers in an inclusive setting (Owens et al., 2002).

Pairing special education teachers with science teachers is a powerful way to use collaboration in the design of educational strategies for disabled students in science. Science teachers generally see their role as reporting student problems or disabilities to specialists, and special education teachers often do not know methodology for teaching science. This can result in the science student receiving only literal help from special educators who either provide extracurricular help, or in-class support during science lessons.

Although it would seem quite reasonable for the two teachers to work together, they often do not. By working in a collaborative setting, each can find greater understanding of the other's job requirements, and they can develop common strategies for making the science classroom accessible.

The New Breed of Coach: Modifying
Instructional Strategies to Ensure Success

Although legendary sports coaches and their methodology remain inspirational to those who follow, it cannot be denied that as the game changes and the players become more highly skilled, new strategies are needed. Coaches who study the game know that foundations are meant to be built on, and they bring a special skill to sports that allows them to modify techniques that result in success. So, too, do effective teachers of science.

Instructional Strategies

Literature in science and disabilities has shown that one of the most important strategies for successful learning by students with disabilities is simply teaching science as a discovery or inquiry process. This is not only for disabled students, but for all students in science at every level. By doing this, science teachers awaken the interest in all students, creating excitement, motivation, and anticipation that might not have been there before. Whether the approach is guided discovery, exploratory, mastery learning, or use of the learning cycle (see Appendix A), if it involves hands-on, minds-on activities, many problems of accessibility are greatly reduced or cease to exist.

The following guidelines for general instructional strategies in the science classroom when teaching students with disabilities, have been compiled from articles and web resources (Keller, 2000a, 2000b; Moeller & Wahl, 2002; Simons & Hepner, 1992; Stefanich, 1995; Stefanich et al., 2001; Stiles, 2000). The more than 800 strategies specific to each of the eight general categories of disabilities (attention deficit, learning disabilities, behavioral disorder, intellectual disorder, communication disorder, motor/orthopedic impairments, hearing impairments, and visual impairments) can be found at the sites listed in the "Additional Resources" at the end of this chapter.

General Courtesies When Teaching Students with Disabilities

For some teachers, meeting a student with a disability is a bit like meeting someone who speaks a different language. At first, there is an awkwardness based on the fear of either committing a discourtesy or not knowing how to respond adequately. These fears are understandable but do not need to be a barrier between the teacher and student with a disability. For the most part, students with disabilities view themselves as normal, like everyone else, and just want an opportunity to enjoy their learning experiences. Following are some general suggestions and guidelines for interacting with disabled students:

- Do not assume that the person is not listening just because you are getting no verbal or visual feedback. Many students with learning disabilities must take time to process what they see or hear. Others need to review it before formulating a response.
- Do not assume that you have to explain everything to students with learning disabilities. They do not necessarily have a problem with general comprehension.
- Be sensitive when using descriptions of students who have disabilities. If the disability is not pertinent to the discussion, do not mention it. Use the word "disability," not "crippled" or "handicapped." A disabling condition might or might not be handicapping. A person who uses a wheelchair has a disability. Not being able to access a building can be handicapping.
- Do not ask a person with a disability to "prove" his or her impairment. For instance, many people give color tests to colorblind persons.
- Consult with the special education specialist to obtain help in understanding the specific nature of the disability for each student.
- Never assess a student's capabilities solely on the basis of his or her IQ or other standardized test scores.
- Make eye contact and always speak directly to the person with a disability, never to his or her companion or interpreter.
- Do not assume that a student with a disability needs help. Ask first. If you offer to help, wait until your help is accepted. It might not be necessary.
- Consider the needs of students with disabilities when planning field trips.
- Give students with learning disabilities priority in registration for classes. Allow course substitution for nonessential course requirements in their major studies.
- A student can have documented intelligence with test scores in the average to superior range with adequate sensory and motor systems and still have a learning disability. Learning disabilities often go undiagnosed, and teacher observation can be a major source of identification.

- Bring to the student's attention science role models who have disabilities similar to the student's. Point out that this individual got ahead by a combination of effort and asking for help when needed.
- Ask the student what you can do to help. Students are usually the best source of ideas for reducing barriers.
- Start with a student's strengths and then strengthen the weaknesses. Disabled students often approach problem solving from different perspectives than do those for whom the regular academic routine is easy.
- Assess the classroom environment and look for ways to remove obstacles and hazards and to make equipment and supplies accessible. This might mean rearranging the room, adding ramps or platforms, or moving seating arrangements to enhance small group work.

Teacher Planning

For students with disabilities, there are some strategies that are helpful when used by science teachers in their lesson planning. Following are general guidelines for all students, but particularly for students with disabilities:

- Communicate with parents, colleagues, special educators, school nurse, community resources, institutes of higher learning, and other specialists for advice and collaboration in helping you to meet the needs of disabled students. They might also have contacts to whom you can be introduced.
- Begin collecting ideas for adding adaptive materials, many of which can be designed and built by the classroom teacher to meet specific needs in his or her classroom. Talk to the school administrator about the purchase of materials that can be beneficial.
- Become familiar with multimodality teaching techniques and strategies. To reach all students, science teachers must learn to adjust their teaching style to accommodate various types of learning. Use professional development money to attend workshops.
- Solicit the help of volunteers in the community to serve as mentors for students who have disabilities.
- Do not lower expectations for students with disabilities. Instead, modify instruction and offer alternative ways for disabled students to achieve high goals.
- Use plans that include instructional objectives and outcomes. Students respond better to this type of approach than they do to mere instructional context. Align objectives to prior knowledge.
- Plan to incorporate several modalities by using auditory, visual, and kinesthetic techniques in your lessons.

Classroom Instruction

Often, students without impairments are able to adapt to sloppy teaching strategies, but that is not necessarily true for students for whom clear communication is essential, regardless of the type of disability. Therefore, the following guidelines for instruction are meant to be applied at all times, for all students.

Keeping instruction varied has been shown to be effective in leading to higher levels of student performance. This is important in instructing students who have disabilities, as teachers cannot always discern the student's limitations. By using more than one technique, teachers help students with disabilities to compensate for learning that was missed because of problems associated with input processing difficulties.

Using models is important as a part of multimodality instruction. Students often use this type of concrete experience to help give meaning to abstract concepts through experience or sensory participation that may be lacking in their background.

By guiding students initially in the inquiry process, teachers can give students with disabilities an opportunity to experience with confidence a type of learning experience that they might not previously have had. Teachers often assume that students with disabilities cannot participate in exploratory or laboratory activities and deny these students the opportunity out of misguided attitudes. Students with disabilities then might perceive science as something they cannot do. By giving them direct opportunities to observe, ask questions, and participate in hands-on science activities with everyone else, teachers help students with disabilities to gain the confidence that science is something that is accessible to them.

Modifying assignments for students who need a different approach improves success rates. Students with motor disabilities, visual impairments, or learning disabilities often need more time for task and test completion. By giving extra time for assignments and assessments, teachers can enhance student learning and achievement. Students also benefit from having a variety of alternatives for activities and presentations of work.

Instructional information is best utilized by all students when it is given in multiple formats. Steps to an activity, lists of required materials, or instructions for completing an activity over time can be displayed on overhead projectors, printed in a large font for insertion into notebooks, or posted at strategic places around the room. Teachers should never rely solely on verbal instruction, especially instructions with multiple steps. Including visual clues will help those who are visual learners and does not cause problems from those who are literal learners. Transparencies can be filed for easy retrieval if students wish to review them or complete their notes.

For students who have difficulty following a lesson or demonstration, it is helpful if the teacher makes notes available for the students to follow. This gives students the opportunity to focus on what is said rather than having to try to write and pay attention at the same time. This is also beneficial for many students who have motor or learning disabilities.

Teachers might want to consider allowing students who have handwriting problems to use laptop computers or other word processors so that they can concentrate on content, vocabulary, and procedures rather than on the writing mechanics.

Making science activities fully accessible enriches the learning experience for everyone. Using equipment that can be used by students with mobility impairment takes little extra time, and simple routes to make pathways for students who need assistance allows students to participate fully, lending support to inclusive learning. With prudent safety precautions, students with disabilities can be full participants in nearly any laboratory activity. We learn by making mistakes; allow students to take reasonable risks. The benefits far outweigh the problems.

Sports figures are heroes in our culture. Young people frequently look up to these men and women who exemplify excellence. This is not often the case for scientists, especially scientists who have disabilities. Yet there are hundreds, perhaps thousands, of examples of disabled scientists who have made significant contributions to the world. Whether teachers have students with disabilities or not, guest scientists who have disabilities act as strong role models and can help to break down stereotypes held by nondisabled students and faculty. Encouraging students to research or learn about people with disabilities who have made contributions in science, math, engineering, and technology also gives new perceptions about people with disabilities and creates inspiring role models for students with disabilities.

Teachers must model the behavior they want to see in their students. Students do mimic behaviors they see in adults. This includes using clear and effective language in its many forms. Teachers should practice these often.

When using technology in the classroom, teachers need to assess the accessibility and appropriateness of online resources for students with disabilities. Some programs might need to be copied and rewritten in larger text. Many programs now have technology for disabled users. Teachers should watch carefully and be ready to modify such things as text size, audio, color enhancement, and icon-to-text ratios for those with visual impairments. Assistive technology, such as touch screens and close-captioned videos, can be implemented to increase accessibility for students with disabilities while often increasing the comprehension of nondisabled students who cannot only listen to audio, but also read the text.

Assessment

To reduce or eliminate the biases that often exist in standard assessments, teachers need to become familiar with and use alternative types of assessment tools with confidence. Existing standardized assessment tools are often misused to track, diagnose, or classify students according to existing perceptions and biases of the tester or the test itself.

Teacher education programs must examine their approach to student assessment and be sure to train future teachers to identify and use authentic assessment, performance-based assessment, and other forms of alternatives assessment. Most traditional tests are designed to be convenient for the administrator, but many students are unable to demonstrate their knowledge and understanding with such assessments. Therefore, for all students to be able to demonstrate their competence, more than one or two types of assessment must be provided as choice for students with varying types of learning modes.

Most traditional assessments are summative. That is, they assess a compiled amount of learned information at the end of a unit of time. However, formative evaluation, or immediate feedback, helps students to understand where their strengths and weaknesses lie, gives opportunity to more effectively correct misconceptions and provides feedback to the teacher about needs for instructional modifications, remediation, or other curricular concerns.

Students with disabilities often fare much better when given opportunities to present what they know rather than responding to a paper-and-pencil test. All students, including those with disabilities, should be allowed flexibility in the mode of examination.

When giving a traditional quiz or test, insist on silence during the assessment to eliminate distractions. Put multiple-choice selections in questions for learning-disabled students (e.g., three choices instead of four or five) and give extra time for completion if needed. Some students work better in a smaller, quieter room; it might be possible for those students to work in a counselor's office or in a library cubby.

Students who have processing difficulties might fare better if given an opportunity to dictate answers rather than write essays. For those who have visual or language difficulties, it might be necessary to read the questions or to provide an auditory tape of the questions.

Before administering tests, use small group or peer tutoring to review, use game format reviews, and provide study guides or concept maps to help direct study. On the tests themselves, consider using graphics or pictorials to help illustrate the problem.

Classroom Design

One can imagine the frustration of coaching a track and field team without a track, jumping pits, or throwing circles. No matter how much they train, the athletes will not be psychologically or physically ready to perform against others who have had appropriate facilities with which to practice.

Likewise, students with disabilities are regularly expected to use science equipment and perform in a classroom that has been designed for the more physically, emotionally, and intellectually able. Some struggle to succeed; a great number either give up or are assigned other tasks while peers enjoy the experience of science exploration.

It is essential that science teachers think about classroom confines for students who have disabilities. If teachers keep in mind that the ultimate goal of students with disabilities is to work independently, then many reasonable modifications will immediately leap to mind when the teacher looks around the classroom.

Most science classrooms are not universal in their design. Therefore, once a disabled student comes into the classroom, there are basic questions a science teacher might consider:

- Are all materials that students use accessible to every student?
- Can every student access at least one work space?
- Is the current seating arrangement reasonable?
- Are directions and safety rules clearly posted in several places and visible to all?
- Are multiple resources available at different learning levels?
- What human resources are available?
- What audiovisual modifications will I need to make?
- Will there be a need for assistive technology? If so, what kinds?

Keep in mind that sometimes minimal cost, not expensive equipment, will be needed to make simple adjustments to the classroom environment. Asking professionals, the students, and parents for advice will help tremendously.

CONCLUSION: Equal Access

There is a new game in town. As the twenty-first century unfolds, research, technology, and new attitudes are opening up educational doors for students with disabilities that have been closed in the past. Access to science activities and careers is greater than ever before for disabled students.

Students with disabilities are capable in science. Throughout history, there have been talented, courageous, and dedicated people with disabilities who have succeeded despite the immense barriers that stood in their way. These role models are testimony to the opportunities that must be given to all students as they search for life goals. If given a chance, students with disabilities can enjoy science and follow career paths that challenge their capabilities.

Legislation has been passed to ensure access for all. Federal, state, and local laws are now in place that ensure participation for all students in the least restrictive environment, and IEPs are the blueprint by which educators can help students to reach their potential. Through collaboration with other teachers, administrators, school health officials, parents, and community resources, teachers have an opportunity to affect, encourage, and promote learning at the highest level for all students.

Modifications might be necessary to remove barriers to access. Although there are scores of adaptations and modifications that are specific to each type of disability, there are general considerations as well. There is a sizable database of resources for teaching students with disabilities, including instructional strategies, classroom design, assessment considerations, adaptive technology, sources for modified science equipment, and legal issues. Information about most of these resources are available on the Internet.

Teachers and administrators are the keys to success. All students deserve equal opportunity to succeed, and it is the school personnel who make it happen. Caring advocates who work in our nation's schools are the foundation for student success. If they can be there for students who have disabilities, help to create an atmosphere of support and independence, and challenge all of their students to reach their goals, they will be the heroes, those "coaches" who made a difference.

The Game in Action

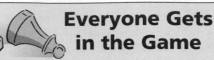

Everyone Gets in the Game

A Very Special Place

Deborah Harris has been a teacher for eleven years, seven in her current position as a sixth grade teacher at Shadowbriar School in Houston, Texas. Before her teaching career, she was a research microbiologist at a chemical company, then a research associate at Baylor College of Medicine. As she put it, "What happens when you take a registered microbiologist with a passion for science and add a love of children? You get a person who wakes up one day and decides what she really wants to do in her life is to teach all children and to teach them to love learning and science!"

Harris not only decided to exchange the lab for a classroom, but also took on the challenge of teaching a wide range of special needs students. Her students at Shadowbriar come from all levels: special education, at-risk, and gifted and talented. As a result of what many would consider an impossible feat of finding success not only with all levels but also in a heterogeneous setting, Harris has garnered several honors for her teaching. She received the *Houston Chronicle*'s award for outstanding teaching and the West Houston Chamber of Commerce Teacher of the Year Award, and she was chosen as the 2001–2002 Lawrence Scadden Teacher of the Year in Science for Students with Disabilities. This annual award, sponsored by Science Education for Students with Disabilities and New Mexico State University's Regional Alliance for Science, Engineering and Mathematics (RASEM) for Students with Disabilities, goes to one teacher in the United States who has shown exemplary teaching in science while working with disabled students.

Accommodations for Students with Disabilities

First and most important, Harris bases her science classes on the inquiry approach, using hands-on activities as often as possible. She notes that she wants all students to be actively included in science education by using an active approach rather than "trying to make science come alive through a book." This approach is considered basic and necessary for effective science teaching in most situations.

"My primary modification," says Harris, "is willingness to work with kids with disabilities and pair them with peer tutors in the lab. Over half of all my science instruction involves hands-on activities, and this is *so* much more friendly for disabled students."

Harris also tries to make a real-world connection for her students. "The excitement and wonder on the children's faces when they participate in their science learning," says Harris, "is worth more than any paper published in (a) book or journal."

Harris sets up her labs to meet the needs of every student—including at-risk students, who need unique accommodations to learn at their potential, and the gifted and talented students who need other accommodations to make learning challenging. "Extra help is provided for my students with physical and learning disabilities by setting up lab groups with peer tutoring available for those that need help to succeed," Harris says. "For students with severe sensory disabilities, such as legal blindness or deafness, lab data are collected on the computer using an extra large font, and lessons are described using auditory enhancers."

Assistive technology is a welcome addition to the twenty-first century classrooms in which inclusion is practiced. Keeping in mind that this classroom is for sixth graders, it is easy to see that such strategies and modifications could be used at other levels, with adjustments for students according to their level of sophistication. Harris reports that with the use of this technology and lab strategies, her special needs students have done "extremely well" in science, and it is her hope that this success will carry over into their other academic classes.

An example of the thoroughness with which Harris thinks about modifications can be seen in the strategies she uses with a remarkably challenged but enthusiastic student who has multiple disabilities. A student who is legally blind would prove challenge enough, but add a wheelchair, being nonverbal, having limited hearing, and having mobility impairment, and this is a student who would cause many teachers to panic—but not Harris. This student is fully included in her science class. How? Some strategies are simply the result of listening to students and parents, who can often make excellent suggestions. Harris positions this particular student so that his good ear is toward her, uses simplified materials for better viewing, pairs the student with others for help in hands-on activities and note taking, and has integrated his communicator within the classroom through a question-and-answer format.

Harris notes with humor that sometimes a good idea has unexpected implications. During a recent test, she noticed that the other students paused to wait for the voice synthesizer to answer a test question before writing *their* answers!

Examples of Modifications in Lessons

During a unit on forces of gravity and motion, Harris invited an engineer and three race car drivers to visit. The drivers brought along their Formula 1 cars! The students were able to see firsthand the real connection of these concepts. Accommodations for her student who uses a wheelchair were made so that he could move directly up to the cars and interact personally with the drivers. He then participated in an activity in which an interactive computer race car game was used to show the scientific laws of motion.

In a forensics activity, students were challenged to apply knowledge of physical and chemical properties of matter to solve a classroom "mystery." Using a variety of lab tests and careful observations of the "crime" scene, students identified the criminal, cause of death, and motive. Modifications for this activity included the following:

- Using small lab groups for each lab activity
- Peer tutoring for each activity

- Use of an enlarged font for the lab detective notebook and lab activity sheets
- Use of a microphone adaptor for the hearing impaired
- Preferential seating for vision-impaired students so that they could see instructions better
- Asking for oral rather than written responses.

These modification did take some time, but once teachers make a particular adaptation for a disability, it then becomes general in its application for future activities. The more it is used, the less time is required for its implementation, and it eventually becomes a part of the standard classroom environment.

In a chemistry activity using "mystery liquids," students were required to identify seven unknown liquids by describing properties of liquids and testing these properties. Properties tested were viscosity, pH, density, and surface tension.

To test these liquids, each group needed to be able to pour, use a medicine dropper, observe properties, and handle and discern color changes in pH paper strips. Not all students were able to physically do all of these tasks, so cooperation was necessary.

Peers tutored and described for students with limited sight, and the use of a microphone adaptor was implemented for a student who was hearing impaired. Data tables were enlarged (72-point font) for easier reading, and data were loaded into the "liberator," a communicator for a student who was nonverbal.

For pouring liquids, students who have reduced motor skills can use large containers or help other students with the pouring. Braille-inscribed science equipment, such as thermometers (which also have large indicator arrows), plastic roll-up meter sticks, and graduated cylinders, is available from science equipment catalogs (see Appendix A).

Keeping a clear pathway between lab tables and equipment is important for wheelchair access. Tables must be high enough for the chair to clear but not so high that the student cannot easily reach the work surface. Written instructions that are visible from anywhere in the room make it easier for learning-disabled students to keep tabs on the steps and goals; and clear, step-by-step instructions for ADHD, autistic, or behaviorally challenged students are very helpful. These can easily be stored or filed for future use.

Activities such as pH testing that involve color change or identification are difficult for colorblind students. Because colorblindness occurs in 4 percent of the population (mostly males), it is very likely that a class of twenty-five students has a student for whom color identification is a challenge. Describing colors to the student while working is helpful, as is using alternatives if possible, such as changing color coding to some other type of identification method.

Although these modifications require time management, much time can be saved by planning ahead, thinking about alternatives for known disabilities, and keeping in touch with the students themselves, who will often have great ideas.

A key to success in the science classroom is for teachers not to diminish expectations for students who have disabilities. Accommodation does not necessarily mean making things easier or removing opportunity. Students who are fortunate enough to have teachers who can make adaptations while challenging the students with high expectations will find success and enjoyment in science.

Attitude Can Make a Difference

It is not enough just to go through the motions in teaching students of any ability, but this is particularly true of teaching students with disabilities. Harris is successful because she believes in what she does, and her enthusiasm naturally carries over into her teaching. According to her principal, Santos Reyes, "Deborah believes that *all* students can become part of the classroom learning; therefore, she sees no limitations for her disabled students." Reyes points out that Harris is effective because she sees no barriers when approaching special needs in her classroom.

This type of attitude is vital in teaching disabled students. As Geerat Vermeij has said, opportunity is important for all students, especially for those whose disabilities might cause others to assume what they cannot achieve, rather than what they can. When we withhold opportunity for a child, whether disabled or not, to discover, explain, and make sense of the surrounding world, "we are depriving the student of a profound source of pleasure and accomplishment." Harris is the type of teacher for whom opportunity is a foundation for all student experiences in science.

Greg Stefanich notes that "a child doesn't care what you know, he just wants to know you care." Harris cares a great deal about her students. Reyes says of Harris, "She not only encourages children within her class but also goes to see them outside of the classroom. She has taken them to movies and attended special events in their lives such as recitals."

One mother notes, "I do believe (my son's) coping skills in this class are a direct result of Mrs. Harris's exceptional patience, understanding, and the hands-on teaching methods she uses extensively, for both her traditional kids and for children, like my son, with severe disabilities."

A Look at Facilities

In a classroom such as Harris's, through which a constant stream of kids with an enormous variety of needs pass each day, one might wonder how a teacher can possibly modify a room enough for everyone. Indeed, where does one start?

Most classrooms are basically similar in size and shape, with standard doors and furniture. To meet the needs of all students, with the idea of creating an atmosphere in which the students can be independent, a teacher must first look at accessibility. This is critical for students with mobility and visual impairments and can also be of importance for those with certain other disabilities such as autism, hearing impairment, and behavioral needs.

Creating a means for safe and easy passage for all students is the first step. Analyze your students' needs and work to create pathways for all students to easily reach supply cabinets, sinks, emergency wash stations, teacher desk, overhead stations, individual work areas, and emergency exits. It might be a good idea to seat students with mobility impairments near the exits in case of emergency, as long as this does not compromise their ability to see, hear, or contribute. Once these pathways are implemented and clear, do not alter them without advance notice, as students will have gotten used to them and will rely on them for ease of movement about the classroom.

If it is necessary to modify a work station, be sure that it has all functions that other students enjoy. Check to ensure that all materials are within reach of all students and that any student can use overhead projectors, have access to easels, write on the boards, and attach information or work to bulletin boards. This might mean lowering chalk and bulletin boards and extending map or screen string pulls to wheelchair level.

Harris says, "My classroom is set up with six lab tables with six chairs at each table. I conduct all of my lessons in cooperative group settings. I feel that *all* students benefit from working together and helping each other, as well as trying out ideas."

Harris reports that her disabled students are always put with groups of four to five other students. They are never isolated. Her students in wheelchairs "just pull up to the table and join in." For a former student with brittle-bone disease who was so small that she had difficulty reaching the table, Harris had a small horseshoe-shaped table that fit her perfectly and simply made another lab group for her there.

Visually impaired students' lab tables are up close to Harris and the overhead, and for hearing impaired students, Harris wears a voice amplifier for their microphone or hearing aid. Visitors who address the class can easily slip the amplifier on as well.

If your school has an outdoor classroom or nature area, determine what must be done for all students to have access. This might mean building a switchback trail, paving an approach, or using sturdy guide cables to direct blind visitors to observation sites. Consider future needs, not just present ones, and remember that you might have visitors who are unable to access your site unless you are proactive in making it accessible.

The students at Pace Middle School in Denver, Colorado, wanted to make an outdoor study site accessible for their disabled peers, so they spent many hours converting a steep slope to a gentler one. Once it was done, all students were able to travel up and down the hill to the nature site.

Inventory your equipment and decide whether you have (or may have) any students for whom they are not comfortable. Buy some modified equipment with your next order from supply catalogs, such as Delta Education (see Appendix A). Keep this equipment in one area, easily accessible for students with disabilities.

Keeping an accessible file of copies of notes and overheads in large type will help students with visual impairments to stay current. This is true for audiotapes or videos of activities for students who might need that type of feedback, including students with learning disabilities.

Teachers will almost certainly have at least one colorblind student every year. By rethinking color codes, they can help those students immensely and not harm students who have normal color vision. Most classrooms rely on color-coding to some extent. Try using symbols, black-and-white patterns, or name labels instead.

Each classroom should have isolated areas in which students who find distractions difficult for concentrating can work, research, read, or work on assessments. Having a busy classroom environment does not mean that it has to be noisy. This is something that the teacher must control early on. Once the guidelines are consistently applied, it does not take long for students of any age to incorporate conversation tones into their everyday activities in the science classroom. Not only will students with learning disabilities or autism find it more comfortable, so will their teacher.

It is not possible to set up a completely accessible classroom all at once. However, by using some of the above guidelines, every teacher can begin to make simple adjustments in anticipation of the enrollment of a student with a disability. If you do not have students with disabilities at the moment, you might want to incorporate informational sessions about disabled people to sensitize your students. This must be done carefully, to avoid stereotyping or creating overly sympathetic and possibly patronizing attitudes. Outside help might be available in the form of disabled adults who can act as consultants. During these sessions, students can be challenged to look for inaccessible areas of the classroom and make suggestions for improvement. If you do have a disabled student, ask him or her in private what might be done to make the science classroom more accessible.

A Matter of Dedication

Effective teachers of students with disabilities are not superhuman. They might be special, but any teacher who understands best practice in science, who is an advocate for all students, and who is committed to making science enjoyable for all students can make the science classroom an inclusive one.

Attitude is all-important. If a teacher thinks that something cannot be done, it probably will not get done. Perseverance is the key to finding a way for all students to have access to science. Many teachers have made incredible things happen in their schools despite a lack of help from peers or administrators. Others have been fortunate to have that backing. In whichever situation you find yourself, take it one step at a time. You will be surprised at how much better it is for your students and for you.

Deborah Harris *is* special. She saw a need and has dedicated her career to helping to meet the needs of all children who come into her classroom. The benefits are obvious. Students with disabilities are capable. Sometimes all they need is the help of a caring adult. Will it be you?

Reflecting on the Game

1. Take a moment to think about and then write a short description of teaching strategies that might be used for gifted students.
2. What hesitations might teachers have when working with students who have disabilities? What are some strategies you might suggest that could help them be more confident?
3. Suppose you have a class that includes students with a variety of emotional, physical, and academic needs. Assuming that you have no curriculum guidelines, design a week-long series of general science lessons for the class. What would your classroom layout be like? Justify your design.
4. Go back to your answer for the first question above, and read your paragraph, but this time eliminate the words "gifted" and "talented." How is education for the gifted viewed differently from education for other students? Discuss reasons why many people believe it is or should be. What are your views, and why?

References

Americans with Disabilities Act (ADA). (1990). PL 101-476.

Cawley, J. F., Kahn, H., & Tedesco, A. (1989). Vocational education and students with learning disabilities. *Journal of Learning Disabilities, 22,* 630–634.

Colburn, A. (1990). If testing's to be the standard, then the price may be too dear. *Education Week, 10*(9), 24–25.

Ferguson, P., & Asch, A. (1989). Lessons from life: Personal and parental perspectives on school, childhood, and disability. In D. Bicklen, A. Ford, & D. Furguson (Eds.), *Disability and Society* (pp. 108–140). Chicago: National Society for the Study of Education.

Glasser, W. (1990). *The quality school: Managing students without coercion.* New York: Harper and Row.

Grandin, T. (2000). *My Experiences with visual thinking, sensory problems, and communication difficulties.* Salem, OR: Center for the Study of Autism.

Grandin, T. (2002). *Dr. Temple Grandin's Web Page.* http://www.grandin.com

Individuals with Disabilities Education Act. (1973). PL 94-142.

Individuals with Disabilities Education Act Amendments. (1997). PL 105-17,20 U.S.C. 1400-et seq., 105th Congress, 1st session.

Keller, Jr., E. C. (2002a). *Strategies for teaching students with learning disabilities.* Morgantown, WV: West Virginia University. http://www.as.wvu.edu/~scidis/learning.html

Keller, Jr., E. C. (2002b). *Inclusion in science education for students with disabilities.* Morgantown, WV: West Virginia University. http://www.as.wvu.edu/~scidis/sitemap.html

Keller, Jr., E. C., & Keller III, E. C. (2001, March). *Using disability strategies on the web.* Paper presented at the NSTA Pre-conference Workshop, St. Louis, MO.

Kyle, Jr., W. C., Bonstetter, R. J., McCloskey, S., & Fults, B. A. (1985). Science through discovery: Children love it. *Science and Children, 23*(2), 39–41.

Lang, H. (2002). Personal communication. National Technical Institute for the Deaf, Rochester Institute of Technology, Rochester, NY. Permission granted to use information.

Lang, T. (1990). Centered on teaching. *Science and Children, 28*(2), 20–23.

Moeller, B., & Wahl, E. (2002). Science for all: Including *each* student. *NSTA Pathways to the Science Standards.* http://www.nsta.org

National Science Foundation (1998). *Breaking barriers: People with disabilities and science and mathematics education.* (NSF 98–70). Arlington, VA: Author.

National Science Teachers Association. (2001/2002). NAEP 2000 science scores show no significant change since 1996. *NSTA Reports!, 13*(3), 1, 3.

No Child Left Behind Act. (2001). Education Bill. H. R. 1.

Owens, K. D., Welton, E. N., & Broadway, F. S. (2002). Getting up to spe-ed: Preservice teacher training for inclusive education. *Journal of Science Education for Students with Disabilities, 9,* 8–14.

Pankiewicz, P. (1992). Hands-on humidity. *The Science Teacher, 59*(1), 38–41.

Paredes, V., & Frazer, L. (1992). *School Climate in AISD.* Austin, TX: Office of Research and Evaluation. (ERIC Document Reproduction Service No. ED 353 677)

Romance, N., & Vitale, M. (1992). A curriculum strategy that expands time for in-depth elementary science instruction by using science-based reading strategies: Effects of a year-long study in fourth grade. *Journal of Research in Science Teaching, 29,* 545–554.

Scruggs, T. E., & Mastropieri, M. A. (1994). Successful mainstreaming in elementary science classes: A qualitative investigation of three reputational cases. *American Educational Research Journal, 31*(4), 785–811.

Shymansky, J. A., Kyle, Jr., W. C., & Alport, J. (1982). How effective were the hands-on science programs of yesterday? *Science and Children, 20*(3), 14–15.

Simons, G. H., & Hepner, N. (1992). The special student in science. *Science Scope, 16*(1), 34–39, 54.

Stefanich, G. (1995). What research says about teaching and instruction for students with disabilities. *Journal of Science for Persons with Disabilities,* Spring, 3–10.

Stefanich, G. P. (2001a, March). *Inclusive science education: Essential considerations.* Paper presented at the National Science Teachers Association annual convention, St. Louis, MO.

Stefanich, G. P. (2001b). On the outside looking in. In G. P. Stefanich, (Ed.), *Science teaching in inclusive classrooms: Theory & foundations.* Cedar Falls, IA: Greg P. Stefanich, Publisher. (NSF grants HRD-953325 and HRD-9988729)

Stefanich, G., Keller, Jr., E., Davison, J., & Payne, C. (2001). Classroom and laboratory modifications for students with disabilities. In G. P. Stefanich, (Ed.), *Science teaching in inclusive classrooms: Models & applications.* Cedar Falls, IA: Greg P. Stefanich, Publisher. (NSF grants HRD-953325 and HRD-9988729)

Stiles, J. (2000, March). *What you can do in science class to help students with disabilities.* Paper presented at the NSTA pre-conference workshop on science and disabilities, Orlando, FL.

Torrance, E. P., & Myers, R. E. (1970). *Creative learning and teaching.* New York: Dodd, Mead and Company.

U.S. Department of Education (1990). *Digest of educational statistics.* Washington, DC: Author.

Vermeij, G. (1997). *Privileged hands: A remarkable scientific life.* New York: W. H. Freeman.

Vermeij, G. (2002, March). From *Science, blindness, and evolution: The common theme is opportunity.* Paper presented at the 2002 "Science-Abled Breakfast" sponsored by Science Education for Students with Disabilities and the National Science Teachers Association, San Diego, CA.

Additional Resources

Barrier-Free Education: http://barrier-free.arch.gatech.edu

Council for Exceptional Children (CEC): http://www.cec.sped.org

C.L.A.S.S. (Creating Laboratory Access for Science Students): http://biology.wright.edu/labgrant/index.html

COMETS (Clearinghouse of Mathematics, Engineering, Technology, and Science): http://www.rit.edu/~comets

DO-IT (Disabilities, Opportunities, Internetworking, and Technology): http://www.washington.edu/doit

ERIC Clearinghouse on Disabilities and Gifted Education: http://www.ericec.org

National Clearinghouse for Professions in Special Education (NCPSE): http://www.special-ed-careers.org

Program ACCESS (Accessing Career Choices in Engineering and the Sciences): http://www.arizona.edu/~access

Playtime Is Science for Students with Disabilities: http://www.edequity.org/playdisab.htm

Project on the Inclusion of Students with Disabilities in Science Education: http://www.as.wvu.edu/~scidis

Science Education for Students with Disabilities: http://www.as.wvu.edu/~scidis/organize/sesd.html

Scientopia: http://www.ee.udel.edu/InfoAccess

Synergy, a publication of the National Science Foundation: http://www.ehr.nsf.gov/index.html

start

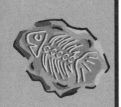

chapter

8

THE NATURE OF SCIENCE:

Understanding How the Game Is Played

Michael P. Clough, Ph.D.
Center for Excellence in
Mathematics and Science
Education, Iowa State University

ABOUT THE AUTHOR: Dr. Michael Clough was an award-winning teacher of high school biology and chemistry for seven years in Illinois and Wisconsin before embarking on graduate study in science education. He is now an assistant professor in the Center for Excellence in Science and Mathematics Education at Iowa State University, where he teaches secondary science methods and the nature of science and science education and supervises science student teachers. The nature of science has always been an integral part of his teaching, at both the high school and college level. Since 1992, he has more than 30 publications and 120 presentations concerning effective teaching, many of which address the nature of science and its implications for science teaching.

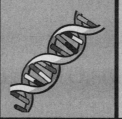

> **Science is a great game. It is inspiring and refreshing. The playing field is the universe itself.**
>
> —Isador I. Rabi
> *Nobel Laureate in Physics, 1944*

CHAPTER WARM-UP

Understanding the game requires an appreciation for the nature of science—its history, sociology, and philosophy along with its contemporary societal niche. Learners' attitudes and conceptions about science are deeply influenced by their understanding of its nature. Teachers of science can facilitate a realistic view of how scientists and the scientific community work by explicitly raising questions and creating situations that compel learners to consider NOS issues.

INTRODUCTION: What Is Meant by the Nature of Science?

In *Never Playing the Game,* Yager (1988) chastised school science instruction for rarely permitting students to investigate an authentic problem, create experiments, analyze data, and formulate possible explanations—that is, to actually play the game of science. He wrote "We pronounce science a fantastic game that all should learn to play [but] our students rarely get to play—rarely get to do real science" (p. 77). Yager's criticism of the way science is taught raises two important questions: In what sense is science like a game, and what is "real science" like?

In *The Game of Science,* McCain and Segal (1981) justified the metaphor by arguing that like a game, "science is challenging, entertaining, and governed by rules" (p. 2). Although scientists and science students likely agree that understanding the natural world is challenging, whether either would describe it as "entertaining" is questionable. Scientists certainly find the natural world fascinating and the quest for knowledge addicting, but the process also entails tedious work and frustration, and students know that significant learning is rewarding but rarely entertaining. Regarding McCain and Segal's third justification, if something akin to rules do exist, what are they and how can they be made clear to students? After all, if students are expected to understand and play the game of real science and teachers are to create an environment in which this will occur, then both need to know something about its character and guidelines.

Rather than speaking of governing rules, the phrase "nature of science" is most often used to describe the interplay of disciplines informing science education about what science is and how it works. As McComas, Clough, and Almazroa (1998a, p. 512) explain,

> The nature of science is a fertile hybrid arena including the history, sociology, and philosophy of science combined with research from the cognitive sciences such as psychology into a rich description of what science is, how it works, how scientists operate as a social group and how society itself both directs and reacts to scientific endeavors. The intersection of the various social studies of science is where the richest view of science is revealed for those who have but a single opportunity to take in the scenery.

Although some characteristics of science are uncontroversial and have clear implications for classroom practice, most are contextual with complex exceptions. Like all analogies, care must be taken in comparing the analog (i.e., the rules) to the target (i.e., the nature of science) too literally. Percy Bridgman, a Nobel prize–winning physicist, is often quoted as saying that "science is doing your damndest, no holds barred." The metaphor of science as a game governed by rules can be maintained if "rules" are thought of as lying somewhere between unyielding regulations and the anarchy suggested by Bridgeman.

Why Understanding the Nature of Science Is Critical

A number of studies document students' misconceptions regarding scientists, how science works, and the nature of scientific knowledge (Clough, 2001; Rowell & Cawthron,

1982; Rubba, Horner, & Smith, 1981; Ryan & Aikenhead, 1992). The significant mis-understandings that both students and teachers hold regarding the nature of science are particularly damaging to general scientific literacy because they likely affect students' attitudes toward science and science classes, and this clearly affects student learning and the selection of further science classes. For example, Sheila Tobias (1990) interviewed a number of successful science students and reported that they became disenchanted with science classes and chose different majors, in part, because science courses ignored the historical, philosophical, and sociological foundations of science. According to McComas et al. (1998a, 1998b), a better understanding of scientists, the scientific community, and how the game of science is played will enhance the following areas.

Understanding of Science's Strengths and Limitations

Misunderstanding the nature of science, many people erroneously apply scientific thinking in areas in which its rules do not apply. For instance, one of the strengths of science is its demand for empirical evidence and naturalistic explanations. This insistence is essential in creating a reliable knowledge base about the natural world. However, just as the rules of football make little sense when applied to baseball, the guiding prescripts of science do not apply or are insufficient in many human endeavors. For instance, faith, not empirical evidence, is at the heart of religion. And although while scientific evidence ought to play a role in many social decisions, it alone is insufficient for making such policy.

Social Decision Making

Complex societal issues require consideration of many factors, such as desired ends, individual and societal values, existing social structures, available resources, and in many cases scientific knowledge. Deciding what role, if any, scientific knowledge should play in these decisions depends in part on accurately understanding the nature of science. Funding decisions regarding science and technology and the controversy over the teaching of biological evolution in public education are obvious examples in which social decision making is affected by individuals' and policymakers' understanding of the nature of science. Understanding how conceptions of science as a way of knowing tacitly affect many other social decision-making processes would certainly make for better public policy.

Instructional Delivery

Understanding the nature of science illuminates the construction and reconstruction of ideas and facilitates an understanding of how students also struggle to make sense of the natural world. Teachers with some background in the history of science will see that many students' ideas are similar to early scientific thinking. McComas et al. (1998b) write, "The persistence of students' naïve ideas in science suggests that teachers could use the historical development of scientific concepts to help illuminate the conceptual journey students must make away from their own naive misconceptions." Furthermore, those who know of the durability of scientific knowledge, while acknowledging that at times it changes for good reasons, will not be confused or cynical when they learn that previously accepted scientific ideas have been modified or discarded.

An understanding of the nature of science will also help teachers to grasp the primacy of scientific theories in guiding research questions, methodologies, observations, interpretations, and conclusions. This understanding has implications for teaching science as inquiry and through inquiry (National Research Council, 1996) and deciding what science content is really fundamental for scientific literacy. Duschl (1987) goes so far as to claim that effective inquiry teaching demands that science teachers have an understanding of the nature of science.

Interest in Science and Science Classes

Issues regarding how the game of science is played might initially seem uninteresting to students. For instance, in a study by Meyling (1997), students who had not experienced explicit nature of science instruction showed little interest in such topics. However, of those students who actually experienced explicit instruction about how scientific knowledge comes to be accepted, two thirds showed further interest in such learning. When the game of science is appropriately conveyed to students as a human adventure, an increase in student interest is not surprising. Rather than seeing science as simply information to be memorized, students begin to see it as a problem-solving activity involving creativity, logic, and social interaction.

Learning of Science Content

Evidence exists suggesting that understanding the character of science assists students in learning science content. For example, Songer and Linn (1991) found that students who understood the tentative nature of science acquired a deeper understanding of thermodynamics than did those who saw science as simply a set of facts. The following student's frustration illustrates how misunderstandings about the nature of science can affect interest in and understanding of science content:

> What is this game that scientists play? They tell me that if I give something a push it will just keep on going forever or until something pushes it back to me. Anybody can see that isn't true. If you don't keep pushing, things stop. Then they say it would be true if the world were without friction, but it isn't, and if there weren't any friction how could I push it in the first place? It seems like they just change the rules all the time. (Rowe & Holland, 1990, p. 87)

Just as in sports, to fully appreciate and understand the game of science and how it is played, students need to be explicitly made aware of the rules and their rationale in the context of experiencing the game.

For these and other reasons, science educators and education organizations and reform documents have for some time emphasized the need for teachers and curricula to accurately portray the nature of science (American Association for the Advancement of Science, 1989; Association for Science Education, 1981; Collette & Chiappetta, 1984; Matthews, 1989, 1994; National Assessment of Educational Progress, 1989; NRC, 1996; National Science Teachers Association, 1982, 2000; Shahn, 1988; Shamos, 1995). The National Science Education Standards (NRC, 1996) place significant attention on the history and nature of science, and in the spring of 1996, NSTA released the high school edition of *Pathways to the Science Standards* (Texley & Wild, 1996), which includes some suggestions and vignettes to more accurately portray the nature of science. Moris Shamos (1995) goes so far as to argue that understanding how science works is the most important component of scientific literacy.

Important "Rules" of Science Appropriate for Middle and High School Students

Although contentious issues exist regarding the nature of science, significant consensus does exist on many issues appropriate for middle and high school students (Eflin, Glennan, & Reisch, 1999; McComas et al., 1998a, 1998b; Smith, Lederman, Bell, McComas, & Clough, 1997). Where consensus does not exist, the key is to convey a plurality of views so that students come to understand the complexities involved in the game of science. In accurately portraying how science is done, the point is not to indoctrinate students, but to educate them about the reasons for differing perspectives (Matthews, 1997). Some of the more important ideas for helping students better understand the nature of science are elaborated below.

Science Is Not the Same as Technology

Many Americans know that although football is related to the game of rugby, the two are not the same. However, most Americans are surprised to learn that American rules football and Australian rules football are just two of several kinds of football. This same sort of confusion occurs regarding what science is. Figure 8.1 will help to illustrate two different forms of science and how they interact with each other and technology.

Evidence exists (Ryan & Aikenhead, 1992) suggesting that students confuse science with technology, leading them to support science because they wrongly see it as providing society with gadgets, vaccines, and other practical outcomes that improve everyday living. Although science and technology do affect each other, basic research is not directly concerned with practical societal outcomes, but rather with an understanding of the natural world for its own sake—akin to playing a game for the love of sport. Scientists conducting basic science might not even consider what societal use may come of their work. However, basic research is responsible for most of the fundamental breakthroughs in our understanding of the natural world, and knowledge that comes from basic research often has unanticipated practical outcomes. For instance, James Watson's *The Double Helix* (1968) made clear that scientists who were working to determine the structure of DNA gave little thought to how the knowledge might be applied, and they certainly could not have foreseen the multiple applications in medicine that

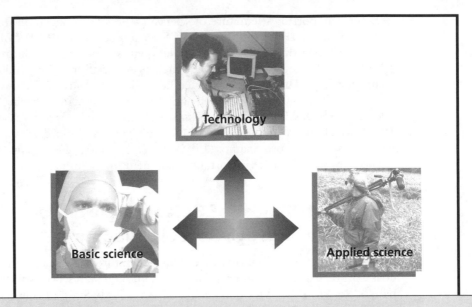

Figure 8.1 Interactions between basic science , applied science, and technology

exist today. And when Thomas Brock went to Yellowstone to study organisms that live in hot springs at temperatures at which most life cannot exist, he could not foresee that decades later, his work would provide the foundation for a process that generates millions of dollars in revenue and is an essential aid to the biotechnology industry (Bednarek, 1993).

Of course, much scientific research *is* done because of the likely benefit it could have in helping to address societal problems. This sort of science is referred to as applied research. The product of basic and applied science is knowledge about the natural world, but technology can be thought of as the more tangible products and processes that are useful in everyday life, industry, and the military. Although technology uses knowledge developed by basic and applied science, it also produces products that promote scientific research, and the knowledge produced by either basic or applied science affects the other as well. If any of the three were missing, the other two would suffer significantly.

In practice, disentangling science from technology and basic science from applied science is difficult, but this illustrates how interdependent the three are. What is important is that students come to see the complex relationships among the three and understand that all must be supported. In 1999, the U.S. budget for research and development (R&D) was nearly a quarter of a trillion dollars. Of this total, approximately 16 percent went to basic science, 23 percent to applied science, and 61 percent to development projects (Payson, 1999). The common misunderstanding of the relationship between basic science, applied science, and technology can have very real societal consequences when funding decisions are made. For instance, the Clinton administration considered curtailing support of basic science because of budget constraints as well as a misunderstanding of basic science's role in promoting technology (Elmer-Dewitt, 1994).

A Universal Ahistorical Scientific Method Does Not Exist

McComas (1996) writes that the most pervasive myth regarding how science works is the notion that all researchers follow a common series of steps. Recent science textbooks have been backing away from listing invariable steps in doing science research, but teachers who were trained in the previous climate often continue teaching this misconception. Medawar (1963) argues that although scientific papers are written in a manner to best communicate and persuade readers of the logic behind the reported work, the format implies to nonscientists that original researchers actually follow a step-by-step method. Conveying a definite form to scientific methodology leads students to believe that experiments are the only route to understanding the natural world, that imagination and creativity play little if any role in research, that the success of science is due to its method, and that this method demarcates science from other human endeavors. None of these assertions hold up to scrutiny. Rather, scientists tend to use whatever methods and approaches will yield insight into a research problem. Many philosophers of science have taken strong stances against a codified scientific method, particularly Paul Feyerabend (1975) in *Against Method*, in which he argues that both the history of science and the relationship between ideas and action support the view that in doing science, "anything goes." Although not all philosophers agree with the extreme anarchy promoted by Feyerabend, Michael Ruse (1999, p. 229), recently wrote,

> Granted, a pragmatic shuffling of theory and data was necessary to bring the two into harmony. But that is the nature of science. Real science is always more like auto mechanics—getting the damned thing to work—than is dreamed of by philosophers in their texts on scientific methodology.

Subjectivity Is a Necessary Part of Science

Hodson (1985, p. 27) argues that the emphasis on a scientific method and the knowledge output of science project an erroneous image of scientists as "objective, open-minded, unbiased and possessing a critical and infallible method." Ryan and Aikenhead (1992) report that 52 percent of the students they surveyed held the naïve view that the best scientists are always very open-minded, logical, unbiased, and objective in their work. Too often, science instruction suggests that scientists make unproblematic observations, that interpretations of data are fairly straightforward, and that the methodology of science results in objective knowledge about the natural world. Gauld (1982, p. 118) contends, "Teaching that scientists possess these characteristics is bad enough but it is abhorrent that science educators should actually attempt to mold children in the same false image." Moreover, such thinking may be at odds with what best facilitates exceptional science (Ryan and Aikenhead, 1992). Although no one has argued that we should teach students to be closed-minded and biased, moving them toward a more realistic understanding of how science and scientists work is desirable.

Because science is a human endeavor, subjectivity cannot be eliminated. That all science must be affected by previously held ideas becomes apparent when one considers that if preconceived notions were not entertained, investigations would never move past collection of data. Without a priori ideas, no basis would exist for determining what sensory input was relevant to an investigation or when a sufficient number of observations had been collected (Cole, 1985; Finley, 1983). What scientists think and see is necessarily influenced by the conceptualizations they bring to bear on their research. Knowledge, besides being a product of investigations, is a tool for making further observations and deriving new knowledge.

A more realistic view of how scientists and the scientific community work includes an understanding of private science, public science, and their interactions. Private science refers to inspiration, intuition, and creative leaps that individual scientists make. Private science can also refer to the dynamics of research teams. The processes and ideas that are born in these close-knit situations can easily result in unwarranted conclusions and unexamined biases, but the process of publicly sharing ideas with the larger community of scientists acts to constrain subjectivity as methodologies and biases are examined and modified by the views of other scientists. Public science tempers the subjective tendencies of private science without eliminating them.

Knowledge Is Not Democratic

Students' and teachers' admirable belief in fair play sometimes spills over into how they believe science should work. However, fair play does not mean giving credibility to all ideas. Discredited ideas such as Aristotelian physics, astrology, a flat earth, geocentricity, and a young earth are not taught, even though a significant portion of the public might believe these ideas. Fairness is not a criterion for selecting what science content is accepted as good knowledge. The scientific community interpreting the best available evidence, not public opinion polls, decides what is good science. The public certainly has a say in technological applications that might affect society, but most people do not possess the expertise to judge the validity of scientific knowledge.

Even within the scientific community, accepted ideas are not determined through voting. How then does the scientific community decide what is good knowledge? Charles Darwin said that his *On the Origin of Species* was "one long argument," and this description also reflects science as a whole. Empirical evidence plays a critical role in creating and justifying scientific knowledge, but it does not decide that knowledge. Argument and persuasion are a necessary part of science because data does not speak. Achieving consensus (a solidarity in sentiment and belief that itself is ill defined) is a complex sociological process that occurs over time, not at some definitive moment.

The Meaning of Theories, Laws, Hypotheses and Scientific Certainty Is Different from Students' Usage of Those Words

The words "theory," "law," and "hypothesis" are frequently used in science classes, yet their appropriate meanings and relationship are rarely conveyed to students. For instance, outside of science, the word "theory" most often is seen as analogous to "guess" or "speculation." Ryan and Aikenhead (1992, p. 571), after collecting the responses of more than 2,000 students in grades 11 and 12, found that "The majority [of students] (64%) expressed a simplistic hierarchical relationship in which hypotheses become theories and theories become laws, depending on the amount of 'proof behind the idea.' " However, although laws and theories are related to one another in complex ways, one *never* becomes the other. Laws are generalizations or universal relationships related to the way that some aspect of the natural world behaves under specific conditions. Scientific theories predict and explain laws (Campbell, 1953) and provide conceptual frameworks for further research (Kuhn, 1970). Interestingly, not only are laws not a higher form of scientific knowledge, but an understanding of laws is incomplete without a theory to explain them.

The scientific community's confidence in ideas concerning the natural world can range from speculative to gaining support to well supported to near certain. Ideas that are speculative or are gaining support but are not yet well supported are often referred to as "hypotheses." Note that "hypothesis" can mean a guess or a well-informed speculation, and these two meanings might refer to a particular instance (an observation), a universal relationship (law), or an explanatory framework (theory). Hence, the word "hypothesis" has at least six different meanings, and students can learn much about the nature of scientific knowledge through analyzing how this loaded word is used in textbooks. Speculative explanatory frameworks (theories) may, over time, become well established, but they are still theories. Speculative invariable relationships (laws) may also become well established, but they remain laws.

Students often see scientific ideas as copies of reality (Ryan & Aikenhead, 1992). Science teachers often perpetuate this view by using loaded words such as "prove" and "true" without making clear to students what the words mean in a science context. Many arguments can be made against the notion of absolute truth in science, but Einstein and Infeld (1938, p. 31) provide an easily understood analogy:

> In our endeavor to understand reality we are somewhat like a man trying to understand the mechanism of a closed watch. If he is ingenious he may form some picture of a mechanism which could be responsible for all the things he observes, but he may never be quite sure his picture is the only one which could explain his observations. He will never be able to compare his picture with the real mechanism and he cannot even imagine the possibility or the meaning of such a comparison.

Because the "watch" can never be opened, asking whether our ideas concerning the natural world are absolutely true is to ask an unanswerable question. Einstein suggested a different view of scientific truth: Truth is what works! Science teachers should acknowledge that even though much scientific knowledge is quite durable, all scientific ideas are open to revision in light of new evidence and interpretations.

Science Has Boundaries

The scientific community tacitly works from three fundamental assumptions: (1) that the natural world is ordered, (2) that humans can come to understand that order, and (3) that understanding that order is inherently good. Working from these and other assumptions, respecting empirical evidence, and demanding naturalistic (i.e., no recourse to the supernatural) explanations, the scientific community has created and continues to create knowledge that is useful for understanding and manipulating the natural world in ways that other knowledge systems cannot.

However, Ryan and Aikenhead's (1992) research indicates that 46 percent of students hold the view that science could rest on the assumption of an interfering deity. This view is one of several that might contribute to the public education controversy over evolution and creationism. In his decision of the court concerning the Arkansas Balanced Treatment for Creation-Science and Evolution-Science Act, Judge William Overton utilized testimony by philosopher of science Michael Ruse regarding the necessary assumption of natural regularity in science (Montagu, 1984, p. 380):

> Creation science as described in Section 4(a) fails to meet [the] essential characteristics [of science]. First, the section revolves around 4(a)(I) which asserts a sudden creation "from nothing." Such a concept is not science because it depends upon a supernatural intervention which is not guided by natural law. It is not explanatory by reference to natural law.

Science does not and cannot deny the existence of the supernatural. Explanations employing supernatural events and/or deities are beyond nature and hence beyond the realm of science. Science deals with the natural world, and consequently, its explanations must be couched in natural expressions with no recourse to the supernatural.

The scientific community's demand for empirical evidence and naturalistic explanations in part account for its success in establishing reliable knowledge about the world. However, these demands also set up boundaries that preclude science from investigating or making claims about that which to many people matters most. For instance, matters of spirituality, morality, and the meaning of life are not amendable to scientific investigation. Dennis Overbye (1993) wrote,

> On God's love science is also silent, and that silence is the wind of liberation. Physicists can neither prove nor disprove that Jesus turned water into wine, only that such a transformation is improbable under the present admittedly provisional physical laws. . . . The fact that science cannot find any purpose to the universe does not mean there is not one. We are free to construct parables for our moral edification.

Understanding the power and limitations of science permits a more accurate assessment of the scientific enterprise's playing field.

Anomalies Do Not Always Result in Rejection of an Idea

Perhaps the most counterintuitive notion from the nature of science is the well-supported view that unsolved puzzles and seemingly refuting evidence do not always result in rejection of an idea. Widely encompassing theories are always faced with anomalies—phenomena that are poorly accounted for or perhaps even contradict the theory. The reasons for this are varied and detailed, but the crux of the matter is that comprehensive theories are not discarded simply because some pieces do not fit. Many historical examples can be found in which contradictory data did not result in abandonment of ideas that we today accept as good science (Chalmers, 1982; Kitcher, 1982; Kuhn, 1970).

For instance, in the nineteenth century, scientists noted that observations of Uranus' orbit departed significantly from that predicted by Newton's gravitational law. Although some scientists at the time speculated that the inverse-square law might not apply at the distance of Uranus, most scientists, noting the enormous success of the Newtonian framework in other affairs, rightfully expected the anomaly to be accounted for without abandoning or modifying Newton's law. In 1835, years after the anomaly in Uranus' orbit was first recognized, the return of Halley's comet sparked the idea that celestial bodies beyond Uranus might exert a force on the planet large enough to explain the planet's orbital discrepancy. This confidence, rather than seeing the anomaly as falsifying a well-supported idea, was key in the prediction and discovery of Neptune in 1846.

Scientific Thinking Often Departs from Everyday Thinking

The frustration expressed earlier in this chapter by the student who (1) denied that objects in motion will forever remain in motion unless acted on by another force and (2) stated that the idealized conditions necessary for that relationship illustrate how scientific thinking is in many ways unnatural. Compelling arguments have been made illustrating the curious, if not bizarre, nature of much scientific thinking. Wolpert (1992) and many other authors (Cromer, 1993; Matthews, 1994; Pinker, 1997; Robinson, 1968; Shamos, 1995; Toulmin, 1972) have argued that science involves a unique way of thinking that significantly departs from everyday thinking. For instance, a cursory look at contemporary science ideas shows them to be anything but common sense. Science ideas are often counterintuitive and cannot be acquired by simply observing phenomena. Much effort along with a priori philosophical presuppositions are necessary to understand the goals, processes, and products of science. Doing science often requires a conscious effort to avoid everyday thinking. Aikenhead (1998) has likened the acceptance of the scientific community's world view to crossing a border to a new culture. For instance, according to Matthews (1994), scientific knowledge is based on assumptions that deny the following ideas:

- The world exists to serve human interests.
- Processes in the natural world bring about some suitable final state.
- Natural processes are activated and controlled by spiritual influences.
- Knowledge comes simply from the observation of things as they are in their natural state.
- Knowledge claims are validated solely by their successful predictions.
- Personal status alone confers authority in defining and maintaining knowledge.
- Knowledge is a fixed and unchanging system.

Yet most students agree with some or all of these assertions. The a priori assumptions of students likely align with the everyday thinking of laypeople, not with those of the scientific community. Effective science teaching will make apparent the scientific community's fundamental assumptions underlying scientific knowledge and, most important, their usefulness so that students can cross into the science culture (at least for the purposes of engaging in science instruction) and understand, not just memorize, scientific understandings of natural phenomena.

Effectively Teaching the Nature of Science

Although major reform documents emphasize the importance of accurately conveying the nature of science to students (AAAS, 1989; McComas & Olson, 1998; NRC, 1996), few teachers do so. Science teachers, reflecting their own science education experiences, possess inaccurate views of the nature of science (Lederman, 1992) and are generally unaware of the social and cultural construction of scientific thought (Brush, 1989). Over thirty years ago, Elkana (1970) stated that science teachers' views concerning the nature of science trailed contemporary philosophical views by more than two decades. DeBoer (1991), in his review of the history of science education, argued that the positivist view of the philosophy of science from the last century still informs much classroom practice and pervades most available curriculum materials. Science textbooks, common cookbook laboratory activities, and most audiovisual materials downplay human influences in research, sanitize the processes that eventually result in knowledge, and portray science as a rhetoric of conclusions. Compounding the problem, science teachers too often simply do not consider the nature of science an important component of science education (Bell, Lederman, & Abd-El-Khalick, 1997; King, 1991).

The irony of this situation is that despite teachers' intentions, they cannot escape conveying an image of the nature of science to their students. Research makes clear that specific teacher practices do affect students' conceptions of the nature of science (Benson, 1984; Dibbs, 1982; Haukoos & Penick, 1983; Lederman, 1986; Zeidler & Lederman, 1989). Cookbook laboratory activities, textbooks that report the end products of science without addressing how the knowledge was developed, misuse of important words that have special meaning in a science setting, and traditional assessment strategies are just some of the ways in which students pick up misconceptions about the game of science. The issue is not whether science teachers will teach about how the game of science is played, only what image of the rules will be conveyed to students. However, instruction that accurately portrays the nature of science to students is not easy, and awareness of particular strategies is critical for creating an effective game plan.

Implicit and Explicit Nature of Science Instruction

Just as knowing how a sport is played does not confer the ability to coach, simply having an accurate understanding of the nature of science is a necessary but insufficient condition for effectively teaching it to students. Planning and implementing lessons is a complex process, and teachers, including those who possess accurate nature of science conceptions, often overlook or downplay nature of science (NOS) instruction. Those who do seriously consider such instruction might believe that if they plan effective inquiry activities, then students will pick up the nature of science that is implicit in those experiences. However, research does not support this commonsense view (Lederman, 1992). Owing to years of science instruction that has consistently conveyed inaccurate portrayals of the nature of science, students have developed deeply held misconceptions that rarely respond to accurate implicit NOS instruction. These expansive yet inaccurate frameworks regarding the characteristics of science and how it works act as filters that blind students to the implicit messages in well-constructed inquiry experiences. Students, like scientists, are not objective, and prior knowledge plays a profound role in making sense of new experiences. Hence, teachers must explicitly draw students' attention to the NOS issues that are inherent in science lessons. Explicitly teaching the nature of science does not mean lecturing about it, but it does mean raising questions and creating situations that compel students to consider NOS issues inherent in laboratory activities, readings, and other science education experiences.

Decontextualized and Contextualized NOS Instruction

Many science textbooks contain a chapter appearing early in the book that addresses how science is done and characteristics necessary for doing science. Unfortunately, these descriptions are almost always erroneous. Rather than use these poor resources, some teachers take this opportunity to explicitly create experiences that more accurately convey the nature of science. For instance, experiences such as discrepant events, puzzle-solving activities (Clough, 1997), "black box" activities, pictorial gestalt switches, and the fossil activity described by Abd-El-Khalick, Bell, and Lederman (1998) and Lederman and Abd-El-Khalick (1998) are often used to introduce important ideas about the nature of science. Activities, readings, and discussions whose sole purpose is to illustrate important ideas about the game of science are examples of what Clough and Olson (2001) refer to as explicit *decontextualized* nature of science instruction. This approach isolates and emphasizes to students fundamental NOS issues in familiar, concrete ways that are not obstructed by unfamiliar science content. This is akin to having an athlete run particular patterns and linking such an activity to playing a sport. However, even though learning skills in isolation is important and easily justified, coaches know that such experiences by themselves do not effectively teach an athlete how a game is played.

Clough and Olson (2001) point out that the above sorts of NOS experiences, even when inserted later between the teaching of science content, remain decontextualized in at least two senses:

> First, such activities may easily be seen by students and teachers as not reflecting authentic science research. That is, the activities may create two conceptions of the nature of science—that illustrated by these sorts of activities and an alternate view associated with authentic science. Much has been written acknowledging that incongruent perspectives can exist side-by-side with no awareness of the contradiction. Second, teachers may see such experiences as "add-ons" and rebel against taking instructional time away from teaching science content. This latter concern was noted by some teachers in a study by Abd-El-Khalick et al. (1998) for not incorporating the nature of science into their teaching. Moreover, these sorts of experiences convey to teachers that effectively teaching the nature of science is a matter of having many activities and resources (Abd-El-Khalick et al., 1998).

So although explicit decontextualized NOS teaching is important in setting a stage for further instruction, it alone is insufficient for developing a robust understand of the nature of science.

Unlike the above experiences, explicit *contextualized* NOS instruction explicitly draws students' attention to important NOS issues entangled in science content and its development (Clough & Olson, 2001). More detailed examples of these sorts of experiences are described by Clough (1997) and include (1) addressing nature of science issues entangled in laboratory activities, (2) presenting science content (e.g. interactive presentations and reading assignments) in a way that accurately reflects its development, (3) the value of historical anecdotes, and (4) the critical role of the teacher. Contextualized NOS is so tightly linked to the science content being learned that conveying how it is *like* science is unnecessary. That is, students are, to the extent possible, *doing science* (i.e., learning science content through their own inquiry) while being explicitly guided to NOS issues in their inquiry. When learning science content through personal inquiry is not appropriate, students explore NOS issues that are inherent in the process scientists went through in piecing together that knowledge (i.e., learning science content as an inquiry process). Teaching science as inquiry and through inquiry is at the heart of most science education reform, and effectively teaching the nature of science is necessarily bound up in this effort (Duschl, 1987).

Game Plan for Accurately Conveying the Game of Science

Understanding the importance of accurately teaching the nature of science, possessing knowledge of important NOS issues, and awareness of explicit decontextualized and contextualized NOS teaching strategies are all critical components in putting together a coherent game plan that will make apparent and tackle students' embedded misconceptions. Teachers are more likely to embrace and promote accurate student understanding of the nature of science if they also have a more concrete picture of what student actions are congruent with that desired state. Articulation of the learning expected of students provides a framework for selecting particular activities, strategies, and teacher behaviors that will move students toward a better understanding of how science works. Clough (1998) provides a list of student actions that are consistent with an understanding of the nature of science. Students who deeply understand the nature of science will do the following:

1. Accurately describe what is meant by "the nature of science"
2. List questions that those who study the nature of science might ask
3. Describe the differences, similarities, and interactions among basic science, applied science, and technology and provide examples of each
4. Describe how laboratory work and puzzle solving activities are alike
5. Articulate why scientific explanations are couched in naturalistic terms with no recourse to the supernatural
6. Describe how science affects society through the technological innovations that flow from it and provide several examples illustrating this
7. Describe how science affects society through the philosophical issues that its ideas raise and provide several examples illustrating this

8. Provide examples of how society affects science and technology
9. Provide arguments against a universal, ahistorical, step-by-step scientific method
10. Explain the value of imagination and creativity in doing science
11. Provide examples of how scientific ideas are not exact descriptions of laboratory data
12. Justify that science ideas, while durable, are not absolutely certain
13. Properly use significant nature of science language (e.g., "law" and "theory")
14. Relate each of the above to laboratory experiences throughout the year
15. Question readings that distort the nature of science

Initially, few if any students will adequately address these issues, but identifying what they do think will help to inform a teacher's game plan. Students tend to share many common NOS misconceptions, making the task of identifying those less daunting. Students' conceptions can be identified through large group discussions, formative written assignments, or available pencil-and-paper tests. Lederman, Wade, and Bell (1998) review the pros and cons of a number of NOS assessment instruments that teachers might consider using with students. Cobern and Loving (1998) provide a detailed description of an engaging NOS card-exchange activity that both introduces students to the nature of science and provides the teacher with key insights into students' thinking on such issues.

Having identified common student thinking, many science teachers choose to initially confront misconceptions with explicit decontextualized experiences. Clough (1997, 1998) illustrates how discrepant experiences, NOS readings such as those found in Table 8.1, and NOS multimedia can be used in these instances. Lederman and Abd-El-Khalick (1998) provide many specific NOS activities that teachers and students will enjoy while also learning much about the nature of science.

However, despite a one- or two-week effort at explicit decontextualized NOS teaching, students often cling to their misconceptions. This tenacity is not surprising in light of overwhelming evidence suggesting that students' understanding is woven into the fabric of their prior experience and is quite useful to them in making sense of those experiences. How, then, are teachers to facilitate more contemporary portrayals of the nature of science? The key is to nurture in students a sense of dissatisfaction with their archaic notions of the nature of science. Clough (1997, 1998) and McComas (1998) provide many examples illustrating how science teachers can maintain pressure on students' misconceptions about the nature of science and facilitate student consideration of more contemporary views.

For instance, properly constructed inquiry laboratory activities provide wonderful opportunities for students to experience and understand much about the nature of scientific research. Because students have typically experienced only cookbook activities and highly structured lab reports, Colburn and Clough (1997) suggest a gradual approach to moving students toward more decision making that will in time more accurately reflect authentic science. Early in the school year, teachers might have students, in groups of two, decide how to convey the results of their laboratory work. This means deciding what to include in the report, whether or not to use data tables and graphs, and the order in which to present the information. Lacking prior experience in making

Table 8.1 Examples of explicit decontextualized NOS readings

Bednarek, D. I. (1993, May 9). Friction: Heat-loving bacterium roils two worlds. Business, academia spar when product of basic research proves practical. *The Milwaukee Journal.*

Begley, S. (1992, November 30). Math has B on its face: The foundations of mathematics have serious flaws. And that may imperil all the sciences. *Newsweek,* p. 73.

Bridgman, P. W. (1960). Explanation. In *The logic of modern physics* (pp. 37–39). New York: Macmillan.

Elmer-Dewitt, P. (1994). Don't tread on my lab. *Time, 143*(4), 44–45.

Feynman, R. P. (1955). The value of science. In *What do you care what other people think?* New York: Norton.

Feynman, R. P. (1966). What is science? A speech to the National Science Teachers Association. *The Physics Teacher, 7*(6), 313–320.

Gyorgyi, A. S. (1964). What is science? *Science, 146*(3649), 1278–1279.

Hoffmann, R. (1993, January–February). For the first time, you can see atoms. *American Scientist,* pp. 11–12.

Klapper, M. H. (1995). Beyond the scientific method. *The Science Teacher, 62*(6), 36–40.

Medawar, P. B. (1973). The pure science. In P. B. Medawar. (1990). *The threat and the glory: Reflections on science and scientists* (pp. 225–227). New York: HarperCollins.

Medawar, P. B. (1973). The cost benefit analysis of pure research. In P. B. Medawar. (1990). *The threat and the glory: Reflections on science and scientists* (pp. 220–224). New York: HarperCollins.

Medawar, P. B. (1963). Is the scientific paper a fraud? In P. B. Medawar. (1990). *The threat and the glory: Reflections on science and scientists* (pp. 228–233). New York: HarperCollins.

National Institutes of Health. (1984). *Why do basic research.* NIH Publication Number 84-660, Bethesda, MD: Author.

Overbye, D. (1993, April 26). Who's afraid of the big bad bang? *Time,* p. 74.

Van Allen, J. A. (1964, February). Science as a human enterprise. *Current Science,* 3–7.

these sorts of decisions, students will likely ask for clarification, but teachers must refrain from directly answering such requests for help. Rather, they should ask students questions such as "What would a reader need to know to follow your work and resulting conclusions?," "How might you present your data in a way that is easiest for the reader to grasp?," and "Who tells a research team exactly how to write their manuscripts for publication?" After students struggle through their initial draft, the teacher would then have them meld into groups of four and share their reports, reflecting on the pros and cons of the different approaches. At this time, a classroom discussion about students' approaches, the pros and cons of each, and how this process mirrors scientists writing their lab reports should occur. Afterward, students write their final draft to turn in. The process deeply engages students in the content illustrated in the lab experience while also explicitly teaching the NOS in a contextualized manner. And teachers have far fewer lab reports to grade!

In future laboratory experiences, the lab and discussion of results take place before the teacher tells students what "should" occur. Lab procedures might have to be rewritten so that they do not convey what is to be expected; this process is illustrated in detail by Clough and Clark (1994a) and Clark, Clough, and Berg (2000). Colburn and Clough (1997) urge postlaboratory discussions in which teachers ask questions such as "What were you investigating?," "What were your results?," "Why do you think the lab procedure was set up in this particular way?," "What interpretations can be made about the data?," and "What have you learned from doing the activity?" Effective use of students' responses and referring back to their lab results set students up for the questions such as "What does your struggle to make sense of the lab results indicate about scientific data?," "Why would scientists looking at data have to go through the same struggle?," and "What does this experience illustrate about the nature of scientific research?" Clough (1997, p. 197) argues that "Student skepticism should be directed back to the laboratory procedure, evidence accumulated, and interpretations made." In experiencing aspects of authentic science, students will at times exhibit the frustration, delight, success and failure, and uncertainty that are inherent in understanding the natural world.

As the school year progresses, more student decision making should be promoted by having the students decide how to go about investigating laboratory research questions. After several such experiences, students can be encouraged to ask their own laboratory research questions and decide how to answer them. How this can be accomplished and the accompanying needed change in the teacher's role (Colburn & Clough, 1997) are extensively illustrated in work by Clough and Clark (1994b), Clark et al. (2000), and Clough (2002). These kinds of experiences provide excellent opportunities to teach students the ways in which scientific papers and science textbooks distort how scientific knowledge is created and comes to be accepted by the scientific community.

Contextualized NOS instruction also demands that readings and teacher talk, so ubiquitous in science education, be examined for their portrayal of the nature of science. Most science textbooks severely distort the nature of science, but a valuable learning experience is to have students critically analyze their textbook's portrayal of the nature of science throughout the school year. Through effective questioning and other means, have students consider how written materials distort or ignore (1) the meaning of words such as "law," "hypothesis," "theory," and "prove"; (2) the human side of science; (3) that assumptions underlying knowledge; (4) the difficulties in research including making sense of data; and (5) the justification for conclusions. The same critical approach should be applied to audiovisual materials.

Some of the readings suggested for explicit decontextualized NOS instruction, if used when teaching science content contained in those articles, are useful in contextualized NOS instruction. Other readings, such as portions of Peter Medawar's (1963) "Is the Scientific Paper a Fraud?" might be perfectly situated after the lab experiences suggested above to illustrate how formal scientific reports and textbooks distort the nature of science. Clough (1997) suggests how portions of *The Double Helix* (Watson,

1968) while teaching genetics, *A Revolution in the Earth Sciences* (Hallam, 1973) when investigating continental drift and plate tectonics, *The Big Splash* (Frank, 1990) when studying the origin of our planet's water, and *Seeing Atoms* (Trefil, 1990) and *For the First Time, You Can See Atoms* (Hoffmann, 1993) when teaching atomic structure, promote an understanding of the nature of science in an explicit contextualized manner.

In all contexts in which teachers talk to students, teachers must be aware that their use of language conveys images of the nature of science (Munby, 1976; Zeidler & Lederman, 1989). The same concerns that surround science textbooks arise in the way many teachers talk about science. Implementing accurate historical examples at teachable moments will also effectively convey a more accurate portrayal of the nature of science. None of this will be easily accomplished, but just as coaches videotape practices and games to assess performance and improve their players' performance, audiotaping and videotaping can help teachers to understand their use of language, what it communicates to students, where historical anecdotes could be useful, how their questions did or did not draw students' attention to the NOS, and how to improve their practice.

Teachers can be assured that their efforts to improve students' understanding will, over time, meet with success. When attempts have been made to include teaching about the history and philosophy of science, they have been found to be effective in improving students' understanding of important issues in the nature of science (Cossman, 1969; Crumb, 1965; Klopfer & Cooley, 1963). Evidence also exists that the game plan advocated in this chapter results in student understandings that are retained long after such instruction ends (Clough, 2001).

CONCLUSION: The Value of Comparing Science to a Game

In teaching about the nature of science, the metaphor of science as a game can be useful in convincing students that outside a science context, they need not personally adopt the rules, but that understanding the rules will help in understanding the processes and content of science. Understanding and using ideas without believing them to be true can be fruitful in many contexts. For instance, in 1867, Friedrich Kekule von Stradonitz, a chemist who is given credit for having suggested a structure for benzene, reputedly wrote, "I have no hesitation in saying that from a philosophical point of view I do not believe in the actual existence of atoms. . . . As a chemist, however, I regard the assumption of atoms as absolutely necessary." Similarly, students can learn about the game of science—its assumptions, processes, and outcomes—without abandoning their personal or cultural belief systems. The increasing diversity in our nation's schools might necessitate this approach if we are to reach the lofty goals set forth in Project 2061 (AAAS, 1989), Benchmarks for Science Literacy (AAAS, 1993), and the National Science Education Standards (NRC, 1996).

The Game in Action

Teaching the Nature of Science, Naturally

Mr. Isaac teaches tenth grade introductory biology and eleventh grade ChemCom chemistry at Clearwater High School in the upper Midwest. Like all teachers, he wants his students to develop a deep understanding of the most fundamental ideas in the subject he teaches. To him, this means far more than accurately reciting the content of the course. It means using science ideas to solve in-school and out-of-school problems, critically analyzing situations, effectively communicating ideas, and other actions listed in Table 8.2. What sets Mr. Isaac apart from many teachers is his insight that the deep understanding of content that so many teachers seek can be achieved only by purposely promoting most, and perhaps all, the student goals in Table 8.2.

Table 8.2 Mr. Isaac's student goals for science education

Students will:

- Convey self-confidence and a positive self-image.
- Use critical thinking skills.
- Convey an understanding of the nature(s) of science.
- Identify and solve problems effectively.
- Use communication and cooperative skills effectively.
- Actively participate in working towards solutions to local, national, and global problems.
- Be creative and curious.
- Set goals, make decisions, and accurately self-evaluate.
- Convey a positive attitude about science.
- Access, retrieve, and use the existing body of scientific knowledge in the process of investigating phenomena.
- Demonstrate deep robust understanding of fundamental science concepts.
- Demonstrate an awareness of the importance of science in many careers.

Emphasizing scientific literacy, Mr. Isaac keeps all his goals for students and their interactions in mind when planning lessons and teaching students. For instance, he knows that students' conceptions about the nature of science significantly affect their attitude toward science, learning of science content, and other desired ends. In conversations early in the school year, he hears students say things such as the following:

- I wouldn't want to major in science because I like to be creative.
- Science is just a bunch of facts.
- It's just a theory, not a law.

- Science ideas are strange.
- Scientists are successful if they correctly follow the scientific method.

These statements reflect just some of his students' misconceptions that were identified in the first week of school through his use of the card-exchange activity (Cobern & Loving, 1998) and selected items from the Views on Science-Technology-Society instrument (Aikenhead & Ryan, 1992; Aikenhead, Ryan, & Fleming, 1989).

Mr. Isaac is painfully aware that teachers cannot escape teaching about the nature of their discipline and that what students learn about the nature of science typically outlasts what they learn about traditional science content. Reflecting back on his own struggles to teach science well, he knows that the popular science textbooks and cookbook activities that he used early in his career conveyed a number of misconceptions to students about the character of science and scientists. In talking with his former students, he has found that at the forefront of their recollection about school science is their impressions of what science and scientists are like.

For these and other reasons, Mr. Isaac puts significant effort into accurately conveying the nature of science to his students but always with his other student goals in mind. Early in the school year, he devotes a week and a half to a unit emphasizing the nature of science. Aware of the unfamiliar and abstract nature of what he intends to convey about how science works, he engages students by using attention-getting activities that play off students' prior experiences. He begins the unit by having students solve everyday brain-teasers. For instance, one puzzle asks students to make the following mathematical statement, constructed with sticks, correct by moving only one stick:

$$VI = II$$

A commonly proposed solution is to slightly move one of the sticks that make up the V so that it forms an X, resulting in

$$XI = II$$

Proponents claim that it represents "eleven equals eleven," but many students balk at the proposed solution, arguing that mixing Roman and Arabic numerals is not appropriate. Advocates snap back that no rule exists forbidding such a solution. This does not satisfy the detractors, and a discussion ensues about what unspoken rules should govern proposed solutions. Mr. Isaac asks students to consider how what they are doing is similar to what doing science is like. He also has students examine the value of having a solution to a puzzle, albeit one with recognized problems, versus no solution at all.

Students also suggest moving any stick and placing it over the equal sign to form "≠". Many students like this solution, but others argue that it does not make the mathematical statement an equality. Advocates of the solution attempt to discredit this point by arguing that the goal is to make the statement correct, not equal. One student is bothered by the solution because any stick may be moved to create an inequality, and that is not a clear solution. Many supporters see this flexibility as adding beauty to the solution. The debate goes back and forth, with advocates lining up in both camps. As frustration mounts, students often want to decide the matter by voting, but Mr. Isaac takes this opportunity to ask how electing an idea will resolve their genuine lack of consensus about the puzzle's solution. The idea that valid scientific knowledge is not determined through majority rule raises in students minds the question of how scientific knowledge does come to be accepted—a complex issue that Mr. Isaac revisits throughout the school year.

Mr. Isaac then asks students to consider for a moment that they represent the scientific community and that, as decades passed, overwhelming consensus had been reached for a particular solution. He follows this with "If most everyone in the scientific community accepts a particular solution to a puzzle, what happens to those few scientists who refuse to abandon other ideas?" Students quickly see that those scientists would be seen as out of touch and ignored. Wanting students to make an important connection between science education and mistaken notions about the nature of science, he asks, "So what would appear and what would be left out of science textbooks that students read in secondary school and college?" Every year Mr. Isaac works to set students up for this insight, and he loves to see their expressions when they see that the accepted solution would appear with no mention of the evidence and arguments that were presented for all solutions as the scientific community wrestled with the puzzle. This obviously makes for a teachable moment concerning how science textbooks, for the most part, distort the nature of science—something of which Mr. Isaac reminds his students throughout the course.

Of course, students want to know what is *the* answer, and Mr. Isaac responds that he doesn't know, but he read in a journal that a group of scientists had proposed the following solution requiring a novel conceptualization of the problem. This group of scientists moved the left hand stick making up the "V" and attached it at the top of the right hand stick so that it sat horizontally over the Roman numeral one:

$$\sqrt{1} = 1$$

Many students are pleased with the newly proposed solution, although others immediately attack it, claiming that square root signs have a stub that forms a little "v" at the bottom. Mr. Isaac then says, "Even if you do not like the solution, what made it so difficult to develop?" After this discussion, he asks, "How would new science textbooks be written if the scientific community now reached consensus that this solution was what nature is like?" Mr. Isaac is pushing students to see that both nature and the scientific community play a role in shaping the ideas that we accept as good knowledge. These and other problem-solving activities such as gestalt switches and black box activities such as the mystery tubes (Lederman & Abd-El-Khalick, 1998) are used to illustrate the following similarities between doing science and puzzle solving (Clough, 1997):

- Creativity, imagination, logic, intuition, serendipity, aesthetics, and personal preferences all play a part in solving puzzles and doing research.
- No universal step-by-step method for deriving solutions exists.

- A puzzles solver's or researcher's prior knowledge determines what solutions are possible and probable. Without a suitable conceptual framework, a researcher is likely to be unable to determine whether a problem exists, how to solve it, or what an appropriate solution would look like.
- An inability to solve a puzzle or settle a research question does not place the puzzle at fault. Rather, it means that the problem's difficulty is greater than the imagination of the researcher.
- The "truth" of a solution is never known for certain, but solutions must at the very least work (account for natural phenomena) to some extent.
- How well a solution works is constrained by what the natural world is actually like, but just as in the puzzle described above, the scientific community, using numerous explicit and implicit criteria, makes judgments in deciding which proposed solution works best.
- Attempting to solve a problem by changing the "rules" (i.e., previously accepted scientific knowledge) is rarely accepted without resistance.
- Until another solution is in hand, entirely abandoning an existing solution, however problematic, makes no sense.

Over the years, Mr. Isaac has accumulated readings and videos that directly target accurate portrayals of the nature of science. He punctuates these experiences with questions that explicitly direct students' attention to important points about the nature of science such as "How is that like science?" and "What about this activity is like what scientists do?" He explicitly says to students that science can be thought of as a game but that to play it, one has to know something about how the game is played. Because the activities and readings during the 1½-week NOS unit are not integrated with science content that students are expected to learn, Mr. Isaac uses them in both his biology and chemistry classes.

Despite this extensive and well-planned effort, Mr. Isaac knows that two weeks of instruction will not fundamentally change his students' notions about the nature of science. Students' misconceptions about the character of science and scientists have developed over many years and are linked in numerous ways to science content they have been taught. Hence, those mistaken notions will not be changed with a short unit that is detached from the science content students are expected to learn. Nonetheless, he uses the unit to raise interest, introduce several fundamental NOS issues in familiar contexts that he will revisit throughout the school year, and communicate the importance that he will place on understanding the nature of science.

For the remainder of the school year, Mr. Isaac integrates the nature of science with the content he teaches in his biology and chemistry courses. For instance, like most biology students struggling to observe cheek cells under the microscope for the first time, his students incorrectly interpret air bubbles as cells. Rather than correct their errors, he asks questions such as "What are the general characteristics of a cell?" and "What makes you think then that what you are observing is a cheek cell?" When more hands go up than he can respond to in a reasonable

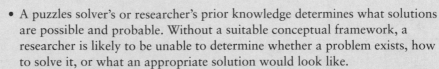

time, Mr. Isaac stops the class, goes to the board, and draws an air bubble and a cheek cell. He says to the class, "In observing your work, in general I see the following two drawings. How can you account for your looking for the same thing but seeing different things?" Students respond that they do not know for certain what a cheek cell looks like. "So what does that indicate about the importance of prior knowledge in observing," Mr. Isaac asks? After students respond, he asks more questions such as "But students are often told that they should be objective in making observations and not let their prior thinking bias their work. Why is that not only impossible, but not desirable? If objectivity is not possible or desirable, what should we be after?" Tying this experience to the puzzle-solving activities helps students better understand the important point that all scientific work is influenced by prior knowledge (i.e., the theory-laden character of science).

When performing laboratory activities in chemistry, Mr. Isaac takes this same approach of using students' experiences and connecting them to issues in the nature of science. Pushing students to interpret data and what that implies about the nature of science soon expands into analyzing laboratory procedures, inventing them, considering where lab questions arise, and eventually having students create their own laboratory questions. When safety or cognitive issues call for more directive laboratory procedures, he asks students to analyze their experiences for how these accurately and inaccurately portray the nature of science. At an appropriate time in the course, students read "Is the Scientific Paper a Fraud?" by Peter Medawar (1963), a paper that Mr. Isaac has adapted to fit his students' reading level.

Of course, Mr. Isaac also presents information to his class, but he does so in a way that better captures the nature of research. In biology, he introduces Mendel's work not as a rhetoric of conclusions but rather as an unfolding story full of issues that convey much about the thrill and frustration of doing science. For instance, what drove Mendel to devote so much time to studying the passing on of traits? What was the historical context of his work? How did Mendel arrive at his ideas? Knowing the importance of language in accurately portraying the nature of science, Mr. Isaac is very careful in his choice of words and phrases. He avoids statements such as "What did the data tell Mendel?" or "What do the data indicate?" Instead, he purposely says, "Note that the data are not talking to Mendel, they're not simply telling him what to think. Instead, Mendel has to *invent* ideas that will *account for* the data. In this case, Mendel *invented* the idea of "factors"—something (he didn't know what) that caused particular traits. Mendel's thinking went something like the following: "While I do not know what these factors are, if we assume they exist I can show how the data I get may be understood in terms of those factors." Furthermore, Mendel could predict the results of particular crosses.

Mr. Isaac emphasizes that the story is even more complex because the data do not reflect the precise ratios that Mendel's factors predicted. Mendel's contemporaries largely rejected his ideas because they had no direct evidence for the existence of factors, nor did many believe that mathematics could be applied to complex biological systems. Mr. Isaac stops and asks students what this illustrates about how science is done. He plays off students' suggestions, posing more questions that raise insights into how scientific progress is a long, complex argument that does not follow the simplistic "scientific method" that is so often found in textbooks.

As the genetics unit progresses, he shows students how existing knowledge drives future research—its questions, procedures, interpretations, and conclusions. For example, Mendel's work was recognized decades later at a time of rapid developments in microscopy. Using more powerful instruments, scientists were peering into cells and began connecting what they observed with Mendel's postulated "factors." This illustrates how technology promotes and is promoted by developments in science, a point that Mr. Isaac raises by asking questions rather than boring students by lecturing. "Scientists soon were investigating what these factors consisted of, and when that answer achieved some consensus," he says and then asks, "What do you suppose scientists began researching?" After playing off students' ideas, he then has them read a small portion of James Watson's *The Double Helix* (1968) in which Watson writes (Stent, 1980, pp. 18–19):

> Of course there were scientists who thought the evidence favoring DNA was inconclusive and preferred to believe that genes were protein molecules. Francis, however, did not worry about these skeptics. Many were cantankerous fools who unfailingly backed the wrong horses. One could not be a successful scientist without realizing that, in contrast to the popular conceptions supported by newspapers and mothers of scientists, a goodly number of scientists are not only narrow-minded and dull, but also just stupid.

Continuing his theme of teaching biology and chemistry in a manner faithful to the nature of science, Mr. Isaac asks questions that have students consider the following:

- How science textbooks inaccurately convey that science ideas are "discovered"— akin to finding gold in the ground
- The necessary role of creativity and imagination in science. He reminds students that Einstein said imagination was often more important than knowledge in doing research.
- What the roles of data, individual scientists, and the broader scientific community are in generating knowledge
- What all this implies about science, scientists, and science education

Ever mindful of his student goals, Mr. Isaac accomplishes all this in ways that force his students to speculate, test and defend ideas, and develop a deeper understanding of science content. Because all the goals are intertwined, he less often resorts to making comparisons to how what occurs in class "is like" science. Because students are learning science in ways that are faithful to how it is done, the connections are more immediate and robust.

In addition to the formative assessment that is ever present in Mr. Isaac's teaching, he also ensures that his summative assessments, laboratory write-ups, and other assignments have portions that address the nature of science. The evidence that he collects indicates that his students are developing the deep understandings of

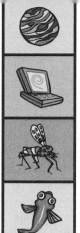

science content and the nature of science that he promotes. To him, the anecdotal evidence is even more compelling. Students increasingly question readings, television programs, and even teachers who distort the nature of science. A group of students have become so interested in the issues raised that they ask about further reading materials and whether he has ever considered teaching a course solely about the nature of science. Although always self-assessing and working to improve his teaching, Mr. Isaac knows that what he does is making a significant difference in the thinking of his students.

Reflecting on the Game

1. What do you believe are the compelling reasons for teaching the nature of science? List the reasons you would provide so that colleagues, administrators, and parents would understand your rationale.
2. Describe the most positive experience you have had in teaching or learning about the nature of science. In your description, be sure to address what occurred in the class and what the teacher's role was.
3. A beginning science teacher asks you to describe the key aspects that

are essential in the successful design and delivery of nature of science instruction. List these key aspects and explain what makes each aspect so important.
4. How might an accurate understanding of the nature of science be helpful to science teachers in sequencing science content to be taught?
5. How might an accurate understanding of the nature of science be helpful to science students learning science content?

References

Abd-El-Khalick, F., Bell, R. L., & Lederman, N. G. (1998). The Nature of science and instructional practice: Making the unnatural natural. *Science Education, 82*(4), 417–436.

Aikenhead, G. S. (1998). Border crossing: Culture, school science, and assimilation of students. In Roberts, Douglas and Ostman, Leif (Eds.), *Problems of Meaning in Science Curriculum.* New York: Columbia University Press. pp. 86–100.

Aikenhead, G. S., & Ryan, A. G. (1992). The development of a new instrument: "Views on science-technology-society" (VOSTS). *Science Education, 76*(5), 477–491.

Aikenhead, G. S., Ryan, A. G., & Fleming, R. W. (1989). *Views on science-technology-society* (Form CDN.mc.5). Saskatoon, Saskatchewan: Department of Curriculum Studies, College of Education, University of Saskatchewan.

American Association for the Advancement of Science. (1989). *Project 2061: Science for all Americans.* Washington, DC: Author.

American Association for the Advancement of Science. (1993). *Benchmarks for science literacy.* New York: Oxford University Press.

Association for Science Education. (1981). *Education through science: An ASE policy statement.* Hatfield, England: Author.

Bednarek, D. I. (1993, May 9). Friction: Heat-loving bacterium roils two worlds. Business, academia spar when product of basic research proves practical, *The Milwaukee Journal*.

Bell, R., Lederman, N. G., & Abd-El-Khalick, F. (1997, January). *Developing and acting upon one's conception of science: The reality of teacher preparation*. Paper presented at the 1997 Association for the Education of Teachers in Science (AETS) Meeting, Cincinnati, OH.

Benson, G. D. (1984). *Teachers' and students' understandings of biology*. Doctoral dissertation, University of Alberta. (ERIC Document Reproduction Service No. ED280683.)

Brush, S. G. (1989). History of science and science education. *Interchange, 20*(2), 60–71.

Campbell, N. (1953). *What is science?* New York: Dover.

Chalmers, A. F. (1982). *What is this thing called science? An account of the nature and status of science and its methods* (2nd ed.) Queensland, Australia: University of Queensland Press.

Clark, R. L., Clough, M. P., & Berg, C. A. (2000). Modifying cookbook labs: A different way of teaching a standard laboratory engages students and promotes understanding. *The Science Teacher, 67*(7), 40–43.

Clough, M. P. (1997). Strategies and activities for initiating and maintaining pressure on students' naïve views concerning the nature of science. *Interchange, 28*(2–3), 191–204.

Clough, M. P. (1998). Integrating the nature of science with student teaching: Rationales and strategies. In W. F. McComas (Ed.), 1998, *The nature of science in science education: Rationales and strategies*. Dordrecht, The Netherlands: Kluwer Academic Publishers. Pp. 197–208.

Clough, M. P. (2001, November). *Longitudinal understanding of the nature of science following a course emphasizing contextualized and decontextualized nature of science instruction*. Paper presented at the 6th International History, Philosophy and Science Teaching Conference with the History of Science Society, Denver, CO.

Clough, M. P. (2002). Using the laboratory to enhance student learning. In R. W. Bybee (Ed.), *Learning science and the science of learning: 2002 NSTA Yearbook*. Washington, DC: National Science Teachers Association.

Clough, M. P., & Clark, R. L. (1994a). Cookbooks and constructivism: A better approach to laboratory activities. *The Science Teacher, 61*(2), 34–37.

Clough, M. P., & Clark, R. L. (1994b). Creative constructivism: Challenge your students with an authentic science experience. *The Science Teacher, 61*(7), 46–49.

Clough, M. P., & Olson, J. K. (2001, November). *Structure of a course promoting contextualized and decontextualized nature of science instruction*. Paper presented at the 6th International History, Philosophy and Science Teaching Conference with the History of Science Society, Denver, CO.

Cobern, W. W., & Loving, C. C. (1998). The card exchange: Introducing the philosophy of science. In W. F. McComas (Ed.), *The nature of science in science education: Rationales and strategies*. Dordrecht, The Netherlands: Kluwer Academic Publishers. Pp. 73–82.

Colburn, A., & Clough, M. P. (1997). Implementing the learning cycle. *The Science Teacher, 64*(5), 30–33.

Cole, K. C. (1985, September). Is there such a thing as scientific objectivity. *Discover*, 98–99.

Collette, A. T., & Chiappetta, E. L. (1984). *Science instruction in the middle and secondary schools*. St. Louis: Times Mirror/Mosby.

Cossman, G. W. (1969). The effects of a course in science and culture for secondary school students. *Journal of Research in Science Teaching, 6*(3), 274–283.

Cromer, A. (1993). *Uncommon sense: The heretical nature of science*. New York: Oxford University Press.

Crumb, G. H. (1965). Understanding of science in high school physics. *Journal of Research in Science Teaching, 3*(3), 246–250.

DeBoer, G. (1991). *A history of ideas in science education: Implications for practice*. New York: Teachers College Press.

Dibbs, D. R. (1982). *An investigation into the nature and consequences of teachers' implicit philosophies of science.* Unpublished doctoral dissertation, University of Aston, Birmingham, UK.

Duschl, R. A. (1987). Improving science teacher education programs through inclusion of history and philosophy of science. In Barufaldi, J. P. (Ed.), *Improving preservice/inservice science teacher education: Future perspectives: The 1987 AETS yearbook.* Location: Association for the Education of Teachers in Science. Pp. 1 23. (Ch. 1)

Einstein, A., & Infeld, L. (1938). *The evolution of physics.* New York: Simon and Schuster.

Eflin, J. T., Glennan, S. & Reisch, G. (1999). The nature of science: A perspective from the philosophy of science. *Journal of Research in Science Teaching, 36*(1), 107–117.

Elkana, Y. (1970). Science, philosophy of science and science teaching. *Educational Philosophy and Theory, 2,* 15–35.

Elmer-Dewitt, P. (1994). Don't tread on my lab. *Time, 143*(4), 44–45.

Feyerabend, P. (1975). *Against method.* London: New Left Books.

Finley, F. N. (1983). Science processes. *Journal of Research in Science Teaching, 20*(1), 47–54.

Frank, L. A. (1990). *The Big Splash.* New York: Birch Lane Press.

Gauld, C. (1982). The scientific attitude and science education: A critical reappraisal. *Science Education, 66*(1), 109–121.

Hallam, A. (1973). *A revolution in the earth sciences: From continental drift to plate tectonics.* Oxford, England: Clarendon Press.

Haukoos, G. D., & Penick, J. E. (1983). The influence of classroom climate on science process and content achievement of community college students. *Journal of Research in Science Teaching, 20*(7), 629–637.

Hodson, D. (1985). Philosophy of science, science and science education. *Studies in Science Education, 12,* 25–57.

Hoffmann, R. (1993, January–February). For the first time, you can see atoms, *American Scientist,* 11–12.

King, B. (1991). Beginning teachers' knowledge of and attitude toward history and philosophy of science. *Science Education, 75,* 135–141.

Kitcher, P. (1982). *Abusing science: The case against creationism.* Cambridge, MA: MIT Press.

Klopfer, L. E., & Cooley, W. W. (1963). The history of science cases for high schools in the development of student understandings of science: A report of the HOSC instruction project. *Journal of Research in Science Teaching, 1*(1), 33–47.

Kuhn, T. S. (1970). *The structure of scientific revolutions.* Chicago: University of Chicago Press.

Lederman, N. G. (1986). Relating teaching behavior and classroom climate to changes in students' conceptions of the nature of science. *Science Education, 70*(1), 3–19.

Lederman, N. G. (1992). Students' and teachers' conceptions of the nature of science: A review of the research. *Journal of Research in Science Teaching, 29*(4), 331–359.

Lederman, N. G., & Abd-El-Khalick, F. S. (1998). Avoiding de-natured science: Activities that promote understandings of the nature of science. In W. F. McComas (Ed.), *The nature of science in science education: Rationales and strategies.* Dordrecht, The Netherlands: Kluwer Academic Publishers. Pp. 83–126.

Lederman, N. G., Wade, P., & Bell, R. L. (1998). Assessing Understanding of the Nature of Science: A Historical Perspective. In W. F. McComas (Ed.), *The nature of science in science education: Rationales and strategies.* Dordrecht, The Netherlands: Kluwer Academic Publishers. Pp. 331–350.

Matthews, M. R. (1989). A role for history and philosophy in science teaching. *Interchange, 20*(2), 3–15.

Matthews, M. (1994). *Science teaching; The role of history and philosophy of science.* New York: Routledge.

Matthews, M. (1997). Editorial. *Science & Education, 6*(4), 323–329.

McCain, G., & Segal, E. M. (1981). *The game of science.* Montery, CA: Brooks/Cole.

McComas, W. F. (1996). Ten myths of science: Reexamining what we think we know about the nature of science. *School Science and Mathematics, 96*(1), 10–16.

McComas, W. F. (Ed.). (1998). *The nature of science in science education: Rationales and strategies.* Dordrecht, The Netherlands: Kluwer Academic Publishers.

McComas, W. F., Clough, M. P., & Almazroa, H. (1998a). The role and character of the nature of science in science education. *Science & Education, 7*(6), 511–532.

McComas, W. F., Clough, M. P., & Almazroa, H. (1998b). The role and character of the nature of science in science education. In W. F. McComas (Ed.), *The nature of science in science education: Rationales and strategies.* Dordrecht, The Netherlands: Kluwer Academic Publishers. Pp. 3–39.

McComas, W. F., & Olson, J. K. (1998). The nature of science in international standards documents. In W. F. McComas (Ed.), *The nature of science in science education: Rationales and strategies.* Dordrecht, The Netherlands: Kluwer Academic Publishers. Pp. 41–52.

Medawar, P. B. (1963). Is the scientific paper a fraud? In P. B. Medawar (1990), *The threat and the glory: Reflections on science and scientists.* New York: HarperCollins.

Meyling, H. (1997). How to change students' conceptions of the epistemology of science. *Science & Education, 6*(4), 397–416.

Montagu, A. (Ed.). (1984). *Science and creationism.* New York: Oxford University Press.

Munby, A. H. (1976). Some implications of language in science education. *Science Education, 60*(1), 115–124.

National Assessment of Educational Progress. (1989). *Science objectives.* Princeton, NJ: Author.

National Research Council. (1996). *National science education standards.* Washington, DC: National Academy Press.

National Science Teachers Association. (1982). *NSTA position statement: Science-technology-society: Science education for the 1980's.* Washington, DC: Author.

National Science Teachers Association. (2000). NSTA position statement: The nature of science. Available: www.nsta.org/159&id=22.

Overbye, D. (1993, April 26). Who's afraid of the big bad bang? *Time,* p. 74.

Payson, S. (1999). *R&D as a percentage of GDP continues upward climb.* Data Brief, National Science Foundation (NSF 99-357). Available: www.nsf.gov/sbe/srs/databrf/sdb99357.pdf

Pinker, S. (1997). *How the mind works* (pp. 302–306). New York: W. W. Norton.

Robinson, J. T. (1968). *The nature of science and science teaching.* Belmont, CA: Wadsworth.

Rowe, M. B., & Holland, C. (1990). The uncommon common sense of science. In Mary Budd Row (Ed.), *What research says to the science teacher: Vol. 6. The process of knowing.* Washington, DC: National Science Teachers Association.

Rowell, J. A., & Cawthron, E. R. (1982). Image of science: An empirical study. *European Journal of Science Education, 4,* 79–94.

Rubba, P. A., Horner, J. K., & Smith, J. M. (1981). A study of two misconceptions about the nature of science among junior high school students. *School Science and Mathematics, 81,* 221–226.

Ruse, M. (1999). *Mystery of mysteries: Is evolution a social construction?* Cambridge, MA: Harvard University Press.

Ryan, A. G., & Aikenhead, G. S. (1992). Students' preconceptions about the epistemology of science. *Science Education, 76*(6), 559–580.

Shahn, E. (1988). On scientific literacy. *Educational Philosophy and Theory, 20*(2), 42–52.

Shamos, M. H. (1995). *The myth of scientific literacy.* New Brunswick, NJ: Rutgers University Press.

Smith, M. U., Lederman, N. G., Bell, R. L., McComas, W. F., & Clough, M. P. (1997). How great is the disagreement about the nature of science? A response to Alters. *Journal of Research in Science Teaching, 34*(10), 1101–1103.

Songer, N., & Linn, M. (1991). How do students' views of science influence knowledge integration? *Journal of Research in Science Teaching, 28*(9), 761–784.

Stent, G. S. (Ed.). (1980). *The double helix: Text, commentary, reviews, and original papers,* Norton Critical Edition. New York: Norton.

Texley, J., & Wild, A. (Eds.). (1996). *Pathways to the science standards: Guidelines for moving the vision into practice,* High School Edition. Washington, DC: National Science Teachers Association.

Tobias, S. (1990). *They're not dumb, they're different: Stalking the second tier.* Tucson, AZ: Research Corporation.

Toulmin, S. (1972). *Human understanding: An inquiry into the aims of science.* Princeton, NJ: Princeton University Press.

Trefil, J. (1990, June). Seeing atoms. *Discover,* pp. 55–60.

Watson, J. D. (1968). *The double helix.* New York: Mentor.

Wolpert, L. (1992). *The unnatural nature of science.* Cambridge, MA: Harvard University Press.

Yager, R. E. (1988). Never playing the game. *The Science Teacher 55*(6), 77.

Zeidler, D., & Lederman, N. (1989). The effects of teachers' language on students' conceptions of the nature of science. *Journal of Research in Science Teaching, 26*(9), 771–783.

Additional Resources

Curd, M. & Cover, J. A. (1998). *Philosophy of science: The central issues.* New York: W. W. Norton.

Duschl, R. A. (1990). *Restructuring science education: The importance of theories and their development.* Teachers College Press. New York.

International History and Philosophy of Science Teaching Group: http://www1.umn.edu/ships/hpst/

McComas, W. F. (Ed.). (1998). *The nature of science in science education: Rationales and strategies.* Dordrecht, The Netherlands: Kluwer Academic Publishers.

Medawar, P. B. (1990). *The threat and the glory: Reflections on science and scientists.* New York: HarperCollins.

Resource Center for Science Teachers Using Sociology, History and Philosophy of Science (SHiPS) http://www1.umn.edu/ships/ SHiPS helps teachers share resources for integrating history, philosophy and sociology in the science classroom. E-mail them at ships@tc.umn.edu for their quarterly news.

start

chapter 9

THE WAVE:
Community Evolution from Spectator to Supporter of Science Education

Jeffrey Weld, Ph.D.
Department of Biology
and Science Education,
University of Northern Iowa

ABOUT THE AUTHOR: Dr. Jeffrey Weld taught high school life and physical science in the Rio Grande Valley of Texas, suburban St. Louis, and rural Iowa before doing graduate study in science education. His interests in learner-centered science have taken the form of NSF-funded curriculum projects, educational video productions, science education organization leadership, local and national consulting, pioneering innovations on campus at the University of Northern Iowa, and a comprehensive research agenda shared through books, magazines, and journals, including *Educational Leadership, Phi Delta Kappan, The Science Teacher, The American Biology Teacher, Education Week,* the *Journal of College Science Teaching,* the *Journal of Science Teacher Education,* the *International Journal of Science Education,* and *Teacher* magazine.

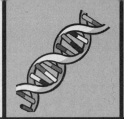

> **What is both surprising and delightful is that spectators are allowed, and even expected, to join in the vocal part of the game.**
>
> —George Bernard Shaw

CHAPTER WARM-UP

The foundation of a modern, successful science education program is fan support from parents, business leaders, school administrators. Twenty-first century science is active, investigative, and relevant to the community, calling more and more on a team of assistant coaches beyond the walls of the lab. Learners in a science-supportive community perform better, enjoy science more, are more confident and more likely to become scientists, and have better relationships with their teachers. It is up to science teachers to initiate this wave of support and reap the benefits of home field advantage.

INTRODUCTION: The Wave

Legend has it that the Wave was born twenty years ago on an overcast Halloween Saturday in Seattle, Washington. Characteristic of the heated rivalry between conference powers Stanford and the University of Washington, the atmosphere at the football game was electric. Ninety thousand fans packed Husky Stadium to cheer on their home team against the visiting Cardinals and their star player, John Elway. On that fateful day, those 90,000 discordant and peripheral individuals were transformed into one teaming mass of undulating purple and gold by cheerleader Rob Weller. With their Huskies down by seventeen points in the third quarter, Weller and band director Bill Bissell coaxed their languid audience to rise section by section in an inspiring crest of enthusiasm that rippled across the stadium. The crowd's collective energy swept like a tsunami across the turf, boosting the beleaguered Huskies to reel off twenty-eight points for the upset victory.

The Wave has caught on; it is now ubiquitous at sporting events, concerts, and political rallies. The Wave's success stems from engagement: Observers become participants who have tangible influence on an outcome. The Wave is about dismantling the anonymity of the crowd while unifying purpose. It is about empowering the passive to become active. Science education needs the Wave.

The Wave in Science Education

Science education has its own version of the stadium, diffuse and modest though it might be, consisting of walls and windows, lab benches and Bunsen burners, computers and bulletin boards. The players operate in a seeming vacuum of fan support, but it is there, if indirect. Beyond the walls are parents and community members who have a keen interest in the performance of science team members. They cheer, wring their hands, wrestle with angst, and leap with joy over achievement. They also puzzle over the game played behind the walls of the lab—how to support it, how it supports them. The supporters of science education can be peripheral, maybe even inconsequential, to the outcome of the game when they have no role to play. Like Huskies fans before the Wave, parents and other citizens of the community might wonder whether their contributions have any effect. Lacking participation, they might even grow critical of the game and its coaches, questioning practices and performance.

The opinion research organization Public Agenda surveyed business leaders about whether high school graduates had the necessary skills to succeed in the workplace. Fifty-eight percent of them believe graduates lack those skills (Public Agenda, 1998). A poll conducted by the educational organization Phi Delta Kappa revealed that most parents were dissatisfied with the nation's schools: The majority gave schools a C or lower in terms of performance (Rose & Gallup, 2001). Fans of science education are unenthusiastic and restless over how the game is progressing. However, evidence suggests that parents are willing to accept part of the responsibility: They admit to being disengaged fans. Most parents blame lack of parental involvement for most of school ills, according to another Public Agenda survey (1999). And of course, the popularity of school choice initiatives across the country attest to disenfranchised clients of education.

Building our fan base, then, should be a primary concern for science educators. We need to establish and maintain the interest and enthusiasm of parents, businesses and industry, and other community members with whom a healthy collaborative exchange can define a winning program. There needs to be a little bit of Rob Weller in all science teachers, who should drum up support for their players and the game they promote by inviting those on the periphery to take an active role in the daily events of the classroom and laboratory.

 ## The Value of Engaged Spectators

Building the Wave

The very foundation of a modern, successful science education program consists of supportive students, parents, business leaders, and school administrators. The road to inquiry science teaching, as defined by the contributors to this collection, can be difficult to navigate even for teachers with the best of intentions when the support of school clients is not there. Indeed, the thirty-year effort toward science education reform has been an arduous journey in part because many families have yet to understand, let alone embrace, the teaching practices born of educational research (Chiappetta, Koballa, & Collette, 1998; Kim & Kellough, 1995). Citizens who have no formal training in education are unaware of accumulated knowledge in learning and cognition or our evolving goals for science education. Without that knowledge, many of the strategies of effective science teachers—investigative learning, student-centered curriculum design, cooperative grouping, problem-solving skill development, authentic assessment—might appear novel to the point of being suspect. A phrase that is often heard by inquiry science teachers who encounter parents at open house or parents' conferences is "This isn't how I learned science." Nor should it be. An exciting dimension of twenty-first century science teaching is the promotion of science literacy within and beyond the laboratory walls to include parents and other community members within the sphere of influence. In an elegantly cyclical fashion, citizens beyond the school become essential contributors to the very inquiry experiences that make science different from, and more effective than, what parents knew.

Efforts to involve the community more integrally in the business of science education date back to the 1980s, when school visionaries suggested that real educational reform would need to involve the entire educational community (Brandwein, 1981; Goodlad, 1984). Historically, private enterprise often interpreted this involvement as being the giver while schools played the role of receiver. Today, the most powerful and successful collaborations recognize that all partners have something to gain (NSF, 1997). This key aspect of a successful science education program has resulted in a prominent place for community building in the National Science Education Standards. Science Teaching Standard D reads: "Teachers of science design and manage learning environments that provide students with the time, space, and resources needed for learning science" (National Research Council, 1996, p. 43). This standard includes an action plan to identify and use resources outside the school:

> The school science program must extend beyond the walls of the school to the resources of the community. Our nation's communities have many specialists, including those in transportation, health-care delivery, communications, computer technologies, music, art, cooking, mechanics, and many other fields that have scientific aspects. . . . these can contribute greatly to the understanding of science and encourage students to further their interests outside of school.

The idea of community networking takes root when the system, building or districtwide, embraces its importance. Although individual teachers can be catalysts, it is beyond their power to fully carry out an action plan for involving the community in science education. The Standards refer to program standards, one of which supports teachers in building collaborative outreach opportunities. Program Standard D states, "The K–12 science program must give students access to appropriate and sufficient resources, including quality teachers, time, materials and equipment, adequate and safe space, and the community" (NRC, 1996, p. 218). This standard too includes an action plan to identify and use resources outside the school:

> Good science programs require access to the world beyond the classroom. Relationships should be developed with local business and industry to allow students and teachers access to people and institutions, and students must be given access to scientists and other professionals . . . to gain access to their expertise.

Before and since the creation of the National Science Education Standards, the National Science Foundation (NSF) funded science education reform initiatives at the local, regional, and national levels. In planning for making changes in the direction of student-centered inquiry in science class, the NSF advised that "valuable plans are the result of a cross-section of people, inside and outside the school system, working together with a common goal of improving all students' access to high quality science programs" (NSF, 1997, p. 17). Generating a wave of support for the science program by engaging parents and community in the day-to-day actions of the learning laboratory is essential to promoting goals such as career awareness, equitable opportunity for all students, the development of skills in reasoning and problem solving, and science content literacy. A community wave of support for science has its own analogous effect of a tsunami of energy sweeping across the turf. This wave, though, drives and sustains achievement in science.

Community Engagement Supports Learning

The potency of community engagement for promoting learning has to do with how people learn. Whether it be students of science or learners of medieval literature, Monopoly or the Macarena, common characteristics of novel knowledge and tasks make them learnable or not. "Learnable" in this educational sense means more than memorization for eventual recall. True learning means an ability to make sense of any new information that relates to what has been learned and to apply new knowledge and skills to solve problems or decipher situational complexities—in other words, synthesis and application (Rutherford & Ahlgren, 1990). So what are these common characteristics that make knowledge and tasks learnable? Anyone who has attempted to learn the Macarena or any other dance step knows them inherently. But the bonanza of educational research on learning and cognition over the last two decades has codified, formalized, and validated them, enabling the vast improvement of teaching (Bransford, Brown, & Cocking, 2000).

First and probably foremost, learning requires that it be relevant to the learner. For the Macarena or any new dance step to come easily to the learner, it has to matter. The imminent threat of an exam following instruction is not enough to surpass the mental threshold for permanent alteration of thoughts and mental processes. Rather, Macarena ability might be instrumental in gaining some broader goal, such as status on the dance floor or physical fitness. Likewise, learning science requires that the skills and knowledge acquired in class have bearing on students' lives outside of academia.

The temptation to delineate the factors that lead to learning in a hierarchical fashion is a false implication that there is an order of importance to them. Though it is not unprecedented in the educational literature to do so, ranking these common characteristics is akin to prioritizing our bodily organs from most important to least. We cannot survive without all of them. Therefore, the second essential characteristic of learnable tasks is that they relate to prior knowledge or belief. Perhaps the dance step is similar to other movements that are familiar to the learner, such as the slide step of a bowler or reaching for an apple. Students of science need to establish such links from what they know currently to the new knowledge that is coming in through their senses.

The senses are a third vital characteristic for learning. The more of the senses are brought to bear on new experiences, the more likely that the event will make lasting impressions. To see how momentum increases proportional to mass as well as to hear it and maybe even feel it provides critical sensory mass for surpassing the mental threshold for true learning. Fourth, a new learning task must be challenging for the learner. Brains are remarkably efficient at filtering the inconsequential and prioritizing the meaningful. Tied closely to relevancy, then, is the notion that new knowledge challenges the learner as something intriguing and important. Furthermore, for true learning to take place, an event must be developmentally appropriate for the learner. Just as the Macarena requires an appropriate degree of coordination, an appreciation for atomic bonding requires that the learner be capable of dwelling in the abstraction of indirect or circumstantial evidence.

Table 9.1 lists the characteristics of the learnable event and how these relate to community engagement.

Community engagement in science education benefits learners by tapping into the characteristics of meaningful learning. Ideas that arise in science class have relevant applications beyond the classroom walls in the worlds of industry, homemaking, and hobby. Students who interact on the community level using science knowledge draw heavily on classroom experiences or ideas when encountering applicable real-world situations. And because those real-world situations are seldom limited to listening or seeing, but involve the full immersion that is typical of real life, they are

Table 9.1 Community engagement meets learnable event characteristics

Learnable Event Characteristics	Community Engagement Feature
Relevance	Tasks, experiences, and knowledge are contextual, applied to real problems that relate to students' lives.
Prior knowledge link	Academic and experiential knowledge are built upon through novel real-world experiences.
Multisensory	Doing typifies community engagement experiences, to include communication and observation, manipulation and solutions.
Challenging	Real-life experiences are complex rather than the distilled models of science class.
Developmentally appropriate	Learners opt to a level and degree of engagement that suits their developmental levels when given autonomy.

multisensory events. Real-life engagements in applications of science are likely to be far more challenging than the contrivances of the school classroom. And when given the option of determining for themselves the level and degree of engagement in community experiences related to science, learners approach novelty governed by their own developmental capabilities.

By establishing relationships within the broader community—the spectators of our game—teachers tap into a powerful mechanism for enhancing learning in science. Community engagement facilitates the goals of modern science education by teaching the way in which people learn. The idea of the power of community engagement for meaningful learning is hardly new. John Dewey (1916) noted long ago,

> Formal instruction easily becomes remote and dead—abstract and bookish. . . . There is a standing danger that the material of formal instruction will be merely the subject matter of the schools, isolated from the subject matter of life-experience. (p. 8)

Dewey's prescience is remarkable in that he had virtually none of the empirical evidence for experiential learning that by today is quite undeniably rich. Broadening our definition of the science class community breaks down the counterproductive isolation Dewey spoke of, thereby accessing students' natural propensity to learn.

Community Engagement Benefits Learners

The sorts of things that facilitate learning exist in a collaborative relationship with the community. It is no wonder, then, that improvements to learners' performance and attitudes manifest themselves when the school walls are figuratively torn down. Sounding suspiciously like an educational panacea, community-linked science classrooms are associated with better academic performance, improved attitudes about science, enhanced esteem and confidence in abilities, increased likelihood of entertaining career options in the sciences, and better relationships between teachers and their students. It's the equivalent of a flurry of touchdowns made as a result of the Wave, but science classes ought not to wait until the third quarter to start the Wave.

In his essay entitled "Seventeen Reasons Why Football Is Better Than High School," Herb Childress (1998) makes a powerful case for stunningly talented kids who are numbingly disengaged in many modern classroom experiences. He states that music, theater, or soccer can be substituted for football, and the seventeen reasons still hold true. For our purposes, "community-based learning" can substitute for "football" to get the same effect. The following are five reasons, then, why community-based learning improves on the prevalent isolated model first described by Dewey nearly a century ago:

1. In community-based learning, teenagers are considered important contributors rather than passive recipients. The very nature of community engagement is the active role assumed by learners. Passive absorption is rarely used and then only in dollops sandwiched between meaningful tasks. Rarely in traditional science classrooms have students been accorded shared control of the lesson or course direction. Players in the game of science education are valued for what they bring to learning tasks. Their playing field is considerably broadened when teachers facilitate connections to the broader community.

2. In community-based learning, players can let the team down. When teachers in isolated classrooms or laboratories tell their students "We're all in this together," they speak in a limited sense merely of themselves and a group of students; the students do not have equal status with the teacher. When the curriculum is broadened to tap into and affect students' local and global communities, the term "we" becomes encompassing and equitable. Students depend not only on each other, but also on significant others—supporters who include parents and local professionals. And in contrast to traditional classrooms, where responsibility is narrowly defined as personal accountability, community engagement requires interpersonal accountability of students.

3. In community-based learning, the unexpected happens all the time. There is an aspect of comforting safety to the science experiences most of us enjoyed as students—predictable learning events such as prescribed labs and routine assessments. For students who engage in investigations or other learning challenges that branch out to involve other stakeholders, predictable routine is replaced by intriguing twists, tangents, and unknowns. This is the fuel for meaningful learning, as described earlier: the relevant and complex nature of real-world problems and issues.

4. In community-based learning, players get to choose their own roles. A student-centered science class is defined by the many essays in this collection to be one in which learner histories, interests, and abilities govern all aspects of the course—its launch points, sequence, pace, depth, and scope. It is contrary to student-centered philosophy for teachers to strictly define roles in a broad sense as teacher

and learner as well as in a narrow sense as learners of stoichiometry by listening, for example. Students can and should sometimes be teachers, and all students should explore key concepts and processes in science through mechanisms suitable to individuals. Using the community as an extended classroom gives students unique pathways to understanding and situates them to possess knowledge that is not widely held and deserves to be taught.

5. In community-based learning, there is lots of individual instruction and encouragement from adults. Science and its societal ramifications are much too complex for any individual, even the most highly trained science teacher, to command. Attempts to be the first and final word in science lead to a familiar tribulation known to every science teacher: having to tackle the material, sometimes the night before class, to stay ahead of students. It is a tall and nonsensical order when expertise beyond the classroom walls exists. What students of science by inquiry need is guidance, not answers, and guidance can be labor intensive. By tapping the expertise of the community, a science teacher delegates some of the responsibility for education to an appropriate team of supporters.

It comes as no surprise, in light of the many benefits of school-community partnerships, that students who enjoy science connected to the outside world outperform those from schools that are isolated from their communities (Staley, 1993). Community involvement in schooling "sets in motion a constellation of activities and improvement that contribute to student achievement" (Hatch, 1998, p. 19). For example, community-oriented programs have demonstrated that participating students experience more psychological, social, and intellectual growth, including positive effects on grades and attendance, than nonparticipating students do (Nolan, Chaney, & Chapman, 1997). The research literature on the benefits of community partnerships are replete with anecdotal successes, including an elementary school where average test scores went from last in the district to third following a school-wide community engagement project and another school where passing rates on a state-mandated test jumped from 27 percent to 61 percent in reading and from 21 percent to 51 percent in math following a similar project (Hatch, 1998). On a more abstract level, students in community-linked learning experiences gain a sense of accomplishment and a confidence borne of having made real and substantive contributions to local or global good (Abbott, 1995; Sandler, Vandergrift, & VerBrugghen, 1995).

Obvious and paramount community partners are parents. Their associations with children's academic lives bring such pervasive benefits that schools can be only fractionally effective in their absence. So well documented is the power of parental involvement that it has become a national priority (Goals 2000, 1998). Consider the overwhelming research evidence: Children whose parents are involved are more likely than other youths to have positive educational outcomes such as improved academic performance, better school attendance, higher aspirations, reduced dropout rates, and increased graduation rates (Chen & Chandler, 2001). This vital factor in education holds true on an international scale; comparisons of students in mathematics and science on the Third International Mathematics and Science Study showed a strong positive relationship with home environmental factors (Smith, Martin, Mullis & Kelly,

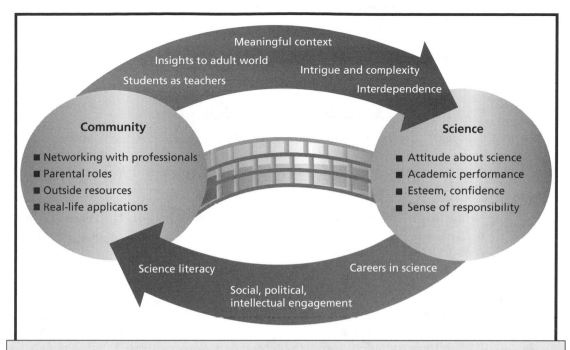

Figure 9.1 Positive feedback loop of community-classroom engagement

2000). It can be unequivocally stated that some measure of parental involvement in children's education is a critical link to achieving high-quality education (as cited in Giddings, 1999).

Schools and science teacher who actively engage parents in the day-to-day events of the class create a positive feedback mechanism whereby parents who participate in their children's education report higher levels of involvement both at home and at school (Vaden-Kiernan & Chandler, 1996). Their children, meanwhile, report a greater degree of enjoyment of science along with increased academic achievement and increased likelihood to be involved in extracurricular activities at the school (Henderson & Berla, 1994). This is the very boost that a wave of community support can provide young players of the game of science (see Figure 9.1). Parental engagement is strong in children's early years in many schools but wanes at grade levels at which children often need it most. For example, school programs that involve parents generally become less strong and comprehensive as children enter higher grade levels (Vaden-Kiernan & Chandler, 1996). Both teachers and parents make the grand and erroneous assumption that a partnership is not as important as children move toward the high school level, when we know that parents remain the most influential persons in students' lives throughout teen and adult years (Kim & Kellough, 1995). And in the most challenging of school settings, where poverty, violence, high dropout rates, and learner apathy prevail, parental involvement is least likely (Moreno, Tharp, & Denk, 1999). Teachers and parents of students at upper grade levels and in challenging school settings need to redouble their efforts toward achieving partnership in pursuit of the many learner benefits of a community wave of support.

Community Engagement Benefits Schools

Although learners and the act of learning itself are the focus of community engagement, teachers and their schools stand to gain a great deal by cultivating partnerships. After all, schools are public institutions that are increasingly held accountable for demonstrable successes by their constituency. To revisit a point that was made earlier, a disconnected fan base can lead to distrust and suspicion, whereas an engaged legion of fans is more likely to support a coach and his or her players. Teachers and schools need parental and community support to achieve any and all educational objectives—from pedagogical to infrastructural.

The goals of student-centered science teachers—things like critical thinking and reasoning, problem solving, and science literacy—are often not intuitively shared by a local citizenry that is more familiar with an antiquated brand of content-driven, didactically delivered science education. So too are the methods of student-centered science teachers foreign to outside observers—things like cooperative learning, open investigation, and higher-order thinking and questioning (NSF, 1997). Not only are modern goals and methods for science held in a limbolike state until parents see reasons to embrace or refute them, but students themselves might at first resist the innovative practices that are defined as inquiry (Bybee, 1993). Teachers and administrators who incorporate research-based practices into their schools and classrooms need the full support of the community to make it happen. Parents and other citizens who are invited to become team members in community-based science programs are transformed into cheerleaders for innovation. Several research studies indicate that family attitudes toward education and their understanding of schools improve as a result of involvement (Bauch, 2000; Sanders, Epstein, & Connors-Tadros, 1999). The mechanisms for fostering a cheerleading cadre of local citizens are detailed in a subsequent section of this chapter. For now, suffice it to say that the single greatest benefit of community engagement for science teachers is the essential support for the very educational practices that utilize the broader community itself.

Those goals and practices mean little if the resources and physical conditions of science classrooms inhibit intrepid teachers' agendas. Numerous success stories of involved communities stepping up to help meet the physical needs of inquiry classrooms attest to the power of collaboration (Abbott, 1995; Hatch, 1998; Lewis & Morris, 1998; Peoples, 2001). Outfitting labs and equipping teachers to carry out modern investigative science classes are key contributions of the community, to be sure. But the personal resources that are accorded to schools by local citizens are invaluable. Science as it applies to everyday living at home, at work, at leisure, and in transportation cannot possibly be represented within the confines of the school science laboratory. Science teachers who are willing to share responsibility for educating their clients with the broader community get the broader community's expertise in return. Teachers cannot be phlebotomists, petroleum geologists, physical therapists, and particle physicists *and* be good teachers. But good teachers know that students need contact and exposure to the professional world of science, so they seek out and cultivate those sorts of relationships. In turn, school and classroom goals and objectives gain the advocacy of many influential allies.

Community Engagement Benefits Parents

The obvious benefit to parents whose children are connected to the community through science experiences is that their children become better students and citizens. However, specific advantages for individual parents accrue as bonus effects of school-community bridges. These effects enhance parents' relationships with schools and with their own children.

Given the myriad ways in which parents can involve themselves in their children's education, some of which are described in a later section of this chapter, the parent/community-school relationship is truly a symbiotic one. Both parties stand to gain a great deal. Parents get an education of their own in the process of helping to educate children. They learn about science, about children in the informative milieu of the school, and about modern schooling itself. Whether parents involve themselves peripherally or centrally in the science classroom, that very association advances their knowledge of the goals and methods of modern science, a critical foundational event for the progression of science education reform (Chiappetta et al., 1998; NSF, 1997). Involved parents are privy to the many successes of effective science teaching and the hurdles that might hinder it. Nascent empathy evolves into support for programs. But more than that, parents' own science literacy grows through involvement with school science. Exemplary science teachers are the resident experts of the community when it comes to the sorts of skills and knowledge citizens should possess for effective participation in a scientific society. Part of the responsibility of that position is to extend that expertise beyond merely the students of the school to include their parents and community members at large. Parent participants in school science programs are treated to many of the same benefits of inquiry science as their children: content within community context, skills of investigation, and applications of science knowledge within the broader sphere of people's lives. As school-community partnerships in science positively influence attitudes, knowledge, and outlooks about science among students, so too can the effect be accorded to parents.

A common lament from citizens of the general population is that they do not understand kids today. Many parents have only a tenuous hold on knowledge of the motivations and interests of their children, particularly as they progress through K–12 schooling (Vaden-Kiernan & Chandler, 1996). Part of the reason for misunderstandings is that the time parents spend with their children has declined by 40 percent since 1960 (Gianetti & Sagarese, 1998). In a poll of middle school teacher in the United States and Canada, half responded "no" to the question "Do you believe parents are well informed with regard to what is happening in their children's lives academically and socially?" There is one type of knowledge on which teachers have an absolute monopoly and about which parents and others in the community are intensely interested: knowledge about children—what they know, what they think, how they interact. Invitations to collaborative with the school science program give parents a rare window into the lives of their own and other children.

In addition to learning about the nature of science learning, about science itself, and about children's academic worlds, parents stand to benefit on a broader level of empowerment when they are part of a school-community team. Relationships with teachers and their schools gives parents a voice in what is often perceived of as an insulated enterprise (Shumow & Lomax, 2001). Voice begets efficacy, and efficacy begets educational advocacy. Educational advocacy among parents of the community can only further the agenda of innovation that has been a theme of this chapter. Parental efficacy brings a significant personal advantage as well: increased likelihood that parents become engaged in other issues and opportunities in their communities (Lewis & Henderson, 1998). Science teachers have a powerful position in an educational network that benefits stakeholders well beyond children in classrooms, and it is teachers who must usually start building the bridge to collaboration. Educational research informs us of that which makes perfect sense: Invitations to become involved in school result in more parental involvement in school (Eccles & Harold, 1994).

Community Engagement Benefits the Community

"Schools are *in* communities, but often not *of* communities" (Bouillion & Gomez, 2001). Partnerships between science teachers and the parents and other citizens they serve render schools of communities. The two become interchangeable: The school is an encompassing community, and the community is certainly a school. And as in the symbiotic relationship of school-parent partnerships, a number of benefits accrue to the community as a whole when it is engaged in school science education. Communities that are accessed by inquiry science classes span micro and macro dimensions, from learner communities of schools to local valence communities to regional satellite communities to a global community. Likewise, the dividend that is reaped from community investment in schools has dimensions ranging from local to global. Those returns ultimately affect the quality of life through an active and informed citizenry who make responsible decisions economically, environmentally, and ethically.

Student-centered inquiry science embraces relevance as the foundation for successful learning, and relevance depends on community linkage. When inquiry science teachers navigate explorations of atoms, aerodynamics, or animal behaviors, they call on community resources for building relevance. These and other science ideas are only half-baked if they end when the students go out the school laboratory door. Application is where any idea in science matters, and applications abound beyond the school walls.

Where the ideas of science are being applied happens to be where students of science need to be delivered by their K–12 schooling experience (NRC, 1996). The relevance of atoms as explanation for any and all materials is important, to be sure, but hardly the end of the story in modern science education. The applied science of atomic energy, of nuclear medicine, or even of particle acceleration in which we can learn more about atoms—that is the degree of relevance required of successful science education. Our increasingly technological society depends on an active and informed citizenry that is capable of, and interested in, wrestling with the tensions between competing ideas in science (Miller, 1996). What percentage of community resources should be devoted to pure versus applied research? What are the ramifications of various technologies on health, welfare, environmental sustainability? School-community partnerships enable depths of pursuit of these complex questions beyond a level that either could do alone. The payoff for communities that invest in this quality of education is a future citizenry that considers all sides, respects divergent opinions, actively engages in vital issues of our times, and responsibly advances the collective culture (Miller, 1996; Rubba & Wiesenmayer, 1993; Staley, 1993).

School-community partnerships are based on investment for a human resource return. Investors are parents, business leaders, community activists, industrial workers, homemakers, and others who can help to balance the mental portfolios of graduates. The investment is time. As a result, our human resources are more ethically balanced, economically productive, politically engaged, and environmentally responsible (Yager, 1996).

A Win-Win Enterprise

A wave of parental and community support provides a number of benefits for students, families, and communities, schools, and teachers (see Figure 9.2). Undeniable evidence of the potent role parents and communities play in the lives of learners takes on a particular urgency when one considers the amount of time teachers spend with students in school. School occupies roughly 14 percent of students' youthful lives, whereas home and community corral 53 percent (Bransford et al., 2000, p. 148). We can only hope that academic dreams take up some fraction of the 33 percent of time students spend sleeping. The many advantages of connecting the learning environment of school with the learning environment of communities can be exponentially increased by erasing boundaries between the two, by which the lion's share of 67 percent of a student's life can be science time!

How to Build a Wave of Support for Science Education

The conception of an effective science program that integrates the community has been a giant step for all stakeholders. The instigator and pivotal role player is the science teacher (NRC, 1996; NSF, 1997; Vaden-Kiernan & Chandler, 1996). In designing or reforming a science program to take a team approach, parental and community involvement must occur simultaneously with other curricular and pedagogical groundwork, rather than elsewhere on a to-do list. This next section describes specific roles, responsibilities, and example bridging that defines school-community partnerships.

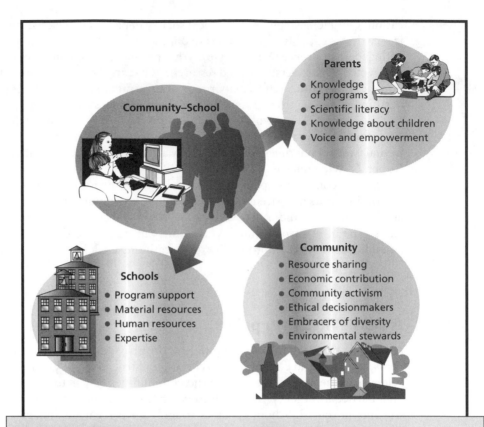

Figure 9.2 Benefits of student engagement in community to home, school, and community

The Science Teacher–Parent Partnership

The very nature of a partnership boils down to individual players bringing skills and specialized knowledge to the relationship, resulting in successes that no individual could realize alone. Partnerships are reciprocal. The many benefits to teachers, parents, and learners in partnership are by now clear. What remains is to clarify the responsibilities, or offerings, each brings to the science education table.

First and foremost, science teachers need to educate their parent partners about how and why they teach science. "Science educators need to do a better job of engaging community support by giving the public an accurate portrayal of the goals of reform" (NSF, 1997, p. 22). Integration of parental expertise and support can hardly be effective in a vacuum of goals and objectives. Science teachers need well-formulated rationales or philosophies, supported by research and elucidated in national standards. The teacher's rationale, which includes justifications for consensus goals for learners and accompanying action plans for attaining those goals, should take the form of a manifesto to be shared with all who have a stake in student learning: administrators, parents, colleagues, and students themselves. The rationale should then be widely disseminated. Goals should be splashed across laboratory walls. Philosophy and supporting documents such as mass media articles on science education reform should be made available to parents at conferences and through electronic or print communications. Teachers should seek out opportunities to speak with parents and parent organizations about these evolving goals and strategies of science education (Giannetti & Sagarese, 1998). Only then are parents in a position to offer support at home and at school for student inquiry. Second, then, science teachers should invite parent participation in the science program—as effective supporters of student learning and as expert resources themselves for the science program.

The national Parent-Teacher Association (PTA) developed a set of six standards for parental involvement in school, each of which carries specific ramifications for successful science partnerships:

1. Regular communication between home and school
2. Support in parenting skills
3. An emphasis on assisting student learning
4. The promotion of volunteering at school
5. Parent involvement in school decision making and advocacy
6. Collaborations with the community to provide needed resources (Sullivan, 1998, p. 44).

These PTA standards describe the reciprocity that makes teacher-parent partnerships mutually beneficial. By communicating the goals and rationale of modern science education with parents (standard 1), teachers support a home learning environment that aids in the achievement of the many benefits of collaboration (standard 2). Parents are more effective advocates for school science (standard 3) when they are invited to actively engage in the science program (standard 4). The many intellectual and physical resources that can be brought to bear in a parent-teacher partnership (standard 5) can have great influence on the curricular directions and decisions made by science teachers (standard 6). A great deal is asked of parents in partnership, which is why a shared philosophy through open and frequent communication is so important. Yet a third responsibility of teachers as partners reflects parents' ultimate motivations for alliance: their children's success. Demonstrable evidence of success for learners of science through inquiry becomes for many parents the "bottom line" in determining their level of engagement in the partnership. Providing such evidence goes well beyond reporting test scores (despite a national fever over standardized exams, as reported elsewhere in this book). Obligation to parents in this regard requires providing tangible evidence of conceptual as well as so-called affective growth as a result of community alliances for science (Weld, 1997). Student-centered science teachers look at assessment through wide-angle lenses and have a profound responsibility for communicating this broad perspective as well as its indicators of student learning, to parents.

Parents, for their side of the bargain, have a responsibility to support science learning on a number of fronts, from mundane to thematic. The many dimensions of parental involvement in a science education partnership include aiding and abetting community-linked science inquiry under the broad umbrella of events called "homework," bringing specific knowledge and expertise to bear in children's science classes, serving as a network of resource acquisition for the science class, and providing community leadership for advocacy of pedagogical and curricular innovations in the science class.

Research indicates that the most powerful role parents can play in their children's academic lives is not school-based involvement, but rather how that learning is supported at home (Finn, 1998). When parents work in concert with science teachers who successfully transmit their rationale for learning and accompany it with invitations for parental involvement, homework takes on an entirely new meaning, becoming much more than simply defining terms or building science fair projects. Instead, an atmosphere of achievement at home fulfills parents' end of the partnership. When parents model the characteristics of successful learners—curiosity, a work ethic, and clear communication, for example—students are more likely to adopt or refine those traits at school (Finn, 1998). In addition to modeling effective learner characteristics, parents in partnership actively organize and monitor their child's time, ensuring adequate devotion to learning tasks as defined through open communication channels of the partnership. They discuss school events, progress, and learner's self-concepts related to science and in turn communicate these unique insights to the science teacher. And of course, parents who are partners in science education help with homework. But the nature of inquiry science homework—data gathering, opinion sampling, expert consulting, report or display creation—requires an informed parent partner who shows interest in the student investigation, helps to locate human or material resources, and asks the sort of questions that guide learners on school tasks (Ho & Willms, 1996; Holliday, 2001; Hoover-Dempsey, Battiato, & Walker, 2001).

Secondary to assistance provided to the science program at home (to be more precise, away from school), parents possess specific knowledge and expertise that are vital to an inquiry science approach. Modern science teaching is investigative and community relevant, which makes it heavily resource dependent. Students need access to viewpoints and expertise on a great variety of subjects that fall within the purview of an academic year of science, and parents are a ready-made human resource pool of willing participants in this aspect of inquiry. They also represent a rich network for the acquisition of material resources. The concentration of supplies in the science lab calls for the casting of nets across the community; parents can be those nets. And when invited to participate in these many ways, parents become involved advocates for the science program, rather than those fans distanced from the playing field who wonder what impact, if any, their presence plays in the science successes of their players. Advocates facilitate the science program by their encouragement, their trumpeting of program goals and methods, and their vote. Teacher and parents are partners in science education, with mutually beneficial responsibilities toward learning, as depicted in Figure 9.3.

The Science Teacher–Community Partnership

Communities have vested interests in the success of local schools, which are the vehicle of economic and civic enrichment. Indeed, on a global scale, schools transmit the human values of sustainable societies: respect, knowledge, and forethought. So it is that the school-community partnership carries great responsibility for working together effectively toward fulfillment of the maxim that we're all in this together. The perspective

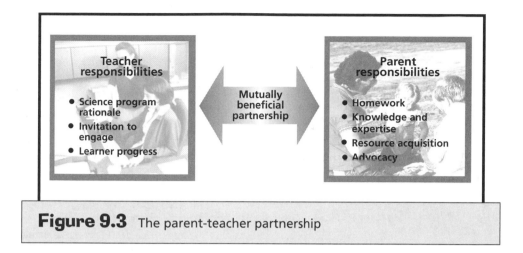

Figure 9.3 The parent-teacher partnership

of community in this partnership spans a range of proximity from the immediate surrounding community to an encompassing international community, all within the domain of responsibility of individual teachers of science. It is a daunting order, made possible through a student-centered inquiry approach to science teaching.

Communities need school science to contribute to the well-being and advancement of the community. That is the science teacher's end of the partnership, and it comes quite naturally by way of community-engaged learners. Students need to educate themselves about the social, political, moral, and physical infrastructure of communities to be contributors. Teachers need to accord their students opportunities to mingle science class knowledge and events with corollary issues of their world beyond the school. Community success depends on this preparatory function of schools. Moreover, communities depend on schools to impart basic skills, attitudes, and knowledge to students for the betterment of the community. These future citizens, parents, and school partners themselves can best contribute when their science education teaches responsibility, sensitivity, creativity, reasoning, and respect along with basic facts and concepts of science.

Communities that value and expect those educational outcomes happen to be the very mechanisms by which they are developed. The responsibility of the community, then, is to be accessible. Science teachers should be able to access the human and material resources of the community, expect program support from the community, and derive professional development from the community toward the realization of those lofty goals. When the science curriculum requires of students a link to their proximate and ultimate communities, experts and institutions need to avail themselves as information and inspiration sources. For effective science teachers to maintain a challenging and relevant program, the community must bring influence to bear financially and politically. And for teachers to build this very bridge of partnership, the community must assume a role of advocate, providing teachers with the necessary professional development to understand and develop community-linked programs. Science teachers and the community are partners in education, with mutually beneficial responsibilities toward learning, as depicted in Figure 9.4.

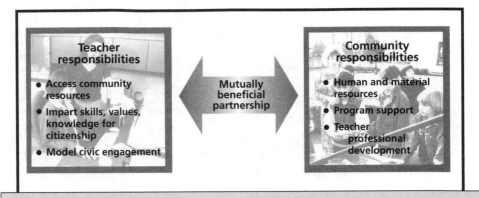

Figure 9.4 The teacher-community partnership

CONCLUSION: The Wave in Science Education

An African proverb resonated famously with the American public when then First Lady Hillary Rodham Clinton invoked it in a speech and later a book of the same title: "It takes a village to raise a child." Ample research on the benefits of school-community partnerships has added empirical credibility to inviting village involvement in children's education. A community that is engaged in the education of its youth can expect of them higher academic achievement, increased motivation, bolstered confidence, heightened probabilities of science career choices, and better relationships with teachers at school. The community reaps even more basic benefits to contributing as a village to the education of students in science: they give back as socially responsible, factually informed, ethically balanced individuals who are ready to assume adult positions in the local and global community. Indeed, it takes a village to educate students of science.

In his book *Martin Manley's Basketball Heaven* (1989), Manley details the statistical effect of the home court advantage: The home team wins 66.7 percent of the time. Considering that the game itself does not change with the venue—court dimensions are constant, hoop heights are consistent, and ball type, size, inflation, are controlled—there is an undeniable fan impact on performance in sports. The effect was observed in a recent football season of the University of Northern Iowa Panthers. An overall record of 5 and 6 overshadowed a remarkable 4 and 1 home field record. Panther fans have standing invitations to engage in support of their team; in return, they cheer, chant, and exhort their players to attain levels of execution that are unachievable without the crowd's wave of enthusiasm.

Schools have a perpetual home field advantage but often fail to take advantage of the fan support for building winning programs. The verdict is in, and the village stands ready. Science teachers need to start the Wave.

The Game in Action

Roadkill and Radon: A Community Wave of Support for Science Education

The collar of Jason's black leather jacket was flipped up so that it was tucked under his long red hair in the back and brushed against his sparse adolescent beard toward the front. He wore reflective sunglasses, the kind with chrome on the outside so you could see only yourself if you looked in Jason's eyes. His feet were propped up on the desk at the back of the lab.

"Is my nose really *that* big?" asked Mr. Ramirez as he pretended to examine himself in the reflection of the sunglasses. "Please take them off in school, Jason, and put your feet down on the floor. I'm afraid you'll tip back and hurt yourself."

"Man! Don't worry about me. Too many people think they have to worry about me. The only person need to worry about Jason is Jason." But when he removed his sunglasses, it was obvious that not enough people were worrying about Jason. His eyes were red and puffy from lack of sleep, his clothes smelled of marijuana smoke, and his grades were barely minimal.

"How did our brainstorming session strike you, Jason?" Mr. Ramirez sat down in an adjacent desk. "Anything on that board sound inspiring?"

"No, man, I ain't into farmers, and I don't give a . . . " Jason glanced at his sidekick, Lanny, and smiled, ". . . about acid rain." Lanny grinned widely at Jason's defiance.

"This is the direction we're heading, my boy, investigating the natural world around you—animals, plants, air, dirt, everything." Mr. Ramirez persisted patiently. "You might as well take advantage of the situation, Jason, and take up something that interests you, even if only in the slightest. Now what might that be?"

"Roadkill, man," said Jason sarcastically. Lanny laughed. Mr. Ramirez scratched his chin, contemplating Jason's *Metallica* T-shirt momentarily. Then he smiled and said, "I think we can run with this, fellows."

Mr. Ramirez's sophomore biology class had been invited to shape the upcoming unit on environmental studies by brainstorming issues—things of local and global importance in the realm of nature and environmental balance. They had come up with quite a list for investigations:

- Radon in our basements and its effect on health
- Emissions from the city's electrical power generating plant
- Acid rain
- Pesticide run off into Lake Red Rock
- Topsoil erosion
- Alien species introductions, especially Asian lady bugs
- The environmental and economic impact of corporate farms in the area
- Pollution emissions from students' cars and trucks
- Water quality
- Deer overpopulation

- Human population growth
- Reintroductions of osprey to the area
- Toxic by-products of a local plastics manufacturer
- Hospital wastes
- Deforestation and wood consumption at a local window manufacturer
- Suburbanization of the city's perimeter
- Roadkill

Next, Mr. Ramirez outlined the parameters for the studies that were to span the coming month. Student groups were charged with developing expert authority on their chosen topics. Several components made up the studies: original laboratory investigations, background research into the global aspect of the topic, local research into the immediate concerns and impact of the topic, and a packaged presentation of all findings for reporting at an eventual environmental colloquium.

At the next class meeting, Mr. Ramirez led two more brainstorming sessions. First, students were invited to offer ideas for resources and strategies for getting to the bottom of their topics. They needed access to telephones for contacting local officials. Mr. Ramirez added that they might consider meeting people face to face. They needed Internet access for regional and global fact finding. They wanted to know what kind of experiments they could do. Mr. Ramirez assured them that between himself and some of the community contacts they would make, experiments could be devised. They considered surveys, interviews, books, magazines, site visits, and field studies as means for gathering information. He had the students craft preliminary plans of action.

They also discussed how this project would be evaluated. Mr. Ramirez started a list of student ideas on key aspects of the study—things like meeting periodic and final deadlines, working together as a team, thoroughness of local impacts of topic, depth of examination of the global side of the topic, relevance and significance of the experiments, considerations of all sides of the issue, clarity and creativity of the presentation. Mr. Ramirez devised a rubric based on student input and shared it with students for final approval. Only a few grumbled at the high expectations. Most of the others embraced the criteria they had devised and were ready to get started.

That night, Mr. Ramirez updated the class website with information for the unit they were about to commence. He posted the assignment parameters, his goals and objectives, and a brief rationale for the unit. He also included their mutually generated grade rubric. He then sent an e-mail to the class list of parents, apprising them of the update to the website, as he does for every unit. Mr. Ramirez made a few suggestions for parental involvement in the unit, from monitoring progress of their children's inquiries and questioning them about findings to making themselves available as citizen-experts for the variety of projects underway to aiding the laboratory through personal or material support. He also shared with parents information about the location and date of the colloquium in which their children would share investigations and encouraged the parents to attend.

With the groundwork laid, the unit unfolded in a flurry of activity. For twenty class days, student teams experimented, researched, interviewed, analyzed, and discussed aspects of their studies. Their support crew was headed by Mr. Ramirez, who facilitated experiments, helped to make contacts with local industry and service representatives, advised on analysis techniques, directed teams toward appropriate resources, and brought divergent teams together when commonalities arose. Others in support roles included school administrators who corraled school resources for the investigators, community citizens who spoke with and helped to educate teams, and parents who provided transportation to sites and motivation and guidance on the home front by providing study space and brain fuel for team meetings.

On any given day of the unit, an observer of Mr. Ramirez's classroom might happen on investigative teams in a variety of roles. The auto emissions group burned strips of copper that had been held in garbage bags full of auto exhaust from student's cars, looking for evidence of halogens in the burned fuel. The acid rain team downloaded data from a school in Vermont that had been contacted for reading the pH of their precipitation in aid of the investigation. The erosion team made an appointment with an area farmer who used buffer strips of natural land between his fields and the river, and after filing permissions from parents, teacher, and administrator, the students paid the farmer a visit. The suburbanization team spoke on the phone with the developer of the town's newest subdivision. He volunteered to take the students over the city in his private plane to get a bird's-eye view of the community's growth. The Lake Red Rock team used computer-interfaced probes to test water samples for dissolved oxygen with the help of one student's father, a chemist. The alien invaders group discussed a book they were reading: Harold Mooney's *Invasive Species in a Changing World*. The deforestation group, as guests of the window factory's plant manager, took a tour of the plant. On the Internet, Jason and Lanny examined data from the Department of Natural Resources on calculated automobile damage expenses associated with collisions with animal on the state's roadways. Then the team made an appointment with a highway engineer whose responsibilities include retrieving carcasses from roadsides across the county.

Mr. Ramirez had weighed the considerable advice he had received from other teachers and a few students that kids like Jason would surely abuse the freedoms of this class. "He is not going to actually meet anyone," they would say, "He's skipping!" or "He's going to fritter away class time on the Internet and end up producing nothing." "We will monitor the situation," Mr. Ramirez assured them.

"It's fourth period, and your hair is wet like you just came from the shower, Jason." Mr. Ramirez was making his rounds in the lab, seizing the opportunity to check in.

"I did," said Jason, "I only get out of bed for this class." A bittersweet revelation, thought Mr. Ramirez.

"You're visiting Mr. Hansen tomorrow at the highway office?" said Mr. Ramirez, monitoring the situation.

"Uh-huh. Lanny and me have a meeting with him during this class."

"Have you completed the permission . . . " Mr. Ramirez hadn't finished the question before Jason filled in the gaps.

"Yeah, we have the forms filled out—Mom, the principal, now just you need to sign. We're taking this downloaded data from the DNR, 'cause it don't tell us which kinds of animals. Plus, we don't know which roads are the worst around here. And Lanny wants to ask him if those deer whistles on car bumpers really work. We're gonna take a video camera and get the whole thing on tape."

Mr. Ramirez breathed a sigh of relief, patted Jason on the shoulder, and said, "Carry on, gentlemen."

By the time the colloquium rolled around, little in the way of surprises awaited Mr. Ramirez, who had spent each class day closely monitoring student progress. Yet the professionalism and thoroughness of these productions continued to amaze him each year. In preparation for the presentations, Mr. Ramirez had sent an e-mail to the parents' list reminding them of the date and time and encouraging them to attend. The community contacts that he had helped to establish were also informed that this was an open forum and their attendance would be valued. Several parents, a hospital administrator, the city's utility director, a Councilman, a wildlife reha-bilitation volunteer, and the school's principal attended the fourth period colloquium.

One by one, student investigative teams recounted their experiments and analy-ses. They navigated their topics and findings using PowerPoint productions, sharing video interview excerpts, diagrams and charts, and summaries of implications. Some augmented their talks with recitations from Walt Whitman; others shared baked goods depicting the earth with an ozone hole; and still others strummed familiar tunes on guitars with original lyrics about radon (to the tune of Elton John's "Levon"— "Radon! You want to fill our basements . . . Leave bedrock far behind . . ."). Their audiences actively participated in discussing findings, sharing common concerns, and suggesting alternative explanations or additional research.

The emissions team took the class on a virtual tour of their town's power plant and then showed discs of petroleum jelly–coated papers that had been distributed through-out the town. Their audience could see how much particulate matter existed on the discs that had been placed near the power plant and at locations to its east compared to west-ern and remotely placed discs. The team shared a chart detailing the current cost of elec-tricity per kilowatt and the estimated cost if the community insisted on additional scrubbers for the smokestacks or the shipment of a higher grade of coal. Lively discus-sion ensued regarding feelings about higher energy costs associated with possible fixes.

The team investigating toxic by-products of plastic manufacturing distributed water bottles to classmates, courtesy of the bottle maker in town. Then they shared findings of environmental "endocrine disruptors" that have affected the sexual traits of animals and are linked to plastic industry chemicals. The team passed around different grades of recycled plastic containers and displayed recycling statistics on a PowerPoint slide. The results of a communitywide survey of plastics use and recycling indicated that a strong convenience factor governed people's intentions. Classmates had strong feelings in all directions about coercion versus volunteerism and awareness in recycling their plas-tics. The consensus sentiment that emerged was the importance of education on this issue.

The alien species introductions team entered the class bedecked with green nylon stockings, and aluminum foil masks with antennae. "Unlike us," they said, "the aliens we're talking about aren't extraterrestrial." Many examples of real aliens were passed around, including plantain, dandelions, bull this-tle, an apple, a honeybee, and an Asian ladybug. Others were depicted on slides: sparrows, kudzu, pheasants, zebra mussels, and many more. To appreciate the problem, they told the class, required that we understand how evolution works. They took their class-mates outside to play a game in which each adapted to some environmental condition and then an alien was introduced that wiped them all out. One of their classmates said that she had never believed in evolution, but when it was put this way, she got it.

Mr. Ramirez called for Jason and Lanny to go next. Their classmates fell silent in expectation of a flop. The roadkill team inserted a videotape into the VCR. Viewers were greeted by "Mr. Roadkill" in his multianimal hide robe and chrome sunglasses. Mr. Roadkill stood before the garage entrance to a local body shop, a smashed-up Ford Explorer to his side. He shared with the students the costs to individuals and to their insurance companies as a result of collisions with animals. The scene switched to a newsroom, where "Lanny Anchordude" stood by a map of the county, pointing out problem roadways for animal-human encounters. Anchordude went "live" to Mr. Roadkill's interview with the highway engineer, who named the most frequently hit animals, listed their population trends over the decade, and shared precautions drivers can take to avoid collisions. Cut to Anchordude and Mr. Roadkill doing an experiment: calculating the speed and distance of an automobile and a raccoon moving perpendicularly across a highway. A stuffed raccoon being dragged across the road by a long string while a car bore down on it provided a graphic lesson in slowing down a little bit to save some furry lives. With that, Jason and Lanny ejected their tape and returned to their desks amid the high-fives and appreciative cheers of their classmates.

On conclusion of the colloquium, Mr. Ramirez thanked the many community representatives in attendance for their interest in and support of the projects. He congratulated the students for their hard work, responsibility, and education on these many important issues. Together, he and the class composed an open letter of thanks to parents and the community, which appeared shortly in the opinion section of their local newspaper. Some of the students felt empowered enough by their projects to write columns for the school paper; others were invited by their parents to speak at the local League of Women Voters meeting and to the Rotary Club. As a result of their environmental studies unit, all of Mr. Ramirez's students were more aware that science spans their lives well beyond school and that real people in real communities deal with this stuff all the time.

Reflecting on the Game

1. How best might the resources (people and locales) of your community be utilized as part of the science curriculum?

2. What strategies can you envision using for promoting the inquiry style of your science class to garner the support of members of your community?

3. What hurdles to parental involvement in the school science program exist, and how might you imagine overcoming those hurdles?

4. Some educators fear that opening up the classroom walls to include the community might introduce classroom management problems. How might the very act of including the community in your curriculum actually diminish management problems?

5. Design a lesson or unit of science that takes advantage of expertise that may exist in student's lives and communities beyond the school.

References

Abbott, J. (1995). Children need communities. *Educational Leadership, 52*(8), 6–10.

Bauch, J. P. (2000). *Parent involvement partnerships with technology.* Nashville, TN: Transparent School Model.

Bouillion, L., & Gomez, L. (2001). Connecting school and community with science learning: Real world problems and school-community partnerships as contextual scaffolds. *Journal of Research in Science Teaching, 38*(8), 878.

Brandwien, P. (1981). *Memorandum: On renewing schooling and education.* New York: Harcourt Brace Jovanovich.

Bransford, J., Brown, A., & Cocking, R., (2000). *How people learn: Brain, mind, experience, and school.* Washington, DC: National Academy Press.

Bybee, R. (1993). *Reforming science education: Social perspectives and personal reflections.* New York: Teachers College Press.

Chen, X., & Chandler, K. (2001). *Efforts by public schools to involve parents in children's education: Do school and parent reports agree?* (NCES 2001-076). Washington, DC: National Center for Educational Statistics.

Chiappetta, E., Koballa, T., & Collette, A. (1998). *Science instruction in the middle and secondary schools* (4th ed.). Upper Saddle River, NJ: Merrill.

Childress, H. (1998). Seventeen reasons why football is better than high school. *Phi Delta Kappan, 79*(8), pp. 616–619.

Dewey, J. (1916). *Democracy and education.* New York: Macmillan.

Eccles, J., & Harold, R. (1994). *Family involvement in childrens' and adolescents' schooling.* Paper presented at the Family-School Links Conference, Pennsylvania State University.

Finn, J. (1998). Parental engagement that makes a difference. *Educational Leadership, 55*(8), 20–24.

Giannetti, C., & Sagarese, M. (1998). Turning parents from critics to allies. *Educational Leadership, 55*(8), 40–43.

Giddings, G., (1999, March). *Influence of culture and home environment on science learning.* Paper presented at the Annual Meeting of the National Association for Research in Science Teaching (NARST), Boston, MA.

Goals 2000. (1998). Educate America Act, Title III, Sec. 302, H.R. 1804.

Goodlad, J. (1984). *A place called school: Prospects for the future.* New York: McGraw-Hill.

Hatch, T. (1998). How community action contributes to achievement. *Educational Leadership, 55*(8), 16–20.

Henderson, A., & Berla, N. (1994). *The family is critical to student achievement.* Columbia, MD: National Committee for Citizens in Education.

Ho, E., & Willms, J. (1996). Effects of parental involvement in eighth grade achievement. *Sociology of Education, 69*(2): 126–141.

Holliday, W. (2001). Homework in science. *Science Scope, 24*(6): 16–19.

Hoover-Dempsey, K., Battiato, A. & Walker, J. (2001). Parental involvement in homework. *Educational Psychologist, 36*(3), 195–209.

Kim, E., & Kellough, R. (1995). *A resource guide for secondary school teaching* (6th ed.). Englewood Cliffs, NJ: Merrill.

Lewis, A., & Henderson, A. (1998). *Building bridges: Across schools and communities, across streams of funding.* Chicago, IL: Cross City Campaign for Urban School Reform.

Lewis, R., & Morris, J. (1998). Communities for children. *Educational Leadership, 55*(8), 34–36.

Manley, M. (1989). *Martin Manley's Basketball heaven.* New York: Doubleday.

Miller, J. (1996). In R. Yager, (Ed.), Scientific literacy for effective citizenship, in *Science, technology, society as reform in science education.* Albany, NY: SUNY Press.

Moreno, N., Tharp, B., & Denk, J. (1999). Parents count. *The Science Teacher, 66*(4): 28–31.

National Research Council (NRC). (1996). *National science education standards.* Washington, DC: National Academy Press.

National Science Foundation. (1997). *Foundations: The challenge and promise of K–8 science education reform* (p. 17). Washington, DC: Author.

Nolan, M. J., Chaney, B., & Chapman, C. (1997). *Student participation in community service activity* (NCES 97-331). Washington, DC: National Center for Educational Statistics.

Peoples, J. (2001). Commentary: Teacher-partners. *The Science Teacher, 68*(3), 10.

Public Agenda, (1998). *Employers and college professors voice frustration over graduates' academic weakness.* New York: Author.

Public Agenda, (1999). *Playing their parts: Parents and teachers talk about parental involvement in public schools,* New York: Author.

Rose, L., & Gallup, A. (2001). The 33rd annual Phi Delta Kappa/Gallup poll of the public's attitudes toward the public schools. *Phi Delta Kappan, 83*(1), pp. 41–58.

Rubba, P., Wiesenmayer, R. (1993). In R. Yager (Ed.), Increased actions by students, in *The science, technology, society movement,* Washington, DC: National Science Teachers Association.

Rutherford, F., & Ahlgren, A. (1990). *Science for all Americans,* New York: Oxford University Press.

Sanders, M., Epstein, J., & Connors-Tadros, L. (1999). *Family partnerships with high schools: The parents' perspective* (CRESPAR Report 32). Baltimore, MD: Johns Hopkins University.

Sandler, L., Vandergrift, J., & VerBrugghen, C. (1995). From desert to garden: Reconnecting dis-

connected youth, *Educational Leadership, 52*(8), 14–17.

Shumow, L., & Lomax, R. (2001). *Parental efficacy: Predictor of parenting behavior and adolescent outcomes.* Paper presented at the Annual Meeting of the American Educational Research Association, Seattle, WA.

Smith, T., Martin, M., Mullis, I., & Kelly, D. (2000). *Profiles of student achievement in science at the TIMSS international benchmarks: U.S. performance and standards in an international context.* Boston, MA: Boston College International Study Center.

Staley, F. (1993). Coordination of STS and community goals. In R. Yager (Ed.), *The Science, Technology, Society Movement,* Washington, DC: National Science Teachers Association.

Sullivan, P. (1998). The PTA's national standards. *Educational Leadership, 55*(8), 43–45.

Vaden-Kiernan, N., & Chandler, K. (1996). *Parents' reports of school practices to involve families* (NCES 97-327). Washington, DC: National Center for Educational Statistics.

Weld, J. (1997). Teaching and learning in science. *Educational Horizons, 76(1), 14–17.*

Yager, R. (1996). History of science/technology/society as reform in the United States, In R. Yager (Ed.), *Science, technology, society as reform in science education.* Albany, NY: SUNY Press.

Additional Resources

The American Educational Research Association's Special Interest Group on Family-School-Community Partnerships www.csos.jhu.edu/fscp/default.htm

Barbour, C., & Barbour, N. (2000). *Families, schools, and communities: Building partnerships for educating children.* Upper Saddle River, NJ: Prentice-Hall.

The California Department of Education's Family-School-Community Partnerships www.cde.ca.gov/fc/family/

A Compact for Learning: An Action Handbook for Family-School Community Partnerships www.ed.gov/PDFDocs/Compact/intro.pdf

Hiatt-Michael, D. B. (Ed.). (2001). *Promising practices for family involvement in schools (family, school, community, partnership issues* (Vol. 1). Greenwich, CT: Information Age Publishing.

chapter

10

TECHNOLOGY

TRANSFORMS THE GAME

OF SCIENCE TEACHING

David R. Wetzel, Ph.D.
Science Education, Bloomsburg
University of Pennsylvania

ABOUT THE AUTHOR: Dr. David Wetzel earned his Ph.D. in science education from George Mason University in 2000. He taught general and physical science in middle school for over five years before designing science and technology curriculum for the Smithsonian Institution/ National Academy of Sciences. Currently, he teaches science education courses at Blooms- burg University of Pennsylvania. Dr. Wetzel's service to science education includes memberships on the board of directors for the National Association for Science, Technology, and Society and the Collaborative for Excellence in Teacher Preparation of Pennsylvania.

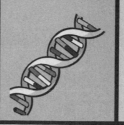

> # I think there is a world market for maybe five computers.
>
> —Thomas Watson, 1943
> *IBM chairman*

CHAPTER WARM-UP

The infusion of technology into the modern science classroom serves not only to support inquiry through data acquisition, manipulation, analysis, and reporting, but also reflects the increasingly technological workplace of professionals within and beyond the sciences. The school technology infusion process has been laborious at times, suffering from a lack of commitment and application. However, research shows—and the standards support—that learners who maximize technological applications in science are more effective inquirers: They possess more diverse investigative and analytical skills, have broader world views, and have more interest in studying science.

INTRODUCTION: Beyond Beakers and Balances

Thirty years ago, science students collected scientific data using traditional instruments such as beakers, balances, thermometers, and spring scales. High-technology tools such as desktop computers did not exist in science classrooms. Calculators and graphing calculators were not available or did not exist. Technological advances have changed the way science is being taught over the past thirty years.

In the past ten to fifteen years, computers have become more commonplace in the science classroom. Today's science classrooms might have as many as eight to ten computers available for student use in scientific investigations. Even with these computers in the science classroom, there is still a place for traditional data instruments. Although electronic devices for collecting and analyzing scientific data have become more common, beakers and balances still have a prominent place in the science lab.

Today's students tend to be more technologically advanced than many science teachers who entered the teaching profession just ten or fifteen years ago. Science students routinely conduct research and collect data using computers and calculator-based technological tools. These tools collect, measure, graph, and organize scientific data in real time, allowing students to spend more of their time developing their understanding of science concepts through observation, inference, classification, prediction, and analysis of the data. The use of such technology allows science teachers to become facilitators of their students learning, supporting inquiry-based teaching and learning from a constructivist perspective. With almost daily advances in technology and an increased availability of economical technological tools for use in science investigations, the use of technology for teaching and learning science content has become very appropriate for helping students develop a greater understanding of science (Flick & Bell, 2000).

Science students use computers for many purposes when investigating scientific phenomena by conducting research on the Internet, using interactive and simulation software for investigation of scientific concepts, and communicating in real time with scientists all around and above the earth. Additionally, students use multimedia software for communication of their conclusions and findings on completion of laboratory investigations. Students use computer- and calculator-based laboratory probeware for data collection, graphical display, and analysis in earth, life, and physical science studies. These are just a few ways in which technology has changed the game of science education over the past thirty years.

The National Educational Technology Standards for Teachers and Students (International Society for Technology in Education, 1998, 2000a, 2000b) provide a sense of what science teachers need to use in preparing their students in developing a better understanding of the nature of science as they use appropriate tools for learning, collaborating, and communicating their understanding. Table 10.1 provides characteristics of how traditional teaching can be influenced when the learning environment includes modern technology.

Table 10.1 Science learning environments that include technology

Traditional Learning Environments	Technology Learning Environments
Teacher-centered instruction	Student-centered learning
Single-sense stimulation	Multisensory stimulation
Single media	Multimedia
Isolated work	Collaborative work
Passive learning	Active, exploratory, inquiry-based learning
Factual, knowledge-based learning	Critical thinking and informed decision making
Isolated, artificial context	Authentic, real-world context
Reactive response	Proactive/planned action

Although we might think of technology as being strictly the use of instructional technology, the use of technology in science teaching includes any tool that is used to make modifications to the natural world to meet human needs. These tools may include high-tech devices that students use to develop a greater understanding of the natural world. Our human need to solve problems or understand the natural world forces us to develop better technologies to conduct scientific research (National Research Council, 1996). As stated in the *National Science Education Standards* (NRC, 1996, p. 24),

> the central distinguishing characteristic between science and technology is a difference in goal: The goal of science is to understand the natural world, and the goal of technology is to make modifications in the world to meet human needs. Technology as design is included in the *Standards* as parallel to science as inquiry. Technology and science are closely related. A single problem often has both scientific and technological aspects. The need to answer questions in the natural world drives the development of technological products; moreover, technological needs can drive scientific research. And technological products, from pencils to computers, provide tools that promote the understanding of natural phenomena.

In the twentieth century, chalkboards, pencils, pens, ditto machines, and overhead projectors were essential technological tools for facilitating teaching and learning. Thermometers, litmus paper, balances, and stopwatches are examples of tools used for collecting scientific data. Although these tools still have a place in science, they have been replaced or supplemented by even better technologies for collecting scientific data. These new technologies include probeware for collecting real-time temperature or pH and photogates for timing. Electronic balances and scales have replaced traditional balances. Overhead projectors are being replaced by computer projection devices. Also, there is no longer any real need to bring the natural world into the classroom in beakers; today's advances in portable technological devices allow students to collect data in the field. These advances in technology allow students and researchers to collect more reliable and accurate data and to observe changes to variables in real time.

This chapter will present a vision of how such technology fits within today's science classrooms, how it influences the players and coaches who teach and learn the game of science education, types of technology used by teachers and students, how these types of technology are used at various grade levels, how technology fits within science and technology standards, and views of where technology will lead us in science education as we move further into the twenty-first century.

Technology's Place in the Game

There is a close relationship between science and technology that extends the idea of teaching and learning through the use of hands-on and "minds-on" activities not only for in-service teacher staff development, but also for preservice teacher preparation and student learning. High technology's place in the science classroom is that of a tool, along with other traditional tools, in a teacher's equipment bag. High-tech tools allow teachers to facilitate their students' learning and understanding of science concepts through the use of inquiry and constructivist teaching techniques. Examples of high-tech tools and resources in a teachers' game bag include electronic balances, fan cars, microscopes, electronic microscopes, computers, the Internet, interactive software, spreadsheets, multimedia presentation software, microcomputer-based laboratory probeware, and calculator-based laboratory probeware.

This close relationship of science and technology as a means of understanding the natural world is pictured in Figure 10.1. The need to understand the natural world fuels advances in technology to support research by scientists and students, giving them the ability to develop a better understanding of the world around us. Technology's place can be further defined as a process and product that supports the National Science Education Standards (NRC, 1996) goal of meeting human needs through modification of our world. Today's technological advances provide unlimited possibilities in science education and supports learning that is as follows:

- *Constructive*—as learners assimilate new ideas with their prior knowledge and experiences to make sense of scientific concepts
- *Contextual*—as learners inquire into real-world investigations or simulations in real time
- *Active*—as learners are engaged in student-centered investigations and their teachers facilitate the learning process
- *Critical thinking*—as learners compile, organize, analyze, synthesize, and draw conclusions based on real-time or simulated data
- *Multisensory*—as learners access and exchange information using a wide variety of media and formats (ISTE, 1998, 2000b, 2000c).

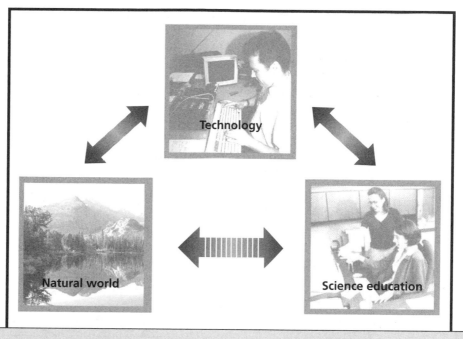

Figure 10.1   The technology bridge and link between understanding the natural world and science education

Investigations that involve the use of technology help students develop a greater understanding of science and allow students to perceive the relevance of how science relates to their own personal experiences (Flick & Bell, 2000). Examples include conducting research using the Internet and organizing data in spreadsheets (Figure 10.2) or databases that facilitate student understanding of scientific concepts. High technology allows enhanced data presentation for drawing more informed conclusions and inferences. Through the use of high technology, students develop a deeper understanding of scientific concepts by controlling and manipulating variables in real time. An example of this is when students use computer or calculator-based laboratory probeware to collect force data and observe how their manipulation of variables influence force in real time through the use of graphical displays. Additionally, the real-time manipulation of variables using interactive software allows students to improve their understanding of how changes in variables influence changes in the findings.

High technology allows teachers to extend their students' learning experiences well beyond classroom walls to include regional, national, global, and even intergalactic domains of knowledge. In 1996, K–12 teachers were allowed to send their students'

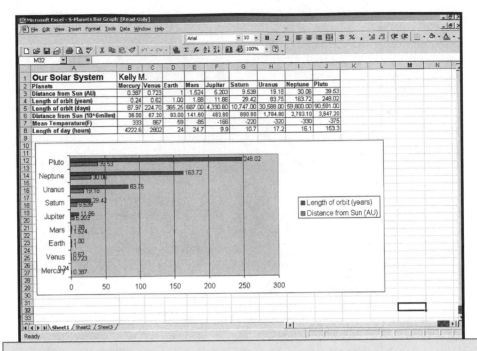

Figure 10.2 Example of a spreadsheet of planetary facts (from Spreadsheet Magic by Pamela Lewis)

signatures to the Jet Propulsion Laboratory to be scanned onto computer disks and then placed onboard the spacecraft Galileo for its journey to and exploration of Jupiter. This facilitated engagement of students' personal experiences with space science exploration through a personal lens. In the following years, they viewed data that the National Aeronautics and Space Administration (NASA) placed on the Internet chronicling Galileo's journey. Students can talk to and observe NASA astronauts aboard the international space station and space shuttle using the Internet and satellite communications in real time, along with observing experiments that the astronauts are conducting in space. Additionally, students can design technologically based scientific experiments that are carried into space onboard these platforms and then use the Internet for data collection, retrieval, and analysis.

Students can collaborate on a global scale in collecting scientific data. One example of this is through the Global Learning and Observations to Benefit the Environment (GLOBE) program (Figure 10.3). This program allows students to collect local environmental data using technological and traditional instruments to share with scientists, teachers, and students around the world. Other examples of how science edu-

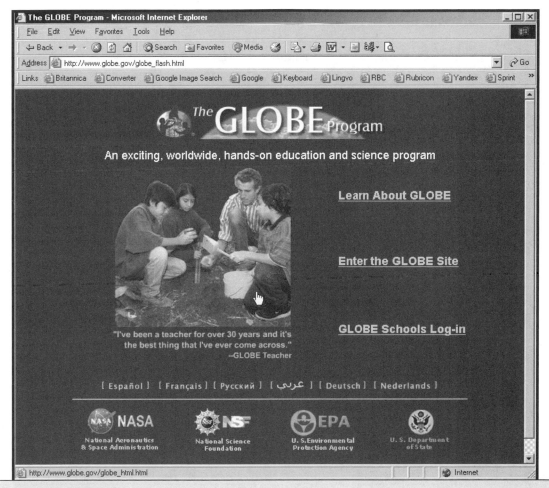

Figure 10.3 GLOBE webpage: www.globe.gov

cation is moving beyond beakers and balances include taking science students out of the classroom on virtual field trips through the use of the Internet to almost any place on earth. These virtual field trips are accomplished through the use of web cams that allow students to visit animals in zoos, sea life in and around Bahaman reefs (Figure 10.4), animals of the African Serengeti (Figure 10.5), and volcanoes of Mexico and Martinique (Figure 10.6).

An additional strategy for the integration of technology in teaching science includes the use of lasers to allow students to study sound and light wave theories (Wetzel & Sterling, 1998). Another strategy allows students to use the Internet to

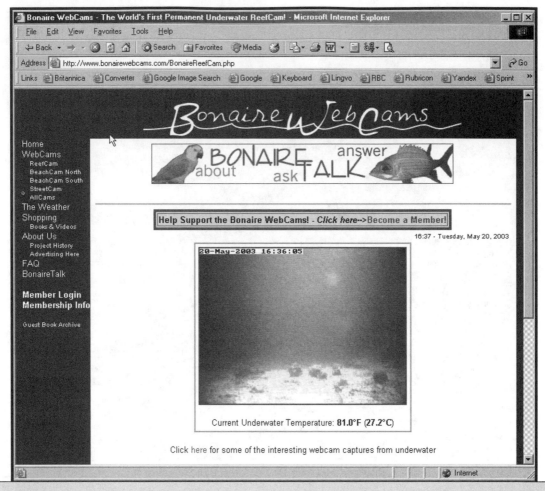

Figure 10.4 The Bonaire ReefCam:
www.bonairewebcams.com/BonaireReefCamLarge.php

complete long-term research related to scientific concepts that they selected to investigate (Wetzel, 1997).

The Climate and Culture of Technology in the Game

The integration of technology in K–12 science is a fact of life in American education. Along with the integration of technology in teaching and learning by teachers, students' ability to use technology is recognized as essential by today's society. Recognizing the responsibility to prepare students to work and live in a technolog-

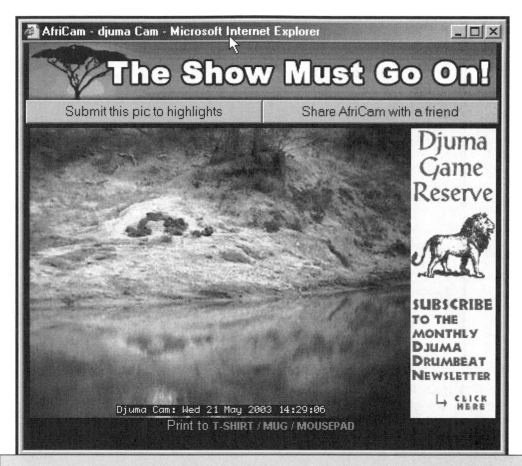

Figure 10.5 Africa Webcam: www.africam.com/public/index.jsp

ical society, national education standards recommend the use of technology in all aspects of teaching and learning science. These standards include the National Science Education Standards (NRC, 1996), Benchmarks for Science Literacy (AAAS, 1993), National Education Technology Standards for Students (ISTE, 1998), and National Education Technology Standards for Teachers (ISTE, 2000a, 2000b). These four standards advocate the use of technology by teachers to encourage their students to become active participants in the learning and investigative science processes. High technology is a modern mainstay of scientists and a ubiquitous part of our lives. An educated citizenry is essential for the judicious use and development of technology. The distinction is made here merely as a means of distinguishing the role of science and technology in a complex pattern of relationships. Whether we choose to modify our environment slightly or alter it radically to live within it, technology

Figure 10.6 Web cam view of the Mount Pelee volcano on the island of Martinique

is a fundamental value chosen by society to facilitate the process (Office of Technology Assessment, 1995).

The separation of technology and science for purposes of study and the tendency to blur the distinctions between technology and science by practice were evident for years in K–12 school curricula. This presented an unrealistic representation of the role of technology in our society and the relationship between technology and science (Zuga, 1991). The artificial separation of technology and science for the purposes of analysis and study does not exist in real-world applications. The relationship between technology and science is symbiotic: Both are necessary for the advancement of human knowledge. Today, the relationships between the activities of scientists and technologists are well established and have forged a collaboration that has modified science research faster than science teachers can identify and describe the advances. The key concern for today's teachers is how to best unify the teaching of science and technology to meet society's goals through the national standards. The integration of science and technology is becoming more common as technological advances have presented teachers with economical and effective tools to use in the classroom with their students.

Teachers' Beliefs and Change Regarding Technology. With the unprecedented amount of technology that is available for use in science classrooms and schools, there is more evidence that teachers are systematically integrating high technology in their classroom curriculum. Schools and districts are operating on a number of fronts to implement technology-based programs. These fronts include a focus on an increased amount of hardware, concern for the integration process, implementation planning processes that strive to meet the needs of teachers, and increased opportunities for professional staff development in the best procedures for integrating technology into the curricula.

To be successful with technology implementation, teachers need to be prepared for changes in pedagogy. These changes require a shift in a teacher's paradigm as he or she implements a new innovation that has an influence on pedagogy (Dexter, Anderson, & Becker, 1999; Fullan, 1991; Honey & Moeller, 1990). The change process might span a period of years, and the recognition of this process by all concerned during the implementation of a new instructional strategy or technological tool is important (Fullan, 1991).

Sustained change follows ownership in a new instructional strategy or technological tool. Fullan's (1991) research findings indicate that it can take two to three years for a new technological tool to be fully implemented and integrated within the science curriculum. Some teachers adapt to the use of a new technological tools quickly; others resist the change altogether. Most teachers will integrate technology into their science classes when provided with appropriate support mechanisms. The ST^3AIRS (staff development, time to learn, trainers that are qualified, transition time, access to hardware and software, involvement of teachers, recognition of teachers, and support for teachers) model (Wetzel, 2002) is one example of a model that has proven to be successful in supporting the integration and implementation of technology in science classrooms.

Teacher Change and Technology. Change is a personal human experience that school systems and change facilitators need to consider when implementing new technologies. To successfully implement a new technological tool, consideration of what the implementation will mean to teachers' personal beliefs and values is paramount. How will it affect their current classroom practices, preparation time, beliefs regarding technology, and values? Many factors directly and indirectly influence teachers' integration of instructional technology (Dexter et al., 1999; Knapp & Glenn, 1996; Honey & Moeller, 1990).

Teachers' beliefs and values regarding change can be a major obstacle. For teachers to conceptually change their teaching strategies and techniques, they need to become dissatisfied with their existing conditions, view change as intelligible, view change as plausible, and find change useful in a variety of new situations (Posner, Strike, Hewson, & Gertzog, 1982).

Effective change must address implementation and integration in concrete and practical terms to reduce the inherent human nature of resistance to change. The novelty or uniqueness of a new technological tool alone will not produce the desired change; only when teachers change their epistemology does change take place. For the implementation of change to be successful, policymakers need to pay attention to teacher's needs, recognize that change takes time, understand that teachers tend to demonstrate growth in relation to their personal feelings and skills, and realize that change is not an event but a process (Hord, Rutherford, Huling-Austin, & Hall, 1987; Wetzel, 2002).

Through time, owing to ever-shifting goals and policies that influence their pedagogy, teachers have developed resilient teaching practices. But because of policy shifts and fads, many educational innovations do not reach institutionalization or stabilization in schools. Teachers who want to change are often not content with the status quo. These are reflective teachers who continually try to do what is best for their students. Schubert and Ayers (1992) contend that only reflective teachers continuously grow.

Wittrock (1974) found that teachers construct or generate meaning though sensory input. Wittrock's findings echo Piaget's (1978) tenet that individuals construct knowledge as they act on objects while trying to make sense of what they have discovered. The generative view of learning yields teacher beliefs and values as key to implementing and integrating new innovations. They construct meaning through their sensory input that may be contradictory to their current contextual influences. The generation of a new teaching method or strategy is based on teachers' existing ideas and sensory input, which often causes a shift in their beliefs and values (Osborne & Wittrock, 1983).

On the basis of their review of case studies of how teachers implemented new programs in their classroom, Tobin and Fraser (1990) concluded that teachers' beliefs about how students learn and what they should learn appear to have the greatest impact on teacher change. Learning to teach focuses more on individual teacher's cognitions, beliefs, and mental processes than on behaviors (Richardson, 1990).

In their research involving 608 teachers, Buck and Horton (1996) found that teachers believed that their teaching had been transformed by the incorporation of high technology in their classroom. These teachers perceived changes in their pedagogy that were threefold. First, they believed that they expected their students to study more complex material and that they taught concepts they had never considered teaching before using instructional technology. Second, the teachers believed that they were able to meet their students' individual needs. The third change was a shift from the traditional teacher-centered learning environment to a student-centered one. These findings suggest that when teachers incorporate instructional technology into their curriculum, there is pedagogical and curricula transformation that improves their students' learning of science concepts.

Influence of Technology on Teaching Science

A teacher's view of how science should be taught is a product of his or her own prior knowledge, development, and experience as teacher. Each teacher's style is influenced by his or her personality and belief system as well. But all teachers' styles are influenced by the context of the organizational structure in which they teach. Teachers might profess valuing independent student accomplishment and successful collaboration among their peers, but statistical records of teachers' behavior typically report that these same teachers still use teacher-centered pedagogy. Brooks and Brooks (1993) found that teachers are predominantly teacher centered and generally behave in a didactic manner, disseminating information to students. This has been suggested to result from a paramount concern with behavioral control and the belief that teacher-centered whole-class lessons are most conducive to quiet classrooms (Becker, 1991).

The use of high technology causes a shift in teacher beliefs and values as they become more student-centered in their teaching. Brooks and Brooks (1993) found that when teachers shift to an interactive manner, they facilitate student learning. This becomes apparent when technology is implemented in the classroom.

Teacher's beliefs are critical to the success of any innovation in education. All teachers have implicit and explicit beliefs about teaching and learning (NRC, 1996). Any change in pedagogy can happen only with a corresponding change in teachers' beliefs about the appropriateness of an innovation. Isenberg's (1990) research indicated that teaching and learning had shifted focus from the observable teacher behaviors to teacher beliefs and their impact on teacher behaviors. This research differs from earlier research that viewed teachers as technicians delivering a prepackaged curriculum. Researchers now acknowledge the powerful influence teacher's beliefs have on curriculum innovations (Cronin-Jones, 1991).

For implementation of new technology to be successful, teachers must believe that the technology is not just an "idea of the month" that will disappear after two or three years. They must believe that their investment of time and energy will improve their teaching and student learning. Teachers must be allowed to experiment with the technology in a low-risk environment and receive constructive feedback. Innovators and researchers must not ignore the complexity of relationships between a belief system and practice. Reform efforts must be grass roots, not top-down or quick fix. This demands extensive intellectual preparation and continual learning on the part of the teachers (Wiske, 1998).

From a Vygotskian perspective, humans develop and change as they interact with others and learn to make use of a culture's tools, both physical and psychological. So the constructions that humans make in their minds originate in interchanges with people and influence their beliefs and values. The transformation from the interpsychological to intrapsychological takes place within a person's "zone of proximal development (ZPD)" (Vygotsky, 1978). Because the teacher is a learner when implementing and integrating an innovation, the teacher who is an expert becomes a novice. In learning new teaching strategies, a teacher's ZPD is concentrated in learning new things that might conflict or support their beliefs and values. Teachers need to be reflective individuals to effectively implement, change, and interact with colleagues and students. Martin (1993, p. 84) argued, "Without time and support for constructive interaction, there is no chance that the teacher will appropriate the new information."

Kuhn's (1970) model regarding changing paradigms in the concept of science teaching involves the belief that in the scientific community there are accepted examples of law, theory, application, and instrumentation. Kuhn's theory of paradigm shifts gives a rationale for changing teachers' beliefs and how these beliefs play a major role in teachers' willingness and ability to change their practices. A change in teachers' practice is brought about through change in their beliefs in learning and teaching. When teachers are faced with disequilibrium in their understandings of teaching and learning, they strive for equilibrium. By sustained experiences with new ideas and collaboration with colleagues, teachers restore that equilibrium by constructing new understandings, and therefore new beliefs, through reflection (Piaget, 1978).

Contextual Barriers to Using Technology

Senge, Kleiner, Roberts, Ross, Roth, and Smith (1999) identified ten challenges to initiating change that influence the use of new technology in teaching science. These challenges influence the growth process in an organization when it implements an innovation that combines inner shifts in teachers' values, aspirations, and behaviors along with outer shifts in processes, strategies, and practices. Senge et al. (1999) referred to this change as "profound change." With profound change, there is learning within the organization as it builds capacity for ongoing change. These ten challenges to profound change in a school organization are as follows:

1. Time to implement the change
2. Adequate support for those implementing the change
3. Relevance of change to the curriculum
4. The administration being consistent and clear about its goals and message regarding the change
5. Fear and anxiety about implementation
6. Assessment of progress in ways that diverge from traditional forms of assessment
7. Isolation and arrogance between believers and nonbelievers of the new innovation
8. Organizational structure and policies that hinder change
9. Inability to transfer knowledge across departmental boundaries
10. Organizational strategies and intended focus that include change as a natural process of the organization

A major challenge to using technology in the teaching of science is assisting teachers in unlearning the beliefs, values, assumptions, and culture that underlie their school's standard operating procedures and practices (Dede, 1998). To be successful beyond initial implementation, school systems need to assist teachers in learning, but also aid them in unlearning their standard organization's operating procedures. The goals of the technology implementation must include organizational changes as teachers learn. A shift in organizational change will sustain change that can be achieved only when it is owned by teachers and not imposed or mandated (Dede, 1998). Research by Becker (2000) has determined common characteristics of K–12 science teachers who use technology for teaching and learning:

- Opportunities for collaboration
- Emphasis on small group work
- Attempts to make computer activities consequential
- Access to professional development activities
- Fewer students per computer in the classroom

How Does Technology Fit the Game Plan?

High technology has changed the way science is taught in K–12 education. Observation, data collection, data analysis, measurement, classifying, inference, communication, and other science process skills are enhanced by infusing such technology in science teaching. Information is gathered, analyzed, and shared much more efficiently when high technology is used. Community-based projects, such as the GLOBE (2002) program enable students to learn science while doing science. Probeware, Internet and Web resources, simulation software, and on-line access to scientists engage students in inquiry-based learning of science. The use of high technology in science teaching and learning is no longer an option; it is essential for connecting students to science on a global scale.

Along with the types of equipment and software discussed in the previous sections, there are other technological resources that are available for use by teachers and students. This technology equipment includes computers, computer peripherals, the Internet, multimedia equipment, interactive software, digital cameras, calculators, probeware, and more. Figure 10.7 provides a representation of the types of technology available for teachers and students to use for learning about science. Although this list is not all-inclusive, it presents a cross section of the types of technological tools that are available and being used in K–12 science classrooms today.

The use of high technology fully engages students and sparks their interest to learn about science. This encourages early learners to develop keen observational, analysis, data organization, presentation, and communication skills as they compare and contrast scientific concepts. For example, students compare and contrast reptile attributes and the habitats in which reptiles live, including human influence on their environment through Internet research or completion of a WebQuest.

WebQuests

K–12 students can use the Internet for research and for contacting their peers or science experts. One example of using the Internet for research is through the use of WebQuests (Dodge, 1995). WebQuests are an inquiry-based activity in which elementary students use resources found on the Internet to solve a problem or study a science concept. Table 10.2 provides websites that contain examples of WebQuests that allow science students to investigate science concepts or problems. Figure 10.8 provides an example of a WebQuest.

The National Science Education Standards (NRC, 1996) and the National Educational Technology Standards (ISTE, 1998, 2000a, 2000b) support teachers in engaging their students in authentic real-world investigations through the appropriate implementation of instructional technology. An ideal method for accomplishing this is through the use of the Internet.

Dodge (1995) developed the idea of WebQuests as a means of using instructional technology to support student exploration with Internet resources. His idea was based on the fact that teachers need an appropriate and effective method for the integration

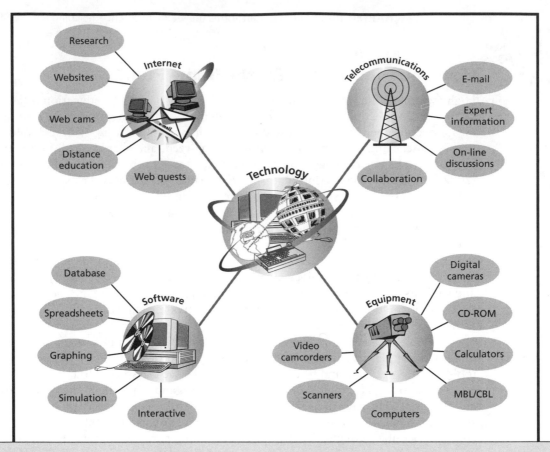

Figure 10.7 Types of technology used in K–12 science education

Table 10.2 Websites of examples of WebQuests in science

http://webquest.sdsu.edu/

Science WebQuests developed by preservice science teachers:

http://facstaff.bloomu.edu/dwetzel

Science WebQuests developed by teachers:

http://facstaff.bloomu.edu/dwetzel

http://edweb.sdsu.edu/webquest/k-3matrix.html (grades K–3)

http://edweb.sdsu.edu/webquest/4-5matrix.html (grades 4–5)

http://edweb.sdsu.edu/webquest/4-5matrix.html (grades 6–8)

http://edweb.sdsu.edu/webquest/9-12matrix.html (grades 9–12)

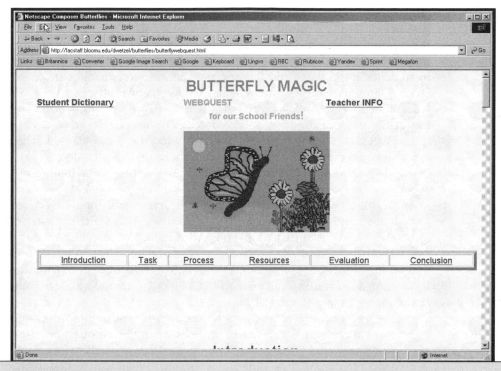

Figure 10.8 Example WebQuest for investigating butterflies in elementary school: facstaff.bloom.edu

of the vast amount of Internet resources to meet curricular objectives. WebQuests are beneficial for student learning of content because teachers integrate the vast resources available on the Internet in a safe and productive way (Yoder, 1999). Another advantage is that this instructional strategy allows teachers to use predetermined websites as their students use the Internet to improve their understanding of science content. WebQuests allow teachers to be creative and use the lure of technology to engage their students in exploration, imagination, problem solving, and promotion of multimedia presentations (Dodge, 1995).

A WebQuest has six basic components that facilitate students' learning during their exploration of a scientific concept or problem-solving objective. These six components are the introduction, task, process, resources, evaluation, and conclusion (Dodge, 1995). Each component has a specific purpose and should be written at the appropriate grade and reading level of students completing the WebQuest. The WebQuest *introduction* sets the stage, sets the hook, and provides background information for the students. The *task* is an authentic scientific concept or problem that is achievable by students within the technology and classroom resources. The *process* is the description of the steps that students need to follow to accomplish the task, location of classroom resources, group assignments, and guidelines for communicating the information that the students synthesize during the completion of the WebQuest. The *resources* are links to Internet websites that support the task, along with additional resources available to students in the classroom. These classroom resources include those in books, reference materials in print or multimedia, and interactive software. The *evaluation* provides students with guidelines that the teacher will use to assess student completion of the task, usually a rubric. The last component is the *conclusion,* which brings closure to the WebQuest and reminds the students what they have learned. The conclusion can also be used as a bridge from one concept to the next (Dodge, 1995).

WebQuests are divided into two categories: short-term and long-term. Short-term WebQuests are completed in one to three days; long-term WebQuests are completed in one to four weeks. A short-term WebQuest has instructional objectives of student knowledge acquisition and technology integration. Along with short-term objectives, long-term WebQuest instructional objectives include research over time, and extension of knowledge over additional concepts and related ideas. Whether through short-term or long-term WebQuest completion, students transform and synthesize what they have learned to create an end product that demonstrates their understanding of a specific concept or idea (Dodge, 1995).

WebQuests have several benefits for science education and student understanding of science concepts. A WebQuest begins with an authentic question or problem that needs to be answered or for which a proposed solution needs to be found. When students are confronted with an issue that is relevant to their world, they are more engaged and motivated by the task. To support this view, WebQuest tasks might include the study of environmental issues, habitat studies, or any science concept. Authentic scientific investigation is engaging and manageable in elementary science, because elementary science teachers' knowledge and understanding of science concepts tend to be bound by their prior knowledge of science and views of science teaching.

A prominent attribute of a WebQuest is the higher-order thinking skills that are required of students for task completion. The question or problem posed is not easily answered by a simple click of the computer mouse. Additionally, the question or problem posed by the teacher through the WebQuest causes students to transform information in a way that allows them to readily communicate their findings to others. Examples include concept maps, webs, multimedia presentations, and posters. Scaffolding of scientific ideas facilitates higher-order thinking skills by the students to support their findings (Dodge, 1995). WebQuests support the science process skills (Padilla, 1990) by having students compare, classify, infer, analyze, and communicate findings related to the scientific question or problem being investigated. Additionally, WebQuests support the learning cycle as students explore a science concept, focus on the concept, and apply the concept to a specific application.

Probeware

Microcomputer-based laboratory (MBL) and calculator-based laboratory (CBL) probeware are systems that use electronic sensor probes for data collection and presentation in graphical form on a computer screen or graphing calculator screen. Sensor probes can be used to electronically collect real-time data for temperature, motion, voltage, and timing with photogates, barometric pressure, humidity, pH, light, and more. MBL probeware uses a computer, interfaces, and sensor probes to collect data in real time. Additionally, CBL probeware is portable, allowing students to gather data in the field—for example, in doing water quality testing—without having to bring samples from the field back to class for testing. The main advantage for using either MBL or CBL probeware is that they allow students to collect data and manipulate variables in real time, so students can spend more time inferring what the data means and drawing conclusions about the data. Figure 10.9 provides a view of changes in water temperature using CBL probeware.

Science-Technology Player's Manual

National Science Education Standards

Through the integration of science and technology, students can develop a better understanding of the natural world. The following list provides a summary of what students need to know regarding the relationship between science and technology:

- Scientific inquiry and technological design have similarities and differences. Scientists propose explanations for questions about the natural world, and engineers propose solutions relating to human problems, needs, and aspirations. Technological solutions are temporary; technologies exist within nature and so cannot contravene physical or biological principles; technological solutions have side effects; and technologies cost, carry risks, and provide benefits.

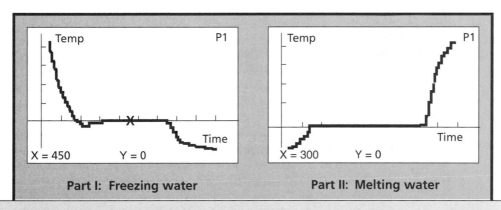

Figure 10.9 Example of measuring temperature changes in water using probeware (from Vernier Software)

- Science and technology are reciprocal. Science helps to drive technology as it addresses questions that demand more sophisticated instruments and provides principles for better instrumentation and technique. Technology is essential to science, because it provides instruments and techniques that enable observations of objects and phenomena that are otherwise unobservable owing to factors such as quantity, distance, location, size, and speed. Technology also provides tools for investigations, inquiry, and analysis.
- Science often advances with the introduction of new technologies. Solving technological problems often results in new scientific knowledge. New technologies often extend the current levels of scientific understanding and introduce new areas of research.
- Scientists and engineers often work in teams, with different individuals doing different things that contribute to the results. This understanding focuses primarily on teams working together and secondarily on the combination of scientist and engineer teams.
- Women and men of all ages, backgrounds, and groups engage in a variety of scientific and technological work.
- Tools help scientists to make better observations, measurements, and equipment for investigations. They help scientists to see, measure, and do things that they could not otherwise see, measure, and do.

National Educational Technology Standards

Science Teachers. Through the use of technology in science teaching, students become empowered to achieve technology skills that will prepare them for life beyond K–12 education. The science teacher is responsible for establishing a classroom environment and preparing learning opportunities that facilitate students' use of technology to learn, communicate, and develop an understanding of science in the natural world. Science teachers need to provide technology-rich experiences throughout all aspects of teaching and learning. The National Educational Technology Standards for Teachers (ISTE, 2000a, 2000b) provide guidelines for producing science students that are capable of understanding the natural world not only through a traditional teaching lens, but also through the real-time and virtual lens of technology.

Science Teacher Preparation. The inclusion of teaching models that include the effective use of technology in science teacher preparation programs are conducive to new teachers using technology in the classroom. The modeling of effective uses of technology for teaching science is best presented in methods courses. Preservice teachers gain basic understanding of technology in their technology education courses, and with this base knowledge, they expand their technology skills by leaning how to apply what they have learned in their science methods courses. Effective preservice science teacher preparation programs present learning environments that join traditional teaching data collection tools, strategies, and techniques with technological tools and technological design to prepare teachers for the twenty-first century.

Science Students. The technology standards for students are divided into six broad categories. Standards within each category are used to allow students to reinforce their understanding of scientific concepts. These categories are as follows:

- Basic operations and concepts
- Social, ethical, and human issues
- Technological productivity tools
- Technology communication tools
- Technology research tools
- Technology problem-solving and decision-making tools (ISTE, 1998)

Examples from these categories include science students' use of telecommunication tools to collaborate on investigations with peers in schools that might be located in other states or countries. Interacting with scientists and other experts around the globe and in space helps to develop an increased understanding of scientific concepts. Students use technology tools to collect, process, and analyze data and report their results of investigations.

American Association for the Advancement of Science

The lessons from history tell us that if technologies, media, and materials are to be productive, the curriculum content and pedagogy that are implemented through them must have promise and value. Some of the technologies in schools today are being introduced without attention to how they actually affect student performance. For example, computer-assisted instruction (CAI) is one of the more popular forms of technology use in schools. However, most CAI programs are highly individualized, a method that has been criticized for increasing the gap between high- and low-achieving students. A simple but crucial question is "How effective was the original instructional approach (in this case, highly individualized instruction) before mediation in the form of computer-assisted instruction?" This factor is critical, especially when the approach has the high acquisition and maintenance costs of CAI (American Association for the Advancement of Science, 1996).

In *Benchmarks for Science Literacy* (AAAS, 1993), the American Association for the Advancement of Science advocates that all science students should understand the relationship between science and technology. The following are examples of what AAAS asserts that each student needs to know at certain grade levels concerning science and technology.

By the end of the second grade, students should know the following:

- Tools are used to do things better or more easily and to do some things that could not otherwise be done at all. In technology, tools are used to observe, measure, and make things.

By the end of the fifth grade, students should know the following:

- Technology enables scientists and others to observe things that are too small or too far away to be seen without them and to study the motion of objects that are moving very rapidly or are hardly moving at all.
- Measuring instruments can be used to gather accurate information for making scientific comparisons of objects and events and for designing and constructing things that will work properly.
- Technology extends the ability of people to change the world: to cut, shape, or put together materials; to move things from one place to another; and to reach farther with their hands, voices, senses, and minds.

By the end of the eighth grade, students should know the following:

- Technology is essential to science for such purposes as access to outer space and other remote locations, sample collection and treatment, measurement, data collection and storage, computation, and communication of information.
- Engineers, architects, and others who engage in design and technology use scientific knowledge to solve practical problems. They usually have to take human values and limitations into account as well.

By the end of the twelfth grade, students should know the following:

- Technological problems often create a demand for new scientific knowledge, and new technologies make it possible for scientists to extend their research in new ways or to undertake entirely new lines of research. The very availability of new technology itself often sparks scientific advances.
- Technology usually affects society more directly than science because technology solves practical problems and serves human needs (and may create new problems and needs). In contrast, science affects society mainly by stimulating and satisfying people's curiosity and occasionally by enlarging or challenging their views of what the world is like.

 ## Technology's Role in the Classroom

Whenever a new technology is introduced into classrooms, its role should be clearly defined before it is used. Too often, it is assumed that students, teachers, administrators, and marketers of the product alike understand the role of a certain technology. Few educational administrators work with teachers and others to clarify how technology will be used in the classroom, and few marketers of high-tech hardware determine the unique needs of specific districts or schools in which their products are to be sold. Failure to define technology's role can have several adverse consequences. For example, if a technology-based program is to be the entire curriculum, then a certain set of evaluation criteria apply for assessing its worth. If this same program is to serve as a tool to support the learning of some other curriculum goal, an entirely different set of evaluation criteria apply. A spreadsheet program, for example, might be the focus of a curriculum unit or an entire course in which the goal is to teach students how to use a spreadsheet program. This same program might be used in a chemistry class because the teacher believes that using spreadsheets improves the quality of students' data collection, analysis, and reporting in laboratory experiments. Used for these two purposes, the same spreadsheet program has vastly different roles. If those roles are not clearly defined, it is impossible to determine how effective a technology is, apart from the specific instructional contexts in which it is used (AAAS, 1996).

There are many sides in the debate over how developing technologies will be integrated into the science classroom to change the way science is taught in K–12 education. This section will focus on three types of new technology that will likely affect science teaching in the near future. Some of these emerging technologies include virtual learning through artificial intelligence, virtual reality, and distributed learning. How virtual learning will influence the evolving game through changing the way teachers teach and students learn as we move into the twenty-first century and beyond will be discussed in the following sections.

Artificial Intelligence

Artificial intelligence (AI) consists of a computer, peripheral hardware, and associated software. This hardware and software is designed for specialized input and output such as sound, sight, touch, speech, and movement. AI technology allows scientific research by permitting students to develop a greater understanding of science concepts through simulation of what is known and what is to be investigated about a science concept. For example, AI simulations can be used to conduct research using on-line databases as a method for testing a hypothesis regarding to the effects of light on plant growth on space stations. This has relevance because among today's students are the future astronauts who might someday visit Mars. Another example of an AI simulation is the study of science-technology-society issues related to human effect on our planet. Students might write new computer programs to test hypotheses about the long-term effects on the earth's environment of humans' current use of technology to change the natural world.

AI has limitations because of the difficulty in analyzing the context of the problem to be solved at times. When students develop programs to use AI to test a hypothesis, they have a difficult time with the complexity of accounting for all variables that are possible when testing their hypotheses. To be successful, AI must replicate all human computational processes. This is a difficult task, and only recently have AI programs been up to the task (May, 1996).

Virtual Reality

Desktop virtual reality (VR) is defined as a three-dimensional, computer-generated synthetic environment that gives a student the sense of being immersed in the environment that is being investigated. Teachers and students can easily create their own VR environment with the use of a computer, a digital camera, and software priced at about $300 (Norton & Sprague, 2001). Examples include students developing their own biological environment to study the effects of pollution on a specific habitat or the growth plants in an environment without gravity. Another example is a VR environment being developed at George Mason University (GMU) in conjunction the National Science Foundation and National Aeronautics and Space Administration (NASA). Their effort has resulted in the development of a VR environment for K–12 students to develop a greater understanding of science concepts through the use NewtonWorld, which allows students to explore Newton's laws of motion and kinetic energy. In the not-too-distant future, NewtonWorld might be available for use in schools as the technology is perfected and becomes more economical. VR environments being developed at GMU have limitations, including the current processing capabilities of computers in schools and the expense. Similar limitations presented equally daunting challenge to the idea of desktop computers in school classrooms just fifteen years ago.

Distributed Learning

Another new technology that has already begun to affect the game of science education is distributed learning, which is defined as using information technologies to extend classroom research. Distributed learning enables students to interpret data collected from virtual communities, artificial environments, webs of knowledge, and sensory input to draw conclusions to support or not support hypotheses (Dede, 1998). As part of distributed learning, webs of knowledge bring together teachers, libraries, reference books, and archived data as sources of information for students to use in their investigations. A second part is the use of virtual communities that allow students to gather expert and peer information through the use of bulletin boards, e-mail, and mailing lists.

Distributed learning takes place today in a limited sense when students visit NASA's Challenger Centers to simulate missions to planet earth. As we move further in to the twenty-first century, technology advances will allow distributed learning to become more commonplace and practical for school science. Teams of students might simulate scientific explorations of Mars or other planets while sitting in their classroom working with collaborators in classrooms in Japan, England, Germany, or other countries.

CONCLUSION: Technological Transformation of the Game of Science Education

The technological world's influence on the game of teaching science has changed the way science is taught in K–12 science classrooms. Over the past thirty years, science students have shifted from predominantly collecting scientific data using traditional instruments such as beakers, balances, thermometers, and spring scales to the use of high-tech tools. Today, computers facilitate data gathering and analysis, Internet research, and multimedia presentation of findings and conclusions. These tools are replacing traditional data collection technology, although traditional tools still have a complementary and primary place as the hardware of science.

This shift in the way data are collected and analyzed and how findings are presented in science classrooms today is evidenced by the way in which science students routinely conduct research and collect data using computers and calculator-based technological tools. These tools collect, measure, graph, and organize scientific data in real time allowing students to spend a greater amount of their time developing their understanding of science concepts through observation, inference, classification, prediction, and analysis of the data. The use of technology allows science teachers to become facilitators of their students learning, which supports inquiry-based teaching from a constructivist perspective.

Even with the rapid technological changes that are taking place today, more technology is on the horizon for the teaching and learning of science. Technologies that will enter the science classroom in the coming years include artificial intelligence, virtual reality, and distributed learning that will enable students to interpret data collected from virtual communities, artificial environments, webs of knowledge, and sensory input, to draw conclusions from research findings to support or not support student hypotheses. These new technologies are only a glimpse of what is to come. The use of high technology in the game of science teaching and learning allows students to develop a greater understanding of science from a local, regional, global, and beyond perspective. As was stated in the National Science Education Standards (NRC, 1996, p. 24) "the goal of technology is to make modifications in the world to meet human needs."

The Game in Action

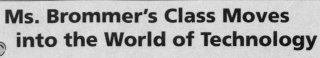

Ms. Brommer's Class Moves into the World of Technology

Ms. Brommer has been teaching eighth grade physical science for the past ten years in a suburban middle school. She teaches five class periods of physical science each school day, with twenty-five students in each class. Two years ago, the school equipped Ms. Brommer's classroom with four computers with access to the Internet through a schoolwide network. She did not use this technology equipment the first year because she did not have the skills or confidence to use computers or the Internet.

Before the last school year, Ms. Brommer's teaching style was characterized as teacher-centered instruction through the traditional model of lecture and demonstration. During the last school year, her teaching style shifted toward a more student-centered instruction style, as she began integrating technology into her curriculum. This shift in her instruction style came about because of her enrollment in a graduate program two years previously to complete a master's degree in science education. As part of the graduate program, she took courses that focused on the integration of technology in the teaching of science. As a result of completing these courses, she gained computer and Internet skills, along with some confidence for integrating this technology in her eighth grade science curriculum.

After dabbling in early attempts to integrate presentation software and the Internet into her curriculum, Ms. Brommer decided to delve more deeply into high technology. Similar to the last school year, she decided to integrate two more new types of technology in her science curriculum. This approach avoided overwhelming her and, in her view, her students. Therefore, she decided that she would integrate calculator-based laboratory (CBL) probeware and WebQuests. She did not want to jeopardize the success she had with previous technology integration and how well her students seemed to develop a better understanding of the science, along with how comfortable she became as a facilitator of science knowledge when using technology.

During the previous school year, she used PowerPoint presentations software to supplement her lesson lectures and demonstrations, along with allowing her students to use this medium to give their own presentations regarding findings from their investigations. She found that the quality of her lectures and demonstrations seemed to be much better, and her students appeared to be more focused on the content she taught. Although Ms. Brommer did not have a projector for her computer, she did have a twenty-seven-inch television that was computer ready, so she connected her computer directly to the television for her students to view presentations. She and her students used the presentation software almost daily. The most important thing that increased her confidence in using presentation software was the positive feedback that she received from her students, other teachers, and the principal.

Another area of technology that Ms. Brommer explored during the previous school year was the use of the Internet to enable her students to locate relevant science information. Although apprehensive at first about allowing her students to use the Internet because she had only recently learned to use it herself, she cautiously permitted them to research science information on the Internet and visit websites that supported her lessons. She quickly discovered that a wealth of information was available to her students that helped them to better understand the science she was teaching. Additionally, her students showed her many science websites that she later used to support her lessons. Her comfort level with the Internet increased as she found that her students enjoyed using the Internet responsibly. Also, as she reflected on her teaching with technology, she discovered that she was becoming more of a facilitator of learning and less a purveyor of science facts and information. This reflective view supported the readings and information that her professors shared with her during her graduate courses.

Two months into the new school year, Ms. Brommer continued to have positive experiences with presentation software and the Internet. She became even more confident in her technology skills and decided that it was time to integrate additional technology into her science curriculum. The next unit in her curriculum was about motion, and a part of this unit focused on speed, so she decided to use another technology tool that she had learned about in her graduate courses: CBL probeware. Additionally, she completed a three-day staff development workshop focusing on the use of CBL probeware to teach science concepts in the physical sciences, specifically the motion detector. To support her effort to integrate this technology, she convinced her principal to allow her to purchase four sets of CBL probeware, four graphing calculators, a view screen (for the overhead), and four motion detectors. This would allow her students to record data and display the motion data in real time.

Studying Motion with CBL Probeware

In previous school years, Ms. Brommer's students used stopwatches to record the time it took a fan car to travel over specific distances across the room and down the hallway. The students would graph their data on graph paper for analysis and then make conclusions based on data from their observations, calculations of average speed, and graphs. Her students always enjoyed building the fan cars from K'NEX® materials, using small fans to provide the constant force necessary to power the fan cars. The students had little trouble collecting the data and constructing their graphs, but using traditional methods of data collection was very time consuming. In many instances, her students were just finishing the graphs and completing average speed calculations when the class period ended. With the pressures of completing the unit within the allotted class time and because of the need to address all appropriate areas of the curriculum before her students had to take the eighth grade proficiency tests in the spring, she rarely had time to allow her students to analyze their graphs for complete understanding of what the average speed curves represented. She always settled on the fact that the investigations, although hands-on, were really not minds-on.

This year, Ms. Brommer decided to take a different approach and use the CBL probeware and motion detectors to collect and display the data through graphs that would allow her students to spend more time analyzing the speed curves for understanding. Her students still built the fan cars and collected their own data, but this time their data were displayed in real-time graphs that they were able to print out for analysis. In her staff development with CBL probeware over the summer, she learned that the graphing calculators had the ability to be connected to a computer and that the graphical display could be enlarged and printed for student analysis. Her students could access the "list" function of the graphing calculators and have the data displayed in table format for completion of data tables. Ms. Brommer had the opportunity to practice a similar investigation during her staff development experience in summer, so she was quite comfortable with using CBL probeware and motion detectors.

When she first introduced CBL probeware with motion detectors to her students, Ms. Brommer used a program called graph matching. This program in the graphing calculator would display a predetermined graph on an overhead screen, using the view screen, for all the students to see. Then students would move forward and backward in front of the motion detector (connected to the CBL) to attempt to match the displayed graph. Students could try to match the graph using either distance or velocity. She discovered that when she used this inquiry-based, student-centered approach to introducing motion to her students, they were better able to understand motion and graph analysis by matching the graphs displayed after a few attempts. Next she let groups of students move around the room holding the graphing calculators and motion detectors to explore motion as they moved closer to or farther away from objects and each other. After this exercise, she reflected that the excitement that she experienced in staff development and her graduate courses regarding using technology was coming to life in her students.

Next she allowed her students to use the CBL probeware with motion detectors to collect data from their fan cars that they had constructed the previous class period. The students printed out their graphs on the graphing calculators using one of the class computers and transferred the data from the calculator data table to a paper form of data table. As the students printed out a graph for each of the three trials they conducted, she observed very serious discussions about the meaning of each speed curve compared to the other trials. Ms. Brommer never experienced this before with students. In the past, the students were too focused on making neat and accurate graphs to have any time to discuss the meaning of the speed curves. After students analyzed their fan cars speed curves, they calculated the average speed for each trial and then averaged the trials to find a more accurate representation of their fan car's average speed.

Next her students wrote a paragraph about what they had observed, what the graph's data represented, and average speed calculations. After the students completed their laboratory investigation, she found that approximately ten minutes of class time remained to permit groups of students to share their findings. When her students completed this investigation using traditional data collection methods, there was rarely any time for students to share their findings and analysis.

As Ms. Brommer reflected back over the laboratory investigation regarding motion, using the CBL probeware with motion detectors to collect the data, she discovered several things. First, her students rapidly grasped the idea of using the CBL probeware to collect their data. They had determined what to do in a matter of minutes, whereas it took her several hours the first time she tried to use the CBL probeware. Second, her students seemed to have a better understanding of what the motion curves represented because there was time at the end of the class period for data analysis. They were allowed to match the graphs displayed on the overhead and then move around the room with the motion detectors in their hands to gain another perspective on what motion graph curves represented. This set the stage for her students to develop a better understanding of their fan car motion curves. Third, although she had to provide some technical assistance at the beginning and during the motion investigation, she found that she became a facilitator of her students learning. She moved from lecture and demonstration to supporting, providing occasional guidance, and asking critical thinking questions as her students investigated motion. Finally, her confidence in using technology for teaching science shifted the way she taught because her students appeared to have a better understanding of the science concepts she was teaching.

Studying Motion Using a WebQuest

The next type of technology Ms. Brommer integrated in her motion unit was a WebQuest. She decided to integrate this type of technology as a capstone for the motion unit because it is an inquiry-based approach for students to study science concepts using the Internet and it would connect many of the concepts that she taught in the unit. In her graduate courses, Ms. Brommer learned about and developed a sample WebQuest on properties of matter. She decided that this type of technology would work well in the unit, considering all the success she had in using the Internet. Also, she had few concerns with her students using the Internet to complete a WebQuest because of its nature and design. A WebQuest permits students to visit only websites that are linked to the resources section for research.

To help Ms. Brommer's students apply their new knowledge about motion in the context of speed, velocity, acceleration, centrifugal force, circular motion, potential energy, kinetic energy, and gravitational force she selected a Roller Coaster WebQuest (www.ashcoteau.org/castille/rollercoaster/index.htm) that was already available on the Internet. She divided her students into groups of four to complete the tasks associated with the WebQuest. One task for her students was to prepare a multimedia presentation about roller coasters, ensuring that most of the motion unit concepts were included in the presentation. She allowed four class periods for research and design. Then she allowed one more class period for group presentations of their work. She had six groups and four computers. For Ms. Brommer, this was not a problem because not all the work for the research and design required use of a computer. Student groups rotated the use of computers for research and presentation preparation. For assessment, the WebQuest included a clear and concise rubric that she used for grading her students' roller coaster designs and presentation, along with inclusion of required motion concepts. Also, the rubric proved to be invaluable to her students because they knew exactly how Ms. Brommer would assess their work, and this resulted in a better-quality presentation of findings produced by the students.

As the students completed the WebQuest, they progressed through the following steps and procedures. First, using the links to additional websites provided in the roller coaster WebQuest, students were able to explore roller coasters around the country. They were able to take virtual roller coaster rides, take virtual roller coaster tours, and study safety devices that were included in roller coasters to further develop their understanding of roller coaster design. Using these supporting website links for their research, students were instructed to develop a drawing of what they thought would be a roller coaster that they would be willing to ride. Their design had to be labeled with all the appropriate motion concepts contained in the roller coaster for connection of motion concepts. Then they scanned their roller coaster designs for inclusion in their groups' multimedia presentation. The final task for each group was a multimedia presentation to share the roller coaster each group designed with the class. Along with presenting the roller coaster, each group's presentations had to include motion concepts that they identified within the design, and then these concepts could be used in other applications that were not roller coasters. Ms. Brommer included this final step as part of the student presentations so that the students could communicate how well they understood motion concepts.

Again Ms. Brommer found herself acting as a facilitator of her students' learning as they applied the science concepts studied in the motion unit. She found using the WebQuest as a capstone to connect most concepts within the unit to be a very successful experience. Her students were more engaged in the WebQuest than she had experienced in the past when she used traditional teaching strategies and did not allow students to use high technology. Further, her students seemed to have a greater understanding of the motion concepts in the unit, as demonstrated in their written assessments and oral communication through multimedia presentations.

Ms. Brommer Reflects on Teaching with Technology

As Ms. Brommer reflected back over her integration of technology in her science curriculum over the past two years, she discovered that there was a permanent shift in the way she taught science. Two years earlier, she would not have dreamed of allowing her students to use the technology. She always thought that high technology required group work because of equipment resources, and she did not like group work because of the noise. She believed that teachers who used this type of student-centered strategy were giving up control of their students' learning and had little classroom control. Also, she would never have allowed the use of the Internet or any other such technology with her students because of her previous view that using high technology some how was cheating or just not right.

Now she was convinced that using high technology caused her to become a facilitator of her students' learning, which allowed them to develop a better understanding of science concepts she taught through hands-on, minds-on investigations. She no longer

relied on her traditional teaching strategies of lecture and demonstration (although she still used these strategies occasionally) because her students would have difficulty understanding science concepts when they were not actively involved in the learning process. She did not feel that she had lost control of her classroom; rather, she felt that she had gained control of her students learning because they were more enthusiastic. Ms. Brommer said to herself, "Now that technology has entered my classroom permanently, my students are really doing science the way scientists do science and most importantly—they understand."

Reflecting on the Game

1. Describe strategies and techniques that you have used, seen, or read about that use the instructional technology tools described in this chapter.
2. Describe strategies and techniques that you have used, seen, or read about that use instructional technology tools not discussed in this chapter.
3. What is your view of how well instructional technology tools facilitate student understanding of science concepts? What evidence do you have to support your view?
4. On the basis of what you have read in this chapter and your experiences, how do you envision instructional technology tools will be used in the science classrooms ten, twenty, or thirty years from today?

References

American Association for the Advancement of Science. (1993). *Benchmarks for science literacy* [Online]. Available: www.project2061.org/tools/benchol/bolframe.htm.

American Association for the Advancement of Science. (1996). *Blueprints* [Online]. Available: www.project2061.org/tools/bluepol/blpframe.htm.

Becker, H. (1991). When powerful tools meet conventional beliefs and institutional constraints. *The Computing Teacher, 18*(8), 6–9.

Becker, H. (2000). Findings from the teaching. Learning, and computing survey: Is Larry Cuban right? *Educational Policy Analysis Archives* [Online]. Available: Epaa.asu.edu/epaa/v8n51.

Brooks, J. G., & Brooks, M. G. (1993). *In search of understanding: The case for the constructivist classroom.* Alexandria, VA: Association for Supervision and Curriculum Development.

Buck, H. J., & Horton, P. B. (1996). Who's using what and how often: An assessment of use of instructional technology in the classroom. *Florida Journal of Education Research, 36*(1), 1–21.

Cronin-Jones, L. L. (1991). Science teacher beliefs and their influence on curriculum implementation. *Journal of Research in Science Teaching, 28*(3), 235–250.

Dede, C. (1998). The scaling-up process for technology-based educational innovations. In

C. Dede (Eds.), *ASCD yearbook: Learning with technology* (pp. 199–215). Alexandria, VA: Association for Supervision and Curriculum Development.

Dexter, S. L., Anderson, R. E., & Becker, H. L. (1999). Teachers' views of computers as catalysts for changes in their teaching practice. *Journal of Research on Computing in Education, 31*(3), 221–239.

Dodge, B. (1995). WebQuests: A technique for Internet-based learning. *Distance Educator, 1*(2), 10–13.

Flick, L., & Bell, R. (2000). Preparing tomorrow's science teachers to use technology: Guidelines for science educators. *Contemporary issues in technology and teacher education.* [Online]. Available: www.citejournal.org/vol1/iss1/currentissues/science/article1/htm.

Fullan, M. (1991). *The new meaning of educational change.* New York: Teachers College Press.

GLOBE. (2002). Global learning and observations to benefit the environment. [Online]. Available: www.globe.gov.

Honey, M., & Moeller, B. (1990). *Teachers' beliefs and technology integration: Different values, different understandings.* New York: Center for Technology in Education.

Hord, S. M., Rutherford, W. L., Huling-Austin, L., & Hall, G. E. (1987). *Taking charge of change.* Alexandria, VA: Association for Supervision and Curriculum Development.

International Society for Technology in Education. (1998). *National educational technology standards for students.* Eugene, OR: Author.

International Society for Technology in Education. (2000a). *National educational technology standards for teachers.* Eugene, OR: Author.

International Society for Technology in Education. (2000b). *National educational technology standards for students: Connecting curriculum and technology.* Eugene, OR: Author.

Isenberg, J. P. (1990). Reviews of research: Teachers' thinking and beliefs and classroom practice. *Childhood Education, 66*(5), 322–327.

Knapp. L. R., & Glenn, A. D. (1996). *Restructuring schools with technology.* Boston: Allyn and Bacon.

Kuhn, T. S. (1970). *The structure of scientific revolutions.* Chicago: University of Chicago Press.

Martin, L. M. W. (1993). Understanding teacher change from a Vygotskian perspective. In P. Kahaney, L. A. M. Perry, & J. Janangelo (Eds.), *Theoretical and critical perspectives on teacher change* (pp. 71–86). Norwood, NJ: Ablex.

May, W. D. (1996). *Edges of reality: Mind vs. computer.* New York: Insight Books.

National Research Council. (1996). *National science education standards.* Washington, DC: Author.

Norton, P., & Sprague, D. (2001). *Technology for teaching.* Boston: Allyn and Bacon.

Osborne, R., & Wittrock, M. (1983). Learning science: A generative process. *Science Education, 67*(4), 489–508.

Office of Technology Assessment, U.S. Congress (OTA). (1995). *Teachers and technology: Making the connection* (OTA-HER-616). Washington, DC: U.S. Government Printing Office.

Padilla, M. J. (1990). *The science process skills.* [On-Line]. Available: www.narst.org/research.skill.htm.

Piaget, J. (1978). *Success and understanding.* Cambridge, MA: Harvard University Press.

Posner, G. J., Strike, K. A., Hewson, P. W., & Gertzog, W. A. (1982). Accommodation of a scientific conception: Toward a theory of conceptual change. *Science Education, 66,* 211–227.

Richardson, V. (1990). Significant and worthwhile change in teaching practice. *Educational Researcher, 19*(7), 10–18.

Schubert, W. H., & Ayers, W. C. (Eds.). (1992). *Teacher lore: Learning from our own experience.* White Plains, NY: Longman.

Senge, P., Kleiner, A., Roberts, C., Ross, R., Roth, G., & Smith, B. (1999). *The dance of change: The challenges to sustaining momentum in learning organizations.* New York: Doubleday/Currency.

Tobin, K., & Fraser, B. J. (1990). What does it mean to be an exemplary science teacher? *Journal of Research in Science Teaching, 27,*(2), 3–25.

Vygotsky, L. S. (1978). *Mind in society: The development of higher psychological process.* Cambridge, MA: Harvard University Press.

Wetzel, D. (1997). Independent student research. *The Science Teacher, 64*(9), 40–43.

Wetzel, D. R. (2002). A model for pedagogical and curricula transformation with technology. *Journal of Computing in Teacher Education, 18*(2), 43–49.

Wetzel, D. R., & Sterling, D. R. (1998). Laser labs. *Science Scope, 22*(3), 34–35.

Wiske, M. (Ed.). (1998). *Teaching for understanding: Linking research with practice.* San Francisco: Jossey-Bass Publishers.

Wittrock, M. C. (1974). Learning is a generative a process. *Educational Psychology, 11,* 87–95.

Yoder, M. B. (1999). The student WebQuest. *Learning and Leading with Technology, 26*(7), 12–15.

Zuga, K. F. (1991). The technology education experience and what it can contribute to STS. *Theory into Practice, 30*(4), 260–266.

Additional Resources

C. Dede (Ed.). (1998). *Learning with technology: ASCD Year Book.* Alexandria, VA: Association for Supervision and Curriculum Development.

Earth and Moon Viewer http://www.fourmilab.to/earthview

Hirschbuhl, J., & Bishop, D. (Eds.). (2002). *Computers in Education.* Guilford, CT: Dushkin.

International Society for Technology in Education. (2000). *Connecting curriculum and technology.* Eugene, OR: Author.

Knapp, L. R., & Glenn, A. D. (1996). *Restructuring Schools with technology.* Boston: Allyn & Bacon.

The Space Place http://spaceplace.jpl.nasa.gov

Water Cycle http://www.muohio.edu/dragonfly/water/index.html

Weather and Air Pollution Web Cams http://www.epa.gov/airnow/webcam.html

Yahooligans http://yahooligans.com/School_Bell, a search engine for Science and Nature websites for students and teachers.

start

chapter

11

TESTING AND ASSESSMENT IN SCIENCE EDUCATION:
Setting Par for the Course

Peter Veronesi, Ph.D.
Science Education, State University
of New York–Brockport

ABOUT THE AUTHOR: Dr. Peter Veronesi is an associate professor at the State University of New York, College at Brockport, where he teaches elementary and secondary science methods. His research interests encompass issues dealing with science teacher education. Dr. Veronesi's work in science student assessment includes NSF-funded professional development initiatives as well as publication and science educator professional organization leadership. He currently serves on the steering committee of the Coalition for Common Sense in Education (CCSE), an organization devoted to educating policymakers and the public regarding trends and practices in student assessment.

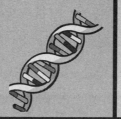

> **We have always found that people are most productive in small teams with the freedom to solve their own problems.**
>
> —John Rollwagen
> *Former CEO of Cray Research*

CHAPTER WARM-UP

Assessment takes different meanings depending on whether you are a reflective teacher, a learner, or a spectator to the game of science education. Though for many, a scorecard mentality equates assessment and testing, science teachers see assessment as an instructional tool for evaluation of performances—both the student's and the teacher's. Enlightened approaches to assessment in science invoke numerous strategies and instruments, often blurring the line between teaching, learning, and assessing. Modern assessment fosters reflection while measuring teaching and learning effectiveness in multiple domains including content, creativity, and reasoning.

INTRODUCTION: Players in Perspective

Brad is the club pro here at the local golf course. Between giving lessons, running the pro shop, and scheduling events such as the Twilight Couples Best Shot, he slips away to play regional tournaments now and then. Brad seldom brings back a trophy. This fact is remarkable only when you consider that he is the best golfer by far at our local course. How good must those guys be who are winning the club tour events? And most of them have never made the cut at a PGA tournament. How good, then, must the professional tour pros be? And most of them never win a major. So just how good are the players we all know by name: Tiger, Phil, Jack, Arnie? They are just a few strokes better than Brad, and when his game is on, there is no difference.

But of course there is. If not for subtle variations in swing mechanics or mental focus, lots of weekend hacks could make the tour. But laying their scorecards side by side next to Annika Sorenstam's or Phil Mickelson's reveals only that it took six or eight extra hits to complete eighteen holes over a three-mile walk. A small difference (or a large one—it doesn't matter) in scores reveals nothing qualitative about golfers and their differences—strengths, weaknesses.

Scorecards are wholly inadequate assessments of all golfers, except the few at the pinnacle. For the rest of us lifelong learners of the game, more authentic assessments that inform our practices and lead to improvement are needed.

The late golf club designer Ely Callaway invoked the name of science in the design and marketing of his instruments of the game; it's only fair then, that golf be invoked metaphorically for the design of instruments of assessment for the game of science education!

Schools of Thought on Assessment

When we look at the American Heritage Dictionary's meaning of the root word *assess*, we find a relevant definition that states:

> **as-sess** (-sessed). 4. To evaluate or praise. See Synonyms to estimate. [MiddleEnglish *assessen*, from Old French *assesser*, from Latin *assidere*, "to sit beside," be an assistant.

So if you follow an English tradition, you evaluate when you assess. However, when you follow an original Latin line of reasoning, to assess means "to sit beside" the person who is showing you something—or, in Brad's case, behind the neophyte golfer. Although these might represent only a subtle, semantically different way of saying the same thing, both interpretations can eventually bring a great disparity between uses when it comes to assessing students' knowledge, understanding, and ability to do science. That is, there are at least two very different schools of thought when the term "assess" is used, and it all depends on whose interests are at stake. There is the scorecard school, and there is the "sit beside and assist" school.

In this chapter, we'll look at past science assessments in the United States, the current status of science assessment, where research says science assessment should be headed, and where it is actually headed. One thing is for sure, the way in which science educators may look at assessment and the way in which the public we serve looks at it can be very different.

The Scorecard Model

Testing in the form of traditional exams had its root in the latter part of the nineteenth century. There are more than 125 years of inertia built into the testing movement (Perrone, 2000). Ironically, the first tests focused largely on written responses and problem solving. The multiple-choice format did not come into wide use until after 1910. By 1936, states such as New York had implemented broad-scale exams in the schools, portending a time when tests would drive the curriculum. Over sixty years later, we have the New York Regent's Exam to contend with.

Science assessment continues to gain headlines, as it might first have in 1970, the year of the very first national science assessment, which was designed to show the first comprehensive data on science understanding in the United States for the 1969–1970 school year. A push for fair and consistent measures of science knowledge spawned the standardized exam, now prevalent in schools. The 1970s also witnessed growth in cognitive psychology, domain-referenced testing, techniques such as multiple matrix sampling, and item response theory that armed test designers with a confidence that large and small groups of students could be deduced to a final, single number, a label (Doran, Lawrenz, and Helgeson, 1994).

Although we have learned much about the most effective forms of science assessment and learning over the past fifty years, the overall way we assess students has changed little. Many stakeholders and policymakers view our education system as an infrastructure such as roads and bridges. As a result, political leaders, on mandate from the lay public, successfully push for economical measures of school performance—broadly applied, ill-fitting tests.

The National Assessment of Educational Progress published results from nationwide tests in 1980 that reinforced and expanded the public perception of a crisis in our public schools. Then the Third International Math and Science Study (TIMSS) attempted to make comparisons between U.S. students' math and science abilities and those of students in other countries in the 1990s (Martin et al., 1999). The TIMSS was criticized for trying to compare different cultures and for fueling the increase in the use of standardized tests (Bracey, 1998). In short, the TIMSS might have been a catalyst leading to the current culture of high-stakes testing used in the name of reform.

The concept is simple enough: Schools exist to teach the next generation, and assessments are needed to find out how well this next generation is learning. Since the early 1970s, a growing body of research has emerged that details the many intricate concerns surrounding assessment and the impact it has on teaching and learning. In an odd, tail-wagging-the-dog twist, however, our assessments often turn out to steer, rather than measure, what we teach. This section deals with the literature surrounding assessment and what research has shown over the years.

There are typical standardized, norm-referenced or criterion-referenced multiple-choice tests, and then there are meaningful assessments that are reflective, constructive, and self-regulated and that have students performing, creating, or producing something (Doran, Lawrenz, and Helgeson, 1994). Assessment tasks should include beginning criteria and expectations and should represent a meaningful instructional activity that is often set in the context of the real world of the student (Herman, 1992). These real-world tasks include (1) challenging, interesting, and reflecting of science instruction, which itself should reflect the goals for science learning, which in turn should reflect good science; (2) reporting systems that reflect science assessments with fidelity; (3) educators at all levels who are aware of the purpose for assessment as well as their clients; and (4) further knowledge and new techniques, created so that assessments of science learning and performance are faithful to the goals of science education and the nature of science (Raizen et al., 1990). The assessment should also provide students the opportunities to express attitudes as well as the more intellectual products and not be drill and practice (Tucker, 1991; Wiggins, 1992).

A focus on test scores and traditional assessments has resulted in many teachers teaching to the test at the expense of authentic learning. Many states have imposed standardized measures of student performance on schools and teachers despite well-known shortcomings in establishing deeper understandings. Regardless of the tendency of traditional assessments to focus on the knowledge level only, states will most likely continue using them because they are cheap and easy to administer (Davis & Armstrong, 1991; Tucker, 1991).

Viewed by thoughtful teachers as nuisances imposed on them by states and local districts in the 1970s, high-stakes tests, such as statewide testing, are now having to be taken very seriously by teachers, students, and parents (Aschbacher & Herman, 1991). To get the highest scores on these high-stakes tests, many teachers ignore real learning in favor of having students focus on the "right answers." Downplaying real learning is a perceived necessity when the right answer (a high score on the A.P. test, the ACT, or the SAT) provides great reward. With renewed interest in minimum competencies, graduation requirements, and college entrance scores, many policy decisions are also being made by using only the results from high-stakes tests, an action that has a direct impact on many lives (Davis & Armstrong, 1991).

For many parents, a good test score means that their child is smart, further reinforcing standardization (Stiggins, 1993; Wiggins, 1989, 1993). In addition, superintendents often urge principals and teachers to raise test scores, overconcerning themselves with the learning that is going on (Shepard, 1989).

While states and their policymakers continue to promote high-stakes tests, several negative aspects of this promotion have emerged, including (1) a narrowing of the curriculum, (2) emphasis on drill and practice toward the test—an outdated form of instruction, (3) rejection of hard-to-teach children by the system, (4) a media focus on scores leading to false impressions regarding the actual understanding and abilities students have in particular areas, (5) misdirection of instruction, and (6) reduction in the professional knowledge and status of teachers (Shepard, 1989).

Have science teachers always been opposed to mass assessment? Actually, no. In science classrooms, traditional assessments have long followed the multiple-choice format and have come to be relied on heavily for many decades. Multiple-choice questions are written most commonly at the knowledge level and are constructed by a single teacher, a team of teachers, or a computer-generated database. These tests are most commonly used to assign grades, diagnose, monitor progress, and plan instruction. But what are they doing for the students or the teachers? Giving multiple-choice assessments requiring only factual recall has been said to be worse than not giving any test at all. It has been this shortcoming that has led to the explosion of interest in the many forms of alternative assessment (Aschbacher & Herman, 1991; Haertel, 1991).

Multiple-choice tests also fall short of addressing the issue of developmental appropriateness, another reason for reform as implied by the following passage (Raizen et al., 1990, p. 30):

> In the case of assessment, if science is taught as only new vocabulary, the implicit message is that science is mostly a matter of memorizing new terms. If factual knowledge is taught, the message is that science is a static body of facts, principles and procedures to be mastered and recalled on demand. If tests call for the student to engage in active exploration and reflection, to pose new questions, and solve new problems, the message can be that science is a mode of disciplined inquiry, applied specialized knowledge, investigative procedures, and rules of evidence for understanding both the natural world and the technologies through which humans have shaped that world to their ends.

Although there are times where quick assessments like these are appropriate, they are often overused. Heavy reliance on low-level multiple-choice examinations brings other negative ramifications:

- Generic standardized multiple-choice tests cannot assess all the instructional goals of any school district.
- The closed nature of a multiple-choice question ensures that students never get appropriate access to more realistic, unstructured tasks and questions.
- The message to students is that a test suggests never having to justify the answer.
- Feedback from an end-of-year test has no implications for that year's teaching and learning.
- Multiple-choice tests that have students selecting a "right" answer never tell teachers whether a student is truly able to use knowledge to fashion high-quality products or performances.
- Multiple-choice tests have a debilitating effect on students who are below the norm on simple recall scales (Wiggins, 1991).

Despite the negatives, many teachers, school districts, and states continue the practice of using mostly standardized (many times low-level) assessments year after year with little change (Berlak, 1992).

Darling-Hammond et al. (1993) state that American schools began using the multiple-choice test as a common means of assessment as school systems long ago took on a factory model approach to education. Adult citizens who experienced factory assessment know only this model of testing (Mitchell, 1992). Few laypeople would find the following test item anything but typical:

Using the metric system, you would measure the length of your classroom in:
a. grams
b. kilometers
c. meters
d. liters

Although "c. meters" is the obvious answer to most, a student in any classroom could correctly select "b. kilometers" though it would most likely be marked wrong. Both can be correct, but only through explanation could a teacher know the student's thinking. Therein lies the problem: Lower-level tests do not require or attest to thinking (Wiggins, 1992). Poorly designed, low-level, multiple-choice tests that included questions like this one were still the most commonly used form of assessment in 1990, and there is little in the literature to reflect any substantial change (Archbald, 1991; Berlak, 1992; National Research Council, 1996; Newmann, Secada, & Wehlage, 1995; Stiggins & Conklin, 1992; Wiggins, 1993).

High-Stakes Versus High-Yield Exams

Gordon and Reese (1997, p. 345) offer a definition of high-stakes testing: "The high stakes test is one which is a standardized achievement test used as a direct measure of accountability for students, educators, schools, or school districts, with significant sanction or reward attached to test results." Barksdale-Ladd and Thomas (2000, p. 384) consider the current and past practices of high-stakes testing movement and its many destructive arms as "an act of unthinking, unilateral educational disarmament." This is inflammatory rhetoric, to be sure, but testing evokes strong feelings on both sides. What are those sides?

There are high-stakes exams, and then there are high-yield exams—tests that show student growth and competency in a broad array of science domains, including concepts, process skills, logic, and attitudes. High-yield exams take many forms and are referred to as *authentic* or *aligned assessments*. The differences in approach to testing could not be greater, and it is unfortunate that teachers themselves might have little input to the evolving testing terrain. A trend has resulted in which teachers are more commonly evaluated almost solely on how well their students perform on standardized tests rather than on how well each individual student may be learning (Hilliard, 2000). Each side in this argument has big weaponry: Pro-testers have a public mandate for school accountability (with an eye toward economy), and pro-learners have Assessment Standards in the form of National Science Education Standards (NRC, 1996).

The Assessment Standards (NRC, 1996, p. 75) provide a meaningful guide for supporting science educators as they learn and grow toward the most appropriate uses for assessment.

1. Assessment Standard A: Assessments must be consistent with the decisions they are designed to inform.
   - Assessments are deliberately designed.
   - Assessments have explicitly stated purposes.
   - The relationship between the decisions and the data is clear.
   - Assessment procedures are internally consistent.
   - Assessments are deliberately designed:
   - Statements about the purposes that the assessment will serve
   - Descriptions of the substance and technical quality of the data to be collected
   - Specifications of the number of students or schools from which data will be obtained
   - Descriptions of the data collection method
   - Descriptions of the method of data interpretation
   - Descriptions of the decisions to be made, including who will make the decisions and by what procedures
2. Assessments Standard B:
   - Achievement and opportunity to learn science must be assessed.
   - Achievement data collected focus on the science content that is most important for students to learn.
   - Opportunity-to-learn data collected focus on the most powerful indicators.
   - Equal attention must be given to the assessment of opportunity to learn and to the assessment of student achievement.
3. Assessment Standard C: The technical quality of the data collected is well matched to the decisions and actions taken on the basis of their interpretation.
   - The feature that is claimed to be measured is actually measured.
   - Assessment tasks are authentic.
   - An individual student's performance is similar on two or more tasks that claim to measure the same aspect of student achievement.
   - Students have adequate opportunity to demonstrate their achievements.
   - Assessment tasks and methods of presenting them provide data that are sufficiently stable to lead to the same decisions if used at different time.
4. Assessment Standard D: Assessment practices must be fair.
   - Assessment tasks must be reviewed for the use of stereotypes, for assumptions that reflect the perspectives or experiences of a particular group, for language that might be offensive to a particular group, and for other features that might distract students from the intended task.
   - Large-scale assessment must use statistical techniques to identify potential bias among subgroups.
   - Assessment tasks must be appropriately modified to accommodate the needs of students with physical disabilities, learning disabilities, or limited English proficiency.
   - Assessment tasks must be set in a variety of contexts, must be engaging to students with different interests and experiences, and must not assume the perspective or experience of a particular gender, racial, or ethnic group.

5. Assessment Standard E: The inferences made from assessments about student achievement and opportunity to learn must be sound.
   - In making inferences from assessment data about student achievement and opportunity to learn science, explicit reference needs to be made to the assumptions on which the inferences are based.

These assessment standards, developed as a consensus bellwether for science education by a team of thousands of science teachers and science teacher educators, provide much needed support to the pro-learners, a group composed almost entirely of those in the education camp. However, the standards carry no mandate, and their implementation varies greatly from district to district, indeed classroom to classroom.

Deborah Perkins-Gough (2000) elaborates on the issues debated between test lovers and test haters. On one hand, simple scores are publicly used as accountability measures for teachers and schools. The scores are seen as politically motivated, something to be sold to the public. These scores also consistently hinder real learning. Proponents of high-stakes tests use the evidence of rising test scores to support their continued use. This promotes an addictive downward spiral, and opponents who focus on meaningful learning point to the loss of real teaching and authentic learning and explain that test scores rise as a result of test preparation rather than real learning (Perkins-Gough, 2000). The alternatives to external pressures and passive acceptance is for teachers, parents, and students to resist such external pressures and look inward, back to the classroom, and to focus once again on learning. Perhaps a story of a frustrated biology teacher details the potential loss of meaningful learning when high-stakes tests await the end of the school year:

> Jill was an excited and dynamic fifth-year biology teacher. She put in the extra mile for her tenth-grade students. Within three years, she was organizing summer field trips for her students, such as hiking in the Adirondacks and whale watching. During the year, she would use a pond that was very close to her school to demonstrate and have her students observe real ecological phenomena and concepts in a natural setting. Then the state imposed strict guidelines for curriculum that would be assessed at year's end with a privately developed, rather secretive biology test. Very quickly, the word got out that if students did not score well on this test, teachers' jobs could be in jeopardy. Jill was faced with a difficult decision; continue on with the investigative format of her biology course while risking gaps in factual knowledge that could jeopardize her students on the standardized exam or resort to more formal instructional methods that covered the content likely to appear on a comprehensive exam. She resigned herself to conforming to the test.

This story provides a window into how meaningful learning is often sacrificed when the stakes are high. Most science teachers want their students to have a meaningful understanding of their science discipline. High-stakes tests hinder this goal by imposing a condition that forces teachers to cover science content rather than have their students uncover the concepts in authentic ways.

Jill is hardly alone in abandoning authentic learning under pressure from testing culture (Zigo, 2001). But the fallout from the forced transition among talented and motivated science teachers can be significant. Some of these consequences can be high stress, low morale, a narrow curriculum, and decreased student love of learning and teaching (Hargrove et al., 2000).

A study in Texas conducted by Gordon and Reese (1997) resulted in a series of suggestions that are intended to bring a focus back to learning and away from the negative impacts of high-stakes testing:

- Policymakers and test developers need to address the negative, unintentional side effects of their tests.
- Professional staff development needs to demonstrate how a rich curriculum can be maintained in lieu of a final test.
- Endless streams of test preparation practices must be avoided.
- Total reliance on a single test score should be replaced by a variety of individualized assessments of student achievement, including various types of authentic assessments and student portfolios.
- The media must get involved with educating the public as to the real meanings of test scores.

Several education organizations have stepped forward to take a stand against high-stakes testing (AERA, 2000; Villaire, 2001), resulting in an extension of Gordon and Reese's suggestions to include careful analyses of many dimensions of this trend. These recommendations are as follows:

- High-stakes decisions (e.g., graduation, or teaching assignment) should not be based on a single test.
- Policymakers must provide schools with adequate resources and opportunities for students to learn;
- A full disclosure of likely negative impacts must be made (e.g., student and teacher stresses, narrowing of curriculum, loss of creativity of instruction).
- Appropriate attention must be given to students with disabilities and other learning problems.
- Ongoing evaluation of both intended and unintended effects of high-stakes testing must occur.

The High Road to High-Yield Assessments

Set to tee off, Glen pulls a 3-wood from his bag. Its titanium head and flexible shaft are brought fully to bear on the small ball atop the tee. Smack! A 220-yard shot. After locating his ball on the fairway, Glen digs into his golf bag to select his next club. At thirty yards out, he selects a pitching wedge to drop the ball close to the pin. He draws back, but only a little. Nice follow-through, and the ball lands five feet from the hole. On the green, Glen selects a putter. He lines up, tap, and plunk! Par. Time only for a celebratory grin, then on to the next hole.

Glen used various clubs to achieve an ultimate goal: getting the ball in the hole. He was skillful at discerning which situation called for which instrument—the right tool for the job. It's no different assessing students in science class; many instruments exist, and it takes an accomplished student of the game to know which is most appropriate and when.

This section explores a few of the major kinds of science assessments that are used to assess student knowledge and skills. The most effective science assessments include model building, concept maps, drawings, writing products (essays, brochures, story lines, letters to companies), science conference/small group debate, inquiries (data, charts, graphs/questions, oral discussion), and portfolios. But first, an explanation of some of the terms associated with assessment is in order:

- *Formative:* The assessment done and used each moment, hour, day, or week that is used immediately to change instruction or monitor progress. It has a flowing or ongoing nature (questions, observation, listening, writing samples).
- *Alternative:* Almost any appropriate assessment that is different from a multiple-choice test format.
- *Authentic:* That which matches what was actually practiced in the classroom and matches the concept or event in real life (designing a real experiment, applying concepts and skills to real problems).
- *Summative:* Used at the end of a thematic or conceptual unit, showing what each student knows and can do at a specified point in time.

The current science education reform movement boils down to students doing science through inquiry (NRC, 1996). This means that a visitor to a science classroom should see, for the most part, students moving around that classroom seeking answers about the natural or designed world. In many cases, the classroom may be outside. In the end, however, the students would be able to communicate a reasonably effective argument, a subject, theme, or concept that is based on data that they have collected. Traditional science learning does not meet this goal because directions are prescribed, and investigations do little more than verify through recipelike protocols. By contrast, students doing meaningful inquiry would be asking their own questions and designing investigations around that question. These types of questions are as infinite as the creativity of the human mind: "How often does a woodpecker feed its young?" "What is the stopping distance of my bicycle at various speeds?" "Which of these soils produce the healthiest plants?" Using questions as starting points, teachers and students then embark on legitimate, productive, and motivating science learning.

The single most important goal of assessment is for students to demonstrate what they know, how they know it, and what they are able to do with this knowledge or skill (Weld, 1992). To ensure the highest degree of congruence between what was taught and what was learned, the most appropriate assessments should be sought. First, it must be decided what is most important for students to know and be able to do.

Once the learning outcomes of any particular science unit have been established, the most appropriate assessment should be developed. A key notion here is that at any given time, goals can vary; they might be emphasized or deemphasized. For example, much of science is about learning to "do" with new skills and ways of thinking. Therefore, students should be given performance assessments to demonstrate the degree to which they can "do."

The assessments that are most effective at truly getting at what students know and can do involve students in asking a question, collecting data, analyzing the data, and interpreting their results. These results are then communicated to a larger group.

This process is how science works; it is the nature of science. To assess inquiry in the most meaningful way requires a science conference atmosphere in which students exhibit their findings to a larger group and respond to relevant questions.

When authentic assessment of true inquiry comes into play, the line between teaching and assessing becomes quite blurred; the assessments that drive this environment must be in place from the start. For example, students entering a science classroom on day one would know that they are required to ask questions and seek reasonable answers to these questions within a given amount of time. Surely, conceptual and process-skill based standards would be in place to act as guides. But these standards can be met and assessed in a variety of meaningful ways, not just a test or quiz. Students who are in science classrooms where the atmosphere is based more solidly on their particular burning issues or questions would be motivated to dig far more deeply into a subject area and emerge as learned scholars. Also, students in this type of classroom would know that they are responsible for presenting their findings to their peers on a regular basis—in a home-grown science conference, for instance.

Having students present their own data to their peers teaches them a great deal about the nature of science and shows them that the teacher values their thought and questions and reinforces these notions by assessing them in a very meaningful way.

Recommendations such as this arise from the National Science Teachers Association's guiding framework on assessment (Doran, Chan, & Tamir, 1998). The NSTA guide extensively details the many components of science assessment, including the rationale for authentic forms of testing.

Key to authentic science assessment is a recognition of the learning theory of constructivism (see Chapter 5) in which a student's prior science knowledge is valued and used to establish growth. In short, constructivism must form the base and the conceptual framework for any authentic assessments that are created and used. That is, students are challenged to use what they know, incorporate any new knowledge, and express their understandings and abilities in creative or novel ways. The more the "ways of showing" are connected to the real world of the student, the more authentic the assessment becomes.

What is a science teacher to do to find out what a student knows and can do? Most science assessments follow one of two paths: formative and summative. Formative assessments detail the day-to-day science knowledge and abilities of students. The stakes are usually low, and students have the opportunity to evaluate their own knowledge and progress. Classroom questions, model building, science conferences, and small group inquiry are but a few methods of formative science assessments that teachers have at their disposal to determine the extent to which the students are "getting it."

Formative and summative evaluation both require that the science teacher consider curricular learning objectives for the school and district then choose the most appropriate assessments to meet the objectives. For example, if inquiry and design are desired learning outcomes, then a student-designed inquiry would be the most appropriate assessment. The teacher would be able to see and hear all the required components of the inquiry. In this case, the student would actually be doing the inquiry and reporting on what was learned—a perfect match for the objective.

Once the needs have been established, the science teacher must begin to design an assessment or choose from the many types that are available and practice the chosen assessments with students. A concept map, for example is a model conceptual framework that is often used successfully by science teachers. However, if a concept map is chosen as an appropriate way for students to show how they are constructing knowledge of a science concept, then this should be a feature of instructional time as well. Hence novel assessments present an opportunity for science teachers to take risks in developing effective instructional methods. Novel assessment choices, like unusual club selection during a golf outing, might just produce unforeseen and favorable results.

Types of Authentic Assessment

Science teachers, like golfers, have broad choice for selection in their bag; unfortunately, many do not have classroom caddies to help bear the load! The effective teachers' assessment bag includes different assessment strategies that fit various goals and learning objectives. Here are a few samples.

Journaling

The journal can be a diarylike series of writing and/or drawings. The student should have a separate book or folder for the journal to maintain a sense of privacy and ownership. Entries can be responses to an instructor's questions or statements, feelings about an activity, or "what did I learn today?" A main feature of journals is the writing component. Students gain practice in their writing skills while communicating their ideas on paper.

The list of positive aspects of student journals is long. For example, considerable transfer of knowledge between subject areas can occur when journals are used. Teachers are better able to respond to individual questions as the journals are read at various times. Long-term improvements within the course and teaching methodology can result as a response from insights gained from students.

Performance Assessments

Performance assessments include process skill-based tasks at the simplest level and complete science investigations at a more complex level. Giving students batteries, bulbs, and wires to create various circuits can demonstrate their ability to show what they know about electricity, for example. When students cannot do performance tasks when they are a learning outcome, there might be a mismatch between the instructional methods and the assessment. Said another way, the students would have to have the opportunity to practice with batteries and bulbs, think through problems, and derive solutions before this performance assessment would match instruction. If students indeed had ample practice with the material and relevant challenge, the task would be authentic to the concept as well as to the teaching.

Baxter, Elder, and Glasser (1996) discussed the role performance assessment can play in improving teaching and learning in a science classroom. While studying a fifth grade classroom on instruction of electrical circuits, the authors discussed one very important notion of science assessment: "Making the thinking of the learners overt provides opportunities for it to be examined, questioned, and realized as an active object of constructive teaching and the focal point of assessment."

Interviewing

The clinical interview has been adopted by researchers who are concerned with the conceptions held by students and is considered the classical tool used in this area. The interview allows the teacher to interact orally with the student, probe for further clarification, and assess students who are unable to communicate as effectively with the written word. If teachers follow some simple guidelines, the interview can be a powerful tool in establishing the student's preconceptual frameworks and evaluating student learning following science instruction.

1. Plan the interview. If possible, use concrete objects, situations, or pictures.
2. Select appropriate questions to ask the student. Ask questions that are designed only to find out what students know about the issue or the concepts involved. Avoid "yes/no" questions. Do not ask questions designed to aid student understanding of the issue. Let students talk without fear of right or wrong. Get them to describe, predict, or explain.
3. Sequence the questions so as to proceed from the easier questions to the more difficult ones. It is important to establish student confidence so the student does not become nervous and uncomfortable during the interview. The real goal is to seek explanations.
4. Students should be given adequate time to answer the questions. If the student fails to respond to the initial question or says that he or she does not understand the question, the question should be restructured so as to give the student a chance to be successful.
5. Whether it is the first time for teacher or student or the tenth, it is important to convey a relaxing presence. Interviewers should project the image that they are human and that they don't know all the answers.
6. In any sequential interview, it is important to refer to prior interviews or relevant intervening instruction. Student ideas should be used. This gives the student a frame of reference from which to respond, making the conversation flow and giving evidence of teacher acceptance.
7. The language of the student should be used when rephrasing questions or probing further. To insist on the "right" word or pronunciation can be confusing and inhibit fuller expression of concepts and propositions. Also, students will sometimes use the wrong label (word) for the right concept (for example, students often say that the earth is shaped like a circle, rather than a sphere). When this occurs, an explanation can be asked for, and the student can supply the correct concept label.

8. Finally, interviews should end on a positive note. The student's cooperation, manners, and answers can be noted; any questions the student might have can be answered. In any case, the interview should end with feelings that will make future interviews an experience to be welcomed and anticipated (Novak & Gowin, 1984).

Portfolios

Portfolios have a strong presence in elementary classrooms because of the self-contained nature of the learning environment, but they can be a rich tool for assessment of science learning at the secondary level as well. Most elementary teachers, for instance, use a portfolio for each student in two ways. Portfolios are used to show a student's "best work." In this way, students are the keepers of what they consider to be representative of "the best of their ability" for any task or assignment for which they have been responsible during the year. The portfolio in this case (a shoebox, manila folder, or suitable container) might contain end-of-unit products or artifacts that students could pull out and explain to a teacher or parent.

Portfolios can also be used effectively to demonstrate student growth over time. Using the portfolio in this manner defines the goal of learning as constant and sustained improvement over time. Looking at student progress over time is what most educators consider their major responsibility.

A portfolio for a science classroom has the potential to be incredibly rich for each student. If used inappropriately, it has the potential to be a waste of time. For example, looking at a portfolio of assessments that include only tests and quizzes would demonstrate that the student can keep up the pace of learning for knowledge only. This might be demonstrated by pulling out various quizzes or tests to peruse them for grades.

However, when used appropriately in a science classroom, students' ability to express their growth in knowledge as well as many other areas can become a rewarding reality for all parties.

Model Building

Model building is an ultimate example of demonstration or application—concepts brought to bear in practical design. Models require resources, both material and space, but the assessment event carries a powerful learning dimension as well, making model building a better use of assessment time than many others. Developmentally, when students construct models to demonstrate nerves in the body or the circulation system, they enhance spatial skills in projective and three-dimensional logic.

Self-Designed Inquiries

Self-designed inquiries can lead to a more fundamental understanding of the nature of science (a topic that is thoroughly discussed in Chapter 8). On a broader level, self-designed inquiries are the quintessential measure of learning in all its dimensions in an inquiry science class: question formulation, experimental design, data analysis, synthesis and application. The products of these inquiries may become part of students' portfolios. These artifacts might include lab write-ups, data, charts, graphs, and written discussion. However, a videotape of a science conference presentation might be included in a student portfolio as well to show the degree to which oral communication skills have been addressed.

Concept Maps

A concept map demonstrates the potential for students to graphically demonstrate their understanding at any given time. Matching short interviews with each concept map provides a whole new level of assessment. When students are explaining what they have drawn, they can clarify their own misconceptions on the spot or can be asked to do so by the teacher. Although the process for using concept maps must be taught to students overtly, their potential for use is limited only by the creativity of the student and teacher and the time available for creating connections between concepts.

To introduce students to concept mapping, they must first be shown the connection for the concept in the real world (see Figure 11.1). The concept must first make sense to them in some way. However, although the concept might be shown or pointed out, it might take years for a valid conceptual framework to emerge in the students' mind.

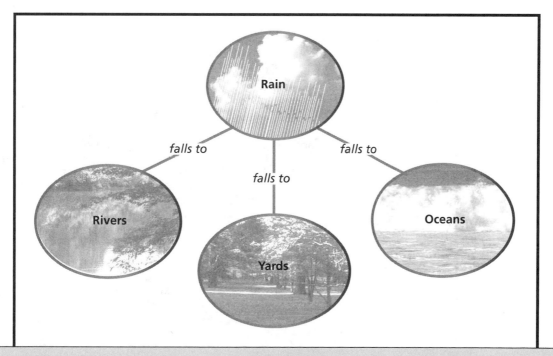

Figure 11.1 An example of a pre-unit concept map related to the water cycle

The students should then be asked to describe the relationship they see to the real-world examples that have been given. These relationships will eventually form the basis for the first concept map. Finally, students are instructed to write these relationships in a form that can be both explained by the student and viewed by another. A key factor is that concept maps become increasingly more complex through time; thus, complexity increase shows increased learning over time (see Figure 11.2). Multiple-staged concept maps can be viewed in portfolios to demonstrate how thinking has changed over time (Novak & Gowin, 1984).

These examples of alternative assessments are only a snapshot of the variety that science teachers have used successfully to help students understand and to understand students. This list is not exhaustive or new, and more effective assessments are surely developed daily by creative teachers in classrooms somewhere. A central tenet of assessment development, though, is that they must teach as well as assess. For example, if a teacher develops an assessment called "The Newscast," in which students work in pairs to deliver a mock news report on a science concept, then, however the students develop their newscast, they are assuredly learning. In this example, a teacher can formatively assess learning by monitoring development of the newscast throughout the week as well as summatively assessing the final newscast itself.

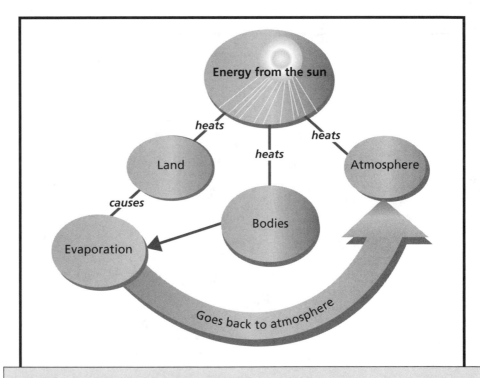

Figure 11.2 A mid-unit concept map (partial)

Good assessments teach, and they are interesting to students in their own right. Alternative or authentic assessing is not risk free, but teachers often begin slowly with a plan to try one new assessment at a time, get good at it, refine it and adapt it to their needs, and possibly move to another one. This process might take the entire career of an individual. In changing or constantly developing the most appropriate assessment, teachers are modeling lifelong learning and demonstrating how effective teaching is an incredibly complex endeavor and requires constant adaptation.

Designing a New Scorecard

Golf coaches know how little is revealed by the scorecard insofar as the growth and improvement of each team member is concerned. Score changes are indicative, to be sure, but they tell virtually nothing of the mechanics of swing, etiquette, or frame of mind. Imagine a coach's scorecard that has room for documenting changes in these nuances that lead to eventual changes in score. How useful such a thing would be for both coach and player! Authentic science assessment too looks beyond scores, to skills, ways of thinking, and attitudes; this calls for redesign of the science scorecard.

Realigning assessment to coincide with the goals of an inquiry science classroom can bring growing pains for students who have been reared on rote memorization tests. At the core of the learning goals for any science teacher are the student's expectations for learning. Expectations for "doing a good job" exist in the minds of every teacher. So that students have a better understanding of what these expectations are, rubrics (authentic science's scorecard) are tools that are developed to show the desired expectations for any task or event. The main goal of a rubric is to provide the student with criteria for success. As with all assessment, rubrics are infinitely subjective and constantly evolving. They are subjective because people (teachers and, ideally, students) decide what is "good," "better," and "best" or "target," "proficient," and "not acceptable," and those decisions change depending on the individual, the classroom, the grade level, the school district, and the state.

On any given task, assignment, or expectation, a student might do what the teacher considers to be an exemplary job. The resulting product might have met each criterion to the highest stated degree so that a student might receive an "A" grade. However, because one student excels on the task this year does not mean that a few more might not do better the next year. Hence, the levels of comparability can indeed change criteria for expectations from year to year. Indeed, these criteria may change from class to class, depending on the nature of the student population or other factors.

An important point to the development of a rubric is that all the expectations are laid out for the student (and, in preferable cases, *by* the students) before any work begins. If the teacher expects ample background knowledge of optics in a poster board on photography, that expectation should be in the rubric.

When rubrics are designed, both the teacher and the students should have input. When students are given voice in rubric design, there is a much greater chance of "buy-in" than if rubric has been given to them with none of their input. This is a central feature of building self-critical lifelong learners in science. Getting student involvement might not be feasible in the design of every rubric, but when students are able to provide some suggestions, the level of engagement in learning and performance rises. In addition, getting student involvement usually provides some of the most creative ideas for the criteria. Table 11.1 and 11.2 show examples of rubrics teachers have used to detail the expectation levels for science learning.

Rubrics can be designed in many different ways. Key elements are simplicity, explicit expectations, and attainable levels of success that students understand. Pro-

Table 11.1 A science experiment or project rubric

Performance Indicators	Outstanding	Passing	Needs Revision
Uses or demonstrates understanding of the significance of the scientific method	Designs and implements an experiment OR Answers a significant question or problem in science	Successfully understands and uses some aspects and methods of experimentation	May complete experiment but is unable to explain the process of the scientific method
Demonstrates skill in scientific inquiry and problem solving	Identifies problems Proposes and implements solutions Evaluates accuracy, design, and outcomes of investigations	Identifies problems Proposes or implements solutions	Unable to identify problem or propose solutions
Uses technology and tools (such as rulers, computers, balances, thermometers, microscopes, magnifiers) to gather and analyze data	Recognizes and limits sources of bias in data, such as observer, sampling, and source biases	Collects, analyzes, and displays data in a variety of ways	Unable to explain data collection processes and the significance of the data collected.
Acquires information from multiple sources, such as print, the Internet, formulas, computer databases and experimentation	Synthesizes information Creates conclusions based on information gathered from a variety of sources	Summarizes the information gathered from the variety of sources and explains its significance	Restates the information; unable to explain
Demonstrates understanding of scientific concepts using appropriate scientific terms	Minimal vocabulary errors	Communication of content is not seriously impaired by vocabulary errors or misuses of scientific terms	Misuses of scientific terms; vocabulary errors interfere with the communication of the content

viding rubrics in advance of learning tasks or units gives students essential knowledge of how to be successful in an inquiry science classroom.

Although grades have always been to some degree a subjective and arbitrary reward system for student work, they remain a reality for most teachers. Rubrics are an effective way for teachers to assign values to work with appropriate rationales for credit.

Table 11.2 A research paper rubric

Performance Indicators	Outstanding	Passing	Needs Revision
Paper has an organizing idea, thesis, or question	Has a clearly defined organizing idea, thesis or question	Organizing idea is discernible; however, it might be too broad or ill defined	No organizing idea or question discernible
Chooses appropriate evidence	Information presented is relevant to organizing idea	Information presented generally supports the organizing idea; may contain irrelevancies	Contains extraneous details and a minimum of supporting evidence
Organizes the paper effectively	Has a clear method of organization, including transitions in which ideas flow logically from each other	Transitions may be abrupt or absent, but reader generally follows the writer's ideas Introduction and conclusion are present but may be weak	Lack of organization seriously impairs the reader's understanding
Collects information from a variety of sources appropriate to the topic	Clearly answers the question "So what?"; writer shows how the evidence supports the writer's argument	Makes limited or weak connections between evidence and theses	Evidence is missing or irrelevant to the argument the writer is making
Cites appropriately, according to one of the agreed-upon conventions (APA, MLA, etc.)	Follows an established format and cites appropriately	Provides some citation but may be inconsistent	No sense of external authority, e.g., plagiarizes
Adheres to conventions of English prose (grammar, paragraphing, punctuation, sentence construction, spelling)	Almost always adheres to the conventions of English	Communication of content is not impaired by grammatical errors	Grammatical errors interfere with the communication of the content of the paper

However, providing a point value to each criterion can create a focus on the grade rather than the intended assignment or project. To avoid this, a teacher must take care to explain why the highest level of expectation is what each student should strive for. It should be noted that rubrics should be limited to three or four levels at a maximum. Each level above three only provides increasing complexities in arbitrary decision making. That is, beyond four levels, the gap of agreement on a proficiency level for any criterion between two people begins to get fuzzy. Reliability simply declines rapidly as criteria levels go beyond three. Said another way, if only two levels (Yes? or No?) exist, the degree of agreement (reliability) between any two people using the rubric becomes very high. ("Does the poster have one or more photos? Yes___ or No ___?")

A grid is an essential part of the authentic model for a meaningful rubric. The model encourages the teacher to be up front with the students in terms of what is expected and at what level or standard the work should be done. The rubric is based on expected outcomes. The instructor asks what is expected of the student and what the student needs to be able to do after having completed the work assigned. These expectations become the outcomes that guide student product or performance. The expected outcomes become strands on the grading rubric. Each of the expected criteria or criteria strands indicate to the student the standards for exemplary work, acceptable work, and work that must be revised. The teacher might ask, "What is one outcome I might expect from a student writing a history of science essay?" One of the most obvious outcomes would be that the student does not make historical errors or that the students shows evidence that a significant scientific event occurred. As a result, the strand for this history of science criterion might appear as shown in Table 11.3.

The teacher might continue to build on this rubric on the basis of the desired outcomes for this particular assignment. The rubric could include other strands such as insights that the student was able to form on the basis of research done, quality of research materials used, ability to reach a defendable conclusion based on clear evidence, and so on. Each idea or outcome would create one strand of the rubric. The descriptions of the standards should be parallel across the page. Another example for this rubric is shown in Table 11.4.

It is less confusing to include only one desired outcome in the descriptors for the standards in each strand. The difficulty otherwise becomes one of deciding how to

Table 11.3 Rubric strand for demonstrating history of science competency

1	2	3
Enough historical errors to render the essay meaningless for useful information	Historical errors distract the reader from the major importance of the information	No major errors in historical fact; shows evidence where scientific breakthrough occurred

Table 11.4 Rubric strand for demonstrating depth of research competency

1	2	3
Little or no evidence of research beyond the basic text	Research goes beyond basic text; indication of use of alternative viewpoints; some additional information would enhance support of writer's central history of science thesis	Indication of multiple use of resources; good use of research to support writer's central history of science thesis

award a value if the student achieves one part of a multiple strand but not all parts. If the strand contains only one idea, then it is rather clear as to whether or not the student achieved the standard or not. All this points to the subjective nature of all assessment tools.

The teacher needs to be sure that all expected outcomes are addressed in the rubric. It is unfair to assess the student on a criterion that is not addressed in the rubric. If one reason for giving the student the rubric in the first place is to demystify the way in which he or she will be assessed, it is not fair to change a rubric without informing the students before the work commences. If the rubric does not contain an outcome that is later deemed important, the teacher should rewrite the rubric.

Rubrics are indeed very subjective, since phrases such as "no major errors" or "less than ten errors" are used. Yet they represent a necessary compromise between evaluating each individual and his or her performance capabilities in a personal and authentic way and navigating the institutional requirement of grading many students in relatively brief periods of time. Rubrics serve the purpose of making papers easier and quicker to evaluate. Students are clear as to what the teacher requires, which causes them to write a better paper or execute a more thorough investigation. Teachers are also clear as to what they are expecting; therefore, reading the paper or report with the clear intent of evaluating what has already been established as standard. No longer does the teacher read papers to discover standards. They have been clearly set forth at the outset.

CONCLUSION: Now, Go Play!

Ultimately, we seek to know whether we've been successful at teaching science as inquiry, that is, as something students do rather than hear about. The accompanying knowledge bases that this style of science calls on go far beyond the capabilities of standardized exams to assess: creativity, experimental design, logical thinking, applications to real-world problems, content within context, and so on. If we were training golfers, it would surely be helpful from a coaching perspective to know far more than the score on the cards at the end of players' rounds. That illuminates virtually nothing of the strengths and weaknesses of players and gives their coach no baseline for planning to help. Likewise, science is a game full of different skills and strategies. How little we know about our students' emerging conceptions of the game simply from scores on tests!

This new wave of assessment in science is referred to as alternative, authentic, accurate, aligned, and active. It seeks to measure students' knowledge of the grammar of science as well as its application to the solving of problems. That focus uniquely defines science assessment as an active endeavor in which the ability to discover is paramount and the content students discover is secondary, though integral, to the process. At the end of a course, students should have command of tools, techniques, and scientific processes. What better way to determine that than to provide an outfitted lab that lacks only a question to be answered? A biology student might be challenged to investigate how thermal pollution affects Euglena. A physics challenge might involve how electrical conductance of various metals can be investigated. Science teachers conduct active, authentic assessment every day in a lab-based course. A multiple-choice exam runs contrary to this process yet remains a prevalent local, state, and national style of assessment. The major impediment to authentic assessment might be the time factor in development and implementation. Yet there is solace in Lockhart's constant of test development. James Lockhart's theorem ($T_d/T_g = c$) states that total time investment (T) in test development (d) and grading (g) is constant (c). Either writing or grading an exam will consume time, and authentic assessment inflates the T_g (Weld, 1992). But ultimately, these assessments are more aligned with what we are attempting to convey to students: that science is a process. Achievement of academic success in science is best measured by doing science.

The ♟ Game in Action

The Evolution of an Assessor

Len is a thirty-year veteran biology teacher in a large, midwestern suburban high school. This story documents the authentic changes navigated by Len as he moved toward authentic assessment of his students.

Between 1975 and 1995, Len considered himself a traditional science teacher. He lectured on a regular basis, followed the text closely, and relied heavily on tests and quizzes. While still using traditional tests, Len began to consider the class period wasted, wondering about more effective uses of the time. He did not doubt the efficiency of the multiple-choice exams at getting to students' content knowledge but felt that there were aspect of their learning that he was missing. Gradually, his reliance on these tests began to lessen as he considered his goals for students and broadened his repertoire of teaching strategies. There eventually came a time when Len used the copy room so rarely that the employee in charge feigned forgetting his name, exclaiming, "Hello stranger, haven't seen you in a while!"

When Len eventually got around to reflecting on his goals for students, he arrived at twelve stated or implied goals:

1. Student self-assessment/evaluation
2. Effective writing and reflection
3. Striving for quality in all work they did
4. Organizing information and presenting it in the most effective ways
5. Hard work
6. Respect
7. Enjoy science class
8. Work well in groups
9. Creativity
10. Progress beyond mere content
11. Positive outlook
12. Critical thinking

When he really sat down and considered the reasons for assessing his students, Len came to three basic motivations:

1. To get students engaged.
2. To know that the assessment is going to be a benefit to his students.
3. To bring him new information about his students that he didn't have before.

Len learned about alternative assessment methods by attending a science educator's conference and reading the literature. Skeptical of trends and reform-of-the-month crazes, Len kept his mind on the goals he had set for his students.

As he experimented with alternative assessments, Len observed that his students were engaged 70 to 80 percent of the time on such tasks as a personal time line, mind mapping, or storyboards. Len asked his students to begin keeping journals, called BioLogs. They used the BioLogs for reflections, presentations, and science conference notes, which provided him with information on student knowledge and understanding that was lacking before. Len developed and adapted each of these assessment practices over a period of years. Eventually, quizzes and tests fell out of line with Len's teaching approach, and alternative methods of evaluation grew out of necessity.

Len's most important goal for his students has become their self-assessments (he also calls them *self-reflections*, though his students mostly call them *self-evaluations*). He tells visitors and parents, "I want them to see what they've learned." Len is very interested in having students look at what they know and understand for themselves, and he is interested in encouraging students to think about what they understood. He uses what he calls "self-checks" so that the students can develop a strategy for filling in the gaps of their own knowledge. Len believes that it is important for students to see and understand what they do not know so that *they* can do something about it rather than him.

Len has his students focus in on and assess themselves in various areas, including expression of thought, listening to each other, understanding, cooperation, creativity, sense of pride, test taking, organization of thought, and communication. Len assesses these qualitative criteria early in the year to ascertain student comfort levels in the various areas. Len points out that the development of these traits at an early time is essential for using assessment that is unfamiliar to the student. Using the following scale, he is able to discover student comfort level:

1. I feel comfortable in activities that call for creativity.
2. I think about how what I learn fits into the big picture.
3. I can clearly communicate my point of view to others, even to those who might not agree with me at the time.

   A. Not yet
   B. Sometimes
   C. Most of the time
   D. Practically always

Len now asks his students early in the year to gauge where they are in terms of many of his goals, including self-assessment. His rationale for using an early check at the start of the year are to have students assess where they are at various skills and to have students begin to think about the kinds of things he would be expecting of them. His hope is to see growth in all the areas stated on the same survey near the end of the year.

Len similarly uses a self-assessment sheet on which students write evidence of their science understanding. He reviews these sheets for possible discrepancies between what each student says and what Len has observed in class or on assessments. So observation becomes a valid form of assessment for him. Most students are mindful of Len's goal for them to be self-reflective. Students typically comment, "I think the self-checks helped me the most. Like after the quarter, the self-checks helped me realize what I didn't know. [My teacher] does more self-evaluations than I've ever had before!"

Len has become a firm believer in self-assessment for himself and that students pick up on that goal and also begin to aim toward it. Student self-evaluation or assessment is also recorded in their BioLogs, which is one of Len's key assessment strategies. Student self-reflections provides Len a window into their thoughts, helping him to realize his goal of student self-evaluation. He states,

> The log assessment has been the most effective strategy for meeting my goal of student self-reflection. In having students keep track of things, writing with some thought, I have used the BioLog to really extended beyond where notebooks used to be.

His view of the traditional science notebook has evolved over a long period of time into a more complex system of student thoughts, ideas, reflections, note, graphs, and feelings. And as Len's view of the student log evolves and grows, his belief in the power it has in helping students better understand biology and his conviction about its constant use also grow. Like many science teachers, Len used to have students keep a simple notebook that contained only facts that had been written down on a chalkboard. For example, he stated,

> I have always been convinced that the notebook/log/journal thing is a really important tool. I always focused on the notes in the past, just the simple taking of notes. When reflective writing in science came out a few years ago, I bought into it so the simple notebooks have evolved into more complex assessment pieces.

In the beginning, many students had some difficulty writing reflectively in their BioLogs. Students indicated the difficulties they encountered, such as simply forgetting to write, not having enough time in class to write, and not knowing exactly what to write. These three factors are a central focus of practice in the beginning of the year so that students learn to think and reflect on that thinking.

The organization of thoughts, ideas, and topics that students have written in their logs needed to be communicated. One of the ways in which Len has his students communicate is via a presentation to the class. He believes that it is important for students to organize information and present it to the class. He states, "If the students make the information clear to the class, they have it."

A practical example of an assessment that Len uses to meet this goal was the Infomercial. The Infomercial is similar to a television commercial and is an activity that Len considered an alternative assessment. Having his students do the Infomercial satisfies his goal for students to organize information and communicate it to others. Assessments of skills of presentation and of content knowledge and application are assessed from group responses to questions from the rest of the class and from Len.

Len's goal of hard work is a valuable component of his assessment ideals. He often states his expectations for hard work to the class: "I'm always looking for evidence of effort." He looks for the evidence in all the assessments that he has students do. During group work, he values assessment of work ethic by recognizing it

as a rubric category and awarding points to members who work hard and take responsibility for the completion of the project. Points are given by having students evaluate themselves on the basis of class-established criteria. Although students sometimes find it socially difficult to use the evaluation forms for group effort, their comments do provide Len with the information he is interested in. Students know that Len considers hard work an important goal: "If he expects you to do something and you're not working like he expects, you might get a lower grade because of it" and "I think [if we try hard] it's like a huge part of our grade because when he puts us in groups, he always wants us to do a lot of work!"

Len believes that assessments such as video productions, newscasts, and Infomercials are appropriate for his goal for expression of creativity. He has been eliciting more student-produced creativity over the years. He feels that he does a lot of things more graphically now. For example, he uses mind maps (similar to concept maps) as a form of assessment.

Because students work on projects in groups from time to time, Len wants their eventual communications to the rest of the class to be transmitted in a comfortable atmosphere. He believes that in creating a safe place for students to express their thoughts, an extremely important goal is accomplished. Len tries various methods to create a safe environment. These methods are apparent during group presentations and classroom discussions. He is accepting of all student responses and asks questions of most groups that he is confident they can answer.

Len's story is not unlike the stories of many other science teachers who have tried and found successful ways of using alternative science assessments. He points out that he has been working toward varying types for many years and that he has needed to adapt them to his situation. He is also convinced that the new methods he has tried are more exciting and learning rich for his students. His movement away from more traditional formats was not easy and did not happen overnight. Yet he saw that the new forms of assessments were more appropriate for his students, and they were adopted and adapted as the years went by.

Reflecting on the Game

1. What are the long-term, perhaps unforeseen consequences of high-stakes standardized tests on teachers and students?

2. How best might science teachers be supported in creating assessments that accurately reflect the nature of science and scientific inquiry?

3. What forces drive the nature of accountability for student understanding of science? How can these forces best be managed by practitioners?

4. How can the impact of the National Science Education Standards, particularly the Assessment Standards, be amplified to prevail as a public policy?

References

AERA. (2000, November). Position statement of The American Educational Research Association. Concerning high-stakes testing in pre k–12 education. *Educational Researcher,* pp. 24–25.

Archbald, D. A. (1991). *Authentic assessment: What it means and how it can help students.* Madison, WI: National Center for Effective Schools Research and Development.

Ashbacher, P. R., & Herman, J. (1991). *Alternative assessments in schools: Report of status and results of local projects.* Los Angeles: Center for Research on Evaluation, Standards, and Student Testing.

Barksdale-Ladd, M. A., & Thomas, K. F. (2000). What's at stake in high-stakes testing: Teachers and parents speak out. *Journal of Teacher Education, 51*(5), 384–397.

Baxter, G. P., Elder, A. D., & Glasser, R. (1996). *Assessment and instruction in the science classroom* (Technical Report #428). Los Angeles: Center for Research on Evaluation, Standards, and Student Testing.

Berlak, H. (1992). Toward the development of a new science of educational testing and assessment. In H. Berlak, F. M. Newmann, E. Adams, D. A. Archbald, T. Burgess, J. Raven, & T. A. Romberg (Eds.), *Toward a new science of educational testing and assessment* (pp. 181–206). Albany, NY: State University of New York Press.

Bracey, G. (1998). Tinkering with TIMSS. *Phi Delta Kappan, 79*(10), pp. 32–36.

Darling-Hammond, L., Snyder, J., Ancess, J., Einbender, L., Goodwin, A. L., & Macdonald, M. B. (1993). *Creating learner-centered accountability.* New York: National Center for Restructuring Education, Schools and Teaching, New York Teachers College.

Davis, A., & Armstrong, J. (1991). State initiatives in assessing science education. In G. Kulm & S. M. Malcom, (Eds.), *Science assessment in the service of reform* (pp. 127–147). Washington, DC: American Association for the Advancement of Science.

Doran, R., Chan, F., & Tamir, P. (1998). *Science education guide to assessment.* Washington, DC: National Science Teachers Association.

Doran, R. L., Lawrenz, F., and Helgeson, S. (1994). Research assessment in science in Dorothy L. Gabel (Ed.), *The handbook of research on science teaching and learning.* New York: Macmillan. Pp. 388–442.

Gordon, S. P., & Reese, M. (1997). High stakes testing: Worth the price? *Journal of School Leadership, 7,* 340–368.

Haertel, E. (1991). Form and function assessing science education. In G. Kulm & S. Malcom (Eds.), *Science assessment in the service of reform.* Washington, DC: American Association for the Advancement of Science.

Hargrove, T. Y., Jones, M. G., Jones, B. D., Hardin, B., Chapman, L., & Davis, M. (2000). Unintended consequences of high-stakes testing in North Carolina. *ERS Spectrum 8*(4), 21–25.

Herman, J. L. (1992). *Accountability and alternative assessment: Research and development issues.* Los Angeles: National Center for Research on Evaluation, Standards, and Student Testing.

Hilliard, A. G. (2000). Excellence in education vs. high-stakes standardized testing. *Journal of Teacher Education, 67*(4), 293–304.

Martin, M., et al. (1999). *Science benchmarking report: TIMSS 1999.* Chestnut Hill, MA: TIMSS International Study Center, Boston College.

Mitchell, R. (1992). *Testing for learning: How new approaches to evaluation can improve American schools.* New York: Free Press.

National Research Council. (1996). *National science education standards.* Washington, DC: National Academy Press.

Newmann, F. A., Secada, W. G., & Wehlage, G. G. (1995). *A guide to authentic instruction and assessment: Vision, standards, and scoring.* Madison, WI: Wisconsin Center for Education Research.

Novak, J. D., & Gowin, B. D. (1984). *Learning how to learn.* Cambridge, England: Cambridge University Press.

Perkins-Gough, D. (2000). Accountability and high-stakes testing: Are we asking the right questions? *ERS Spectrum, 18*(4), 4–11.

Perrone, V. (2000). *Lessons for new teachers* (pp. 149–173). New York: McGraw-Hill.

Raizen, S. A., Baron, J. B., Champagne, A. B., Haertel, E., Mullis, I. V. S., & Oakes, J. (1990). *Assessment in science education: The middle years*. Andover, MA: Network of Innovative Schools.

Shepard, L. A. (1989). Why we need better assessments. *Educational Leadership, 46*(7), 4–9.

Stiggins, R. J. (1993). Two disciplines of educational assessment. *Measurement and Evaluation in Counseling and Development, 26*(1), 93–104.

Stiggins, R. J., & Conklin, N. F. (1992). *In teachers' hands: Investigating the practices of classroom assessment*. Albany, NY: State University of New York.

Tucker, M. S. (1991). Why assessment is issue number one. In G. Kulm & S. M. Malcom (Eds.), *Science assessment in the service of reform*. Washington, DC: American Association for the Advancement of Science.

Villaire, T. (2001). High-stakes testing: Is it fair to our students? *Our Children, the National PTA Magazine, 26*(7), pp. 5–10.

Weld, J. (1992). Measuring a sense for science. *Educational Leadership, 50*(1), 76.

Wiggins, G. (1989). The futility of trying to teach everything of importance. *Educational Leadership, 47*(3), 44–48, 57–59.

Wiggins, G. (1991). *Toward one system of education: Assessing to improve, not merely audit.* (Education Commission of the States Working Paper). Denver, CO: State Policy and Assessment in Higher Education.

Wiggins, G. (1992). Creating tests worth taking. *Educational Leadership, 49*(8), 26–33.

Wiggins, G. (1993). *Assessing student performance: Exploring the purpose and limits of testing*. San Francisco: Jossey-Bass.

Zigo, D. (2001). Constructing firebreaks against high-stakes testing. *English Education, 3*(33), 214–232.

Additional Resources

Carter, G., & Berenson, S. (1996). Authentic assessment: Vehicle for reform. In J. Rhoton & P. Bowers (Eds.), *Issues in science education*. Arlington, VA: National Science Teachers Association Press.

Doran, R., Lawrenz, F., & Helgeson, S. (1994). Research on assessment in science. In D. Gabel (Ed.), *Handbook of Research on Science Teaching and Learning*. New York: Macmillan.

Hein, E., & Lee, S. (2000). Assessment of science inquiry. In *Inquiry Thoughts, Views, and Strategies for the K–5 Classroom*. Washington, DC:

National Science Foundation. (Publication #nsf99148).

Raizen, S., Baron, J., Champagne, A., Haertel, E., Mullis, I., & Oakes, J. (1989). *Assessment in science education: The middle years*. Washington, DC: National Center for Improving Science Education.

Performance Assessment Links in Science (PALS) http://pals.sri.com/

WestEd Assessment Resources www.wested.org/cs/wew/view/top/2

PART FOUR

Reflecting on the Game

start

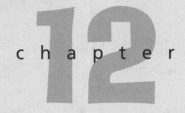

chapter

12

REFLECTING

ON THE GAME:
Action Research
in Science Education

John W. Tillotson, Ph.D.
Department of Science Teaching,
Syracuse University

ABOUT THE AUTHOR: Dr. John W. Tillotson is a former high school chemistry teacher and currently a member of his community's school board. After earning bachelor's and master's degrees in chemistry, Dr. Tillotson earned a Ph.D. in science education and joined Syracuse University as a dual associate professor in the Department of Science Teaching and the Teaching and Leadership Program. His research interests include studying the impact of science teacher education programs on preservice teachers and the influence of educational standards on science teaching and learning in high needs rural schools.

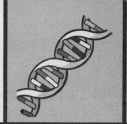

Moses Ochanji
Department of Science Teaching,
Syracuse University

ABOUT THE AUTHOR: Moses Ochanji graduated from Kenyatta University in Kenya with a bachelor of science degree in physics and a master of education degree in science education. He taught high school physics and mathematics in various schools in Kenya and worked as a curriculum specialist with the Department of Adult Education–Kenya. He is currently a Ph.D. candidate in science education and a teaching assistant in the Department of Science Teaching at Syracuse University.

Thomas J. Diana, Jr.
Department of Science Teaching,
Syracuse University

ABOUT THE AUTHOR: Thomas Diana, Jr., is currently a first-year doctoral student and teaching assistant at Syracuse University in the Department of Science Teaching. He received his master of science degree from Syracuse University in science education and is certified to teach biology in New York State. He received a bachelor's degree in biology from Utica College of Syracuse University.

> ## Champions keep playing until they get it right.
>
> —Billie Jean King

CHAPTER WARM-UP

Continuous improvement through reflection characterizes excellent teachers. Labeled action research, this formalized reflection on one's own teaching, student learning, or the dynamic school environment as a whole provides a basis for action toward continuous improvement. Teachers who inform their practices through action research are more able to articulate intentions and test assumptions. They become more critical observers of their classrooms and of the current research in their field. In short, teachers who cyclically alter practices on the basis of the insights of their research embody the unique professionalism of science education while modeling inquiry as a lifelong pursuit.

INTRODUCTION: What Is the Game?

Science education has many similarities to the sports world. Numerous connections can be made by comparing the American sport of basketball to the science education field. Each basketball team, either professional or amateur, is made up of numerous players, each of whom has various skills and abilities from which the team benefits. Similarly, a science classroom is composed of many "players," all of whom have diverse learning styles and different talents that benefit the teaching/learning outcome. They also have variations in experience and possible skill deficiencies to improve on through practice and from instruction of the "coach." It is the coach's responsibility to build a relationship with each and every one of the players and to be knowledgeable about each player's skills and deficiencies. The coach as the leader of the team guides the players in both practice and the game. It is also the coach's responsibility to bring the best out in each one of his or her players and to lead them in succeeding for their entire careers. In comparison, in a science classroom, the teacher can be equated to the coach of the students. It is the teacher's responsibility to guide the students through the science education game and give them the tools they need to perform on their own for the rest of their lives.

Teaching and coaching are professions that require constant reflection and continuous change. Consider the basketball coach who modifies the lineup, alters the game plan, and switches defenses in response to constant reflection on the progress of the game. In science education, a teacher must become a reflective practitioner. Altering lesson plans, modifying lab exercises, and utilizing alternative forms of assessment are examples of what is needed for a science educator to embrace change in the classroom to improve his or her overall teaching performance in addition to the students' overall achievement. Moreover, in basketball, the coach is constantly seeking advice from assistant and bench coaches, creating a collaborative effort with them and the team. In science education, action research can be used to create this same collaborative environment between other teachers and administrators. In this chapter, we discuss the process and benefits of teachers engaging in a reflective process when acting as coaches in the game of science education.

What Is Action Research and How Does It Create an Environment for Coaching the Game of Science?

Action research is a form of inquiry that can range from the individual teacher to the classroom to the entire school. It is conducted to examine numerous issues consisting of inquiries to gain data on teacher practices, student achievement, and curriculum changes. One common thread in all forms of action research is that it is a vehicle by which education can be examined and change can be implemented according to the data collected. It seeks to establish a basis for taking action. Action research is a form of continual professional development for educators. It consists of educators studying their teaching practices, examining current and past research conducted in the field, comparing what they discover from their results to their current strategies in the classroom, and making changes to improve their practices according to the results achieved (Calhoun, 2002).

Past research has shown that conducting collaborative action research has numerous benefits. As was mentioned earlier, action research can be utilized to make schoolwide improvements, to promote reflection and self-assessment of educators, and to enhance decision making of teachers and administrators (Glanz, 1999). One common problem that is associated with science education is the failure of research to influence practice. This research-practice gap is one issue that science educators and science education researchers need to address (Pekarek et al., 1996). Recently, a past president of the National Association for Research in Science Teaching (NARST) explained that many K–12 science teachers perceive action research as being almost nonexistent in their daily teaching practices (Koballa, 1997). Action research is one method for bridging this research-practice gap by creating more collaboration between university researchers and K–12 science educators.

Why Play the Game?

Action research can bring many benefits to the science classroom and the entire school. Carrying out collaborative action research leads to both individual and team success. One group of researchers studying a set of teachers' perceptions following their action research project found that the teachers believed that they became reflective practitioners. They reported a need for seeking reasons for their everyday actions (Johnson & Button, 1998). This feeling of personal growth and success in changing to a reflective educator can be achieved through action research.

During the season, basketball coaches are continually examining statistics of the games, watching videotapes of the team's performance, and studying the match-ups for the next game. In the off-season, basketball coaches are constantly performing research in an effort to improve their team's performance. They attend basketball workshops, participate in basketball camps, and recruit new players. All of these actions count toward the coach's professional development. Although science teachers do not typically recruit their players, they can perform research to continually examine methods that can be implemented into science education toward self-directed professional development. Action research is one method for science educators to connect their teaching to the national science education standards. In the national science education standards, teacher research is part of the professional development standards that are needed to succeed in the reform of science education (NRC, 1996).

Through action research, teacher researchers generate new knowledge. Although many times this knowledge is for their own practice, it might also be for the immediate community of teachers in the school in addition to the larger community of educators in a school district.

Collaborative action research is a way of knowing for science educators (Cochran-Smith & Lytle, 1993). This self-directed inquiry by science educators can be used to create a lifelong learning environment, one in which the teacher becomes the creator of knowledge and not just the disseminator of knowledge. Through action research, the collaboration between teachers is increased, and the communication between teachers and administrators can be equally increased. This reform in professional development is an extension of personal growth in educators of all disciplines and is used to create change in their classroom and other educational settings.

Cochran-Smith and Lytle (1993) summarize the benefits for teachers who perform action research and describe how these teachers become transformed following action research. These include the following:

- Being transformed into theorists who articulate their intentions, test their assumptions, and find connections to their practice
- Transforming their perceptions as writers and educators

- Becoming critical observers of their classroom
- Becoming critical readers of current research conducted in their field
- Working jointly with their students to answer questions important to both

Playing the game through action research in science education can also promote student growth and development. Past research has determined a set of norms that support student growth and development. These norms include the following:

- Collegiality
- Experimentation
- High expectations
- Trust and confidence
- Tangible support
- Reaching out to the knowledge base
- Appreciation and recognition
- Caring, celebration, and humor
- Protection of what is important
- Involvement of stakeholders in decision making
- Traditions
- Honest, open communications (Saphier & King, 1985, as quoted in Sagor 1992, p. 6)

Collaborative action research is a tool that can be used to uphold these norms throughout a school. Science education, like basketball, is constantly changing. Implementing action research at both a classroom and a schoolwide level is needed to carry out this change. Conducting action research, like basketball, has some set plays that need to take place for it to be successful.

 ## Action Research: An Individual or Team Effort

The sport of basketball is one that can be played on an individual or team basis. Often, basketball players spend countless hours practicing alone in an effort to improve their shooting or dribbling skills. Likewise, players routinely participate in pickup games at the park or in the driveway with other individuals that might feature a shooting contest such as the game of "Horse" or a one-on-one competition of some sort. Ultimately, these individual and group practice efforts lead to the development of the important knowledge and skills of the game of basketball and improve the overall performance of the basketball team during formal competitions. Action research too can be carried out in a variety of fashions depending on the nature of the problem being investigated and the action researcher's intentions. The following sections will outline the various forms that action research can take, the stages of an action research investigation, and the goals and outcomes associated with each model.

As Koballa (1997) has pointed out, the major dilemma of traditional research on teaching is that it often fails to inform classroom practice. The expansion of action research at the K–12 classroom level represents a powerful model for improving the way teachers teach and the way students learn (Calhoun, 1994; Cox & Craig, 1997;

Sagor, 1992; Tillotson, 1998). The terms that are used to describe classroom-based research are diverse. In the literature, this form of inquiry is often referred to as *teacher research* or *practitioner research*. Regardless of the term that is used to describe the endeavor, action research represents a systematic form of inquiry carried out by teachers and administrators who seek answers to classroom-based problems and issues. The results of such investigations are particularly relevant to practicing educators because they are focused directly on classroom phenomena. Thus, the applications of these research results are both immediate and practical. Cochran-Smith and Lytle (1993, p. 59) note,

> Teacher research is concerned with the questions that arise from the lived experiences of teachers and the everyday life of teaching expressed in a language that emanates from practice. Teachers are concerned about the consequences of their actions, and teacher research is often prompted by teachers' desires to know more about the dynamic interplay of classroom events. Hence teacher research is well positioned to produce precisely the kind of knowledge currently needed in the field.

Many educators have provided outlines or frameworks for examining the different forms of action research and the purpose that each of these types of inquiry can serve. Cochran-Smith and Lytle (1993) categorize teacher research as being either empirical or conceptual in its focus. Empirical research involves the "collection, analysis, and interpretation of data" (p. 27). They describe three types of empirical teacher research. Type I involves journals in which teachers study their classroom experiences over time by recording observations, interpreting events, and reflecting on the impact of their practices. For example, a science teacher might keep a journal over the course of the school year about the apparent impact of using problem-based laboratory experiments versus the traditional verification laboratory activities on students' attitudes toward science.

Type 2 teacher research involves oral inquiries in which "two or more teachers jointly research their experiences by examining particular issues, educational concepts, texts (including students' work), and other data about students" (Cochran-Smith & Lytle, 1993, p. 30). An example of this type of teacher inquiry might be a faculty and staff review of a student with a learning disability in a high school biology class. Each member of the faculty and staff who works with the student would provide a systematic and detailed review of the student's performance and a commentary on successful strategies for assisting the student. This process might involve the English teacher, who could provide insight into the student's writing skills; the special education teacher, who might suggest curricular adaptations to best support the student; and the school counselor, who might suggest strategies for providing emotional support and encouragement to help make the student successful.

Cochran-Smith and Lytle (1993) describe Type 3 teacher research as being classroom or school studies in which the goal is for educators to examine practice-based issues using a wide variety of information and data collected through various means. Calhoun (1994) and Sagor (1992) have further broken down this type of inquiry by identifying three distinct variations of teacher research that are arguably the most commonly recognized versions of action research. One type is the teacher-as-researcher model in which an individual teacher or administrator identifies a problem that is specific to that setting and conducts classroom-based research that pertains primarily to the individual setting in which it was carried out. For example, a chemistry teacher who experiments with two different strategies for introducing students to the concept of gas laws might gather data from students and form conclusions that pertain specifically to that science classroom. Although the outcomes of this inquiry might be potentially interesting to other science teachers, the goal of the teacher in carrying out the action research study was to inform practice in her own classroom.

Another type of inquiry is collaborative action research in which a group of researchers tackle a problem they share across multiple classrooms (Calhoun, 1994; Sagor, 1992). Here, two or more teachers design and conduct classroom research that examines a problem or issue that affects multiple classroom environments. In this form of inquiry, groups of teachers come together to identify a topic that is of concern to all members of the team. The group then sets out to systematically collect various types of data from multiple classrooms that can be pooled together to gain a deeper understanding of the issue and to help formulate meaningful solutions that can be implemented in a number of classrooms. An example might be a case in which the entire group of high school physics teachers is interested in how they can better understand the problems that their students experience with poor algebraic skills in solving mathematical problems in the course. The team could collaboratively brainstorm ways to gather information on this problem from each of their individual classrooms that could later be aggregated and analyzed to help the team decide which strategies might work best for improving students' skills in solving algebraic equations. In this example, the team of physics teachers might also collaborate with math teachers to help them in identifying promising strategies to implement that could be studied to see which ones had the most positive impact on student performance.

The third type that Calhoun (1994) identifies is known as schoolwide action research. Under this model, a school community focus is adopted in which the breadth and content of the study are expanded. The emphasis is on having all students in the school benefit from the collective research effort. Other educators have offered slightly different models in describing the aims of action research in schools (see Carr & Kemmis, 1986; Noffke, 1997; Richardson, 1994).

Calhoun (1994) notes that with schoolwide action research, there are three main purposes that guide these efforts. First, the goal is to improve the school organization's ability to solve educational problems. The second is for the research investigation to make improvements with regard to equity so that all students benefit from the results of the inquiry, not just those few who are taught by a select number of teachers who might engage in the action research project. The third aspect of schoolwide action research is that the investigation must be carried out with the intention of improving conditions across the entire school, meaning that the breadth and scope of the inquiries themselves are more substantial than those in the other two forms of action research. In this type of inquiry, the focus of a schoolwide action research project might be improving students' literacy skills across all subjects. Thus, science teachers would collaborate with other teachers and administrators to collectively investigate and formulate solutions related to the goal of improving overall student literacy in the school district.

Not all teacher research falls under the empirical framework. Cochran-Smith and Lytle (1993, p. 27) suggest that this form of inquiry can also be conceptual, involving "theoretical or philosophical work or the analysis of ideas." They refer to this form of action research as Type 4, in which essays written by teachers examine the nature of school policies, practices, and characteristics, including the action research effort itself. Here, teachers create essays that represent a collection of reflections on student performance, teacher behaviors, published works, or school policies that might lead to making specific assertions about what should be changed on the basis of a careful scrutiny of the data gathered. For example, a teacher might develop an essay that provides a theoretical analysis of how particular educational reform efforts have affected her school district through an examination of the way in which the school district's professional development program has infused new ideas and innovations into the existing framework of the school's professional culture.

Regardless of which variation of action research a K–12 educator ultimately chooses, the process by which the study is designed and carried out typically follows a series of well-defined steps. These steps are part of a cyclical process that will be described in greater detail in the following sections.

Action Research: Developing the Playbook

Any coach knows that simply tossing a basketball to a youngster doesn't automatically result in a polished player who knows the rules of the game or has the fundamental skills necessary to be successful. Beginning basketball players need time and support in learning the basics of the game and how it is played in various contexts. Similarly, K–12 educators must first understand how action research is conducted and the skills that must be developed before they can successfully carry out their own inquiry investigation. Without proper guidance and support, both basketball and action research can be frustrating and unfulfilling experiences.

One of the most critical aspects of the action research process is problem selection. Choosing the type of classroom-based inquiry to engage in is usually governed by the nature of the topic that is selected for study. Science teachers who are interested in examining their classroom practices, and the impact they have on students typically gather a variety of data throughout the school year that help in this evaluation process. This is known as a reflective form of action research (Feldman, 1996). Here, the teacher uses specific data collected from the classroom to inform the choices he or she makes about instruction. The reflection process is continuous and ongoing and often spawns new ideas for subsequent action research projects.

Action research can also be geared toward addressing specific school issues through a problem-solving approach (Feldman, 1996). In this case, teachers or administrators focus on a specific problem of interest in the school that has been identified as being significant. The action researcher asks questions about the problem, develops a plan for gathering informative data, and carefully analyzes the results of those data to make the most informed choices about how to resolve the issue.

Practice Makes Perfect: How Action Research Makes Better Players

Although there is no single, rigid procedure that must be adhered to, there is a general pattern that most practitioner-oriented investigations follow. Calhoun (1994) and Sagor (1992) offer similar five-step action research models.

Problem Formulation

As a coach prepares for a game, she identifies areas of the team's performance that need the most improvement for the team to win. In doing so, she consults with her assistant coaches and reviews individual and team performances in recent events. Let's say the team's defense has had trouble stopping the opponents from getting the three-point shot. Having identified the team's strengths and weaknesses, the coach then develops a game plan that players work on in practice and attempt to implement during the next game.

The same process is true for action researchers. In the problem formulation stage, researchers identify what they already know about an issue or problem, what they still need to know about it, and their understanding of the key variables affecting the situation. It is important that the research questions have attainable results and that the phenomena falls within the action researcher's scope of influence (Cox & Craig, 1997). Equally important is that the action researcher must be both concerned about and interested in studying the problem that is identified.

Developing ideas for an action research study is often best achieved through brainstorming at faculty meetings and by reading examples of classroom investigations found in various books and journals (see Table 12.1 for a list of references featuring examples of action research studies).

Data Collection

Once the coach has identified the team's problem (e.g., an inability to defend against the three-point shot), she must gather sets of data that will help her to determine the effectiveness of the strategies used to correct this weakness. These data might include videotapes of previous games, game statistics, observations made by the coach and her assistants, and feedback from players on the team.

In this stage of the process, action researchers must also assemble sets of data from all possible sources that will aid them in answering each research question. The researchers must determine the sample population(s) to be accessed, the scope and length of the data collection effort, and the various types of data that will be needed

Table 12.1 Resources for action researchers

Burnaford, G., Fischer, J., & Hobson, D. (1996). *Teachers doing research: Practical possibilities.* Mahwah, NJ: Lawrence Erlbaum Associates.

Hustler, D., Cassidy, A., & Cuff, E. C. (1986). *Action research in classrooms and schools.* London: Allen & Unwin.

Noffke, S. E., & Stevenson, R. B. (1995). *Educational action research: Becoming practically critical.* New York: Teachers College Press.

Wells, G., et al. (1994). *Changing schools from within: Creating communities of inquiry.* Portsmouth, NH: Heinemann.

to complete the study successfully. In general, the most reliable and valid results are obtained when researchers gather a minimum of three sets of data for each research question posed to triangulate the findings (Bogdan & Biklen, 1998; Sagor, 1992). Appropriate sources of data might include existing sources, such as student work (portfolios) or archival evidence; tools for capturing everyday life: logs, journals, videotapes of lessons, photographs, and shadowing research subjects; and tools for questioning subjects: interviews, written surveys, tests and quizzes, and focus groups.

Data Analysis

After all of the game data have been compiled, the coach and her staff begin to analyze the information by looking for patterns or trends. She might look to see whether certain player combinations on defense were more effective than others at stopping the outside shooting of the opponents. She might examine whether or not certain defensive formations were more effective at preventing particular players on the other team from getting open for too many shots at the basket. Taking these results into consideration, the coach then revises her game plan once again on the basis of the new information that has been gathered.

Similarly, once the data have been assembled for each research question, the action researcher must then begin the exciting task of analysis. This stage of the process yields the most rewards as meaningful information on how to improve practice or resolve an issue is uncovered. The researcher must systematically examine all data looking for patterns, trends, significance, and correlations. Conclusions are drawn and suggestions are made on the basis of this careful analysis phase.

There have been debates about the rigor involved in teacher research and the sophistication of the research methods involved (Cochran-Smith & Lytle, 1993). Although some argue that action research should be closely modeled after traditional university-based research paradigms, others have made the case that teacher research represents a different kind of knowledge that is not bound by the rules and procedures that are used in university-directed research on teaching (Bissex & Bullock, 1987; Kincheloe, 1991).

Reporting Results

Once a coach has analyzed her team's data, she often shares these results with the players, her assistant coaches, and the media. By reporting the findings, she is conveying her intention to continually improve the team's performance. She demonstrates a willingness to examine all pertinent variables in a careful, systematic fashion.

The action researcher is also obligated to share the findings of the investigation in all possible forums. This sharing step ensures that others know the outcomes of the practitioner-oriented research within the school community, as they might also stand to benefit from this knowledge. Even when the research involves a single teacher gathering data from one classroom, the potential for other teachers to learn from the careful investigation of this problem or issue is very high.

The reporting stage also promotes a spirit of risk taking and innovation within the school community and emphasizes the importance of continuous improvement efforts. The sharing of action research results empowers teachers as both learners and inquirers and leads to a reduction in the research-practice gap in schools (Cox & Craig, 1997). In some cases, action researchers publish their findings in various educational journals as a means of further contributing to the existing research base in education (Richardson, 1994). In conducting action research, teachers generate knowledge that can be shared both locally and publicly, according to Cochran-Smith and Lytle (1993). They contend that local knowledge is that which can be used for purposes of improving a teacher's own practice or for the immediate community of teachers, while public knowledge is that which stands to benefit the larger community of educators.

Action Planning

Having studied the problem of poor defense, the coach uses the information to generate a new game plan for each subsequent contest. This revised game plan will also get modified later as new information is uncovered after each game. New defensive strategies are put in place and evaluated. Thus, the process repeats itself over and over again as new problems are identified.

The power of action research to improve science teaching and learning in schools lies within the planning stage. It is here that a strategy is formulated to take action based on the results of the investigation. These action plans can include changes in current teaching and assessment practices, alterations in existing school and /or classroom policies, and new mechanisms for studying problems or issues within the school community.

It is critical that the action research endeavor be recognized as a cyclical process (Calhoun, 1994; Cox & Craig, 1997; Sagor, 1992; Tillotson, 1998). Each stage of the action research model directly informs the others, leading to new studies being born from existing ones. This cyclical process occurs in all types of action research, regardless of whether it follows the teacher-as-researcher, collaborative action research, or schoolwide action research model and whether it is empirically based or conceptual in nature. Table 12.2 provides an example of an action research study that demonstrates this process.

Table 12.2 Action research: A practical example

Setting	A rural high school in upstate New York that qualifies as a high-needs district. Two secondary chemistry teachers are collaborating on an action research project geared toward helping students achieve the NYS Math, Science and Technology Standards. They have created an inquiry-based unit on gas laws that involves students in collecting real data, analyzing the data, communicating their findings, and applying this knowledge to new situations. The teachers decided to teach parts of the unit in a traditional lecture/notes format and the other part in a more student-centered, inquiry format via a learning cycle approach. They then compared student outcomes in both cases.
Research problem	How will students react to nontraditional styles of instruction during the newly developed unit on gas laws?
	Will an inquiry-based teaching approach using the learning cycle format assist students in applying their knowledge to new situations?
Data collection	A pre-unit and post-unit student questionnaire that measured students' attitudes toward learning science, learning style preferences, and preferred teaching style was administered.
	Observational data were collected throughout the teaching of the gas laws unit.
	Interviews were done with a sample of students from each class.
	Assessment data were gathered on students' conceptual understanding via a brief quiz and the unit exam. Student performance on items pertaining to gas laws from the New York State Regents Exam administered at the end of the year was also considered.
Data analysis	The teachers compared pre-unit and post-unit results on the surveys, quizzes, and unit exams, as well as the Regents Exam.
	They looked for patterns and trends in the observational data that both individuals had collected.
	Interview responses were categorized and grouped by type.
	Findings suggest that students routinely had better attitudes toward science learning during the inquiry-based lessons using the learning cycle. Students preferred to have hands-on experiences as opposed to notes and lectures. The quiz and exam scores showed that students were successful in applying the knowledge they had learned in the realigned gas laws unit to novel situations. Some students needed more teacher guidance than others during the inquiry activities.
Report	The teachers jointly authored an action research report that they shared with the teaching staff, district curriculum coordinator, building principal, superintendent, and board of education. In the report, they emphasized what they investigated, what they collected as evidence, and what they learned from the process. They also identified what the next phase of action research cycle would examine.
Action planning	The teachers decided that students needed additional opportunities to practice with inquiry-oriented activities that require them to organize their own data and apply problem-solving strategies. A revised plan for gathering research data was also developed.

Connecting Action Research with the Literature Base

Although there is ample evidence to suggest that K–12 teachers place limited value on the educational research literature, action research experts advise that the existing literature is often a rich source of information and ideas that can positively impact teacher research (Calhoun, 1994; Cochran-Smith & Lytle, 1993; Sagor, 1992). Sagor (2000, p. 143) identifies five ways in which the professional literature in education can be used to enhance an action research investigation in all five stages of the model. These include identifying topics in the professional literature that relate to or match the area of interest; gathering research reports, research syntheses, articles, videotapes, and so on; organizing materials for study; analyzing and interpreting the information in these materials as aids to understanding and action; and determining the most promising actions.

Achieving Higher Standards Through Action Research

As our nation strives to promote increasingly higher standards of academic excellence, it is clear that our science teachers must take a more active role in the generation of applied educational research. A close examination of the recommendations found in the leading science education reform documents reveals a strong emphasis on the value of expanding teacher research initiatives. The Board of Directors for the National Science Teachers Association (NSTA) (Kyle, Linn, Bitner, Mitchener, & Perry, 1991) made recommendations concerning action research that included the following:

- There is a need to create an investigative society.
- Teachers must be engaged as action researchers.
- Research must be conducted that is close to the classroom.
- Collaborative research between individuals in universities and schools must occur regularly.

Likewise, the National Center for Science Teaching and Learning reports that for meaningful changes in practice to occur, increased collaboration between researchers and practitioners is necessary (Berlin & Krajcik, 1994). This report further states that if teachers are to use and value educational research, they must become a greater part of the process, making contributions to the existing research base. Through this process, real problems identified by classroom practitioners must become part of the science education reform agenda. As Bissex and Bullock (1987, p. xi) point out, "By becoming researchers, teachers take control over their classrooms and professional lives in ways that confound the traditional definition of teacher and offer proof that education can reform itself from within."

Barriers to the Game

Throughout a basketball game, the players and coaches must monitor such things as blocked shots, technical fouls, and turnovers to the other team. These are some of the obstacles that teams must overcome to succeed at winning the game. Similarly, in the game of action research, teacher researchers need to overcome some of the obstacles that research has shown to be impediments to implementing action research into everyday practice.

One of the problems that teachers face is the amount of time it takes to implement action research. Every teacher knows that the grind of everyday practice is grueling enough without the added burden of a collaborative research project (Calhoun, 2002). The problem of finding the time to collaborate with other teachers can be solved with the help from administrators. With increased collaboration between teachers and administrators, a framework can be constructed to set aside time for teachers to collaborate on their action research project. With backing from other colleagues and administrators, the added time and effort needed to conduct an inquiry oriented action research project can be successfully hurdled.

Within the problem formulation section of the action research cycle, there is another concern that teacher researchers need to address. Many teachers are not familiar with the educational research on some of the issues they wish to examine. Often, teachers inquire about the same problems and issues that other science educators have been experiencing for a long time. Before teachers define the problem that they want to examine, they would do well to review the research literature to assist them in their problem formulation (Johnson & Button, 1998). Another suggestion is to use teaching dilemmas to identify action research topics. By creating reflective journals of their successes and failures in the science classroom, teachers can refer back to their written dialogue and get assistance for their problem formulation. Teachers also need time to simply think about the problems that they want to examine.

One helpful suggestion, provided by Sagor (2000), is for teachers to avoid the problem of diverting finite time and energy to low-priority efforts by being "selfish" about their research focus. Richard Sagor believes that teachers who have a passionate personal concern about an issue in science education will be more likely to pursue an action research project to seek answers and solutions to their problem. This selfish act is similar to that of the coach of the basketball team instructing his or her star player to keep the ball for the last shot of the game. By being selfish about their action research projects, science educators are more likely to build a winning program.

Reform in education does not take place overnight. As one education researcher explains, "No substantive issue in education has a 'quick fix' solution" (Thompson, 1996, p. 76). Action research is no different in the educational spectrum. Action research should be a continuous process, and not just a one-time trial. Action research should be conducted on a regular basis. As was mentioned earlier, to do this, teachers need to have personal interest in the action research project and they need time to carry out the cycle. In addition, teachers also need to be given choice about their inquiry projects for them to achieve personal growth from the project (Chandler-Olcott, 2002).

Another barrier to science educators implementing action research into their everyday practice is the accountability issue involved. Science educators need to be comfortable with collecting data and reporting the results of their own classroom. One way in which science teachers can be at ease about putting their science classroom in the spotlight is to have the backing and support of administrators. By having an active collaboration between teachers and administrators, teacher researchers will be more comfortable reporting their results, some of which might yield apparent weakness in their teaching practices. It is important to note that even though they might find weaknesses in their teaching practices, this new knowledge of their classroom can be utilized to implement changes to correct these shortcomings. Teacher researchers can now use the data they collect to attempt new strategies or include new curriculum to address these problems.

Another pitfall that teacher researchers can encounter is the perception that science teachers are already teaching according to current standards and according to science education reform sentiment. This hurdle can be leaped by having teachers attempt to perform action research projects that are personal to them. When they carry out their projects, science educators will most likely see that they can improve on their current practices.

Maximizing the Score: Range of Applications for Action Research

Most would agree that for change to be successful and positive, those who carry out the change must be involved and engaged in the process itself. By engaging practitioners in the change process, action research provides ownership and often results in a sense of efficacy. In recent years, researchers exploring K–12 issues have identified several outcomes of participation in action research. For instance, they have found that educators grow professionally and intellectually and establish more meaningful relationships with their learners using action research. They feel a sense of empowerment and increased self-esteem. They are also more open to change, are more reflective about practice and decision making, and are better problem solvers (Cochran-Smith & Lytle, 1993). Overall, they have greater expertise in the field and a fresher attitude toward the educational process (Bennett, 1994).

Action research can address a number of applications. These applications can be viewed from the perspective of individual teacher research verses schoolwide or collaborative research.

Individual Teacher Action Research

Action research carried out by an individual teacher often focuses on understanding the students, or the classroom climate. The classroom climate may include aspects of the classroom such as curriculum, methods of teachers, or even ways of grouping students. This goal can be achieved by examining students' beliefs and their interpretations of classroom life. A teacher might conduct case studies of students and their perceptions of school and classroom activities. Such inquiries would require an educator to interview, survey, and observe students.

Individual teachers might also carry out action research with the aim of improving the classroom curriculum and developing the requisite teaching skills. To accomplish this goal, a teacher could examine how different classroom activities influence student learning. For example, a teacher might audiotape class sessions, conduct a survey to discover what students think about assessment procedures, or keep careful notes during student conferences to determine whether students' sense of responsibility for their learning increases.

Schoolwide Action Research: Decision Making and School Improvement

The climate in most of our nation's schools is strained. Teachers and administrators are struggling to achieve new mandates while dealing with factors such as limited financial resources, teacher shortages, and a population of students whose educational and emotional needs are greater than those of any past generation. Action research represents one powerful tool for improving the quality of teaching and learning within a school community.

Past research on school effectiveness has shown that in the most successful schools teachers are likely to discuss teaching and learning issues with one another on a regular basis, collaborate on the preparation of materials, critique each other's work, and jointly design lessons (Little 1982).

The success of action research in any school depends on a number of conditions. First, faculty and administrators must be committed to changing the status quo. Second, there must be a clear understanding about how decisions will be made and implemented, based on what is learned from each action research initiative. Third, study groups or small teams of researchers should spearhead the effort and should meet often to consider progress and review the objectives of the investigation. The school administration must play a role in making sure that all the players are brought on board and involved at all levels of planning for the action research project.

The application of schoolwide action research lies in examining the consequences of team or school policies and programs. One goal that is central to this type of research is trying to understand what other teachers, staff members, parents, administrators, and community members think about a school's policies and programs. For example, an educator could analyze data from observations, interviews, or surveys regarding teachers' use of computers, special programs to help struggling students, or various methods of communicating with parents.

For administrators who want to use action research to improve their skills and their schools, the following guidelines are suggested:

- Learn the basic procedures of action research and build a network of staff members and administrators who know and understand the process. Accomplish this through a clear understanding that action research is a tool for decision making and school improvement.

- Facilitate learning about action research by affiliating with institutions of higher learning and professional organizations that can help to introduce the concept. In the beginning, provide direct incentives for the staff to conduct formal action research. Initial incentives might include release time, staff development credits, and stipends. However, it is important to remember that the time to talk with one another about teaching and learning can also be an incentive. Educators in every school are concerned about programs and policies that will improve learning. Use action research to keep a strong focus on answering practical questions about improving instruction.
- Share the results of research with the entire staff when annual improvement plans are being developed. Use recommendations derived from the research to help in brainstorming further initiatives.

Teachers and administrators are the heart of every school. They help to plan and implement programs created for students' benefit, and they have daily one-on-one contact with the students. Because they see the problems firsthand, they are familiar with what programs or areas need to be evaluated, and they know what questions seem most important to ask. Having teachers participate in research teams increases the likelihood that they will support changes that need to be made, and having administrators participate enables them to understand how to use evidence when making policy decisions. Collaborative action research can help us to understand our institutions.

Action Research as Professional Development Tool

Preservice Teacher Development

Many teacher education programs now require preservice student teachers to carry out action research projects during their student teaching placements. The goals of conducting research as a teacher are to continue to grow as a reflective practitioner, to be thoughtful and deliberate about the choices made, and to learn more about the students and subjects taught. Case studies show that when action research projects are introduced in the internship setting, they provide an opportunity for focused, deliberate learning that evolves out of the curiosity and genuine interest of the teacher participants (Rock & Levin, 2002). Action research experiences provide opportunities for preservice teachers to gain valuable insights into themselves as teachers, their students, the curriculum, teaching, and their roles and responsibilities as teachers.

At Syracuse University, science education preservice teachers carry out action research projects during their student teaching. The greatest impact has been in partner schools where conversations related to teacher research have developed. Student teachers discuss their inquiry projects with their host-teachers and other school staff members. Often, the host-teacher has knowledge that is shared with the student teacher, consequently improving the study. A growing number of student teachers and their host-teachers are engaging in teacher research together. The student teachers are expected to communicate with the school's leadership team and to explain their research questions and methodology. Some schools might ask the student teachers and their hosting teachers to present their projects to the staff at a faculty meeting. These meetings have stimulated further conversations about research at the schools.

At the end of the student teaching session, the student teachers present their research projects at conferences of their colleagues, teachers, and administrators and teacher educators. The conference serves to make the research conducted in the partner schools, both by teachers and student teachers, important. The student teachers take the whole process very seriously, and the studies they report show that they are learning from it. A few of these have been published in science teaching–related journals.

It is important not only to train preservice teachers in the process of action research, but also to provide them with opportunities to observe their mentor teachers engaging in these practices. Cochran-Smith (1991, p. 307) states, "the only way for beginners to learn to be both educators and activists is to struggle over time in the company of experienced teachers who are themselves committed to collaboration and reform in their own classrooms." Those learning to coach the game also need to study the way the game is played.

In-Service Teacher Professional Development

Constructivism is beginning to transform the ways in which professional development activities are structured and facilitated in many preservice and inservice settings. Current constructivist thought on the professional development of teachers states that teachers should be actively pursuing their own questions, building on their own knowledge base, and interacting with the social environment. Darling-Hammond and McLaughlin (1995) believe that effective professional development means that teachers must be provided with opportunities to reflect critically on their practice to construct new knowledge and beliefs about content, pedagogy, and learners. Teachers therefore need to be given ample opportunities to learn in constructivist settings and construct for themselves educational visions through which they can reflect on educational practices. Action research lends itself to one such opportunity that teachers can follow to learn and construct their own knowledge about the settings in which they work.

Whether an individual, a small group, or an entire school faculty undertakes action research, part of its promise is the ability to build the capacity of individuals and organizations to move beyond current understandings and practices. By participating in action research, participants live the problem-solving process themselves and model it for their students. They focus on the collection of data to diagnose problems, they conduct a disciplined search for alternative solutions, they take collective action, and they conscientiously monitor whether and how well a "solution" works.

For those seeking whole-school improvement, both in terms of student learning and in terms of the conditions of the professional workplace, action research places disciplined inquiry (i.e., research) in the context of focused efforts to improve the quality of the school and its performance (i.e., action). The integrity of the process for site-based school improvement lies in the union of the researchers and action takers. Its ultimate aim is to have all faculty members and eventually students and parents involved in research on student learning.

Action Research as a Link Between the University and the Classroom

Our understanding of the complexities of teaching in schools can only be enhanced by collaborative efforts that join university faculty and classroom practitioners in applied action research. Such efforts provide practitioners with technical support and offer university researchers a dose of practical reality concerning school-based issues (Calhoun, 1994). In fact, no longer is it possible or wise for universities to conduct educational research that serves no one other than themselves and other researchers. Classroom science teachers can no longer ignore current knowledge on effective practice and continue to use outdated and ineffective techniques. Action research provides a vehicle for bridging the gap between research and practice. Substantial evidence exists that "when teachers have the time and opportunity to describe their own views about teaching and learning, to conduct research on their own teaching, and to compare, contrast, and revise their views, they come to understand the nature of exemplary science teaching" (NRC, 1996, p. 67).

Just as coaches must continually modify and adjust their game plans, so too must science teachers commit to providing their students with the most effective learning experiences possible. That can happen only when the lines between classroom teachers and university researchers become so blurred that we value equally the contributions each group makes to the knowledge base.

CONCLUSION: Proactive Problem Solvers

This chapter has outlined the process in which teachers as strategic informants in the game of science education can study their own game toward a purpose of self and student improvement. However, studying the game does not necessarily and directly transform to improved performance. The process can take longer than expected, as the focus of the study might require improving any one of myriad elements of the game.

Briscoe and Wells (2002) studied teachers engaged in action research and identified three important things that a teacher interested in improving their professional situation needs to consider. First, on a personal level, willingness on the part of the teacher researcher to risk the uncertainty associated with change is necessary. The process of studying the game is not without risks. However, facing the initial risks provides the teacher with a weapon to tackle further fears. By engaging in action research, a teacher gains a commitment to continue classroom research and the change process.

Second, the importance of reflection on one's beliefs about teaching and learning is an important factor in understanding changes in practice that are initiated in the research process. It is well documented in the literature that the process of change and associated reflection is initiated and accompanied by a change in beliefs about teaching and learning (Christenson et al., 2002). Engaging in research can initiate conflict when long-held beliefs about teaching and learning come into question. Will-ingness to question one's beliefs is an important resource for pursuing action research.

Third, the teacher as researcher must come to understand that change takes place not only in the teacher, but in other classroom participants as well. Students and the teacher together must negotiate an understanding of what is intended by the change that is brought about by classroom research. In the case of schoolwide research, the school administration needs to bring all players to negotiate the change process. This ensures ownership of the effected change.

State and national education standards now place great responsibility on the teacher. By and large, the teacher decides what content and methods to use to meet education goals. Clearly, teachers must now get proactively involved in the research process to become problem solvers and decision makers who feel empowered in their own work. Action research provides teachers and administrators with an opportunity to study their own game and implement changes that are of most meaning to the players.

The Game in Action

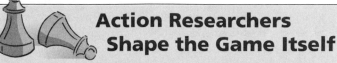

Action Researchers Shape the Game Itself

In a course entitled Teacher Development in Science, teacher candidates at Syracuse University conduct collaborative action research so that they will have the capability for lifelong learning with regard to science teaching long after they leave the program. Action research is used as a means of asking and answering meaningful questions about the real problems they will confront in teaching science. This approach is consistent with the vision of the Standards *in which it is argued that "When teachers have the time and opportunity to describe their own views about learning and teaching, to conduct research on their own teaching, and to compare, contrast, and revise their views, they come to understand the nature of exemplary science teaching" (NRC, 1996, p. 67).*

The students are required to follow Sagor's (1992) five-step process for conducting collaborative action research, as his text is a very user-friendly document that is critical for these novice researchers' success. Sagor's steps include (1) problem formulation, (2) data collection, (3) data analysis, (4) reporting of results, and (5) action planning (Sagor, 1992, p. 10). The following are example studies conducted by students who participated in Teacher Development in Science.

A Study of Lab Design

Gregory grew interested in comparing student performance on inquiry-based labs versus cookbook-type labs while student teaching in an area high school. While constructing the project, he was teaching four biology classes about the processes of diffusion and osmosis. His first step was to modify two labs to reinforce the concepts of diffusion and osmosis. The labs that he modified were the Egg Lab and the Potato Lab. The Egg Lab demonstrated the diffusion of water into and out of a shelled egg. The shelled egg is placed into a variety of solutions that cause water to diffuse into and out of the egg. The Potato Lab also demonstrates the osmosis of water into and out of a cell. The potato pieces are placed in a pure water solution as well as a salt-water solution, resulting in an increase or decrease in mass.

Both labs were modified to be inquiry-based investigations. Two biology classes completed the inquiry-based Egg Lab, and the other two classes completed the traditional type of Egg Lab. The objectives for both forms of the labs remained the same. However, the inquiry-based labs required students to create their own procedures and data tables based on the situations they were given. The students were given a control and were required to obtain answers to five key questions using methods of their own design. They had to decide how to adjust the variables and test against the control, and they used the key questions to spur their ideas.

Immediately after completing the labs, students took a five-question quiz to assess their basic understanding of diffusion and osmosis. The key ideas assessed had been directly incorporated within the objectives of both styles of lab. The following day, the two classes that had completed the inquiry-based Egg Lab were given the traditional type of Potato Lab. The two classes that had previously completed the traditional Egg Lab were then given the inquiry-based Potato Lab. After completing each lab, all students took a second quiz that assessed concepts reinforced throughout both types of labs. Once again, all students took the same quiz, regardless of what type of lab they had just completed.

The intent of this assessment was to observe whether or not students who completed the inquiry-based labs had higher or lower quiz scores than those who completed the traditional labs. Each quiz was designed on the basis of identical objectives from each style of lab. The results of the students' quiz scores were as follows:

- The average quiz score of the forty-four students who completed the inquiry-based Egg Lab was 55 percent.
- The average quiz score of the forty-four students who completed the traditional Egg Lab was 62 percent.
- The average quiz score of the forty-four students who completed the inquiry-based Potato Lab was 74 percent.
- The average quiz score of the forty-four students who completed the traditional Potato Lab was 82 percent.

The second component of the investigation was to gain insight into how students felt about inquiry-based labs. On completion of each inquiry-based lab, each student answered the following two questions: Do you feel that you have learned more from this style of lab than you would have from a traditional, step-by-step type of lab? Would you like to do more do-it-yourself labs in the future? Students were briefed on the differences between these two types of labs before the interview. The final component of data collection was a brief survey of fourteen faculty members who taught various science-related courses. The survey was designed to gain insight into how often these teachers used inquiry-based labs in their classrooms, whether or not they thought their students were learning more from these types of labs, and whether or not they thought their students enjoyed these types of labs more than the traditional types of labs.

The results of the two interview questions given to all students immediately after completion of one of the inquiry-based labs were as follows:

- Do you feel you have learned more from this style of lab than from a traditional, step-by-step lab? Out of eight-eight students, 57 percent stated yes, and 43 percent stated no.
- Would you like more labs in the future to be in this sort of do-it-yourself style? Of eight-eight students, 46 percent stated yes, 36 percent stated no, 12 percent stated some of the time, and 6 percent stated that they did not care.
- How often they use inquiry-based labs in their science classrooms. Of fourteen teachers, none said "almost always," three said "often," two responded "not very often," eight chose "sometimes," and one said "never."
- Do you feel that your students learn more from inquiry-based labs than from traditional types of labs? 86 percent of the teachers said yes, and 14 percent said no.
- Do you feel that your students enjoy completing inquiry-based labs more than traditional types of labs? 50 percent of the teachers said yes, and 50 percent said no.

After analyzing the results, a majority of teachers in the science department had anticipated the quiz scores of the inquiry-based cohort to be higher than the traditional cohort. The results demonstrated the opposite of what was anticipated. Many factors might have affected these results. The students were used to being led through labs by a step-by-step procedure. The majority of them had never completed labs of this style before and often complained of not knowing what they were supposed to do. Many also complained of having to think during the inquiry-based labs. This alone caused many students to give up, even though many seemed to enjoy the challenge this type of lab presented. Most of the students who did poorly on the quizzes were also the students who stated that they did not learn more from inquiry-based labs and would not like more of these types of labs in the future. If the students had more experience with these types of labs and a better understanding of what they were aiming to accomplish, the quiz score results might have been significantly different.

Although the quiz results were not what were expected, there were still benefits gained from the research, especially from the results of the two student interview questions. The higher percentage of students who stated that they learned more and would like more inquiry-based labs in the future demonstrated significant interest in these types of labs, which made the departmentwide goal seem worthy of pursuing. Gregory completed Sagor's five-step process by disseminating the results of his study through a national science teachers' journal (Booth, 2001).

Investigating the Value of Prior Knowledge

Susan sought to determine the relevance of laboratory activities in the high school science curriculum. Specifically, she was interested in examining laboratory exercises that were taught during her student teaching. She formulated the problem by examining the lab exercises that were taught, with a critical eye toward whether or not there was a relationship between the students' prior experiences that they brought to the classroom and their lab experience in science class. To gain an accurate description of the students' perceptions, several data collection strategies were conducted.

As Sagor (1992) points out, it is important to use three sources of data when conducting classroom-based action research. Triangulation of data will give the teacher researcher a reliable and valid source of data to which the following steps of the cycle can be carried out. Susan used four sources of data throughout the action research project: written surveys administered to the students, students' grade reports (homework, quizzes, lab reports, and tests), observations of lab sessions, and informal interviews with the students.

Following the collection of data from seventy-five students in all five science disciplines (earth science, biology, chemistry, physics, and integrated science), Susan analyzed the data. Basic statistical analysis was conducted on each of the data sources taken. Some of the comments that the students made during the interviews were as follows:

"Do experiments that we could do at home or that we can use in everyday activities."

"I really need more time to complete the lab, because when I run out of time, I usually don't finish the lab."

"Take things a little slower to make sure that everybody understands."

Knowing some of the students' perceptions, Susan could adjust the science curriculum and possibly some teaching strategies to ensure that a positive learning environment was in place so that all students could perform in science class. The results of her classroom-based action research projects were as follows:

- Lab activities are related to real-life situations but not in enough depth to promote concept understanding.
- Lab activities enhance concept knowledge.
- Students are rarely involved in the design of lab exercises.
- Most lab exercises are "cookbook" in nature.

The results of the action research project were presented at a local science teachers' poster session. This enabled Susan to display her action research project and entertain questions from other science education professionals.

Following the reporting of the results achieved from the action research project, the last step in the cycle is action planning. With the knowledge that was gained, Susan planned the following actions for future science lab exercises:

- Design and engage students in inquiry-based lab activities.
- Incorporate cooperative groups into the lab exercises to increase the collaboration between students.
- Incorporate at least one lesson per unit to include students' prior knowledge into the curriculum. (e.g., field trips, service learning projects, presentations regarding local issues).

A Study of the Impact of Program Change

Elliot's student teaching experience was in a city high school in Syracuse, New York. Traditionally, students at this school enrolled in regents earth science in the ninth grade, regents biology in the tenth grade, and regents chemistry in the eleventh grade. After students completed these three sciences, they were eligible to take advanced science courses. Students could choose from AP chemistry or physics, SUPA (Syracuse University Project Advance, a course that gives the students advance credits from Syracuse University) psychology, and/or SUPA biology. Students who took AP classes went to college with a stronger background in those subject areas. Some colleges exempted these students from classes on the basis of the students' AP performance. Students who participated in SUPA classes were registered at Syracuse University and received eight college credits from Syracuse University for these courses. Because the courses appear on an official Syracuse University transcript, SUPA credits were transferable to most four-year colleges. Because students could not take the advanced science courses until they had completed all three regents sciences, they were forced to choose among the four advanced courses during their senior year of high school. Teachers of the advanced courses ended up competing for students for their classes. To allow students to take more advanced courses, the high school decided to allow selected sophomores to take regents biology and chemistry simultaneously in the tenth grade.

Elliot worked with the chemistry and biology teacher to design a study that would provide answers to the questions that needed to be answered before this project could be implemented. The research questions were as follows:

- Given that biology and chemistry are both work-intensive classes by themselves, would students be able to keep up with the work for both the classes as well as their commitments to other classes and activities?
- How were the current students performing compared to those who took biology and chemistry separately?
- How would the joint courses affect the students' grade point average?
- What would be the impact of pulling out high-achieving students from regular classes to participate in the regents classes?

Data to answer these questions were collected in several ways. Students were surveyed about their attitudes toward the courses and science and about how the program was affecting their academic and extracurricular lives. The teachers of all subjects were surveyed about their opinions of the program, the level of their classes during the year compared to previous years and the expected impact of their program in their classrooms. In addition, data from previous scores in chemistry and biology were compared to the current grades of the students in the pilot program.

The results showed that the students who favored taking chemistry and biology together were concerned about the amount of work that the joint courses would bring. Most of the teachers did not understand why this program was important, they feared that the science courses were receiving more attention than other AP courses such as Latin or history, and the science teachers reported significant drop in motivation among the students who were not selected for the early regents classes.

The study suggested a need for improved communication between teachers of various disciplines, a screening procedure to identify the students who could enroll in the biology-chemistry combination class, and repeated surveys on students in the combination class.

Conclusion

In spite of the many differing opinions on how the reform of science education can become a reality, there is little debate about the importance of high-quality professional development opportunities for preservice and in-service science teachers. As we rethink our national goals for science education and the mechanisms by which we can achieve them, we must also rethink the way in which we prepare teachers. Overemphasis on highly technical skills related to teaching while avoiding any connection to advances made in understanding teaching and learning theory is not the solution to our problems.

We hope that the examples we have used here illustrate the power of action research in promoting the cycle of excellence in preservice and inservice teacher education.

Reflecting on the Game

1. Why do you think the research-practice gap exists in education? In what ways does action research help to bridge this gap?

2. What role might action research play in the professional development of science educators at all levels?

3. What factors in schools would support the use of action research to promote improvements in science teaching and learning? What factors would likely inhibit the use of action research? What strategies could be used to overcome these barriers?

4. Describe the various forms of actions research and the purpose each serves. Who are the key participants in each type of action research?

5. What are the characteristics of a well-designed action research study?

References

Bennett, C. K. (1994). Promoting teacher reflection through action research: What do teachers think? *Journal of Staff Development, 15*(1), 34–38.

Berlin, D. F., & Krajcik, J. (Eds.). (1994). *What are appropriate relationships between practice and research in science education?* Report from the Science Education Research Agenda (SERAC) Working Conference at the National Center for Science Teaching and Learning, Columbus, OH.

Bissex, G., & Bullock, R. (1987). *Seeing for ourselves: Case study research by teachers of writing.* Portsmouth, NH: Heinemann.

Bogdan, R., & Biklen, S. (1998). *Qualitative research for education* (3rd ed.). Boston: Allyn and Bacon.

Booth, G. (2001). Is inquiry the answer? *The Science Teacher, 68*(7), 57–60.

Briscoe, C., & Wells, E. (2002). Reforming primary science assessment practices: A case study of one teacher's professional development through action research. *Science Education, 86*(3), 417–435.

Calhoun, E. F. (1994). *How to use action research in the self-renewing school.* Alexandria, VA: Association for Supervision and Curriculum Development.

Calhoun, E. F. (2002). Action research for school improvement. *Educational Leadership, 59*(6), 18–24.

Carr, W., & Kemmis, S. (1986). *Becoming critical: Education, knowledge and action research.* Philadelphia, PA: Falmer Press.

Chandler-Olcott, K. (2002). Teacher research as a self-extending system for practitioners. *Teacher Education Quarterly, 29*(1), 23–37.

Christenson, M., Slutsky, R., Bendau, S., Covert, J., Dyer, J., Risko, G., & Johnston, M. (2002). The rocky road of teachers becoming action researchers, *Teaching and Teacher Education, 18*(3), 259–272.

Cochran-Smith, M. (1991). Learning to teaching against the grain. *Harvard Educational Review, 61*(3), 279–310.

Cochran-Smith, M., & Lytle, S. (1993). *Inside/outside: Teacher research and knowledge.* New York: Teachers College Press.

Cox, A. M., & Craig, D. V. (1997). Action research. *The Science Teacher, 64*(9), 50–53.

Darling-Hammond, L., & McLaughlin, J. (1995). Policies that support professional development in an era of reform. *Phi Delta Kappan, 76*(8), 587–604.

Feldman, A. (1996). Enhancing the practice of physics teachers: Mechanisms for the generation of sharing knowledge and understanding in collaborative action research. *Journal of Research in Science Teaching, 33*(5), 513–540.

Glanz, J. (1999). Action research. *Journal of Staff Development, 20*(3), 22–23.

Johnson, M. J., & Button, K. (1998). Action research paves the way for continuous improvement. *Journal of Staff Development, 19*(1), 48–51.

Kincheloe, J. (1991). *Teachers as researchers: Qualitative inquiry as a path to empowerment.* London: Falmer Press.

Koballa, T. (1997). Two communities: One challenge. *NARST News, 40*(2), 3–4.

Kyle, W. C., Linn, M. C., Bitner, B. L., Mitchener, C. P., & Perry, B. (1991). The role of research in science teaching. *Science Education, 75*(4), 413–418.

Little, J. W. (1982). Norms of collegiality and experimentation: Work-place conditions of school success. *American Educational Research Journal, 19*(3), 325–340.

National Research Council (NRC). (1996). *National science education standards.* Washington, DC: National Academy Press.

Noffke, S. E. (1997). Professional, personal, and political dimensions of action research. In M. W. Apple (Ed.), *Review of Research in Education* (pp. 305–343). Washington, DC: American Educational Research Association.

Pekarek, R., et al. (1996). The research-practice gap in science education. *Journal of Research in Science Teaching, 33*(2), 111–113.

Richardson, V. (1994). Conducting research on practice. *Educational Researcher, 23*(5), 5–10.

Rock, T. C., & Levin, B. B. (2002, Winter). Collaborative action research projects: Enhancing preservice teacher development in the professional development schools. *Teacher Education Quarterly,* pp. 7–21.

Sagor, R. (1992). *How to conduct collaborative action research.* Alexandria, VA: Association for Supervision and Curriculum Development.

Sagor, R. (2000). *Guiding school improvement with action research.* Alexandria, VA: Association for Supervision and Curriculum Development.

Saphier, J., & King, M. (1985). Good seeds grow in strong cultures. *Educational Leadership, 42*(6), 67–74.

Thompson, S. (1996). How action research can put teachers and parents on the same team. *Educational Horizons, 74*, 70–76.

Tillotson, J. W. (1998). *A cycle of excellence in science teacher development.* Paper presented at the annual meeting of the Association for the Education of Teachers in Science, Minneapolis, MN.

Additional Resources

Altrichter, H., Posch, P., & Somekh, B. (1993). *Teachers investigate their work: An introduction to action research.* New York: Routledge.

Arhar, J., Holly, M. L., & Kasten, W. C. (2000). *Action research for teachers: Traveling the yellow brick road.* Upper Saddle River, NJ: Prentice-Hall.

Burnaford, G., Fischer, J., & Hobson, D. (1996). *Teachers doing research: Practical possibilities.* Mahwah, NJ: Lawrence Earlbaum Associates.

Cox-Peterson, A. M. (2001). Empowering science teachers as researchers and inquirers. *Journal of Science Teacher Education, 12*(2), 107–122.

Hogan, K., & Berkowitz, A. R. (2000). Teachers as inquiry learners. *Journal of Science Teacher Education, 11*(1), 1–25.

McNiff, J. (1993). *Teaching as learning: An action research approach.* New York: Routledge.

The Teacher as Researcher Special Interest Group Showcase on Action Research www.teacheras researcher.org/

start

chapter

13

THE FUTURE OF THE GAME OF SCIENCE EDUCATION

Robert E. Yager, Ph.D.
Science Education, The University of Iowa

ABOUT THE AUTHOR: Dr. Robert Yager served as president of seven national organizations, including the National Science Teachers Association, the National Association of Research in Science Education, and the National Association for Science, Technology, and Society. He has directed over 100 National Science Foundation projects targeting science education and has published over 500 research reports, chapters, books, and curriculum materials. Dr. Yager's leadership in science education spans the globe; he has worked with science teachers in Korea, Taiwan, Israel, Estonia, Australia, Malaysia, Indonesia, Germany, and Egypt. He is now in his fifth decade of professional service at the University of Iowa, where he began as a science teacher at the laboratory school in 1956.

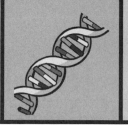

One might reasonably expect the Chairman to know what his corporation will be 10 years from now. He doesn't. One could, within reason, expect the Chairman to be able to predict how technology will transform his business a decade hence. But no, stumped again. Here is what he does know: something startling, intriguing and profound is afoot.

—Robert E. Allen
Former Chairman & CEO, AT&T

CHAPTER WARM-UP

Historically, schools have conformed to, rather than defined, societal trends while science has advanced by great leaps to alter our lives and work. The school-science interface has been awkwardly straddled by science educators who have erred toward conformity over advancement, emphasizing trivial facts over encompassing ideas and producing a few science specialists instead of a populace of the scientifically literate. A mandate for reform, fueled both by a windfall of research on learning and a new consensus embracing science for all, places science class on the cusp of a societal trend where learners gain the essential traits for a brave new world: critical, analytical, cooperative skills steeped in conceptual understanding, with the capability to apply these skills and knowledge to the problems and opportunities awaiting our students in our future.

INTRODUCTION: History Informs the Future

Science education has enjoyed rapid growth, public attention and support, and a great variation in coaching styles over the past century. The game that is now played and the current coaching staff and players can be better understood by viewing the past, concentrating on the immediate past from which they came. A review of this past is offered as we ponder the current game and extrapolate where we will be in another quarter of a century.

Education is a creation of society, and the American tradition is that education (and the institutions created to do the educating) are controlled by the citizens of each school district with its own board elected from the citizenry. This board, like boards of athletics, sets the policies, employs the coaching staff, and establishes standards and rules, oversees the financing, and reviews evidence of how the goals are being met. Unlike a board of athletics, school board members often have little expertise concerning the research that should guide the profession. Instead, schools respond to the decrees of a citizen board that often does not question the status quo or consider new evidence related to significant choices. And many school employees and members of the community assume that education is approached in schools and classrooms without considering its use in life beyond the school itself. In fact, relevant learning experiences are rarely in evidence outside specific classrooms and departments in a school.

Societies have changed dramatically over the past 200 years; schools, by contrast, have remained rather static. Teachers in elementary schools are seldom specialists and must develop rules and assist student learning in a variety of subjects over the school day (all typical courses comprising what humans know and what they identify as essential for passing to the new generation). Early in the twentieth century, K–8 teachers were responsible for all subjects and often for all grade levels. Then specialization and new rules often occurred in the high school (grades 9–12); in recent times, however, this situation is extended to middle schools (often grades 6–8).

Keeping Up with the Times

Every society has struggled with the problem of how to prepare the next generation for a future that has yet to be invented. Invariably, the rules of the game and the players tend not to change until society advances so far that it demands that schools change to prepare students for the current society, not the one of past years. Societies generally support an education that produces learners who are prepared for life, work, and further specialization at the next academic level. In the first 150 years of U.S. history, Hurd (Hurd, 1986) has reported forty major reform efforts, all designed for a new game, that is, to make schools and learning more immediately practical and useful to reflect the current culture in place of the one from yesteryears. Not only has the game changed, but so have the needed competencies from the coaches: the teachers.

In the last twenty years, there have been over 100 national reports that termed the situation one of crisis for science education in K–12 schools and undergraduate science programs in colleges. These reports invariably call for immediate changes that would improve the quality of education and produce excellence. Interestingly, however, the direction and substance of the suggestions that are made to improve and to achieve excellence vary greatly. And few, if any, have recognized the importance of scientific changes and new requirements for knowledge and skills that could arise from coherent policies for systemic reform of the whole of education. Few have considered the purposes, the scope, and the required teaching that could result in improved high school and college graduates. Students do not possess the essential knowledge and intellectual skills to live healthful and responsive personal lives, to act as responsible citizens assisting with major societal decisions, and/or to enter the workforce in ways that will increase economic productivity. And there is evidence that college graduates are not much better after four more years of collegiate study. Existing programs are woefully inadequate for preparing students to use information and skills taught in their daily living, work toward resolution of societal problems, or perform in a technologically driven economy.

Does Anybody Really Know What Time It Is?

Key issues for real reforms deal with the stated purposes of science education, an appropriate context for the science curricula, an identification of essential science content, and the conditions that enhance learning. These issues never reach the public, they are rarely debated, and there is no consensus as cries for reform (often related to improved test scores) arise from official reports, the media, revised courses and whole curricula. It is almost like a new game for which there are no willing players and no spectators.

Since the 1970s, Americans have been bombarded with reports that indicate major societal and cultural changes—changes that should have impacted education. Hurd (1986) indicated major sources for the societal/cultural changes that have occurred. He has noted that these breaks with the past have been described as a "cultural mutation" (Kenneth Boulding), a "discontinuity" (Peter Drucker), a "watershed" (Jonas Salk), the birth of a "post-industrial" society (Daniel Bell), a new "information age" (John Naisbitt), a "third wave" (Alvin Toffler), and a time "between two ages" (Zbigniew Brzezinski). The magnitude of these social transitions indicates what Alfred North Whitehead described as "likely to happen only once or twice in a century." Toffler's *Future Shock* made the general public aware of these changes, and Charles Silberman's *Crisis in the Classroom* made educators aware of an impending need for "the remaking of American education." Both of these books were published in 1970 and became best-sellers. Over thirty years later, the questions regarding what this "new age" means for the new game of education in the sciences remains before us.

During these same years, science as a human enterprise has changed dramatically. Science and technology have become an integrated system using the same methodologies. J. Robert Oppenheimer described science and technology as "two sides of a single coin." Today scientific research depends both on adequate theories and instrumentation. Many times, advances in science arise from technology, making the old definition of technology as the application of science completely obsolete.

As Science Advances, Science Teaching Lags

Scientific research has become more interdisciplinary, moving light years from the defined disciplines of physics, chemistry, biology, and earth science. Such disciplines no longer exist. As today's problems are considered, expertise from a great variety of disciplines and subdisciplines is needed. Much research in science and technology is mounted by research teams often involving over 100 "experts." Over 70,000 different journals now exist to report the findings of scientific and technological research; no one person can read, understand, and use all of them in a lifetime.

Even with such significant changes in society and in science and technology, the typical K–12 courses continue to be defined and presented in broad disciplines that have no meaning in the practice of current science and technology. Even when the public relates social purposes and human welfare to research and innovation, schools retain the structure of another age and reduce to teaching of "basics" that are not basic to dealing with current problems. The basics might not be appropriate for inclusion until they are needed. Instead, the basic concepts and glamorized skills are taught because they "will be" needed by students—a condition that is rarely realized by over 99 percent of high school graduates. This is like using old rules for a completely new game. It would never occur in the athletic arena.

Science teaching and science textbooks often ignore the interface between science and society. They ignore the links between the natural and social sciences and between nature and people. They ignore the research concerning learning and teaching. It should be obvious that when science and technology are related to social and human problems, issues of values and ethics inevitably arise; science and technology are never value free or ethically neutral for either scientists or citizens. A serious criticism of science teaching is that students complete courses with a paucity of values essential for responsible decision making or for choosing positive directions for life and learning. Teaching students a particular set of values is not the objective. This would be like preparing an athletic team only for one immediate task: defeating the next team. Rather, the aim of teaching value-laden science is to provide students with opportunities to integrate valid scientific information into the making of ethical judgments. This should apply regardless of the situation or particular conditions.

Science Education Permutations

In the United States, school programs stabilized in the 1920s, and high school emerged with a common curriculum. In the case of science, biology was born as a single course, replacing many individual courses in anatomy, physiology, botany, zoology, and others. These were times, too, when organizations such as the American Association for the Advancement of Science (AAAS) began to influence science in schools. In 1928, AAAS recommended that high school science should "function more completely in the lives of people generally and to emphasize a sense of moral obligation that will prevent newly acquired knowledge and method of science from serving base ends" (Hurd, 1986, p. 354). In 1932, the National Society for the Study of Education recommended that school science focus more upon understanding broad concepts and principles of science that have societal applications. The committee recommended that science education emphasize real problems in teaching about the practical and cultural aspects of science (Whipple, 1932).

The Progressive Education Association was active in seemingly similar advances. John Dewey's research and writings were at a peak. Peddiwell's (1939) Saber-Tooth Curriculum was a popular attempt to change school programs to meet the immediate needs of society. World War II brought a focus on "Big Science" and the introduction of applications courses. In 1942, the National Council of Science Teachers recommended that science education be clearly related to our culture, contemporary living, and social/economic issues. Science teachers recommended that courses be organized around broad social problems that engage students in critical thinking. Such thinking characterized science coaching styles throughout the 1940s. The 46th Yearbook of the National Society for the Study of Education called for science being "functional" with applications related to personal and social experiences of students. All of these efforts were like preparation for a new game designed to produce better learners for playing the game for an enriched life (Noll, 1947).

The late 1950s produced one anomaly to what reformers have recommended in our history of nearly 250 years. The Soviet exploits in space ushered in massive reforms—a new game—that called for fundamental changes in school science that were drastically different from any of the past reforms. The concern for Soviet successes in space prompted more attention and public support for improving science education than did either World War I or II or the Korean and Vietnam conflicts.

The science reforms of the late 1950s and 1960s were led by scientists whose aim was to change the game in ways that all would experience and know the science that scientists know and practice the skills scientists use in their knowing of the objects and events comprising the natural universe. The efforts centered on producing visions of what scientists in their various disciplines saw as the big ideas of their disciplines that could provide the frameworks for new courses in schools. There was little attempt to relate the teaching and the content to social problems. There was an assumption that science as known to scientists would be appropriate and inherently interesting to all. It was assumed that preparing new players would create a team able to win in terms of scientific advancement.

There were attempts to rid school science of technology (television, transportation, communication, home appliances). Technology careers were removed from science and incorporated into vocational programs for the non-college-bound students. Teaching science as inquiry was also a major focus. However, that tended to be taught by direct instruction and in terms of more open-ended laboratories—still prescribed and directed by textbooks and laboratory manuals prepared by scientists.

Textbooks were not questioned. In fact, they were conceived as a way of changing what teachers teach, and as always, they aimed to include the needed teaching approaches to ensure that the reforms would succeed. There was talk of "teacher-proof" curricula.

All of these reforms had faded by the mid-1970s. The public support for school science and the massive reform efforts of the preceeding fifteen years were gone. Many people even blamed science for the political, societal, and environmental crises that characterized the times.

 ## True Winds of Change

In the late 1960s, the long-term movement to reform science education was revitalized by the Advisory Committee for Science Education of the National Science Foundation (NSF) (1965). This committee recommended a curriculum that related science and technology to human and social affairs. The advisory committee sought for students of science an appreciation for the role of science and its use in solving the problems of society. The committee recognized that this goal called for an interdisciplinary, problem-solving approach to teaching rather than a discipline-specific approach.

The curriculum development projects supported by the National Science Foundation began to change with reform-minded science educators in key positions at NSF and in many states (in a sense, new athletic boards were in charge of major funding to accomplish the reform of coaching in classrooms). There was a call for more research information to accompany this new development and the realization that teaching must change—perhaps more than the curricula. In that climate, the new leadership in Washington decided that study, research, and new evidence were needed before mounting major new games and recruiting new coaches to lead such games.

Project Synthesis was funded in 1978 (Harms & Yager, 1981). It included four goal clusters and became the rallying cry for new games, rules, and coaches. The four goal areas included the following:

Goal Cluster 1: Personal needs. Science education should prepare individuals to utilize science for improving their own lives and for coping with an increasingly technological world.

Goal Cluster II: Societal issues. Science education should produce informed citizens prepared to deal responsibly with science-related societal issues.

Goal Cluster III: Career awareness. Science education should give all students an awareness of the nature and scope of a wide variety of science and technology-related careers open to students of varying aptitudes and interests.

Goal Cluster IV: Academic preparation. Science education should allow students who are likely to pursue science academically as well as professionally to acquire the academic knowledge appropriate for their needs.

Harms and Yager (1981, p. 119) summarized the situation in the 1980s at the end of the final report of Project Synthesis:

Not only is there an increased need to understand large national issues, there is also an increasing need to understand the way science and technology affect us as individuals. Thus, a new challenge for science education emerges. The question is this: "Can we shift our goals, programs and practices from the current over-whelming emphasis on academic preparation for science careers for a few students to an emphasis on preparing all students to grapple successfully with science and technology in their own everyday lives, as well as to participate knowledgeably in the important science-related decisions our country will have to make in the future?"

Although the research base for Project Synthesis and the funding for new materials and new staff development effort were important changes, the media and school leaders often sought quick fixes. The American public was ready to improve science education; there were calls to save the schools, preserve the nation, and "require" more or better learning. These concerns resulted in many legislative and administrative actions that ignored the real problems, the real needs, and the available research.

The actions included requiring more science courses, lengthening the school day and the increasing the number of days in a school year, requiring testing for students and teachers using business models to change responsibilities, improving laboratory materials and equipment, purchasing computers, encouraging teachers to work in research laboratories in industry and universities, making courses more rigorous, increasing the number of topics covered and associated details, giving tests more frequently, and establishing mandatory attendance rules. Basically, there were more mandates, more requirements, more testing (often not related to goals an/or instruction). Societal and government leaders did not understand learning, but they determined the rules and demanded specified performances in the game.

It was assumed that administrative rules would result in better funding, better student learning, and better preparation for collegiate study. Fortunately, there have been many efforts that have been concerned with purposeful, meaningful organization of school programs (e.g., around major social ideas), improved instruction, and assessment related to all three.

Birth of Meaningful Reform

The National Science Teachers Association used the Project Synthesis research to initiate a *Search for Excellence in Science Education Program* that sought out schools and school personnel in which the desired state conditions were in evidence. The four focuses for Synthesis resulted in corresponding searches, including elementary science, physical science, life science, inquiry, and science-technology-society. A volume was produced that described approximately ten situations that are most like the synthesis descriptions of excellence (Penick & Yager, 1983). An NSF grant provided opportunity for an in-depth study of six national centers. This study produced some results about conditions in which reforms were undertaken, focusing on purpose, context, organization, instruction, and assessment.

By 1983, a new national crisis had engulfed the political and educational establishments. This was the economic crisis that threatened the very foundation of the public education system. Rather than returning to the massive reform of curricula and the efforts to help teachers, funds were expended to study human learning. This became the focus of all our reform efforts as cognitive science was born and our knowledge expanded concerning how humans learn. As the twentieth century ended, the National Research Council of the National Academy of Science (probably the world's most prestigious science society) produced two books, *How People Learn: Brain, Mind, Experience, and School* (Bransford, Brown, & Cocking, 2000) and *How People Learn: Bridging Research and Practice* (Donovan, Bransford, & Pellegrino, 1999). These volumes provide more rules and new information for policymakers, administrators, and teachers that need to be used as these people assume leadership for, and the preparation of, new and existing teachers for new games for a new millennium.

Mindful Science Teaching

The study of the mind in the last few decades has had many important implications for the education community. It has produced new course design, new strategies for teaching, and new means of assessing learning. The study of human learning has produced a new focus on interdisciplinary approaches. Now such studies are central as reforms are contemplated—reforms that will result in more and better learning. Educators and cognitive scientists are finally working together to promote new leaning in educational settings and beyond. Never before has there been a time when evidence from such a variety of disciplines has converged and promised to bring new techniques and approaches into focus. The NRC book *How People Learn* (Bransford et al., 2000) advances the following notions, which most affect the reforms:

- Research from cognitive psychology has increased our understanding of the nature of competent performance and the principles of knowledge organization that underlie people's abilities to solve problems in a wide variety of areas, including mathematics, science, literature, social studies, and history.
- Developmental researchers have shown that young children understand a great deal about basic principles of biology and physical causality and about number, narrative, and personal intent and that these capabilities make it possible to create innovative curricula that introduce important concepts for advanced reasoning at early ages.
- Research on learning and transfer has uncovered important principles for structuring learning experiences that enable people to use what they have learned in new settings.
- Work in social psychology, cognitive psychology, and anthropology is making it clear that all learning takes place in settings that have particular sets of cultural and social norms and expectations and that these settings influence learning and transfer in powerful ways.
- Neuroscience is beginning to provide evidence for many principles of learning that have emerged from laboratory research, and it is showing how learning changes the physical structure of the brain and, with it, the functional organization of the brain.
- Collaborative studies of the design and evaluation of learning environments among cognitive and developmental psychologists and educators are yielding new knowledge about the nature of learning and teaching as it takes place in a variety of settings. In addition, researchers are discovering ways to learn from the

wisdom of practice that comes from successful teachers who can share their expertise.

- Emerging technologies are leading to the development of many new opportunities to guide and enhance learning that were unimagined even a few years ago.

Indeed there is a new game that is increasing in popularity. It is attracting new players who need new coaches ready to lead, inspire, and aid at winning the game.

Formerly, education focused on the acquisition of literacy skills. There were few attempts to get students to think or analyze critically, to express themselves clearly and forcefully, or to solve complex problems in the areas of mathematics and science. Now these higher-order skills and more complex forms of literacy are expected for all people to deal with current problems. Such skills are necessary for the workplace. They are needed for meaningful participation in the democratic processes that characterize the new millennium. Knowing has shifted from the ability to remember and repeat information to being able to locate it and use it. These skills have not been taught, expected, or developed during the past century in schools around the world.

The NRC monograph *How People Learn* (Bransford et al., 2000) offers general, research-guided principles for dealing with learners and learning. These include the following:

- Understanding the essential features of the problems of various school subjects will lead to better reasoning and problem solving.
- Transfer and wide application of learning are most likely to occur when learners achieve an organized and coherent understanding of the material.
- Learning and understanding can be facilitated in learners by emphasizing organized, coherent bodies of knowledge (in which specific facts and details are embedded) and by helping them use what they learn.
- Education needs to provide children with sufficient mastery of the details of particular subject matters so that they have a foundation for further exploration within those domains.
- The predominant indicator of expert status is the amount of time spent learning and working in a subject area to gain mastery of the content. Secondarily, the more one knows about a subject, the easier it is to learn additional knowledge.

This same publication summarized the research on teachers and teaching:

- Teachers need expertise in both subject matter content and in teaching.
- Teachers need to develop understanding of the theories of knowledge (epistemologies) that guide the subject matter disciplines in which they work.
- Teachers need a knowledge base (an epistemology) of pedagogy, including knowledge of how cultural beliefs and the personal characteristics of learners influence learning.
- Teachers are learners and the principles of learning and transfer for student learners apply to teachers.

- Teachers need opportunities to learn about children's cognitive development and children's development of thought (children's epistemologies) to know how teaching practices build on learners' prior knowledge.
- Teachers need to develop models of their own professional development that are based on lifelong learning, rather than on an "updating" model of learning, to have frameworks to guide their career planning.

Although the research is less specific and quantitative, the NRC summarizes the findings about necessary learning environments for a new game of science education. In many ways, this is now critical research, since it is apparent that the context for learning may be more important than an elaboration of concepts and skills to be learned. This research identifying the importance of context indicates that supportive learning environments, which are the social and organizational structures in which students and teachers operate, need to focus on the characteristics of classroom environments that affect learning. Classroom environments can be positively influenced by opportunities to interact with others who affect learners, particularly families and community members, around school-based learning goals. Furthermore, the tools of technology are creating new learning environments, which need to be assessed carefully, including the cognitive, social, and learning consequences of using these new tools (Bransford et al., 2000). Our new breed of coaches must know how people learn so that they can prepare professionals (the team) for performance in the new millennium.

A Shared Standard for Excellence

The Natural Science Education Standards represent another major set of rules and visions for new games as new reforms are envisioned. The National Standards were also produced by the National Research Council (1996) and represent four years of work and the expenditure of seven million dollars to provide consensus as to the visions offered for the needed improvements. The new game is organized around four new goals—not so unlike those central to Project Synthesis. These include the expectation that students must do the following:

1. Experience the richness and excitement of knowing about and understanding the natural world
2. Use appropriate scientific processes and principles in making personal decisions
3. Engage intelligently in public discourse and debate about matters of scientific and technological concern
4. Increase their economic productivity through the use of knowledge, understanding, and skills of the scientifically literate person in their careers (NRC, 1996)

The National Standards also focus on the needed changes in teachers (our coaches of the new school). Interestingly, it was easier to gain approval and acceptance of these changes in teaching than was the case for content offered as central. The "more emphasis" conditions meet with favor among all stakeholders, yet there are few instances in which the conditions exist in most classrooms. We remain optimistic that the changes to the "more emphasis" conditions will be the necessary component for reforms to succeed. The specific changes in teaching that illustrate where we are in the current year are contrasted as follows:

Less Emphasis On	More Emphasis On
Treating all students alike and responding to the group as a whole	Understanding and responding to individual student's interests, strengths, experiences, and needs
Rigidly following curriculum	Selecting and adapting curriculum
Focusing on student acquisition of information	Focusing on student understanding and use of scientific knowledge, ideas, and inquiry processes
Presenting scientific knowledge through lecture, text, and demonstration	Guiding students in active and extended scientific inquiry
Asking for recitation of acquired knowledge	Providing opportunities for scientific discussion and debate among students
Testing students for factual information at the end of the unit or chapter	Continuously assessing student understanding
Maintaining responsibility and authority	Sharing responsibility for learning with students
Supporting competition	Supporting a classroom community with cooperation, shared responsibility, and respect
Working alone	Working with other teachers to enhance the science program (NRC, 1996, p. 52)

To accomplish the changes in teaching, extensive "coach development workshops" will be necessary. The NSES also developed a less/more emphasis series of contrasts indicating how staff development programs must change. These illustrate new ways of dealing with the continuing improvements of the coaching staff. These contrasts from NSES are as follows:

Less Emphasis on	More Emphasis on
Transmission of teaching knowledge and skills by lectures	Inquiry into teaching and learning
Learning science by lecture and reading	Learning science through investigation and inquiry
Separation of science and teaching knowledge	Integration of science and teaching knowledge
Separation of theory and practice	Integration of theory and practice in school settings

Individual learning	Collegial and collaborative learning
Fragmented, one-shot sessions	Long-term coherent plans
Courses and workshops	A variety of professional development activities
Reliance on external expertise	Mix of internal and external expertise
Staff developers as educators	Staff developers as facilitators, consultants and planners
Teacher as technician	Teacher as intellectual, reflective practitioner
Teacher as consumer of knowledge about teaching	Teacher as producer of knowledge about teaching
Teacher as follower	Teacher as leader
Teacher as an individual based in a classroom	Teacher as a member of a collegial professional community
Teacher as target of change	Teacher as source and facilitator of change (NRC, 1996, p. 72)

If changes in teaching and ways teachers are prepared are changed, assessment strategies must change as well. The National Standards again includes the same less/more emphasis to permit a complete description of the needed changes while reflecting the current statistics (i.e., the less emphasis descriptor). Such assessment is needed to provide the evidence that the new programs demand better and more informed players. The emphasis contrasts concerning assessment of the success with school science are as follows:

Less Emphasis on	**More Emphasis on**
Assessing what is easily measured	Assessing what is most highly valued
Assessing discrete knowledge	Assessing rich, well-structured knowledge
Assessing scientific knowledge	Assessing scientific understanding and reasoning
Assessing to learn what students do not know	Assessing to learn what students do understand
Assessing only achievement	Assessing achievement and opportunity to learn
End-of-term assessments by teachers	Students engaged in ongoing assessment of their work and that of others
Development of external assessments by measurement experts alone	Teachers involved in the development of external assessments (NRC, 1996, p. 100)

Too often, only a concern for content or curriculum is considered in discussions of reform. Textbooks and supplementary materials are produced on the assumption that they will affect the teaching and that continuing staff development is not important. The National Standards try to minimize an elaboration of traditional content and indicate that curriculum development should occur in the schools. But there are seventeen content standards that do indicate major changes in the content that are needed:

Less Emphasis on	More Emphasis on
Knowing scientific facts and information	Understanding scientific concepts and developing abilities of inquiry
Studying subject matter disciplines (physical, life, earth sciences) for their own sake	Learning subject matter disciplines in the context of inquiry, technology, science in personal and social perspectives, and history and nature of science
Separating science knowledge and science process	Integrating all aspects of science content
Covering many science topics	Studying a few fundamental science concepts
Implementing inquiry as a set of processes	Implementing inquiry as instructional strategies, abilities, and ideas to be learned
Activities that demonstrate and verify science content	Activities that investigate and analyze science questions
Investigations confined to one class period	Investigations over extended periods of time
Process skills out of context	Process skills in context
Emphasis on individual process skills such as observation or inference	Using multiple process skills: manipulation, cognitive, procedural
Getting an answer	Using evidence and strategies for developing or revising an explanation
Science as exploration and experiment	Science as argument and explanation
Providing answers to questions about science content	Communicating science explanations
Individuals and groups of students analyzing and synthesizing data without defending a conclusion	Groups of students often analyzing and synthesizing data after defending conclusions
Doing few investigations to leave time to cover large amounts of content	Doing more investigations to develop understanding, ability, values of inquiry and knowledge of science content
Concluding inquiries with the result of the experiment	Applying the results of experiments to scientific arguments and explanations

| Management of materials and equipment | Management of ideas and information |
| Private communication of student ideas and conclusions to teacher | Public communication of student ideas and work to classmates (NRC, 1996, p. 113) |

The science standards also include information about the common problems associated with science programs and those affecting the whole system. There are eleven changes that are envisioned if the reforms are to succeed and continue to improve:

Less Emphasis on	More Emphasis on
Developing science programs at different grade levels independently of one another	Coordinating the development of the K–12 science program across grade levels
Using assessments unrelated to curriculum and teaching	Aligning curriculum, teaching, and assessment
Maintaining current resource allocations for books	Allocating resources necessary for hands-on inquiry teaching aligned with the Standards
Textbook- and lecture-driven curriculum	Curriculum that supports the Standards and includes a variety of components, such as laboratories emphasizing inquiry and field trips
Broad coverage of unconnected factual information	Curriculum that includes natural phenomena and science-related social issues that students encounter in everyday life
Treating science as a subject isolated from other school subjects	Connecting science to other school subjects, such as mathematics and social studies
Science learning opportunities that favor one group of students	Providing challenging opportunities for all students to learn science
Limiting hiring decisions to the administration	Involving successful teachers of science in the hiring process
Maintaining the isolation of teachers	Treating teachers as professionals whose work requires opportunities for continual learning and networking
Supporting competition	Promoting collegiality among teachers as a team to improve the school
Teachers as followers	Teachers as decision makers (NRC, 1996, p. 224)

The NSES visions of needed changes produce basic rules that are vastly different from those defining the reform game of the 1960s. These four central ideas for current reforms include the following:

1. A broader definition for science content that is important and useful for all learners with the aim of achieving universal scientific literacy. Science content is envisioned as including eight facets, normally unifying science concepts and processes in everyday use; basic themes of life, physical, and earth/space science; science and technology; science for meeting personal and secretarial challenges; and the philosophy and history of science.

2. Science cast in real-world contexts, often in terms of problems, current issues, question arising from personal curiosity. Most traditional teaching, courses, student activities seem unrelated to the real world of the students and their daily lives. A context for learning has been elevated to equal if not greater importance than the concepts and processes that have characterized science education debates for nearly 100 years (i.e., a two-dimensional view of our field).

3. The inclusion of technology with science is important in terms of students seeing the relevance and importance of science. Science and technology are intertwined; neither can exist in current society without the other.

4. Enlarging the list of stakeholders and developing a collaborative approach to science learning, study, and schools is central to current reform efforts. We no longer focus on curriculum materials prepared centrally for all to use. Students, teachers, and others must have ownership if the science that is studied is to be learned.

Science Education as Scientists See It

The American Association for the Advancement of Science, the largest organization of scientists in the United States, has sponsored Project 2061, an ambitious challenge to affect this game of science education. The AAAS's first formal act was to produce *Science for All Americans* (AAAS, 1990), which provides the rationale for Project 2061 and a wonderful view of what changes are needed. The AAAS offers a new game that many teams around the world are choosing to play. This means that there are many coaches studying the game and preparing the players.

One of the major contributions is the identification of common themes as science, mathematics, and technology are connected. Some important themes pervade these fields repeatedly, regardless of the facet of the natural world that captures interest. These are the ideas that transcend disciplinary boundaries and prove fruitful in explaining, in theorizing, in observing, and in designing. These common themes include systems, models, constancy and change, and scale.

A brief look at each theme provides a sense of direction for teaching and learning. Of course, what is missing is a situation and/or context in which the themes have real meanings at a point in time, in a given community, in the personal experiences of learners. Following is a quote from *Science for All Americans* (AAAS, 1991, p. 179) describing each theme:

Systems. Any collection of things that have some influence on one another can be thought of as a system. The things can be almost anything, including objects, organisms, machines, processes, ideas, numbers, or organizations. Thinking of a collection of things as a system draws our attention to what needs to be included among the parts to make sense of it, to how its parts interact with one another, and to how the system as a whole relates to other systems. Thinking in terms of systems implies that each part is fully understandable only in relation to the rest of the system.

Models. A model of something is a simplified imitation of it that we hope can help us understand it better. A model may be a device, a plan, a drawing, an equation, a computer program, or even just a mental image. Whether models are physical, mathematical, or conceptual, their value lies in suggesting how things either do work or might work. For example, once the heart has been likened to a pump to explain what it does, the inference may be made that the engineering principles used in designing pumps could be helpful in understanding heart disease. When a model does not mimic the phenomenon well, the nature of the discrepancy is a clue to how the model can be improved. Models may also mislead, however, suggesting characteristics that are not really shared with what is being modeled. Fire was long taken as a model of energy transformation in the sun, for example, but nothing in the sun turned out to be burning.

Constancy. In science, mathematics, and engineering, there is great interest in ways in which systems do not change. In trying to understand systems, we look for simplifying principles, and aspects of systems that do not change are clearly simplifying. In designing systems, we often want to ensure that some characteristics of them remain predictably the same.

Patterns of Change. Patterns of change are of special interest in the sciences: Descriptions of change are important for predicting what will happen; analysis of change is essential for understanding what is going on, as well as for predicting what will happen; and control of change is essential for the design of technological systems. We can distinguish three general categories: (1) changes that are steady trends, (2) changes that occur in cycles, and (3) changes that are irregular. A system may have all three kinds of change occurring together.

Evolution. The general idea of evolution, which dates back at least to ancient Greece, is that the present arises from the materials and forms of the past, more or less gradually, and in explicable ways. This is how the solar system, the face of the earth, and life forms on earth have evolved from their earliest states and continue to evolve. The idea of evolution applies also, although perhaps more loosely, to language, literature, music, political parties, nations, science, mathematics, and technological design. Each new development in these human endeavors has grown out of the forms that preceded them, and those earlier forms themselves had evolved from still earlier forms.

Scale. The ranges of magnitudes in our universe—sizes, durations, speeds, and so on—are immense. Many of the discoveries of physical science are virtually incomprehensible to us because they involve phenomena on scales far removed from human experience. We can measure, say, the speed of light, the distance to the nearest stars, the number of stars in the galaxy, and the age of the sun, but these magnitudes are far greater than we can comprehend intuitively. In the other direction, we can determine the size of atoms, their vast numbers, and how quickly interactions among them occur, but these extremes also exceed our powers of intuitive comprehension. Our limited perceptions and information-processing capacities simply cannot handle the whole range. Nevertheless, we can represent such magnitudes in abstract mathematical terms (for example, billions of billions) and seek relationships among them that make sense.

Each of these themes provides a description of new games that should transform science. Each provides a transdisciplinary view of science—a human activity in which all are involved at some level. Carl Sagan realized this when he commented that every human starts out a scientist, full of curiosity and awe of the natural world and anxious to make meaning of it (NRC, 1998).

Science for All Americans also stresses the importance of habits of the mind in science education. There are habits that every coach helps all players develop if they are to be proficient in this game of science (AAAS, 1991, p. 183):

> Throughout history, people have concerned themselves with the transmission of shared values, attitudes, and skills from one generation to the next. All three were taught long before formal schooling was invented. Even today, it is evident that family, religion, peers, books, news and entertainment media, and general life experiences are the chief influences in shaping people's views of knowledge, learning, and other aspects of life. Science, mathematics, and technology—in the context of schooling—can also play a key role in the process, for they are built upon a distinctive set of values, they reflect and respond to the values of society generally, and they are increasingly influential in shaping shared cultural values. Thus, to the degree that schooling concerns itself with values and attitudes—a matter of great sensitivity in a society that prizes cultural diversity and individuality and is wary of ideology—it must take scientific values and attitudes into account when preparing young people for life beyond school.
>
> Similarly, there are certain thinking skills associated with science, mathematics, and technology that young people need to develop during their school years. These are mostly, but not exclusively, mathematical and logical skills that are essential tools for both formal and informal learning and for a lifetime of participation in society as a whole.
>
> Taken together, these values, attitudes, and skills can be thought of as habits of mind because they all relate directly to a person's outlook on knowledge and learning and ways of thinking and acting.

These habits of the mind indicate a new game that must be played, and new coaches are needed to help develop such a team. Basically, most typical instruction (the "less emphasis" descriptors listed earlier) does not result in any real learning, and certainly, most instruction does not mirror the vision for instruction in science as elaborated in the National Science Education Standards or in Project 2061. For the sake of our collective future, we must resolve the problems related to teaching if we are to advance and realize the current visions in any significant way. It will require a new game with new roles.

A Recipe for Science Education's Future

Reinsmith (1993) has posited ten factors for learning that must be discussed, debated, and contextualized for every science teacher. These include many new coaching strategies to be widely adopted in support of science education's advancement.

1. Learning first takes place by a process much like osmosis.
2. Authentic learning comes through the trial and error.

3. Students will learn only what they have some proclivity for or interest in.
4. No one will formally learn something unless that person believes that he or she can learn it.
5. Learning cannot take place outside an appropriate context.
6. Real learning connotes use.
7. No one knows how learning moves from imitation to intrinsic ownership, from external modeling to internalization and competence.
8. The more learning is like play, the more absorbing it will be.
9. For authentic learning to happen, time should occasionally be wasted, tangents pursued, side paths followed.
10. Traditional tests are very poor indicators of whether an individual has really learned something.

We now know that the minds of most K–12 students are not engaged—probably in any of the courses in the total curriculum, certainly not in science. Perrone (1994) has surveyed the literature and offers eight ways in which the minds of students can be engaged, a condition that is necessary if our new games for science teaching are to succeed. These are all indicators of the importance of context and the school environment in the new education game. The new coaches help students to experience real mind engagement as outlined by Perrone. His points include the following:

1. Students help to define the content.
2. Students have time to wonder and to find a particular direction that interests them.
3. Topics have a "strange" quality—something common seen in a new way, evoking a "lingering question."
4. Teachers permit—even encourage—different forms of expression and respect students' views.
5. Teachers are passionate about their work. The richest activities are those invented by teachers and their students.
6. Students create original and public products; they gain some form of "expertness."
7. Students do something, such as participate in a political action, write a letter to the editor, work with the homeless.
8. Students sense that the results of their work are not predetermined or fully predictable.

STS: Playing Field of the Future

The science-technology-society (STS) initiatives of the last twenty years probably provide the most documented successes for moving us forward in the twenty-first century in ways outlined here. These efforts were well underway before the extensive research support from the cognitive sciences. Basically STS programs are ones that do the following:

- Seek out and use student questions and ideas to guide lessons and whole instructional units.
- Accept and encourage student initiation of ideas.

- Promote student leadership, collaboration, location of information, and taking actions as a result of the learning process.
- Use student thinking, experiences, and interests to drive lessons (even if this means altering the teacher's plans).
- Encourage the use of alternative sources for information from both written materials and experts.
- Use open-ended questions and encourage students to elaborate on their questions and their responses.
- Encourage students to suggest causes for events and situations, and encourage them to predict consequences.
- Encourage students to test their own ideas, that is, answer their questions, encourage them to propose their own ideas as to causes, and predict consequences of their ideas and experiments.
- Seek out student ideas before presenting teacher ideas or before studying ideas from textbooks or other sources.
- Encourage students to challenge each other's conceptualizations and ideas.
- Use cooperative learning strategies that emphasize collaboration, respect individuality, and use division of labor.
- Allow adequate time for reflection and analysis.
- Respect and use all ideas that students generate.
- Encourage self-analysis, collection of real evidence to support ideas, and reformulation of ideas in light of new experiences and evidence (NSTA, 1990–1991).

If reforms and the potential claimed for STS in education are to be realized, then many challenges must be met. Greatest among these are changes in instruction that are central to current reforms in science education. These are changes that can produce a future citizenry that is capable of realizing a better world, a citizenry that is capable and motivated to create a future we want. This is the promise offered by STS instruction.

STS means broadening what is included in science in most educational settings: schools and colleges. Instead of posing science as what current scientists believe to be accurate interpretations of the natural world and/or as the tools used by these same scientists to determine the accuracy of such interpretations, STS requires that science be studied in a real-world context. This real-world context or situation becomes the motivation for learning and the glue to ensure that the learning is real and useful in the lives of learners. STS also means including technology (the study of the human-made world), which in turn enhances the learning of the natural sciences. Technology affects the daily lives of all learners more than does basic science. Science is not seen merely as information and skills organized by discipline specialists as important ideas and attributes that all must experience and master simply because professionals have so defined them.

There are some specific challenges that must be met if STS is to realize its potential as educational reform. For example, textbooks are slow to change. In many countries, they are controlled by the government. When the government decides to change, many teachers feel unprepared to use new texts that change radically. When teachers and schools choose the texts, the majority tend to purchase books that are little different from the old ones. National tests attempt to measure the effectiveness of what is taught (or what is in the curriculum), not what should be taught. Furthermore, they test for the ideas and understandings that arise from direct instruction. It is rare to test for student use of skills and concepts in new contexts (situations). Research scientists often do not accept the broader view of science that is deemed more appropriate for all learners. They have retained a more restricted definition of science to correspond to their work at the research frontiers of their own disciplines. Hence, practicing scientists must use their own critical thinking skills in considering changes in the way education commonly occurs in classrooms and laboratories at all levels around the world if real reforms are to occur.

Though it is difficult to advance the changes needed to implement an STS approach in most educational settings, current efforts are impressive enough to envision a future in which the challenges of today have been met. STS provides us with a way of achieving scientific literacy for all. This occurs when the following reform features are followed:

- The definition of appropriate science content in K–12 science classrooms must be broadened.
- Instruction and curriculum must be seen as locally relevant; concepts and skills should be useful in the daily lives of learners.
- Equal billing for technology and science should be given; the distinction between the two human endeavors must be reduced and the commonalities emphasized.
- Collaboration is needed in providing a learning environment for all learners: those in a school, the community, and the whole of humanity.
- Focus must be on students who meet the four goals for the game of science in schools. Students must be taught to experience the thrill and excitement of knowing and understanding the natural world, use appropriate skills and principles in making personal decisions, engage in public discussion and debate about societal and technologic concerns, and increase their economic productivity through knowing, understanding, and using science in their careers.

These are the new goals for winning the science game in the future. Reports are clear in showing the advantages of STS instruction, which also results in changes in curriculum structure.

Curricular and Assessment Domains

Six curriculum and assessment domains are recognized as basic to STS, as discussed thoroughly in Chapter 3 of this book: the concept domain, process domain, application domain, attitude domain, creativity domain, and world view domain. When all six domains are taken seriously in terms of organizing material and implementing the needed forms of instruction, the advantage of STS can be readily seen.

In studies of the effects of STS instruction, many specific results in each of the above domains illustrate the advantages. When students' adjusted means on a battery of assessments for each domain are compared, the benefits of STS over traditional text-driven approaches are striking (Liu & Yager, 1997; Yager & Weld,

Table 13.1 Results of student learning in each domain in STS and non-STS classes

Grade	STS Mean	S.D.	Non-STS Mean	S.D.	T-test	STS Mean	S.D.	Non-STS Mean	S.D.	T-test
	Concept Domain					Process Domain				
6	72.3	18.3	49.6	14.8	29.1*	73.4	26.9	46.8	16.2	27.9*
7	73.4	19.2	49.3	15.3	32.1*	74.6	27.3	48.6	14.7	24.2*
8	72.8	17.9	50.3	15.2	29.6*	75.3	27.2	49.4	15.1	31.3*
	Creativity Domain					Attitudinal Domain				
6	70.8	17.3	50.9	16.2	90.1*	58.9	29.4	46.5	15.5	29.4*
7	72.3	18.3	52.4	15.8	82.5*	57.4	28.3	49.1	16.1	30.6*
8	70.6	17.5	52.3	15.3	76.5*	56.6	27.2	52.2	15.8	21.7*
	Application Domain					WorldView Domain				
6	60.4	16.8	50.9	15.9	29.4*	80.2	17.2	62.1	14.8	38.9*
7	62.1	17.3	48.9	16.0	28.3*	83.3	19.3	66.3	18.1	45.2*
8	59.5	17.0	49.3	15.4	20.9*	83.1	20.1	67.4	17.4	39.7*

*Significant at .01.

1999). Table 13.1 indicates specific results from a study of over 6,000 students in grades 6, 7, and 8 who were taught science as STS or as a traditional, lecture-based course.

The results of STS instruction in six domains have been well established. Extensive research indicates that the teaching approaches result in superior learning for students of all abilities in all domains. Interestingly, the concept domain—even when utilizing recall-type tests—results in higher performance achievement among the young investigators of an STS approach contrasted to their traditionally lectured peers. Figure 13.1 provides a model to illustrate learning goals, contexts for content, and assessment using STS.

CONCLUSION: Optimistic Horizons

Do these solutions—National Standards, Project 2061, learning research, and STS—suggest optimism concerning new efforts for reform? Will the new game results in massive improvements in real learning? Five situations provide the hope and emerging evidence that our current efforts at reform are on the mark and succeeding. They

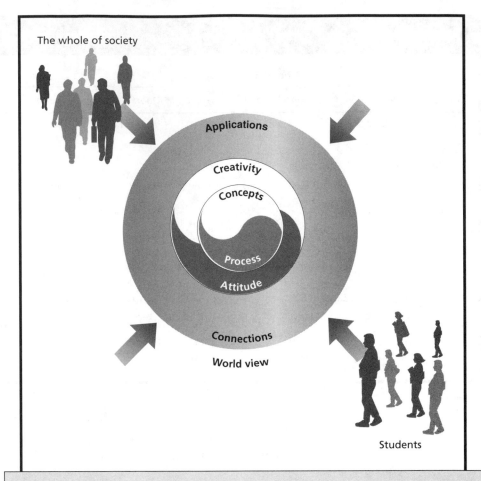

Figure 13.1 Domains for teaching and assessing science learning

also indicate areas for questioning and follow-up research. Continued efforts in evaluating and renewing our expertise in each area suggest that the next several years will be exciting ones that will allow us to envision even more inconceivable improvements and exciting possibilities to assess our successes.

First of all, we now realize the power of collaboration and the importance of all stakeholders being involved in creating the visions and in the efforts to realize them. This certainly was (and is) the position of Project 2061 Science for All Americans (AAAS, 1990) and the rationale for systemic reforms and the teacher education collaboratives supported by the NSF. As more people establish systemic reform projects and as the funding continues and encourages the moves, change will occur more quickly. It will be reinforced with the evidence that assessment provides when it is more broadly conceived to meet all the goals.

A second factor attributing to the likely success for realizing our immediate goals for the next few years will be changes in teaching and the effect these changes will have on students. Such students will be more scientifically literate and will possess scientific habits of the mind. The successes will demand changes in instruction in which information is often personally collected and used in making even more decisions, establishing new goals, and determining new ways of meeting them. We need to recognize that all of these essential aspects of science are missing in most school programs. Student questions rarely frame instruction; students rarely are asked to predict possible answers; students rarely design their own experiments to test the validity of their answers; students seldom debate the conclusiveness of their answers or experiments; students rarely compare the results of their work to others as evidence. Many activities are now conceived to be open-ended; however, it is rare to find open entry and choice for designing experiments and collecting evidence instead of doing what a lab sheet or other set of directions dictate. Some would argue that typical instruction in schools where science concepts are taught directly to students causes most students to miss these most important aspects of the human enterprise called science.

Every teacher, every student, every human must be empowered to wonder, to suggest explanations, to devise ways of testing personal and class hunches that are offered to explain the objects or events in question, to collect and analyze evidence, to communicate the process and the results to others. Research must not be left only to the professionals. Action research in schools and in the daily lives of students needs to be central to science teaching and learning. To learn science means to engage in it as opposed to learning about what others have done.

A third reason for optimism that we will succeed with current reforms is the latest research on human learning. Our knowledge of how all people learn puts us in a powerful position to succeed in ways never before possible. We must make teaching more of a focus and utilize research about teaching instead of viewing our mission as merely transmitting the conceptions of nature which scientists now accept as valid explanations. We want and need people who can think, solve problems, and make decisions based on evidence and reasoning. If the current research is put to use by science teachers and other school leaders, the next decades will be golden times as we succeed in developing a citizenry that is scientifically and technologically literate. We will have defined it operationally, and we will have evidence of success. Such a condition will hasten others to the task and to achieving similar results.

A fourth basis for optimism is the wonder and success of computer technology. Never has a technological advance been so important in human affairs. Surely, the future will be shaped as computer technology advances, in many respects allowing everyone to do more than would be possible in terms of time and use of the human brain. Computers allow us to locate information with speed and efficiency; they analyze and report data; they allow us to see things happen that would normally take a lifetime. Our imaginations have only begun to tap the potential of this technological achievement. But the answer is not merely procuring more computers. It is first creating a need and a reason. Again, it is defining a problem and determining the best ways possible to get answers that can be tested, refined, and made part of the continuing progression leading to learning and more learning.

A final factor that provides optimism for even greater successes with meeting the goals of scientific literacy for all is a new focus on science teacher education. Recently, I headed two major research efforts funded by the U.S. Department of Education—Salish I and Salish II—(Salish Research Consortium, 1997). These studies reveal the following nine findings:

1. Most new science teachers use little of what teacher education programs promote during their initial years of teaching.
2. Few teacher education programs are utilizing what we know about science as envisioned by the National Science Education Standards.
3. Programs are poorly conceived in terms of sequential experiences with science teaching; these are unrelated to the general education and science courses that comprise most of a bachelor's program.
4. There are few ties between preservice and in-service efforts.
5. Support for teacher education reforms have been largely unrecognized and underfunded; only in the last few years has this situation been altered.
6. Significant changes in teacher education majors can be made during a single year, when part of a collaborative research project.
7. There is strength in the diversity of institutions and faculty involved with science teacher education.
8. Changes in science instruction at colleges must be substantial if real improvements are to occur in schools.
9. Collaboration in terms of experimentation and interpretation of results is extremely powerful.

The points for optimism outline needed research in science education if the current successes with science education are to occur generally over the next quarter of a century. The climate has never been better for realizing current reform visions, funds are available, national standards are in place, state leaders have endorsed the new directions, and international attention and efforts are in concert with national initiatives. But science teachers must take on major responsibility for changing their teaching and transforming it into a science. They must ask questions about science, about processes, about varied contexts for learning. They must help students question better, to propose ideas that respond to questions, to design tests, to help them establish the validity of their explanations, to help them to communicate their results and the interpretations offered as evidences for success. And most important, students must be helped to use their learning in new contexts and thereby provide real evidence that learning has actually occurred. When science has been learned, it becomes a functional part of the learner. It indicates the importance of continued learning for an entire lifetime for all—especially for teachers who are encouraging it as their professional calling.

Certainly, we are involved with a new game; we need coaches who are ready for a new generation of students, a new culture in a new millennium, new goals for education in the sciences, new ways to assess success, and new views of K–12 programs and the system involved to achieve scientific and technological literacy for all. The new game is the most exciting we have seen throughout history. We need better coaches as we all advance to a new level—a new degree of success, a new game. The future of science education depends on it.

Reflecting on the Game

1. What kinds of materials are needed to realize the learnings associated with current reform efforts? How would current materials need to change?
2. If the U.S. science curriculum is a mile wide and an inch thick, what can be done to change such a description? Do current standardized tests in the United States match the structure of the typical curriculum and typical courses?
3. What kinds of experiments could be planned to meet the problems of the old games of science education while also preparing for new games to match the stated goals of the national and international efforts to achieve programs that lead to greater student learning and students who have scientific literacy?
4. Who should help to develop exercises and procedures for playing successfully the new games that characterize real science?
5. How can you and colleagues plan different instruction that would be designed to produce the kind of person (learner) that is outlined in the new goals for science in schools?

References

Advisory Committee for Science Education. (1970). *Science education: The task ahead for the National Science Foundation.* Washington, DC: National Science Foundation.

American Association for the Advancement of Science. (1990). *Science for all Americans: Project 2061.* Washington, DC: Author.

Bransford, J., Brown, A., & Cocking, R. (2000). *How people learn: Brain, mind, experience, and school.* Washington, DC: National Academy Press.

Donovan, M., Bransford, J., & Pellegrino, J. (1999). *How people learn: Bridging research and practice.* Washington, DC: National Academy Press.

Harms, N., & R. Yager (Eds.). (1981). *What research says to the science teacher* (Vol. 3). Washington, DC: National Science Teachers Association.

Hurd, P. D. (1986). Perspectives for the reform of science education. *Phi Delta Kappan, 67*(5), 353–358.

Liu, C.-T., & Yager, R. E. (1997). The Iowa scope, sequence, and coordination project: A middle school science reform program approved by the National Diffusion Network. *Research in Middle Level Education Quarterly, 20*(4), 77–105.

National Research Council. (1996). *National science education standards.* Washington, DC: National Academy Press.

National Research Council. (1998). *Every child a scientist: Achieving scientific literacy for all.* Washington, DC: National Academy Press.

National Science Foundation. (1965). *Science education in the schools of the United States* (Report to the House Subcommittee on Science Research and Development). Washington, DC: U.S. Government Printing Office.

National Science Teachers Association. (1990–1991). Science/technology/society: A new effort for providing appropriate science for all (Position Statement). In *NSTA handbook* (pp. 47–48). Washington, DC: Author.

National Science Teachers Association. (2002). *NSTA Reports: NSF centers work to improve science teaching and learning* (Vol. 13, pp. 28–29). Washington, DC: Author.

Noll, V. (1947). *Science education in American schools. 46th yearbook of the National Society for the Study of Education.* Washington, DC: National Society for the Study of Education.

Peddiwell, J. A. (1939). *Saber-Tooth curriculum.* York, PA: Maple Press.

Penick, J., & Yager, R. (1983). The search for excellence in science education. *Phi Delta Kappan, 64*(9), 621–623.

Perrone, V. (1994). How to engage students in learning. *Educational Leadership, 51*(5), 11–13.

Reinsmith, W. A. (1993). Ten fundamental truths about learning. *The National Teaching and Learning Forum, 2*(4), 7–8.

Salish Research Consortium. (1997). *Secondary science and mathematics teacher preparation programs: Influences on new teachers and their students. Final report of the Salish I research project, (SALISH I).* Iowa City, IA: The University of Iowa, Science Education Center. [U.S. Department of Education Grant No. R168U30004]

Silberman, C. (1970). *Crisis in the classroom: The re-making of American education.* New York: Random House.

Toffler, A. (1970). *Future Shock.* New York: Bantam-Doubleday-Dell Publishers.

Whipple, G. M. (1932). *A program for science teaching. 31st yearbook of the National Society for the Study of Education.* Washington, DC: National Society for the Study of Education.

Yager, R. E., & Weld, J. D. (1999). Scope, sequence and coordination: The Iowa project, a national reform effort in the USA. *International Journal of Science Education, 21*(2), 169–194.

Additional Resources

Lind, D., & Kral, R. (Producers). Lawrence, C. L., & Yager, R. E. (Directors). (1998). *A state of change: Images of reform in Iowa.* (Available from the Annenberg/CPB Math and Science Collection, 901 E Street, NW, Washington, DC 20004-2037)

Smith, P. S., Banilower, E. R., McMahon, K. C., & Weiss, I. R. (2002). *The national survey of science and mathematics education.* http://2000survey.horizon-research.com/reports/

Yager, R. E., & Harms, N. C. (Eds.). (1981). *What research says to the science teacher* (Vol. 3). Washington, DC: National Science Teachers Association.

Yager, R. E. (Ed.). (1993). *What research says to the science teacher: Vol. 7. The science, technology, society movement.* Washington, DC: National Science Teachers Association.

Yager, R. E. (Ed.). (1996). *Science/technology/society as reform in science education.* Albany, NY: State University of New York Press.

Yager, R. E. (2002). *Achieving the visions of the national science education standards* (Occasional Research Paper). The Iowa Academy of Education, FINE (First In the Nation in Education) Foundation.

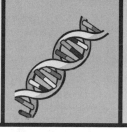

appendix A

BUILDING THE STUDENT-CENTERED CLASSROOM

Robin Lee Harris, Ph.D.
Department of Earth Science
and Science Education,
Buffalo State College

ABOUT THE AUTHOR:
Dr. Robin Harris started her science career studying invertebrate marine ecology in San Diego and in the Mediterranean Sea. In 1983, she returned to the United States to launch a teaching career in science, mathematics, and English spanning grade levels from pre-K to college students. After earning a Ph.D. in science education, Dr. Harris joined Buffalo State College, where she teaches science methods courses, general science courses, and graduate courses in evaluation and research. She is active in local and national science teacher organizations and maintains a vibrant research agenda investigating student conceptual change, teacher beliefs and practices, and constructivist learning theory.

> # In theory there is no difference between theory and practice. In practice there is.
>
> —Yogi Berra
> *Former major league baseball*
> *player and manager*

INTRODUCTION: Student-Centered Science Under Construction

Let's explore the craft of creating a student-centered science classroom, one that coalesces knowledge of learning theories, standards, and research-based practices. Creating it is only half the fun, sustaining a student-centered environment, with emphasis on the many choices teachers must make regarding teaching strategies, curricular options, and instructional models, is the other task at hand here. Teachers, of course, set the tone for a student-centered science class by using the many tools at their disposal. Learners themselves determine the timeliness and utility of those tools. The deceptive ease with which good science teachers appear to orchestrate an inquiry classroom belies a complex navigational program that is established at the outset and continuously modified over time and through experience.

Teachers in Student-Centered Classrooms

Teachers who build student-centered classrooms embrace the idea that their students come to their classroom with prior knowledge about how the natural world works, that personal learning styles vary, and that there are variations in student interests and abilities. With this fundamental constructivist appreciation of students, teachers set personal and classroom goals, design standards-based instruction and create a learning environment that nurtures the learner.

Teacher Characteristics

The habits of mind and practice of winning science teachers can serve as a model for the preparation or professional development of all science teachers. Studies of top educators of science reveal that they share many of the following qualities (Penick, Yager, et al., 1986):

- Attend and make presentations at professional meetings and in-services
- Lecture far less than teachers in general
- Stress a process-approach science
- Use professional journals in their teaching
- Profess more enthusiasm for science teaching as their careers progress
- Gain inspiration from other teachers, their students, and others
- Are aware of national curricular materials
- Feel well qualified to teach science
- Put in far more than minimal time
- Are involved in extracurricular assignments
- Have high expectations for their students

The qualities of student-centered science teachers spring from their beliefs about teaching and learning, which ultimately manifest themselves in a core set of goals and actions and that guide their practices.

Goal Setting

The following seven items are a distilled collection the goals that science teachers often claim to hold for their students of science (Penick & Bonnstetter, 1993):

1. Have a positive attitude toward science.
2. Use their knowledge in identifying and solving problems.
3. Be more creative.
4. Communicate science effectively.
5. Feel that some of their knowledge is useful and applicable.
6. Take action based on evidence and knowledge.
7. Know how to learn science.

As step 1, the establishment of goals aligned with standards representing the consensus view of the science education community is vital. However, defining the mechanisms—actions that take place in the classroom on a daily basis—is the only sure-fire way to ensure progress toward those noble goals. Step 2, then, is to figure out enough about our student clientele to effectively execute a game plan that achieves those goals. Only then can we clarify the mechanics—the day-to-day interactions and curricular choices of a student-centered classroom.

Learners in Student-Centered Classrooms

Learning styles, a relatively novel way of discussing the uniqueness among students, were based on the work of Gardner (1983) and Dunn and Dunn (1987). Learning styles are students' preferred ways of learning and processing information. They bottle up the "cognitive, affective and physiological traits that influence the way learners interact with, and respond to the learning environment," (Jacobsen, Eggen, & Kauchak, 2002, p. 250).

Gardner (1983) described eight types of intelligence, though overlap undoubtedly exists among individuals (Table A.1). Each type of intelligence is said to have one or more of three abilities accompanying it: the ability to create a product or service valued in one's culture, the ability to problem solve, and the ability to acquire new knowledge. In making use of the multiple intelligences theory in teaching, it has been suggested that teachers do three things:

1. Cultivate desired skills in our students.
2. Provide a variety of ways to approach learning objectives.
3. Make instruction individualized (Nicholson-Nelson, 1998).

How learning styles manifest themselves in a student-centered classroom is a matter of recognizing the cognitive diversity among students and crafting learning ex-

Table A.1 Summary of Gardner's multiple intelligences with identifying characteristics

Intelligence	Learner Self-Description	Learning Opportunities
Body-kinesthetic	I live an active lifestyle. Arts and crafts are enjoyable pastimes. I have a feel for that.	Hands-on learning, drama, dance, action games
Linguistic	I write for pleasure. It is easy for me to explain my ideas to others. I hear you.	Storytelling, choral reading, journal writing
Logical-mathematical	Structure helps me be successful. Step-by-step directions are a big help. Prove it to me.	Brain teasers, problem solving, number games
Musical	Moving to a beat is easy for me. I focus in on noise and sounds. I'm tuned in.	Songs that teach, moving to rhythm, reciting poetry that has rhythm
Naturalistic	I enjoy working in a garden. I believe preserving our National Parks is important. I'll recycle that.	Experimentation, exploration, investigations, science issues, inquiry,
Spatial	Rearranging a room is fun for me. I am good at reading maps and blueprints. I get the picture.	Visuals, art, mind-mapping, imagination games
Intrapersonal	Working alone can be just as productive as working in a group. Fairness is important to me. I'll think about it.	Individualized instruction, independent study
Interpersonal	I learn best interacting with others. Television and radio talk shows are enjoyable. Let's make a deal.	Cooperative learning, competitive learning, community involvement, simulations, role-play

Source: Marks-Tarlow (1996).

periences that accommodate such diversity. Science teachers do well to encourage learners to develop strengths in several different styles. An understanding of and appreciation for learning styles is a prerequisite for achieving those goals of student-centered teachers.

On Equity

Now that we have established that all learners are different in terms of learning style, it is time to consider treating them fairly (though not necessarily equally, as clarified in Chapter 4). If teachers endorse a goal for all students to have a fair opportunity to achieve in science, then we all must be sure to relay this message through how we act to our students. How do teachers show equity in their classroom interactions? Equity shows up in day-to-day interactions, in the way questions are asked and responded to, in the way problems are handled, in the way reinforcement is offered, and in the way knowledge and skills are assessed. Following are eight guidelines for fairly interacting with students:

1. Provide students with opportunities to show their expertise in the subject. Acknowledge students and give them feedback.
2. Use wait time effectively.
3. Listen to students.
4. Distribute questions and verbal exchange fairly.
5. Ask the sorts of questions that elicit thought rather than quick answers.
6. Provide students with analytical feedback for all of their work.
7. Assess student learning in a variety of ways.
8. Use physical presence or proximity to let students know they are a valued presence in the classroom (Grayson & Martin, 1997).

Promoting the Skills of Inquiry

Now that the importance of learner appreciation for learning styles and a sense of fairness has been established, the business of teaching an inquiry style, student-centered environment can begin to take shape. When you boil it down, science class is about learning three basic kinds of scientific skills and understandings: concepts, processes, and the nature of science. "Students need to learn the principles and concepts of science, acquire the reasoning and procedural skills of scientists, and understand the nature of science," (Olson & Loucks-Horsley, 2000, p. xiii). What makes our jobs as science educators challenging is that these understandings are not innate for many of our students.

Consider the work of practicing scientists as a guide for designing the inquiry classroom with its three basic types of understandings. Scientists conduct investigations for many reasons: They work on replicating other scientists' investigations; they build models that are used to explain ideas; they explore unexplored parts of our planet, our solar system, and our universe; they search out answers to questions about human disease. They are, in a nutshell, curious. Student-centered teachers help learners to extend their natural curiosity into scientific ways of knowing for targeting concepts, processes, and the very nature of science itself.

Consider the evidence that curious inquirers of science gather. Real-world scientific evidence is usually subject to a strict set of criteria. For example, proposed explanations must be logical, their methods must be replicable, their explanations must be open to questioning and modification, and their foundation must square with historical or current scientific consensus. Evidence is the cornerstone of scientific inquiry. Maintaining the integrity of evidence is the responsibility of each scientist, and so should it be for each student. Scientists communicate and defend their findings to their peers. In the scientific arena, explanations are debated, are defended, often grow, and often change. That sounds like something we need our learners of science to be doing too, reflecting the nature of science itself in the daily milieu of the science classroom.

Assembling the Inquiry Toolbox

The student-centered science class is a remarkably complex and lively setting in which the teacher's goals for learners are predicated on a foundation of learner differences along with an essential fairness. These goals revolve around central ideas that make up science literacy: knowledge and skills associated with science concepts, processes, and the nature of science itself. Finally, the student-centered science teacher can take direct action toward meeting those noble goals for students by crafting effective interactive strategies, effective curricula, and effective ways for organizing the science class.

Questioning Strategies

Arguably the single greatest action that student-centered teachers of inquiry science can take is to develop effective interactive strategies, namely, questioning. Teachers vary the kinds of questions they use depending on the outcomes they desire. Questions can be categorized as lower-order or higher-order, convergent, divergent, probing, and learner-centered. All these types of questions have a place in the student-centered classroom to lead discussions, to start and end investigations, and for assessment.

Convergent questions have finite answers. They are "knowledge" questions on Bloom's knowledge-comprehension-application-analysis-synthesis-evaluation hierarchy (Table A.2). These questions might require little thinking on the part of students. Consider vocabulary or recall questions to be convergent, such as the example "the product of mass and velocity is . . . ?" Convergent questions have their place but should be complemented and outnumbered by other types of questioning.

Divergent questions have several possible answers. Depending on the sort of divergent question that is asked, there could be answers at all levels of thinking on Bloom's scale. Divergent questions can be used effectively to open a discussion. Open-ended essays are a type of divergent question that is often used in assessment. Divergent questions start most student-centered learning units. An example of a divergent question is "How are mammals different from reptiles?" It takes practice to incor-

Table A.2 Blooms taxonomy and higher-order thinking skills questions	
Bloom's Taxonomy Level	**Sample Question Starters**
Recall	Convergent single-answer questions
Comprehension	Describe the relationship between
	Compare . . . and . . .
	How do you know . . .
Application	Can you make . . .
	Use the knowledge you have about . . . to work with this new set of data
Analysis	What are the parts that make up . . .
Synthesis	Combine these elements to. . . .
Evaluation	Choose one of . . . and defend your reasons with data from our investigations

Source: Bloom, B. S. (1956).

porate divergent questions, and all of the question types that follow, into the daily classroom dialogue.

Probing questions are the curve ball of questioning. They test the learner's conceptual knowledge and ability to articulate that knowledge to others. Because deep understanding of concepts is a consensus goal in modern science education, probing questions should be commonly observed in student-centered science classrooms. An example of a probing question is "How would altitude influence the time and heat needed to boil a pot of water?" Probing is one strategy that can be used to assess and enhance deep understanding.

Reflective questions are those that require active thinking about thinking or learning. They are metacognitive—thinking about thinking—questions. They elicit long pauses and initiate extensive dialogue after they are asked. Reflective questions seek evidence: "How did you solve that problem?" or "How did you make that decision?" or "Why did you organize your response in the way you did?" They allow learners an opportunity to think about how they conducted themselves. This can lead to pattern recognition and deeper understanding of concepts and skills (Bransford, Brown, & Cocking, 2000).

Learner-centered questions make the discussion more relevant to the individual. Learner-centered questions focus on an individual's point of view or way of looking at a discussion idea. The teacher refers to an individual's point of view when wanting others to expand their thinking or reconsider their own. For example, while discussing a local issue, students might take several different sides. The teacher might ask that students consider the points of view of industrialists and environmentalists toward an issue, for example. The objective is that students will eventually recognize each other's viewpoints and direct questions and responses to them. (Kasulis, 1982).

Effective questioning takes practice. It also requires appropriate responses if the dialogue is to proceed beyond the initial question. Wait time is essential following any question designed to elicit thought on the part of students (Rowe, 1986). Nonjudgmental, welcoming responses on the part of teachers figures prominently in the continuation of exchange of ideas beyond an initial question. The quality of dialogue in the student-centered classroom sets the tone for developing critical analysis skills on the part of students and provides a valued assessment mechanism for the teacher. But inextricably linked to quality interchange in an inquiry science class is the quality of the curriculum itself.

Inquiry Curriculum

This section examines how teachers put research, standards, and instructional strategies together. Each sample curricular model described here relies heavily on the constructivist tenet that social exchange and group work promote deeper understanding, all the while reflecting science as it is done in the real world. Though the three models described have slightly different foci, they have far more in common by establishing relevancy and active investigation as primary.

Issue-Based: Science, Technology and Society. Issue-based explorations are the heart of student-centered science classrooms. They start out with the identification of an issue of local importance. Then local resources are tapped to help resolve problems. Students actively seek the information that they use to help them resolve problems. The teacher's role is one of facilitator or coach, helping students to acquire information. Students begin by using their knowledge base and then build on it to work through an issue. A question is asked, ideas are brainstormed, primary and secondary research is conducted, results are shared and debated, and a resolution of the issue is made. Sometimes it is a continuum of choices; other times it is a simple decision (Harris-Freedman, 1999). Because students explore local issues, they learn about social responsibility. They also learn how to make decisions based on multiple factors. Issues are never cut-and-dried; they have fuzzy areas. This style of instruction helps students to grow in their capacity to work with multiple responses (Yager, 1996). The idea that science, technology and society (STS) are interconnected is an outcome of this style of instruction. STS is an integrative, inclusive style of thinking. Teaching with STS ideas in mind helps students to understand their personal world through a science context. It helps them to see careers and social responsibilities that are a part of being a citizen of a community. It helps students to develop attitudes of stewardship and responsibility (Yager, 1996).

Event-Based. Event-based explorations usually start with an unusual physical phenomenon, such as a hurricane, earthquake, or tornado. Students use secondary materials to learn about the various facets of this event. This type of exploration is usually set up to integrate sciences and societal perspectives as students work through the minute-by-minute events that take place during a hurricane, for example. Event-based instruction allows teachers to bring weather and other hazardous conditions into classrooms for students who might never have experienced them. It helps to develop social awareness alongside of the sciences involved with each type of event.

Problem-Based. Problem-based explorations are just that: Students seek to solve problems, puzzles, or questions. This is the classic "I wonder . . . ?" type of exploration. The best problem-based issues are those that are rich in context and related to real-world situations. They will also be connected to the science principles that are the heart of instruction (Allen & Duch, 1998). Students work to identify concepts and principles that they need to know to solve a problem. They work in cooperative groups in which several skills are developed. These skills include critical thinking, analysis, evaluation and use of appropriate resources, effective communication, content knowledge and intellectual skill growth, and lifelong learning (Allen & Duch, 1998, p. 1). Inquiry skills and understandings are used to develop possible solutions to the problem.

Instructional Models

Choices of interactive styles and of curricular models are but a part of the whole student-centered classroom picture. Organization of the daily classroom sequence of events can facilitate or hinder inquiry. Like the curricular models above, the two learning models below share more philosophically than they differ: entry to conceptual understanding by establishing prior knowledge and beliefs, guided explorations of concepts, open exploration, application, and evaluation.

The Learning Cycle. Three phases make up the learning cycle: exploration, concept introduction, and concept application. During exploration, students use their prior knowledge to interact with a new situation, ideas, or new materials through activity or discussion. During concept introduction, students' questions from the exploration phase are addressed. Concepts are introduced and discussed, and connections are made to the initial explorations. During the concept application phase, students apply the newly learned concepts to a novel situation. This is the phase in which practice and time spent with several different kinds of examples allow students to create new patterns in their minds. In addition to the three phases of this instructional sequence, evaluation is inserted into each phase in the form of informal and formal feedback from teacher to student and from student to student, spurred through high-quality questioning (Trowbridge, Bybee, & Powell, 2000).

The 5-E Model. Five phases define the 5-E model: engagement, exploration, explanation, elaboration, and evaluation. In engagement, students are invited to ask questions, define problems, or analyze demonstrations. Successful engagement results in students asking questions and showing motivation to work on their tasks. This phase is an ideal assessment opportunity for teachers to establish students' prior knowledge.

In the exploration phase, students have a common base of experiences that are geared toward building understanding and long-term learning. A variety of activities or investigations take place. Here is where students have the time to begin to build a conceptual foundation, readying them for the next phase.

During explanation, common vocabulary is developed. Clear, comprehensible explanations of the concepts being studied are shared. Students share their explanations built from prior phases toward a common scientific vocabulary and understanding.

The next phase, elaboration, is similar to the concept application phase of the learning cycle. Students are given novel and extended activities to solidify their new understandings. Students apply their new knowledge in comprehending unique situations, extending subject competency. During this phase, many naïve ideas and misconceptions can be dispelled.

The final phase is evaluation. At this time and during all other phases, students receive feedback on their work in written or oral format. Students are also invited to evaluate their own work, directed and facilitated by a teacher who is skilled in the questioning styles of inquiry.

CONCLUSION: A Work in Progress

Ours is a lively, risky, exciting profession and a lifelong endeavor to develop effective strategies for instruction and assessment. The establishment of goals for our students that reflect a national consensus for science literacy for all establishes a baseline focus on all that we do with and for our students. Then as we prioritize a recognition of each of our students as a unique learner deserving of fair opportunities to pursue science, a scaffold is in place for constructing a student-centered inquiry experience. From the toolbox of professional science educators, actions suitable for achieving those goals can be selected, determining the quality of dialogue and exchange and the depth of experience with the concepts and processes that define science as a discipline. Building a student-centered science class is a continual work in progress but doubtless a labor of love.

References

Allen, D. E., & Duch, B. J. (1998). *Thinking toward solutions: Problem-based learning activities for general biology.* Fort Worth, TX: Saunders College Publishing, Harcourt Brace College Publishers.

Bloom, B. S. (1956). Taxonomy of educational objectives. *Handbook I, Cognitive domain.* New York: David McKay.

Bransford, J. D., Brown, A. L., & Cocking., R. R. (Eds.). (2000). *How people learn: Brain, mind experience and school.* Washington, DC: National Academy Press.

Dunn, R., & Dunn, K. (1987). Dispelling outmoded beliefs about student learning. *Educational Leadership, 44*(6), 55–62.

Gardner, H. (1983). *Frames of mind: The theory of multiple intelligences.* New York: Basic Books.

Grayson, D. A., & Martin, M. D. (1997). *Generating expectations for student achievement: An equitable approach to educational excellence* (3rd ed.). Canyon Lake, CA: GrayMill.

Harris-Freedman, R. L. (1999). *Science and writing connections.* White Plains, NY: Dale Seymour Publications.

Jacobsen, D. A., Eggen, P., & Kauchak, D. (2002). *Methods for teaching: Promoting student learning* (6th ed.). Upper Saddle River, NJ: Merrill Prentice Hall.

Kasulis, T. (1982). Questioning. In M. M. Gullette (Ed.), *The art and craft of teaching* (pp. 38–48). Cambridge, MA: Harvard-Danforth Center for Teaching and Learning.

Marks-Tarlow, T. (1996). *Creativity inside out: Learning through multiple intelligences.* Menlo Park, CA: Addison Wesley.

Nicholson-Nelson, K. (1998). *Developing students' multiple intelligences.* New York: Scholastic Professional Books.

Olson, S., & Loucks-Horsley, S. (2000). *Inquiry and the national science education standards: A guide for teaching and learning.* Washington, DC: National Academy Press.

Penick, J. E., & Bonnstetter, R. J. (1993). Classroom climate and instruction: New goals demand new approaches. *Journal of Science Education and Technology, 2*(2), 91–97.

Penick, J. E., Yager, R. E., et al. (1986). Teachers make exemplary programs. *Educational Leadership, 44*(2), 14–20.

Rowe, M. B. (1986). Wait-time: Slowing down may be a way of speeding up. *Journal of Teacher Education, 37*(1), 43–50.

Trowbridge, L. W., Bybee, R. W., & Powell, J. C. (2000). *Teaching secondary school science: Strategies for developing scientific literacy* (7th ed.). Upper Saddle River, NJ: Prentice Hall.

Yager, R. E. (1996). Science/technology/society as reform in science education. Albany, NY: State University of New York Press.

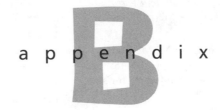

THE TEACHING STANDARDS OF THE NATIONAL SCIENCE EDUCATION STANDARDS

Teaching Standard A: Teachers of Science plan an inquiry-based science program for their students. In doing this, teachers

- Develop a framework of yearlong and short-term goals for students.
- Select science content and adapt and design curricula to meet the interests, knowledge, understanding, abilities, and experiences of students.
- Select teaching and assessment strategies that support the development of student understanding and nurture a community of science learners.
- Work together as colleagues within and across disciplines and grade levels.

Teaching Standard B: Teachers of science guide and facilitate learning. In doing this, teachers

- Focus and support inquiries while interacting with students.
- Orchestrate discourse among students about scientific ideas.
- Challenge students to accept and share responsibility for their own learning.
- Recognize and respond to student diversity and encourage all students to participate fully in science learning.
- Encourage and model the skills of inquiry, as well as the curiosity, openness to new ideas and data, and skepticism that characterize science.

Teaching Standard C: Teachers of science engage in ongoing assessment of their teaching and of student learning. In doing this, teachers

- Use multiple methods and systematically gather data about student understanding and ability.
- Analyze assessment data to guide teaching.
- Guide students in self-assessment.
- Use student data, observations of teaching, and interactions with colleagues to reflect on and improve teaching practice.
- Use student data, observations of teaching, and interactions with colleagues to report student achievement and opportunities to learn to students, teachers, parents, policymakers, and the general public.

Teaching Standard D: Teachers of science design and manage learning environments that provide students with the time, space, and resources needed for learning science. In doing this, teachers

- Structure the time available so that students are able to engage in extended investigations.
- Create a setting for student work that is flexible and supportive of science inquiry.
- Ensure a safe working environment.
- Make the available science tools, materials, media, and technological resources accessible to students.
- Identify and use resources outside the school.
- Engage students in designing the learning environment.

Teaching Standard E: TEACHING STANDARD E: Teachers of science develop communities of science learners that reflect the intellectual rigor of scientific inquiry and the attitudes and social values conducive to science learning. In doing this, teachers

- Display and demand respect for the diverse ideas, skills, and experiences of all students.
- Enable students to have a significant voice in decisions about the content and context of their work and require students to take responsibility for the learning of all members of the community.
- Nurture collaboration among students.
- Structure and facilitate ongoing formal and informal discussion based on a shared understanding of rules of scientific discourse.
- Model and emphasize the skills, attitudes, and values of scientific inquiry.

Teaching Standard F: TEACHING STANDARD F: Teachers of science actively participate in the ongoing planning and development of the school science program. In doing this, teachers

- Plan and develop the school science program.
- Participate in decisions concerning the allocation of time and other resources to the science program.
- Participate fully in planning and implementing professional growth and development strategies for themselves and their colleagues.

[From National Research Council. (1996). *National Science Education Standards* (pp. 27–52). Washington, DC: National Academy Press.

Index